planting

principles for starting new churches

second edition

louie e. bustle \\ gustavo a. crocker

global mission
church of the nazarene
lenexa, kansas

Planting: Principles for Starting New Churches
Deeper Life Publications
By Louie E. Bustle & Gustavo Crocker

Copyright © 2010 by Premier Publishing
(Print) ISBN: 978-1-935900-07-8
(Kindle) ISBN: 978-1-935900-06-1
(ePub) ISBN: 978-1-935900-05-4
Printed in the United States of America
Cover Design: Matt Johnson

contents

foreword

Principles for Starting New Churches is a long overdue book on a subject that is close to my heart. Having been a church planter at the start of my full-time ministry, I am quite aware of what it's like for someone to pioneer a new church with no people, no property and no money!

Louie Bustle and Gustavo Crocker are both visionaries who know how to lead. Both of these authors are among the best strategic thinkers in the church world today. They both have a worldview influenced by their missionary service and understand how to plant a church in any area of the world, despite the challenges of culture, geography or the global economy.

This book is a must read for those who feel the call to step into new frontiers of ministry and plant a church. It is loaded with vital information on how to structure and build a strong local church. Its pages are filled with ideas, plans, programs and methods for those who are willing to step out in faith to build a great church. It also helps the reader find various models and methods that work in different cultures and settings.

The genius of the book is its simplicity. Principles for Starting New Churches is written on a level that anyone can understand and identify with. With confidence the authors tell us that God can use anyone to plant a church. In fact, all God needs is your willingness!

As I read this book, I was once again reminded that church planting is the best way for church denominations to grow and evangelize. New churches assimilate better and reach more new people for Christ. As church leaders we must join with Louie Bustle and Gustavo Crocker in a worldwide endeavor to plant more churches.

-Stan Toler

General Superintendent, Church of the Nazarene

Bestselling Author

introduction

Where does planting a church begin? Surely it begins with understanding what you need to do and why you need to do it. In the next several sections, this book will help you address the former, but first let's address the latter.

Think back to the time in your life when you made a commitment to Christ. Where were you and how did you get there? We have often asked pastors and leaders that same question: "How did you get into the church?" Like most of us, many of them were introduced to the church by people in whom they had confidence. Friends bringing friends to Jesus is certainly a New Testament concept.

Almost all of the rest said they were saved in churches that were started close to their homes. That makes sense—after all, where do you grocery shop? Where do you get gas? Most likely at the nearest store or station. Most people polled lived within a 10-block radius of the church where they were saved. They were invited to a church, attended, accepted the Lord and made that church their home. But what if there had been no church in that 10-block radius? No church in a 20 or 30-block radius?

There is a famous movie quote that says, "If you build it, he will come." While we don't look to Hollywood for our spiritual inspiration, one thing is for sure: If it's never built, they can't come. Imagine that your home church had simply never existed because someone felt it was too expensive, too discouraging, too much work to establish it. How would that have impacted your life and the lives of all the people in that congregation? Let us not fall into the trap of thinking that there are enough churches in existence and if someone wants us, it's up to them to find us. Just like in the parable of the lost sheep, it's our job to go looking for them.

"Church planting is a mission for the lay people—not the lay people of tomorrow or the future generation of lay people, but today's congregation. Me. You. Now."

Put simply, church planting is a mission to live out the love we have received, to be living evidence of a grace that operates above and beyond our daily human existence. Jesus put it this way in Acts 1:8: "You will receive power when the Holy Spirit comes on you; and you will be my witnesses in Jerusalem, and in all Judea and in all Samaria, and to the ends of the earth." To be witnesses of this truth we live in and live out every day—that is our mission. We plant churches because there are so many who need to see that evidence and grace in action. Today's challenge is not only to bring the people to the church but also to take the church to the people. Planting new centers of hope and grace are part of the plan, and we must engage in such a plan with a burning passion for our mission.

Whose job is it to plant churches? Surely someone who has a degree from a seminary somewhere who is highly trained, highly skilled and heavily gifted. Or is it? If we look to the New Testament for our guidance, we see the early church exploding in its power, size and effectiveness, even with very few trained leaders. We have been awakened to the responsibility of all pastors to mentor others for leadership, for every church to start a new church and for every member to win new people to Jesus Christ. Church planting is a mission for the lay people— not the lay people of tomorrow or the future generation of lay people, but today's congregation. Me. You. Now.

How easy it is to look at the conditions and social trends around us and assume the task is not even worth attempting. Questions of practicality plague us. Many are asking:

- "How can we build a church today when the cost is so staggering?"

- "People's hearts are so hard—how can the Church win them?"

- "How is it possible to evangelize to the protected, high-rise apartment complexes or the busy centers of urban sprawl?"

God has answers for the impossible questions we are asking, and He wants to build His kingdom through His chosen children around the world. In Ephesians 3:20, the apostle Paul declares, "Now to him who is able to do immeasurably more than all we ask or imagine, according to his power that is at work within us." Our driving passion is found in allowing God to love others through us. Only then will we take part in God's mission of saving the lost.

The church must dare to do the impossible. We must learn to ask largely and think big for God. We hope that in these few pages you will be challenged and equipped to take part in this mission and be a church planter.

> *"Growth is nothing to fear. Rather, it is the natural result of living out the calling placed on our lives by the Great Commission."*

passion

as the lyrics to Bob Dylan's song say, "The times, they are a-changin'." The world is a very different place than it was even 20 years ago. Technology capabilities have revolutionized cultures, and the changes, in many ways, are only beginning. As cultures and societies change and grow, so must our approach to evangelism and ministry.

Unfortunately, many Christians believe that the only way to keep up with the changing needs of our culture is by pouring large amounts of money into planting a few, expensive churches. While there is a place for all kinds of churches, the concept of the megachurch has become the ideal model for too many pastors, who have come to us saying, "If I had more money, I would have better growth!"

However, a church can have all the money in the world and still be spiritually dead. Where does that leave us? A study of social trends tells us that people long for connection with one another. The same technology that advances our standard of living isolates us at the same time—270 friends on Facebook do not a true friendship make. The postmodern generation in particular is ripe for connection. The church is the ideal place to find such a connection. That was something the members of the early church knew. When asked for money at the Temple's entrance, Peter responded to the crippled man, "Silver or gold I do not have, but what I have I give to you" (Acts 3:6). His natural response was to offer the man the same grace, hope and healing he had received. Our natural response is to do the same, by founding new places where people can encounter the Gospel alive and at work.

As we grow in our relationship with God both as individuals and as the body of Christ, the natural result is growth. We desire to see others find what we have found. We are, as some have put it, beggars pointing to the bread. The first disciples working in the early church are the best model for church growth that we have available to us. Even in a social atmosphere of persecution and governmental oppression, the disciples continued to spread the word and invite others into fellowship with Jesus, "And the Lord added to their number daily those who were being saved" (Acts 2:47b).

Dr. Phineas F. Bresee is another historical figure whose faith and fearlessness laid the foundation for today's Church of the Nazarene. He had a vision that included the world, sending missionaries and pastors and starting churches everywhere possible. He also had a vision for building his Glory Barn on the local scene. He wanted a church with a vision for genuine relationships and salvation as it preached the holiness doctrine that the Word of God emphasizes.

This leads us back to the question posed in the Introduction: Whose job is it to plant churches? The church planting philosophy of the Church of the Nazarene has gone through several changes. In many instances we have given the responsibility of starting new churches to the district superintendents. The pastors' responsibilities have been primarily in the local churches. However, it is impossible for the district superintendents alone to start all the new churches. This is a task for all believers! Even if you're not called to be a pastor, you are called to be a witness—an instrument in God's hand as He writes the story of salvation.

This is not to say that pastors are removed from the action. Pastors play a key role in the planting process. They set the conditions, challenge the people and establish a plan of growth for the local church, as well as for new churches. But this is key to the success of a church planting initiative: There must also be a mobilized laity. Take note of the system of growth and development the apostle Paul initiated. He sent people, called of God, to minister in satellite churches, prayer cells and celebration services. They started small churches and prepared pastors. They took the "seminary by extension" to the people. Some pastors were full time, some were bi-vocational and others were lay pastors who started congregations.

Growth is nothing to fear. Rather, it is the natural result of living out the calling placed on our lives by the Great Commission. Will you be an instrument, used of God, to fulfill His plan for building the Kingdom by planting churches?

"God honors a mission-minded church with growth when its people are building the Kingdom."

planters

et's begin by understanding what kind of church planter you are called to be. There are two types of church planters. The first is the apostolic, or catalytic, church planter. This person is called by God to start churches but not to continue to pastor those churches after they are established. The second is the pioneer church planter who lays the foundation and continues on as the pastor to the congregation.

the catalytic church planter

There was a time when the role of missionaries was to establish and pastor one congregation at a time. The new mission realities, however, demand that missionaries on foreign fields become facilitators of catalytic church planting. Missionaries used to start a church and pastor it for four years before going on home assignment. At that time, they turned the church over to another pastor. This has not proven to be the best utilization of mission funds. Therefore, the emphasis has been put upon a missionary being a catalytic church planter, supervising and training 5 to 10 pioneer leaders to pastor the church plants. These leaders may have little or no experience, but the day-to-day training with the catalytic church planter equips them for the work to which God has called them. This church planting method has yielded an impressive harvest in most mission areas outside of North America.

> *"Some of the most receptive areas for new churches are the growing edges of a city or town . . . they are looking for new friends and possibly a new congregation."*

The catalytic church planter can also be effective in North America and other post-Christian parts of the world. Each church can start a new church. The pastor of the mother church is the catalytic church planter. He/she uses the mother church as a base from which to start new churches, along with men and women who have been called to the ministry of church planting. This enables the pastor to maintain ministry in the mother church at the same time.

Let's examine some examples of catalytic church planting and briefly discuss the methods used. During a two-year period Marcos Hatchett started six new churches in Santiago, Dominican Republic. Pastors for each of those new churches came from the mother church. At the same time, the mother church provided several pastors for other churches on the district. While starting these new churches, the mother church grew in attendance from around 80 to over 200 and became one of the strongest churches in the country.

Jesus Bernat from North Uruguay also caught the vision. His church has experienced phenomenal growth in the process of starting several daughter congregations. The men who pastored these churches were called to preach from Bernat's local congregation. In that way, brother Bemat was able to influence Kingdom growth at a much faster rate.

In Bangladesh, the Church of the Nazarene started with two congregations in 1994. By 2010, thanks to the leaders' emphasis on catalytic church planting and church mobilization, the Church of the Nazarene in Bangladesh has reached 1,260 organized churches and is planning more than 2,000 new works that are in the process of being developed and organized.

> *"When God's people pray, doors are opened in the community."*

In Western Europe, where churches struggle amid postmodern, post-Christian environments that claim little need for faith, Reverend Annemarie Snijders is a catalytic leader who is seeing her communities transformed. Drawn to ministry since age 21, Snijders attended European Nazarene College in Germany before becoming a pastor's wife. She then earned her MA in world evangelism, preparing to become a pastor herself. In Veenendaal, Netherlands, she felt called to start a Nazarene church, emphasizing God's grace and love. Services began in 2004. Focused on building lasting relationships, the church invites others to "taste and see" unconditional love. Snijders rejoices as people discover Christ, thankful for the community of faith she calls "vulnerable, vibrant and alive."

God honors a mission-minded church with growth

when its people are building the Kingdom. There is no need to give up a great number of members to start daughter churches. A church and its pastor may want to give a few members to a new congregation, but at the same time plan for growth in the mother church. On the other hand, the new pastor and his/her family may be the only members needed to start the new congregation.

the pioneer church planter

The second kind of church planter is the pioneer. Throughout its history, the Church of the Nazarene has had many pioneer church planters. This church planter feels a call to leave his/her comfortable position and move to new areas and start new churches with the intention of remaining with that congregation after its establishment. Many pastors have spent their lives in pioneer church planting. Miguel Peña was such a man. In his short ministry in Latin America he established three excellent congregations by leaving an organized church and moving to a new area.

God does call specific leaders to this ministry. One of the beautiful things about being a pioneer church planter is that you do not need to have a great amount of experience. This is especially true if there is a sponsoring church and a support network to help. All of us can be involved in church planting. The New Testament structure of church planting was multiplication of congregations and districts. Acts 2:46, 5:42 and Colossians 4:15 all speak of house churches. Acts 9:31 speaks of groups of churches in various districts. The idea was to develop a movement where the Word of God could perpetuate growth and churches could be established in the faith and increase daily, as seen in Acts 16:5 and 2:47.

> *"Church planters are those who see the lostness of their neighbors and community through the eyes of Christ."*

Where does a church planter start? Usually, it is best to begin with contact persons, either through the local church or through the people who requested that the church begin in their area. Another way to start might be through a strategy and feasibility study of needs and possibilities for starting a church in a new area. This is accomplished through a community survey. A community survey is vitally important whenever starting a new congregation. Mapping out the area, noting where other churches are located, pinpointing the availability of public transportation, utilities and zoning are all involved in a total community survey. Of course, the receptivity of an area is of vital importance.

A good place to look for areas that may be receptive of new churches are the growing edges of a city or town. When people move into new areas, they are more receptive because they have given up their friends (and in some cases their established church) and are looking for new friends and possibly a new congregation. If they have not been attending church, they will be more receptive at the time of their move or during a crisis period in their lives than at any other time. That is when the church needs to be there to help them establish their lives in Christ. Appropriate timing should not be underestimated.

God does open doors in special ways. He leads and guides His people through open doors and by direct communication as they talk to Him. Prayer is of vital importance in all aspects of the church, including planting. When God's people pray, doors are opened in the community.

Church planters are those who see the lostness of their neighbors and community through the eyes of Christ. They are moved to open their homes and start a new church.

God can call anyone to do this.

"Choosing the church planting method that is the most relevant to the local culture is critical for the success of your church plant."

models

There is no single model that applies to all cultures, contexts and ministry realities. The following list is a limited compilation of models that we have observed at work in various contexts of the world. Some of them are more effective in pioneer areas while others are more effective in areas where Christianity may have been in existence for a long time but where the church is in stage of decline. The recommendation is to use the models that better fit the context and the ministry realities you'll be facing. Prayer, consultation and good missiology will be extremely helpful in determining the best method to use (see the included Suggested Reading list for more on this). In addition, there may be cases in which the solution is a combination of the models outlined below.

The Church of the Nazarene in Razgrad, Bulgaria, has been at work for more than a decade. Since the very beginning the local church, under the leadership of Pastor Nikolaj, decided that they would reach out not only to their urban community, but also to the dozens of small villages within driving distance of the town. To do so, the leadership team identified four leaders who had been trained in basic evangelism and church planting. These leaders were given the responsibility of reaching a minimum of four villages in the surrounding areas. So far, they have planted five churches that connect monthly with the founding church, the hub.

the hub model

The principle of the hub model is simple: A local congregation becomes the center of development for various simultaneous church plants in the vicinity by providing leadership, ministry support, discipleship and fellowship, until such a time that each of the church plants reaches a stage of development that will allow it to become self-running.

While there are variations of the model, most of the successful hub-based church plants follow these basic criteria:

- The sponsoring church (hub) prayerfully commits to simultaneously reach several towns, villages, city sectors, etc., according to need, access, contacts, strategic location, etc.

- The hub identifies catalytic leaders with potential

for church planting.

- The pastor and the leadership of the hub church train these leaders. The church planters don't need to be professionally trained in ministry and/or church planting; they will grow along with the new church plants.

- The hub pastor joins the church planters on visits to the various communities where initial contacts, ministry potential, invitations, etc., are available. Normally, the church planters assess the type of activity that is more appropriate to gathering a group of disciples. Small Bible studies, coffeehouses, cultural gatherings, film showings, etc., are important to developing the basic critical mass needed. The hub pastor rotates his/her visits so that church planters continue to be mentored.

- These points of contact (the small Bible Studies, coffeehouses, cultural gatherings, film showings, etc.,) meet during the week and their meetings become increasingly regular (from once every other week to weekly on a specific day of the week).

- The church planters go back to the hub congregation for normal ministry activities (weekend services, prayer times and training) and their own edification.

- As the new church plants develop, they begin meeting regularly and leaders of the hub church visit them regularly to provide a sense of fellowship.

- At the beginning, and as distance and conditions allow, participants at the new church plants attend the hub church once a month to experience a broader celebration and fellowship.

- The church plants can take two different

leadership forms: a) the church planter becomes the pastor and leads the congregation with a church planting mindset, or b) the church planter identifies a local leader from the church plant and equips him/her as the local pastor.

- Church planting movements that have used the hub model host the weekly gatherings in the following progression:
    - Weekday studies and prayer
    - Weekend fellowship of the points of contact
    - Monthly gathering/celebration of the church groups
    - Empowerment and release of the church groups for mission-type work

the daughter church model

Landivar Church of the Nazarene in Guatemala City, Guatemala, has a long history of successful church planting. When one looks at the history of the local church, it may appear as if it has experienced spotty growth and development. Rather than growing steadily and moving from one membership size to the next, the church shows ups and downs in membership throughout its more than 50 years of history. The same is true for its finances. The reality behind these numbers, however, is quite different. The Landivar church of the Nazarene has planted, funded and resourced at least six daughter churches during its first years of organization. All of these daughter churches are vibrant congregations today that continue giving life to new congregations with the same missional DNA of the mother church.

The Crocker family in El Milagro was at the center of one such church plant. When Mrs. Crocker, a long-time

Nazarene, suffered a stroke that kept her from traveling across town by bus to join her church in Landivar, she and her husband, along with their oldest daughter, faced the dilemma of fellowship versus identity. On the one hand, they knew they needed fellowship with a body of believers, and since they were unable to travel to meet with their local church, one option was for them to attend another evangelical church nearby. On the other hand, they were deeply rooted in the doctrine of holiness that they had embraced and experienced with the Church of the Nazarene. So what does a shut-in family do when there is no Nazarene church nearby? Simple. They plant one at home!

Familiarized with the church planting DNA of the Landivar church, the family invited the pastor and the Landivar church to sponsor a daughter church in their home. Today, following its humble beginnings as a house church, the El Milagro Church of the Nazarene in Guatemala has more than 200 members, with their own pastor and leadership team, and a beautiful facility, built by the original members themselves. The founders are now with the Lord but the legacy of a grown daughter church still continues.

The daughter church is one of the most natural church planting models. The principle is that the mother church "gives blood" to start a daughter congregation and then nurtures it until it reaches adolescence and eventual adulthood. The daughter church still has the mother's DNA but it operates in full interdependency. Again, there may be multiple variations, but the experiences that we have observed help us identify at least the following criteria:

- A daughter church generally starts because of particular conditions in the area:
    - A church family that moved to another part of town or to another city
    - A group of families that commute to the mother church from a similar area of the city or town
    - A burden by a group of believers in the mother church about a particular location in the city or town. These believers are willing to move their fellowship to a certain location, etc.

- The mother church must be willing to give up some of its key members in order to give life to a new congregation (hence the term "giving blood").

- This group of members who come from the mother church becomes the core of the daughter church that will eventually expand into the new church. The mother church supports them during the initial stages of the church plant. It is important to note that the core group must have a welcoming mindset to allow new neighbors to join them as part of the new congregation. Failed attempts to start a daughter church have often been connected to the core being so tight (because of their natural need for self-preservation and fellowship) that they close themselves off to new arrivals.

- The mother church must commit to initial investments on behalf of the daughter church (key leaders, instruments, furniture, transportation and even facilities, if possible). This is as natural as the investment that parents make in their children during their formative years.

- The leadership of the mother church must walk alongside the daughter church until such a time that the new church is ready to walk on its own. Planting the church is not enough. The mother church must help the daughter church during the first steps toward maturity. Conversely, the mother church must be willing to let go of the daughter church. The timely release is key to the healthy life of the new congregation.

the arrowhead model

The arrowhead model operates by finding the key local believers who will become the center for church planting in a given area. Once these key believers are identified and discipled (the arrowhead) the rest of the elements of the sponsoring church or organization are added in increasing measure until the church establishes roots in the community.

The arrowhead metaphor has been chosen to demonstrate the different roles that key leaders can have to achieve the same goal of planting a new congregation. There are at least five distinct steps involved in planting churches using this model:

1. **Identify the "man or woman of peace"[1] in the target community.** The church planters visit the community and, through prayer and interaction, identify those who, thanks to God's prevenient grace, are ready to become His followers. Once identified, these new believers are discipled. They represent the tip of the arrowhead, or the "man or woman of peace."

2. **Send discipling disciples.** A support team is sent that will work with the pioneer church planter to assist him/her with discipleship and follow up. These discipling disciples become a system of support for the new church plant. They provide support but they do not become part of the new church plant. Included in this group is local laity who will eventually be trained as church planters themselves. This support group is the area just beyond the arrowhead's tip.

1. See Luke 10:1-9

3. Equip teams of workers. Most churches have more than one worship leader, musician, Sunday school teacher, etc. These local leaders join the support team in the new church plant and assist them with the initial formal services and/or activities. While these teams of workers start by doing the ministry themselves, they immediately identify and train people in the new church plant to assume these ministry roles in the new church—worship, discipleship, etc. The teams of workers remain part of the catalytic planting team and not part of the new church. This leadership force represents the middle of the arrowhead's design.

4. Pastoral and congregational visits. The sponsoring church or district maintains close contact with the new plant during the initial stages of its life. It is important for the pastor of the sponsoring church or the district leadership (if the new plant has been started by more than one congregation) to organize constant visits to the new plant with the purpose of sharing the Word of God, providing moral support and giving the sense of connectedness. In some cases, the sponsoring church (or churches) arranges visits to the new location with the purpose of congregational exchange.

5. **Support networks.** New church plants need all kinds of support networks during their first months of life. The sponsoring congregation or organization provides many of the initial resources such as prayer, basic discipleship materials, music and basic furnishings. In most cases, local groups grow to a point where they are ready to move from a living room to a rental location or their own building. While it is important for the new local congregation to take ownership regarding decisions about

location and facilities, it is always important for the extended Nazarene family to make itself available and pool resources to help the new church plant access land, joint construction projects, etc. These support networks affirm the new church plant as part of a larger, supportive family.

Let's take a look at an example of the arrowhead model at work. The church planting movement of the Church of the Nazarene in Bangladesh was originally established by using the arrowhead model. Using evangelistic and community engagement tools such as the Jesus Film and Child Development Centers, leaders of the church in Dhaka identified areas where there was potential for church planting.

After several months of contact with the poorest communities in the north of the country, Santoj[2] came in contact with Prakash[3], a Hindu community leader with many networks and contacts in the entire zone. Prakash

2. Name changed to protect identity
3. Name changed to protect identity

was antagonistic toward Christianity, to the point that he had threatened to kill the leaders of the church. However, he soon became open to Santoj's witness because Santoj was genuinely helping the neglected children in the village. Through this witness and because of God's prevenient grace, Prakash received Christ and was the first person baptized in the area. He became the catalytic leader for the establishment of the church in one of the fastest growing areas of the world.

Even though the Bangladesh miracle cannot be tagged to one single church planting model, the principle of the arrowhead was key in the establishment and expansion of the church.

the corridor model

When he was the regional director for the Church of the Nazarene in South America, Dr. Bruno Radi had the vision to plant churches in the towns that lay along the road that connected two major cities that he continuously commuted to and from. The road between Pilar, Buenos Aires, Argentina, and Bragado served as a 180 km corridor to dozens of small towns in that part of the country. Applying the gravity models and location theories that most retail stores use in North America to locate their super-centers, Bruno implemented a unique and successful church planting model that helped plant more than five churches in the area.

Using seminary students and lay leaders from the local church as church planters, the team mapped the key locations along the corridor and identified five areas of potential church plants. Each of the leaders conducted a demographic study of their assigned location and its surroundings. They determined age, religion, social dynamics, trends, preferences and potential tools to use in each location. Then, as the time of the launch arrived, church planting teams were ready to connect the corridor.

Each weekend the teams left the local church in Pilar and headed toward Bragado. As they drove, teams were dropped off in five towns along the road. These teams were left with evangelism and church planting tools, plans and specific instructions. Their role was to implement over the weekend the local plans they had previously devised (showing the Jesus Film, conducting sport clinics, concerts, visiting the parks, medical brigades, etc.). As contacts emerged, the team members followed up with them and organized them into groups, according to the realities and responses they faced. At the end of the weekend, the convoy returned from Bragado to Pilar, collecting the church planting teams and getting ready for planning the next week's response. The process was repeated several times until a formal small group gathering and/or mission had been established in each town, local leaders had been identified, and a formal church-planting plan was in place.

Two years later, the project resulted in five fully organized churches in the identified locations. These churches went on to start several daughter churches each, and now the project has become one fully organized district, the Buenos Aires West District of the Church of the Nazarene.

Even though the corridor model has not been widely implemented in Christian church planting movements, other religious groups and primarily commercial ventures have used it to maximize coverage in connecting geographical areas. For church plants, the model requires at least the following criteria:

- There must be a leadership team that is committed to developing a geographical strategy and to investing in its implementation.

- A sponsoring church or a district must be willing to set aside human and financial resources to facilitate the initial months of ministry.

- Eventually, these local church planters must develop local missionary skills that can then be used by the sponsoring church to plant daughter churches in its own periphery.

- Continuity and persistence are paramount for this model to succeed.

- Each location must have at least two workers assigned to church planting work (the Matthew chapter 10 instructions are key for these workers).

the small group model

People in post-Christian environments are somehow leary of churches that meet in traditional church buildings. In places like Europe, North America and Australia, to name a few, the average person has developed a disdain for anything that happens around the institutional church. Yet, they are hungry for relationships, for fellowship, for meaning, for love. While the church building may not be relevant to them, they long to be a part of a group that cares for them. Scripture clearly directs the church body to fill this need, and through the church body, God plans to bring them the redeeming message of Christ's salvation. In such cases, small groups help establish the church as a springboard for Christian fellowship of new and old believers alike.

In Cali, Colombia, the Church of the Nazarene has one of the largest congregations in the world; it has been developed using the small group model. Pastor Adalberto Herrera attributes the growth of his 12,000+ member congregation to the hundreds of small groups that gather every week for prayer, discipleship and fellowship.

In North America, the small group model has been proven successful as a church-planting tool. A small group is typically made up of three or more people, under the leadership of discipling disciples who meet regularly during the week to share about their lives, support one another, pray together, worship God and study biblical truths. Each group has a host and a leader (or one person may host and lead). Groups meet in a number of different locations according to the social preferences of those who participate—coffee shops, restaurants, sports gatherings, workplaces and even a church room. However, the preference is that these informal gatherings move to more formalized meetings in homes.

As these groups develop, some of them become church plants themselves. Others become a referral point for unchurched people who would, step-by-step, feel more comfortable with the idea of faith gatherings and would eventually join the sponsoring congregation.

A successful small group plant model has the following characteristics:

- It focuses on outreach to those outside of the church. There are also small groups that are designed to provide spiritual growth and Bible study for believers in the congregation.

- It gathers in locations that meet the needs of the prospective believers (homes, coffee shops, restaurants, etc.).

- It builds and increasingly nurtures the sense of community.

- It focuses on its own multiplication. A church plant can emerge from either the growth of a small group or the gathering of several small groups into a fellowship of like-minded believers.

- It fosters mutually supportive relationships and accountability.

- It starts with a volunteer leader from the sponsoring church but it normally develops its own leaders from within.

- It strengthens the concept of corporate solidarity that results from Christian conversion.

the house church model

Aziz[4] is the leader of a vibrant church planting ministry in an area of the world that is violently hostile toward Christians. Because of the risk and prohibitions associated with planting official churches in these countries, Aziz and his team have used the house church model as the key to reach thousands of people who would otherwise be lost in darkness and oppression.

The methods of the house church plant vary according to the cultural and religious restrictions in a given location and the levels of risk for the church planters and the hosts. However, there are some principles that can be observed when planting house churches in closed environments:

4. Name changed to protect identity

- Find a reliable and trustworthy contact in the community who will be the host of the house church. These point leaders are normally identified by the local network of believers and not by external entities.

- Disciple the hosts first.

- Train the host in personal evangelism and discipleship.

- Emphasize the call for repentance and belief in Christ.

- While hosts act as leaders of the church plant, church planters focus on training, discipleship and the administration of the sacraments (house church believers cannot attend open congregations for the sake of the sacraments, for example).

- Treat the house church as a church. Even with just two or three people, it has the God-given potential to grow and reproduce! The nucleus of the new church is forming.

- Avoid the temptation of bringing the new believers into the church planting team. The team serves as the catalyst, helping to give birth to an indigenous church.

- Following the example of the early church, house church movements begin as small gatherings meeting in natural settings such as homes, open courtyards, under trees, etc. Rather than growing into large gatherings, growth is channeled into the multiplication of new churches.

The house church model, a variation of the small group model in the West, has also proved to be effective in reaching cities and neighborhoods in North America, Europe and

Australia. In their study on house churches, Towns, Stetzer and Bird ("Seven Characteristics of House Churches") suggest that the house church is perhaps one of the most appealing means to reach the cities in post-Christian environments because, when properly implemented, house churches are:

- Communities of convictions
- Learning communities
- Faith-formation communities
- Value-formation communities
- Mentoring agencies
- Belonging communities
- Providers of self-identity

Regardless of which method you use, choosing the church planting method that is the most relevant to the local culture is critical for the success of your church plant.

"Trusting people, particularly new converts, is one of the best ways to train them for the work of the ministry."

starting

alex Abraham, the CEO of Operation Agape in India, has contributed the English "7 Es" for successful missional outreach. These recommendations can also be applied for successful church planting:

> 1. **End Vision**—Begin with the end in mind. This answers the question, "How would one know that the church planting goals for a given area had been reached?"
>
> 2. **Entry Strategy**—Different roles but the same goal. Identify strategic doors of getting to the communities and neighborhoods to reach.

3. **Evangelism**—Utilize all creative means possible to reach the people who do not know Christ.

4. **Effective Discipleship**—Make the best resources available to move from addition to multiplication as fast as possible.

5. **Establish Churches**—Churches have to be planted so the Gospel can continue to flourish for years to come.

6. **Equip Leaders**—These leaders are equipped by the sponsoring local churches and then sent out to various neighborhoods and communities.

7. **Evaluation and Accountability**—An evaluation will be conducted at least annually and will be communicated to various leaders and ministry boards.

A new church means a new identity. As a church planting team, ask yourselves, "What kind of church do we plan to start?" Each new church must establish an identity in the community where it is going to work. Here are several things that are of vital importance in the formation of a positive identity:

- Include the name of the community where the church is located and choose a name for the group. This will give the group a sense of initial identity.

- Establish holiness as a biblical doctrine and as an evangelism tool. This distinguishes the Church of the Nazarene from many other churches.

- Establish a church that is interested in church growth and missions. We are a dynamic church with a mission to the whole world.

- Emphasize love as a key element in the life of the church. Embracing everyone must be part of the DNA of the church.

- Emphasize biblical worship that is informed by the core values of the church.

If these things are established, the community will see the new church as a positive influence.

The next question to ask yourselves is, "What kind of church is needed?" Paul Orjala, when teaching seminary students in the principles of church planting, summarized the main needs of a relevant church. To him, a church that is needed in the community is a church that would:

- Bring a person to salvation and the assurance of that salvation.

- Help solve personal problems.

- Help solve community problems.

- Change lives.

- Give meaning to lives.

- Provide fellowship for the lonely.

- Provide a place of service.

- Provide guidelines for living.

Getting started correctly is essential for growth. Even when people in a community are responsive, it is important to continually meet their perceived needs. Your approach must appeal to their value system and encourage their faith and trust in you. When you have become their friends, the possibilities are much greater that they will accept the Gospel you present. Pastors need to train their young people to make friends so they can bring friends to the church and to Jesus Christ.

Next you need to answer the question, "Where will we begin services?" It may be that you will want to rent a place such as a school or a store building. Even shopping centers have been used effectively for beginning congregations. You may want to start at a coffee shop or someone may offer his/her home or garage.

Finally, ask yourselves, "What kinds of gatherings will we have at the beginning?" There are many ways to begin a church. The Bible study is one of the most popular methods, but good beginnings have also evolved from prayer cells, evangelistic campaigns, cultural gatherings and neighborhood canvasses.

Successful church planters have effectively used local church groups to help canvass and invite people to come to special services in the new church. There are many people who would be willing to assist in such a way to start a new church. Many of the churches in South America, for example, were started by using youth groups from nearby Nazarene churches to visit and witness in the community. In the evening they sang during the evangelistic services and had the opportunity to welcome the people they had visited with.

Usually several people came to know Jesus Christ during the first week and formed the nucleus of a new congregation.

The pioneer church planter will want to develop exciting, spiritual services for the new congregation, which will include:

1. **Attractive gatherings.** People will want to go to church because there is something that draws them to worship and serve the Lord.

2. **The power of God.** People need to sense the presence of God in the services. Ritual alone will not be enough to keep people attending regularly.

3. **Involvement.** Involve your people in all kinds of ministries. If there is not a job for them to do, create a meaningful one.

4. **Solid biblical, evangelistic preaching.** People are hungry for the kind of preaching that

challenges and inspires them to learn and do the will of God.

5. **Worshipful music.** A church without music is a church that stifles growth. Where appropriate, find ways to develop the musical ability of your people to create a music atmosphere in which they will want to be involved.

6. **People inviting people.** Your people must be friendly and want to see the church grow. A church that expresses genuine love will reach people quickly.

7. **Meaningful impact on the community.** A church exists to minister to both the spiritual and physical needs of the community where it is planted. Meaningful engagement in the community ensures ongoing presence and vitality.

To establish the new congregation, leaders are essential. They are needed in the Sunday school, the youth organization, the community outreach, cell groups and Bible studies. No person can be an entire orchestra. Developing leaders and training new converts will be one of your most important responsibilities in training and equipping the people for the work of the ministry (Ephesians 4:12). Your responsibilities will also include discipleship programs, which offer on-the-job training.

One of the most important words in the vocabulary of the minister is trust. Trusting people, particularly new converts, is one of the best ways to train them for the work of the ministry. Delegating responsibility and the authority to carry through helps lay people to understand and accept their biblical role in the church.

"People generally want to be part of a moving organization, not a little group that may dwindle and die as time goes on."

organize

When planning to plant a church, keep in mind that there is also the larger body of the Church of the Nazarene to consider. The first step in the process of planting a church is to approach your district superintendent. In most cases, a district superintendent will welcome the announcement that a new work is being planted or sponsored and will enthusiastically give supervision to the project. In any event, he/she should be apprised of the plans. Supervision of the project will continue to be his/her responsibility. (Occasionally district leaders, through reluctance to release control or give permission, may easily kill initiative for church planting. The church planter(s) must be convinced of God's direction so as not to be easily deterred.)

Regular reports to the district superintendent by the church planter and/or sponsor pastor are, of course, a part of the Church of the Nazarene's program. Authorization to organize the new work into a fully organized church must come from the district superintendent.

Contrary to the current theory that "organizing a church is the easiest way to kill it," it has been our experience that the timely organization of a church can secure its longevity. Depending on the conditions, church planting efforts usually plan for a church to become organized within six months. Organization gives form to the group and makes it an integral part of a larger body such as a district. Psychologically, it helps the people by making them responsible and serious about developing a vibrant church. People generally want to be part of a moving organization, not a little group that may dwindle and die as time goes on. We have seen many churches die because they were not organized early enough in the process.

The following guidelines are useful for pastors who strive to organize new church plants:

1. To organize a church there is the need for approximately 15 stable members to form a solid leadership and ministry team and carry on the full functions of a church. These need to be tithing members. Tithing and stewardship are essential in the ownership of the local church by the local believers.

2. A regular, stable gathering place is necessary to allow people to have a sense of stability and belonging. The gathering facility may be:
   - Rented
   - In a home with a long-term commitment
   - A building owned by the church

3. Services (of appropriate form) should be conducted regularly.

4. The church should learn to participate in the connectional ministries of the Church of the Nazarene by responsibly investing in district and global mission financial responsibilities.

5. There should be maturity in evangelism.

6. The church should have a pastor, accepted by the leadership and recognized as the leader of that congregation. This could be one of the following:
   - An ordained elder
   - A licensed minister
   - A supply pastor
   - A lay pastor

Occasionally, the ideal does not emerge and one of the above conditions is not met. This does not necessarily spell out a death sentence. Perhaps it will be necessary to reevaluate and apply new measures with renewed perseverance. There are existing churches that might have been stillborn had they been organized prematurely without the essential ingredients for a viable church. It is important to discern God's timetable, still keeping the goal of organization alive.

"Every pastor should be consistently developing new methods, growing and maturing."

qualities

We are pastors in the making. After years of ministry we continue learning new things every day. Every pastor should be consistently developing new methods, growing through continuing education and maturing in his/her relationship with God.

Dr. V. H. Lewis used to say, "You would think with the beautifulness of heaven and the awfulness of hell, we Nazarenes could do something for the Kingdom." With this motivation, catalytic leaders develop certain qualities in the pastors under their leadership. Some of the pastoral qualities that are essential in a church-planting pastor are:

1. **Develop common sense.** This quality is at the top of the list. Without the ability to reason sanely, it is difficult to be an effective pastor. Every pastor should strive to develop his/her best potential in this area.

2. Develop the ability to get along with people.
Good relationships with people are of vital
importance. I have often said that if some
missionaries and pastors did not have to work
with people, they would be great ministers.
Of course, that is said with tongue in cheek
because if you cannot work with people, you will
have no ministry at all.

3. Develop vision. A leader without vision cannot
lead. The ability to see what can be done, even
in adverse circumstances, is a quality that is
necessary for the development of a church.

4. Be filled with God's Holy Spirit. The greatest
preachers of the doctrine of holiness are those
whom God has filled with His Holy Spirit in the
cleansing, purifying work of grace. You can know
that God has done this work in you. He can do

the impossible through you because His Holy Spirit is operating, giving you power to be a faithful pastor.

5. **Develop the ability to preach.** The ability to prepare and deliver messages can be learned in a homiletics class. The skill to organize words and to communicate increases with practice. However, the message touches the hearts of the people only as the Holy Spirit takes your words and anoints them. His power makes the difference between a message that is just a speech and a message that is a true work of grace.

6. **Develop the desire to work for the Lord.** There is no room for lazy pastors in the kingdom of God. Time for study, counseling, visitation and all of the other responsibilities of a pastor must be organized into a regular schedule. Visitation is especially important. The more visits made

by pastors and people, the more contacts the church has for growth.

7. **Develop the ability to inspire your people to build the kingdom of God.** This requires that you will trust them in the building of the Kingdom. We have come to believe that one of the greatest responsibilities in leadership is to inspire people to do the impossible for the Kingdom.

8. **Develop evangelism as the center of your ministry and your church.** Many times we get so involved in building the church that we forget about evangelism. We have known of churches that raised two million dollars in a year's time but only won 10 to 15 new people to Jesus during that year. Priorities need to be re-examined when this happens.

9. Develop intentional worship experiences in the local church. You may not have musical ability but you can find people who do. Delegate this responsibility and give supervision to creating the right atmosphere in the gatherings through music that is culturally relevant and biblically centered.

10. Engage in lively gatherings. Your gatherings should attract rather than repel people. God does not often reveal himself in dead, dragging church gatherings. Where God is, there is life. The Church of the Nazarene believes that church gatherings must appeal to people who are looking for something real.

11. Develop your congregation's gifts. The more people you can involve in the life of the church, the more you will win for the Kingdom. The more your people are visiting and working for the Lord, the more they will love the church.

12. Develop humility concerning your position.
A pastor who has an ego problem fights for his/her position and wants to receive the credit for building a great church. That kind of person is not a Kingdom builder.

13. Develop the ability to preach the doctrine of holiness in a dynamic way. Holiness is not something that is tagged on to the Gospel. Holiness is at the center of the Gospel. We are all saved to live holy lives. Through the experience of sanctification, God enables us to live without a civil war in our own hearts. The presentation of holiness will turn your congregation into a New Testament, biblical church.

14. Expect each gathering to be special. There is no such thing as a normal church service. Every time your new church gathers, there must be an expectation from the congregation, and from you, that God is going to do something special in that gathering.

15. **Take risks.** Calculated risks are part of entrepreneurship. Pastors must be entrepreneurs. If there are no risks involved, there are no gains. This means trusting people and trying new programs. It means being willing to fail in order to succeed. However, your risks must be calculated, so you will know how to work out your plan and plan your work.

16. **Develop the ability to organize.** The ability to organize time is of major importance, as is the ability to organize the people to do the work of the Kingdom. Pastors can develop organizational abilities if they have the desire and the motivation to do so.

17. Develop the ability to set goals. Pastors with vision will set challenging goals for themselves and for their church. Some churches are like automobiles without drivers. They have no goals, nor anyone to guide them. The goals of a congregation should be:

    a. Definite: Calculate your goals so that it will take faith to reach them, but don't make them so high that they are impossible to reach even with a miracle of God.

    b. Precise: Many times we talk about growing the church when we should be talking about how.

    c. Clear: There should be no question as to what the goal is.

d. Reachable: Setting goals that are beyond the reality to actually attain can be demoralizing to your church plant.

e. Grounded in faith: If we are the Church, we should be about the business of God and faith. Our goals should be too.

f. God-given: Setting goals that aren't according to God's plans will be detrimental to your effort.

"You would think with the beautifulness of heaven and the awfulness of hell, we Nazarenes could do something for the Kingdom."

Many times a pastor is afraid to set goals for fear he/she will not be able to reach them. This fear is caused by a lack of confidence in himself/herself and his/her abilities. Proper self-esteem will overcome these fears. We challenge you to find some good books on how to set goals and how to reach them. It will help in this new adventure of starting a new church.

18. **Reproduce yourself.** The last challenge is to reproduce yourself as a church planter and pastor. This is a biblical principle we find throughout scripture. God wants us to build the Kingdom through reproduction. As we begin to look for new people for the ministry, we will be able to develop new pastors for the Kingdom.

As a pastor you must strive to be all that God wants you to be so you can lead your people to be all God wants them to be.

"The pastor who is a good administrator sets the stage for growth in the church."

responsibilities

the pastor who is a good administrator sets the stage for growth in the church. It is not enough to go through the motions of conducting services. Some administrative responsibilities that may help in this church planting adventure are outlined here.

1. **Promote.** Promotion is very important for a salesman or leader, even in the secular world. We have the responsibility to keep the challenge of the Great Commission before our people. This does not mean giving long announcements, but it does mean promoting and giving importance to what you want to see accomplished within your congregation.

2. **Manage your time.** As previously stated, time management is key for a pastor because his/her responsibilities are many and varied. It would be wonderful if you could do as the apostles

in Acts 6, spending all your time in prayer and proclaiming the Word. You cannot. But you will be able to delegate and organize time for prayer and study. These are the most important priorities of your pastoral activities. Without them, your church will not grow.

Make the most of every day. As you organize your time and your church, you will accomplish much for the Kingdom. God helps us as we strive to do as much as possible for Him.

The following outline suggests a plan for organization of your varied responsibilities.

- Office work
    - Prayer
    - Bible study
        - Personal
        - Sermon preparation—
          develop seed thoughts for

future messages as well.

- Develop a filing system for Sunday school, church services, visitation, etc.
- Prepare reports for the district superintendent and/or the overseeing pastor who is helping you to start this church and for the district assembly.

- Organization of the Church
    - Training of teachers and leaders
    - Missionary Society
    - Youth organization
    - Prayer cells
    - Bible studies
    - Ushers

- Other responsibilities
    - Oversee by delegating the maintenance of the building.

- Oversee the visitation program.
- Oversee the altar workers, teaching them how to guide people in praying for salvation and sanctification and how to give counsel at the altar.
- Oversee the organization of church services, putting as many people to work as possible in each service.
- Prepare a membership class. We would suggest you conduct a membership class every week, possibly during Sunday school, consisting of four to eight sessions. We have used four lessons covering:
  - History of the Church of the Nazarene
  - Organization
  - General and special rules
  - Doctrine

- Set a membership Sunday every
  month if possible, or at least
  every three months. Make that
  an important day in the life of
  your church and promote it.
  Some important requirements for
  members are:

  - Believe the doctrine of the
    Church of the Nazarene.
  - Be faithful in attendance.
  - Be faithful in tithes and
    offerings.
  - Read the Manual of the
    church carefully.

3. Plan to receive members. Set your dates, and
work toward that goal. Of course, you will have
to prepare them for the reception.

4. Evangelize. Mass evangelism in the local church
as well as personal evangelism by you and

your members in homes and businesses will bring in new members and help them grow and reproduce.

5. **Disciple.** Within three months of a person's conversion, he/she should be discipled and ready for reception into membership. If a person is not ready for membership, establish another time period so he/she will be working toward that goal. Continue to work with him/her until he/she has completed the membership class and can meet the requirements for membership.

6. **Pray for the salvation** of those outside of your church body. Not only the pastor, but also the church, needs to be praying that God will bring more sheep into the flock—not for the sake of numbers or reports, but for the sake of their salvation.

7. **Use contextualized, effective involvement programs.** Get your people involved in winning others. God saves us not to sit on the benches but to receive power to become witnesses (Acts 1:8).

8. **Strengthen the congregation.** Acts 14:21-22 explains the importance of strengthening the disciples and encouraging them to remain true to the faith.

- Utilize them.
    - Involve them in decisions.
    - Give them ownership.
    - Equip them (Ephesians 4:12).
- Feed them through good preaching.
- Help them to grow by
    - Developing good habits.
    - Studying the Word of God.
    - Learning discipline.
    - Public testimony.

- Make sure they have a real experience of transformation in Christ.
    - Encourage them to seek the infilling of the Holy Spirit.
    - Motivate them.
- Love them
    - Through fellowship.
    - Through encouragement.
    - By being there when they need you.
    - By praying for them by name during the week.
- Teach them to lead others to Christ.
    - At the altar
    - Outside the church
- Keep a good up-to-date list of your members and a record of their walk with Christ.
- Train your members to:
    - Manage the business of the church in general.
    - Manage the money of the church.

- Receive the monthly report of the pastor, which will give the state of the church, its direction, and its goals.
- Receive the report of the treasurer.
- Become responsible for the pastor and his/her salary.

"With the help of the Holy Spirit, keep your personal life without spot or blemish as an example of holiness, if you expect people to follow you to a holy God."

- Serve on committees. (At the beginning, the pastor will probably want to use the regular board because of lack of personnel. However, he/she should not be afraid to use new people.)

- Visit. Visiting is a very important responsibility of the pastor. In this day we are hearing pastors say that it does not pay to visit. That is not true, and such advice should not be taken seriously. Certainly it is easier not to visit, but your church will not grow unless someone is visiting. True, as the church grows larger, the pastor will have less and less contact with established members. But members of longer standing, equipped for ministry themselves, will by that time be ready to share the responsibilities of ministry.
  - What constitutes a visit? The visit does not have to be long. You may even want to call ahead and make an appointment in these busy days. You can make many contacts, inviting people and dealing with their spiritual needs.

- What do you talk about?
    - Their family
    - Their activities
    - The activities of the church
    - Possibly even yourself and your family
    - Their spiritual needs.
- Try to get to their hearts through personal evangelism in the home. Remember that you will need to win them to yourself before you can win them to Jesus.
- Read the Bible.
- Pray with them before you leave their home.
- Invite them to church.
- Continue to visit or delegate visitation. Remember that developing the follow-up program is of utmost importance, not only

with new people you have visited but especially with people who have visited the church.

9. **Meet the need.** Develop your services to meet the need where you are. If most of your visitors come to the weekend morning service, you probably should prepare to meet the evangelistic needs of the congregation then, rather than on the evening services and vice-versa. All of the services should be prepared with the special needs of your people in mind.

10. **Be ready spiritually.** You are the preacher, God's ambassador to appeal to others with the message of reconciliation. You are the instrument of the Holy Spirit to deliver the message of God. Be ready spiritually to deliver not only a message, but your soul and heart as you represent an all-powerful God.

11. Holy living. With the help of the Holy Spirit, keep your personal life without spot or blemish as an example of holiness, if you expect people to follow you to a holy God. Live what you preach, and preach what you live.

12. Prepare for evangelism. Build the awareness in your church that humanity is lost and without God. It is the church's responsibility to lead people to a forgiving, life-changing God.

- Preach until your people carry a burden for the lostness of man.
- Transfer your vision to your people.
- Change your strategy from a "come" structure to a "go" structure for the church. Many times people have started a church, put up a beautiful sign, sat back and prayed, "God send them in." That mentality must be changed to, "Church, let's go, as the Great Commission bids us, into all the world and preach the Gospel."

- Challenge your people to pray and carry a burden for each worship service and for other members of the body of Christ.
- Invest time in studying. A person is what he/she reads. Set apart funds monthly for purchasing books that will help you in your ministry and build your library.
- Be a friendly pastor.

13. **Pastor as evangelist.** The greatest evangelist you will have in your church is you. Certainly, you will want to invite evangelists to come and hold revival services in your church. However, Sunday by Sunday you are the evangelist. We have heard many pastors say, "I have so much to do, and God has called me to pastor. I do not have the ability to be an evangelist as well." That is true. However, you can develop a style of evangelistic preaching that will build

your church much faster and make you a better preacher of the Word. The following things may help you:

- Preach with power—remember the importance of what you're preaching.
- Preach solid doctrine—holiness never misses.
- Preach for a decision.
- Preach with the power of the Holy Spirit.

14. **Invite to the altar.** Make an appealing invitation for people to come to Christ. Nazarenes have used the altar effectively for many years. More recently, people are less and less reluctant to use the altar because more churches are introducing the open altar approach. We need to develop the idea that the altar is the church family's central meeting place with God.

- Make your intentions clear. Let people know what the altar is for. Help people feel like coming there to kneel is the right decision.
- Prepare the atmosphere for an altar call. That may mean musical ensembles, solos, and/or congregational singing. Music should be well prepared and suited to the message. Give the people time to think, pray and search their hearts.
- Do not force the invitation. Make the people feel comfortable, and give the Holy Spirit time to deal with their hearts.
- Have your altar workers prepared and ready, and have all of your people praying with or for the seekers.

15. **Holiness is central.** Preach holiness as the central message of the Gospel. It is, of course, one of the most important messages you will preach. Remember that holiness is not just another theme of the Church of the Nazarene or of the Bible. It will bring conviction for sin that has been committed, but it will also lift your sanctified people to a higher level in Christ and a closer relationship with Him. Lead your people to the place where they not only receive the Holy Spirit but are able to give a definite testimony of God's sanctifying grace.

"The church is always built by faith and the sacrifice of men and women with a burning desire to see the kingdom of God go forward."

support

for the last several years, many of our church planters have had a built-in dependence on districts and district finances. If we are to win the world for Jesus, the church must change this philosophy. The newly formed group must accept support of itself and its pastor. A few new churches will have pastors who are supported for a while by the district or by sponsoring local churches. However, most new churches will have to be pastored by bi-vocational pastors or lay pastors who are willing to sacrifice their time and energy for the sake of God's kingdom.

As the pastor, you are an employee of the local church, not the district. If the district or mother church is able to help with finances, it should be for a limited time, to be cut back in stages with a deadline for final cut off. This helps the new pastor to challenge the new congregation to faithfully give their tithes and offerings to support their church.

A good book on stewardship would be a wise investment. As part of a discipleship course a pastor can teach that stewardship begins with the giving of time, but also includes the giving of tithes and offerings for the building of the Kingdom. This is God's chosen way to build His Church around the world. Giving is an integral part of our life in Christ and should be done joyfully. He has given us 90% to spend wisely. Ten percent goes back to Him, along with love offerings as God enables and the Holy Spirit prompts.

The church is always built by faith and the sacrifice of men and women with a burning desire to see the kingdom of God go forward. God will build His church through great stewards for the Kingdom's sake. We should not be against a minister receiving a decent wage; we want our pastors to receive as much as possible. At the same time, pastors must be willing to live at the basic level of the people they are serving.

Bi-vocational pastors have been used of God in wonderful ways to build His Kingdom. Some of the greatest days of the Church of the Nazarene happened when people would move, get a job and begin a new church. Many of the old timers even pitched tents and gave their time to start Churches of the Nazarene in new areas.

Once again the Church of the Nazarene is changing its concept and emphasis, using more and more lay pastors or bi-vocational pastors. Of course, if God has called someone to a full-time pastorate, he/she must not settle for working a full-time secular job and pastoring on the side. Pastoring must be the priority while the secular work operates as the financial support system. As soon as the church is able to pay an adequate salary, he/she needs to cut loose from his/her secular job and work full time for the Kingdom.

Many who read this booklet will be bi-vocational men or women. If you can be successful in the secular world, you will almost always be a success in the church world. That dedication and work ethic will reveal itself in church growth and success in planting new churches.

conclusion

Suppose you want to plant a new church. What steps do you need to take? We cannot give you all the answers in a few sentences, but we can give you some basic principles, most of which would be valid in any situation.

1. Contact your local pastor and tell him/her of your desire to plant a new church. See if he/she will sponsor you and help you make the contacts for planting a new congregation.
2. Work with your leadership for permission and legitimacy. Get their guidance concerning where, when and how you could start a church on that district. Tell them of your plans and desires and why you think there is a need for this church planting venture. It's possible that the leadership

can help you in some way, even financially, to begin that church.

3. Make your plans once you have permission. Begin to make contacts and find a place to gather. Begin with the type of gatherings you feel are most appropriate for that particular place and situation. Sometimes we make it too hard, or at least much harder than it really is, to begin a new church.

4. Secure people to pray for you in your new adventure. Prayer is one of the most important factors in building the Kingdom.

5. Remember, God is on your side, and He has promised never to leave you or forsake you.

As you plant this church, look to future possibilities for sponsoring another when your congregation becomes stable and self-supporting. It's a great way to build the Kingdom and fulfill the Great Commission. May God's richest blessings be upon you as you do His will.

suggestions

Bustle, Louie E. *Keys For Church Growth*, Kansas City, Missouri: Beacon Hill Press, 1990.

Calguy, R. *The Principles and Practice of Indigenous Church Planting*. Nashville, Tennessee: Broadman Press, 1981.

Estep, Michael R., ed. *Great Commission Church Planting Sourcebook*. Kansas City, Missouri: Nazarene Publishing House and Church Growth. Inc., 1989.

Estep. Michael R., ed. *Great Commission Church Planting Strategy*. Kansas City, Missouri: Nazarene Publishing House, 1988.

Hesselgrave, David J. *Planting Churches Cross-Culturally. A Guide for Home and Foreign Missions*. Grand Rapids, Michigan: Baker Book House, n.d.

Hodges, Melvin. *Growing Young Churches.* Chicago: Moody Press, 1970.

Jones, Ezra Earl. *Strategies for New Churches.* New York: Harper & Row Publishers, 1987.

Maner, Robert E. *Making the Small Groups Within the Church.* Kansas City, Missouri: Beacon Hill Press, 1980.

POLITICS WITHOUT
PARLIAMENTS
1629-1640

POLITICS
WITHOUT
PARLIAMENTS
—••*1629-1640*••—

ESTHER S. COPE
University of Nebraska – Lincoln

LONDON
ALLEN & UNWIN
Boston   Sydney

Allen & Unwin (Publishers) Ltd,
40 Museum Street, London WC1A 1LU, UK

Allen & Unwin (Publishers) Ltd,
Park Lane, Hemel Hempstead, Herts HP2 4TE, UK

Allen & Unwin, Inc.,
8 Winchester Place, Winchester, Mass. 01890, USA

Allen & Unwin (Australia) Ltd,
8 Napier Street, North Sydney, NSW 2060, Australia

First published in 1987

British Library Cataloguing in Publication Data

Cope, Esther S.
    Politics without parliaments, 1629–1640.
1. Great Britain—Politics and
government—1625–1649
I. Title
941.06'2   DA395
ISBN 0–04–941020–2

Library of Congress Cataloging-in-Publication Data

Cope, Esther S.
    Politics without parliaments, 1629–1640.
Bibliography: p.
Includes index.
1. Great Britain—Politics and government—1625–
1649. I. Title.
DA395.C66   1986   941.06'3   86–10935
ISBN 0–04–941020–2 (alk. paper)

Set in 11 on 12 point Sabon by V & M Graphics Ltd, Aylesbury, Bucks
and printed in Great Britain by Billings & Sons Limited, London and Worcester

Contents

Acknowledgements

This project developed from questions I encountered first in a study of the Short Parliament of 1640 and then in my biography of Lord Montagu. I began to concentrate my attention on the 1630s during the spring of 1979 when I was at the Folger Shakespeare Library on a research leave granted by the Research Council of the University of Nebraska–Lincoln. The Research Council also assisted me with the purchase of microfilm and xerox copies of manuscripts and in the summer of 1981 gave me a Holmes Memorial Faculty Fellowship. A leave during the fall semester of 1981 from Happold Funds at the University of Nebraska–Lincoln and a Huntington–National Endowment for the Humanities Fellowship during the spring of 1982 gave me the time and freedom essential for writing a draft of the book. I am grateful to the Regents, administration, and particularly Max Larsen, former Dean of Arts and Sciences, at the University of Nebraska–Lincoln for their parts in making it possible for me to have a full year to devote to research.

To the staffs at the Folger and Huntington I owe an especial debt. The Huntington's provision of a quiet office was an invaluable contribution to my writing. Fellow readers at both the Huntington and the Folger have contributed to this project in more ways than they know. Maija Cole welcomed me to the Yale Center for Parliamentary History on several occasions and in between answered my queries by letter. Among the other repositories where librarians and archivists have gone out of their way to assist me are: Houghton, Widener, and Law Libraries at Harvard; Institute of Historical Research; British Library; Public Record Office; Bodleian Library;

County Record Offices in Bedford, Cornwall, Devon, East Sussex, Kent, Northampton, Nottingham, Shropshire, and Somerset; City Archives of York; University of Nottingham; Massachusetts Historical Society; the Library of Congress; and the University of Nebraska–Lincoln Libraries.

The footnotes tell a tale of talks with and references from many scholars, only a few of whom I shall mention here. Others not specifically named in the footnotes have encouraged me with their expressions of interest. Lois Schwoerer sustained me during a year when administrative and family responsibilities left little time and energy for research. My family and non-historian friends also deserve thanks for their support and understanding. Wellington the Cat showed remarkable patience during my long hours at the desk, even longer absences in libraries and endless days at the computer.

Richard Cust, Barbara Donagan, Caroline Hibbard, Sears McGee, and Linda Popofsky all shared with me unpublished papers of their own. Barbara Donagan read and commented on Chapter 2. Elizabeth Foster, Conrad Russell and John Morrill read a draft of the entire book. Their sharp eyes and thoughtful responses have been of inestimable help. The final version is, of course, my responsibility.

I am especially grateful to Sandra Pershing, Joan Curtis, Lona Haskins, Barbara Michaels and Linda Dykstra of the History Department at the University of Nebraska–Lincoln. They struggled together to follow my arrows and type one good draft. Margaret Cullinane and Laurel Volpe came to my rescue and typed a revised version. G. G. Meisels, Dean of Arts and Sciences, University of Nebraska–Lincoln, managed to find funds for typing at a critical moment.

This book includes some material I published in *The Life of a Public Man: Edward, First Baron Montagu of Boughton, 1562–1644* (Philadelphia, Pa: American Philosophical Society, 1981); 'Public images of Parliament during its absence', *Legislative Studies Quarterly*, vol. 7, no. 2 (1982), pp. 221–34; and 'Politics without Parliament: the dispute about muster masters' fees in Shropshire in the 1630s', *Huntington Library Quarterly*, vol. 45, no. 4 (1982), pp. 271–84.

Abbreviations

Alum. Cant.	J. Venn, *Alumni Cantabrigiensis* (Cambridge: Cambridge University Press, 1924).
BIHR	*Bulletin of the Institute of Historical Research.*
Birch	T. Birch (ed.), *The Court and Times of Charles I*, 2 vols (London: Henry Colburn, 1848).
BL	British Library, London.
Bodl.	Bodleian Library, Oxford.
CD 1628	R. Johnson, M. Cole, *et al.* (eds), *Commons Debates, 1628* (New Haven, Conn.: Yale University Press, 1977).
CD 1629	W. Notestein and F. H. Relf (eds), *Commons Debates, 1629* (Minneapolis, Minn.: University of Minnesota Press, 1921).
Cl C	Clifton Manuscripts, University of Nottingham Library.
Cope and Coates	E. S. Cope and W. H. Coates (eds), *Proceedings of the Short Parliament of 1640*, Royal Historical Society, Camden Fourth Series, vol. 19 (1977).
Cope, *Montagu*	E. S. Cope, *The Life of a Public Man: Edward, First Baron Montagu of Boughton, 1562–1644* (Philadelphia, Pa: American Philosophical Society, 1981).
CSPDom.	*Calendar of State Papers, Domestic Series* (London, 1856–97).
CSPVen.	*Calendar of State Papers and Manuscripts Relating to English Affairs Existing in the Archives and Collections of Venice and Other Libraries of Northern Italy* (London, 1864–1947).
DeL'Isle	Historical Manuscripts Commission, *Report on the MSS of the Right Honourable Viscount DeL'Isle,*

	V.C. at Penshurst Palace, Kent, Vol. 6; Sidney Papers, 1626–1698 (London, 1966).
DNB	*Dictionary of National Biography.*
EHR	*English Historical Review.*
El	Ellesmere Manuscripts, Henry E. Huntington Library and Art Gallery, San Marino.
HA	Hastings Manuscripts, Henry E. Huntington Library and Art Gallery, San Marino.
Harley Letters	T. T. Lewis (ed.), *The Letters of the Lady Brilliana Harley*, Camden Society, vol. 58 (1854).
Harvard	Widener Library, Harvard University.
HEH	Henry E. Huntington Library and Art Gallery, San Marino.
HMC	Historical Manuscripts Commission.
Holles	Letters of John Holles, earl of Clare, University of Nottingham, MSS (NeC 15404–5), Yale Center for Parliamentary History Film.
HN	Henry E. Huntington Library and Art Gallery, San Marino, preface to call number for early printed books.
JBS	*Journal of British Studies.*
Keeler	M. F. Keeler, *The Long Parliament* (Philadelphia: American Philosophical Society, 1954).
Knowler	W. Knowler (ed.), *The Earl of Strafford's Letters and Despatches*, 2 vols, (London, 1739).
Knyvett	B. Schofield (ed.), *The Knyvett Letters, 1620–1644*, Norfolk Record Society, vol. 20 (1949).
Laud, *Works*	W. Scott and J. Bliss (eds), *The Works of William Laud*, 7 vols in 9 (Oxford: Parker Society, 1847–60).
Montagu MSS	Manuscripts in the collection of the Duke of Buccleuch and Queensberry.
PC	Privy Council Registers, Public Record Office, London.
PCR	*Privy Council Registers*, reproduced in facsimile (London, 1967–8).
PRO	Public Record Office, London.
Rous	M. A. E. Green (ed.), *Diary of John Rous*, Camden Society, vol. 66 (1856).
Rye, Corr.	Rye Corporation, Correspondence, East Sussex Record Office.
SP	State Papers, Domestic, Public Record Office, London.

ST	T. B. Howell (ed.), *Complete Collection of State Trials* (London, 1816).
STC	*A Short-Title Catalogue of Books printed in England and Ireland and of English Books printed abroad, 1475–1640*, eds A. W. Pollard and G. R. Redgrave (London, 1926).
STC W	*A Short-Title Catalogue of Books printed in England, Scotland, Ireland, Wales, and British America, and of English Books printed in Other Countries, 1641–1700*, ed. D. Wing (New York, 1945–51).
STT	Manuscripts from the Collections of the Temples of Stow, Henry E. Huntington Library and Art Gallery, San Marino.
TRHS	*Transactions of the Royal Historical Society.*
Whiteway	Diary of William Whiteway, British Library, Egerton MS 784, Yale Center for Parliamentary History Film.
Woodforde	Diary of Robert Woodforde, Historical Manuscripts Commission, *Ninth Report*, app., part ii.
WP	*Winthrop Papers* (Massachusetts Historical Society, 1929).
Yale	Yale Center for Parliamentary History.
Yonge	Diary of Walter Yonge, British Library, Additional MS 35331, Yale Center for Parliamentary History Film.

Introduction

Charles I dissolved his third Parliament in March 1628/9 and did not summon another for eleven years. Although James I had waited four years after 1610 and seven after 1614 before calling the Lords and Commons, neither he nor any other monarch during the previous century had allowed such a long interval without them to elapse. Charles returned to personal rule after holding an abortive three-week session in the spring of 1640, but the demands of war and popular discontent prompted him to meet what would become the Long Parliament in November of the same year. His era of nonparliamentary government quickly became identified as a period in history.

Throughout the winter of 1640–1 MPs talked of grievances that had accumulated during the 'intermission of parliaments' and were a consequence of it. They complained of the allowance of Popery, Arminianism and other innovations in religion, of violations of property by imposition of charges and judicial proceedings and of much more including the very absence of Parliament. From their perspective the 'Short Parliament' that had met some months earlier had merely added disappointment to the burdens the English already faced. They listed its dissolution along with other incidents from the 1630s as evidence of the ineptitude and wrongdoing of the earl of Strafford, Archbishop Laud, and the others who as bishops, judges and councillors had been advising the king.[1]

The parliamentarians' view of the 1630s differs significantly from that presented by some of their contemporaries who applauded Charles's efforts to crack down on Puritanism, sedition and disrespect for his prerogative. Poets praised Charles I for bringing England peace and prosperity. The benefits of his reign seemed striking when contrasted with the devastation and suffering experienced by people in war-torn Germany. When the earl of Clarendon wrote his *History of the Rebellion*, he asked why his countrymen were not satisfied with the advantages they had.[2]

Historians who have studied the 1630s in the centuries since have wrestled with the conflicting interpretations of the period and its relationship to the civil wars of the 1640s.[3] The primary purpose of this volume is to delineate and assess the nature of politics in the counties and towns of England during the eleven years between 1629 and 1640 when no Parliament met. Parliament's unique role in bringing monarch and people together to consider each other's needs meant that politics changed in its absence.[4] Without a forum where they could freely discuss public affairs with individuals from the entire kingdom those in England who were concerned about the condition of Church and commonwealth found they must either address the king directly and risk his displeasure, or use institutions and tactics designed for other purposes or become observers rather than participants in the political process.

This book argues that the English, especially those who were prominent in their communities between 1629 and 1640, were informed about public issues. The frequent parliaments of the 1620s had allowed people from all over the kingdom to exchange views and had instructed those at Westminster and beyond about questions of religion and government. By the end of the decade news of events at home and abroad circulated widely. The English, educated about the functions of Parliament, aware that it served political as well as legislative, revenue-raising and judicial purposes and acquainted with details of its proceedings from the minutiae of ceremonies, procedure, and the dress or conduct of MPs to the content of speeches, action on bills, and the relations between king, Lords and Commons, had an interest in politics that did not cease when no Parliament was sitting.[5]

Without Parliament the setting for politics was necessarily local and informal. Many of the individuals who had been and might again be MPs were leaders in the counties and towns. There, as lieutenants and deputy lieutenants, sheriffs, justices of the peace, mayors, aldermen and burgesses, they had some opportunities to interpret, impede, or facilitate the business that came before them.

Although their responsibilities were administrative and judicial – the king and council expected them to execute orders – their knowledge, experience, intermediary position between crown and populace, and the official and unofficial papers reporting their conduct make them critical figures for this study.

Property, status and connections gave both those who held positions of responsibility and others resources for political action in the absence of Parliament. Through such informal means and through litigation the laity could undertake the very difficult business of trying to influence the ecclesiastical hierarchy. Petitions were a tactic that virtually anyone could employ, but even though they emphasized the king's power and the petitioners' dependence, they were not without danger for subscribers.[6] Likelihood of punishment was much greater for anyone who held public meetings, participated in demonstrations, gave speeches, printed tracts, or formed organizations for political purposes. Those who wished to express opinions had to choose whether they were willing to incur penalties or whether they should avoid straightforward statements and attempt to achieve their goal by other means.[7] The choice was difficult. Although Charles I tended to regard extra-parliamentary politics as opposition, the severity of his treatment of would-be politicians was not always predictable. Evidence about open and explicit politics during the 1630s must be supplemented by and analysed with that concerning more subtle manoeuvring.

The political sophistication of the local leaders enabled them to calculate their moves. Hesitant to engage in activities that might smack of outright defiance of royal authority, they demonstrated their attitudes through symbolic acts. Often they appear more compliant than they were. Despite their lack of formal organization, their diverse priorities, their conservative rhetoric and their relatively small numbers, they represented a significant body of potential resistance to the rule of Charles I. Their opposition became stronger and more explicit in 1639 and 1640. The first Bishops' War added new grievances to those already existing and made manifest connections between particular grievances. The dissolution of the Short Parliament of 1640 deprived the English of an opportunity for expressing their concerns in the traditionally accepted manner. Doubts about policies and practices grew into fears of arbitrary government. When the Scots invaded England that August, pressure for reform increased. More and more people responded to the king's appeal for their help in defending the kingdom with calls for relief of grievances through Parliament.

Through its examination of the conduct of politics in the 1630s this book provides evidence about the issues that prompted political action. It shows that localism, religious convictions, and constitutional precepts affected responses to royal policies; so did personal ambition and factional rivalries. While few persons explicitly challenged the government of Charles I on constitutional grounds, a greater number had experiences that made them anxious about the security of their heritage. Many felt their religion was in danger. Fear of Popery, frustration in defending their rights or in advancing their interests made them lose confidence in both ruler and regime. The realities of politics in the early seventeenth century defy the neat categorization that scholars would find convenient. Individuals might have more than one reason for opposing policy. They might, for example, resent the intrusions of Laudian ecclesiastical visitors, worry that the visitors' demands were leading the kingdom down the road to Popery, and ask where authority over religion lay. Tactical considerations in the presentation of political views also blurred lines distinguishing among constitutional, religious, local and other bases of political action.

The relationship between country and court and between community and nation was itself complex. Charles I's subjects did not think merely in terms of their own 'countries', and when they talked of 'country', they sometimes meant county and sometimes division, parish, village or neighbourhood. Local issues and problems provided the context in which they encountered royal policy. Disputes within, between and among counties, towns, hundreds and parishes attenuated unified resistance to 'outside' interference. Local quarrels and customs could nevertheless serve as defence against centralization and/or a base for opposing policy, but coexisting with parochialism were broader interests nourished by readily available information about developments at court, elsewhere in England, and on the continent. Breadth of perspective, understanding of particular issues, and priorities varied from individual to individual and from circumstance to circumstance. Although the absence of parliaments gave politics away from the court a necessarily local format during the 1630s, local and national concerns were frequently joined.[8]

Dislike of specific policies and practices, misgivings about the direction in which the kingdom was heading, and a virtual lack of heartfelt affection for the king himself influenced political attitudes. Charles's inability to arouse the love of his subjects and his inclination to be suspicious of their efforts to affect policy had an overwhelming impact on the political environment of his reign. To assess politics without parliaments between 1629 and 1640 we must consider more than the revenue collected by the crown, constitution-alist arguments, or outbreaks of violence. Neither the Whig view of a revolutionary party struggling against eleven years of tyranny nor a revisionist alternative of only minor challenges to a generally successful personal rule by Charles represents an accurate description of the period.[9]

In taking up the admittedly difficult task of tracing the political activities of the men who served as leaders of town and country during the 1630s this book proceeds by examining evidence about their lives and especially about their role in governing their communities. Because the bulk of the sources are personal, administrative and judicial, they provide little explicit information about politics and thus add another covering layer to whatever obfuscation individuals may have used to conceal their own political aims. Conclusions will at times be tentative. Even when a broad perspective shows that words and deeds have political implications not manifest from the immediate context or ordinarily associated with administration, justice, or estate management, we cannot always be certain whether politics were conscious. Much ultimately depends upon interpretation.

The methodological problems that a history of politics without parliaments presents have deterred scholars from attempting to examine reactions to royal policy in England during the 1630s. The increasing availability of family papers and governmental records for research and the growing number of studies of particular commun-ities that have been completed give the investigator of politics 'in the country' between 1629 and 1640 access to more data. The work of historians and social scientists on 'non-elites' and 'non-institutionalized' politics and on politics in developing nations suggests new techniques and approaches.[10] An examination of politics in England during the eleven years of Charles I's personal rule is now feasible.

Until we have some notion about politics without parliaments, we cannot assess the significance of parliaments in the early seventeenth century. Without knowing how Charles's subjects responded to the policies and projects by which he tried to raise money, defend the kingdom and preserve the Church of England, we cannot understand the origins of the civil war of the 1640s. We need to be able to measure the English political temperature during the 1630s. How does it compare with that during the years of nonparliamentary government in the reign of James I? Did Charles I's subjects believe that he had made a firm decision to rule without parliaments or did they think that he might soon find reason to summon another? The existence of political activity in the country during the absence of parliaments is not in itself an indication either of the presence of revolutionaries or of divisions that would lead to war. By studying politics we can put disputes in perspective and distinguish minor quarrels from more serious conflicts.

This book seeks to contribute to our understanding of the period through its analysis of the conduct of politics in the absence of parliaments. In taking the eleven years of the king's personal rule for its parameters it is not accepting the claim that the dissolution of 1629 put England on a 'high road' to civil war. It makes no assumption about the validity of the MPs' contentions about the significance of the absence of parliaments. Establishing a basis for assessing those contentions is one of its aims.

The book begins with an examination of the aftermath of the dissolution of Parliament in 1629. The first chapter includes, in addition to a study of politics during the year following the breakup of Parliament, an overview of reactions to the absence of parliaments during the remainder of the decade. The next three chapters treat successively religion, defence, and projects and procedures. In each of these areas controversies erupted. By separating these topics into discrete chapters some of the interconnections between issues may be obscured, and yet during much of the 1630s the English reacted to royal policies on their merits rather than as facets of an overarching scheme of government. Letters and papers testify to the scrutiny that local governors, familiar with law and procedure, gave to particular projects and to instructions sent to them by the crown. Individuals often took greater interest in some measures than in others. The topical organization followed in these three chapters permits comparison and contrast of reactions to religious measures with those to shipmoney or distraint of knighthood. The scheme partially conceals the role that specific people played in the politics of the period, but the conclusion addresses this question and assesses the relative importance of localism, constitutionalism and religion in opposition.

The Anglo-Scottish conflicts of 1639 and 1640 brought together the collection of grievances and problems that were the focus of politics during the 1630s. The fifth chapter reverts to the chronological approach of the first and looks at politics from the outbreak of the first Bishops' War in 1639 until the summoning of the Long Parliament in the autumn of 1640. The war marked a turning point because it endowed the issues of the previous period with new meaning. It gave the English a new framework for understanding their recent political history, a new basis for analysing their government, and new cause for political action. Their perspective developed further with the failure of the brief Parliament that met in the spring of 1640 to accomplish business. Politics intensified during that summer and turned to focus upon demands for a Parliament. The chapter thus serves to gather up threads from the preceding chapters. A conclusion makes more general and more extensive observations about the nature and significance of politics without parliaments.

This book is not a comprehensive study of the 1630s. It directs its attention to public perceptions of policies rather than to the policies themselves or to the development and adoption of policies by the king and his advisers. Its judgements about Charles I stem from the reactions of his subjects to his rule. The court, that is the officials and others who were frequently with the king, appears here not in its own right but as a focus of interest for those who were removed from it. The poets from whose pens came panegyrics of the king or of the peace and prosperity enjoyed during the 1630s are likewise peripheral to this study. The conventions of poetry and the concepts of duty poets espoused linked them far more closely with the crown than with the people. Though not courtiers, most of those treated in these pages are themselves an elite. Only in a limited sense is this a study of popular politics. It concentrates upon the impact popular politics had upon local leaders' responses to royal policies and practices rather than treating the concerns and needs of the population as a whole and considering the ways in which these were expressed.[11]

The data upon which this analysis of politics of the king's leading subjects is based came in part from my own research and in part from the research of other historians. (A list of sources appears below.)

The principal primary sources I have used are the records of government and the papers of individuals and families. Both kinds of sources provide abundant documentation of the activities of the men who held positions of responsibility in the towns and counties of England. Books, especially sermons and tracts which were printed at the time, are my third type of material. I have looked at many of the books printed between 1629 and 1640 as well as primary source materials which have been printed since then. In my manuscript research I have focused my attention upon four major regional areas: the north, centred upon York (City Archives); the midlands with an emphasis upon Nottinghamshire (Clifton MSS) and Northampton-shire (Montagu MSS); the Welsh border, especially Shropshire (Shrewsbury, Bridgnorth, and Ludlow MSS; Ellesmere MSS); and the west country, primarily Somerset (Quarter Sessions Records; Phelips MSS) and Devon (Quarter Sessions Records; Exeter City MSS; Yonge diary). Supplementing this, I have looked at Corporation MSS from Rye, on the south coast; the Temple MSS which contain material about local affairs in Buckinghamshire and Warwickshire; and the Hastings MSS for Huntingdonshire, Leicestershire and Rutland. For London, the southeast, East Anglia, and Cheshire and Lancashire, I am relying primarily on printed records and the work of other historians.

NOTES

1   See, for example, Pym's speech of 7 November 1640 in W. Notestein (ed.), *The Journal of Sir Simonds D'Ewes from the Beginning of the Long Parliament to the Opening of the Trial of the Earl of Strafford* (New Haven, Conn.: Yale University Press, 1923), pp. 7–11. Also see speeches of Rudyerd (J. Rushworth, *Historical Collections* (London, 1721), Vol. 4, p. 26), Bagshaw (ibid., p. 27), D'Ewes (*Journal*, ed. Notestein, p. 5) and the charges against Strafford, Laud and Lord Keeper Finch (*ST*, Vol. 3, pp. 1387–8; Vol. 4, pp. 11–14, 326–30).

2   Edward Hyde, earl of Clarendon, *History of the Rebellion*, ed. W. D. Macray (Oxford: Clarendon Press, 1888), e.g. 1.12, 146–8, 162. See also R. Anselment, 'Clarendon and the Caroline myth of peace', *JBS*, vol. 23, no. 1 (1984), pp. 37–54.

3   To date virtually all the studies of the 1630s have appeared either within more general histories of the early Stuart era or as part of specialized studies of people or problems of the period. Hugh Kearney reviewed *The Eleven Years' Tyranny of Charles I* in a pamphlet published for the Historical Association

in 1962 (Aids for Teachers Series, no. 9). Kevin Sharpe is currently working on a comprehensive study of court, policy, and country in the 1630s. He sets forth his view of the era in his essay, 'The personal rule of Charles I', *Before the English Civil War*, ed. H. Tomlinson (London: Macmillan, 1983), pp. 53–78.

4   Elton makes this point for the Tudor period in 'Tudor Government: the points of contact: 1. Parliament', *TRHS*, Fifth Series, vol. 24 (1974), pp. 183–200.

5   Conrad Russell takes a narrower view of the significance of early Stuart parliaments in 'Parliamentary history in perspective', *History*, vol. 61, no. 201 (1976), pp. 1–27. See also his 'The nature of a parliament in early Stuart England', in *Before the English Civil War*, pp. 123–50, and the differing interpretations of T. K. Rabb and D. M. Hirst in 'Revisionism revised: two perspectives on early Stuart parliamentary history', *Past and Present*, vol. 92 (1981), pp. 55–99.

6   e.g. the fate of the Northamptonshire gentlemen who presented the petition from some of their neighbours concerning the suspension and deprivation of ministers in February 1604/5 (Cope, *Montagu*, pp. 37–42). Concerning petitioning and the importance of county petitions to Parliament between 1640 and 1642, see A. Fletcher, *The Outbreak of the English Civil War* (New York: New York University Press, 1981), pp. xxv–xxvii and ch. 6.

7   Morrill discusses this briefly in 'The religious context of the English Civil War', *TRHS*, Fifth Series, vol. 34 (1984), p. 159.

8   Arguments such as those of Alan Everitt in *The Community of Kent and the Great Rebellion* (Leicester: Leicester University Press, 1966) and John Morrill in *The Revolt of the Provinces* (London: Allen & Unwin, 1976) need to be qualified by Clive Holmes, 'The county community in Stuart historiography', *JBS*, vol. 19, no. 1 (1980), pp. 54–73, by Anthony Fletcher, 'National and local awareness in the county communities', in *Before the English Civil War*, pp. 151–74, and by the work of Richard Cust among others. I am grateful to Cust for sharing with me an unpublished paper, 'The opposition to the Loan: I. News and opinion in the 1620s'.

9   The revisionists have been more visible than the Whigs in recent years. They tend to emphasize the monarchy's accomplishments and faction and politics at court. See, for example, Kevin Sharpe, 'Faction at the early Stuart court', *History Today*, (October 1983), pp. 39–46; also his 'Personal rule', in *Before the English Civil War*, pp. 53–78. The anti-revisionists themselves reject the Whig label and stress the importance of opposition both in Parliament and in the country. See, for example, the article by Rabb and Hirst in *Past and Present* (1981), cited above.

10 Even though the local leaders who are the principal figures in this study were in many respects an elite, they share characteristics of non-elites such as women or minorities today because except in Parliament they were outside established political structures. Evidence about their political opinions and activities, like those of non-elites, does not appear in an organized form in the public records. It has to be gathered from a variety of sources. John Brewer's illumination of non-institutionalized politics in the eighteenth century (*Party*

Ideology and Popular Politics at the Accession of George III (Cambridge: Cambridge University Press, 1976), is suggestive although both the politics and the sources for that period are quite different from what they are in the seventeenth century. Among the work on developing nations, see R. Jackson and C. Rosbert, *Personal Rule and Black Africa* (Berkeley, Calif.: University of California Press, 1982), esp. pp. x, 1–2, 5; M. Fortes and E. E. Evans-Pritchard, *African Political Systems* (Oxford: Oxford University Press, 1940), esp. pp. 11–13; M. J. Swartz, 'Process in administration and political action', in M. J. Swartz (ed.), *Local-Level Politics: Social and Cultural Perspectives* (Chicago: University of Chicago Press, 1968), pp. 227–8; also J. A. Barnes, 'Networks and political process', in *Local-Level Politics*, p. 107. My colleague Dane Kennedy advised me about work on Africa.

11 A full-scale study of popular politics is a project in itself. Such a study should draw upon non-written evidence and methods such as those employed by Keith Thomas in *Religion and the Decline of Magic* (London: Weidenfeld & Nicolson, 1971), and by David Underdown in 'The problem of popular allegiance in the English Civil War', *TRHS*, Fifth Series, vol. 31, pp. 69–94. B. Sharp, *In Contempt of All Authority* (Berkeley, Calif.: University of California Press, 1980) looks at popular politics in the context of revolts and riots, but he relies primarily upon analysis of written material.

1

1629: The Aftermath of Parliament

On 2 March 1628/9 King Charles I adjourned Parliament. Eight days later he went one step farther and dissolved the assembly. Before another Parliament could meet, elections would have to occur. The abrupt dissolution was Charles's third during the four years that he had reigned, and on each occasion his action gave rise to fears that the realm would suffer because, without a Parliament, he and his people would have no way to resolve their political differences. Parliament, as Sir Benjamin Rudyard put it in 1640, was the 'bedd of reconciliation' between king and subject.[1]

The breakup of Charles's third Parliament did not come as a complete surprise to the political community. Complaints about violations of the Petition of Right and about the apparent toleration of Arminian clergy marked the second session of that Parliament from its very beginning in late January 1628/9. On 25 February after the House of Commons had questioned officers of the Customs concerning the seizure of goods from merchants who had refused to pay tonnage and poundage, the king ordered the Commons to adjourn for a week.[2] Sir Thomas Barrington wrote his mother that the 'probabillytie' of dissolution was causing 'generall sadness'.[3]

The prophecies of the Parliament's failure soon proved self-fulfilling. Determined not to go home before taking steps toward redressing the grievances of their countrymen, Sir John Eliot and several other members of the Lower House prepared resolutions protesting about royal religious and fiscal policies and brought these to the House on 2 March when the adjournment was to have ended.[4] Black Rod's appearance on the same day with an order from the king for the House to adjourn once more threw the Commons into an uproar. Amid the commotion Eliot and his friends held Speaker John Finch in his chair and thereby prevented his compliance with the royal command long enough for their resolutions to be passed by acclamation. Their victory was a pyrrhic one. Charles declared their resistance and the accompanying disorder in the Commons sufficient reason for dissolving the Parliament.[5]

Memories of the aftermath of the dissolutions of the Parliaments of 1625 and 1626 offered people little comfort in March 1628/9. Although the Parliament had enacted many private bills during its first session when it had also passed the Petition of Right, it had left undone some important pieces of public business, including voting the king tonnage and poundage. In the turmoil on 2 March the Commons had denounced persons who collected or paid the levy without parliamentary sanction.[6] Yet until another Parliament met, those who refused payment faced the same fate that had befallen resisting merchants during the preceding years. The judgement against the Five Knights imprisoned in 1627 for declining to lend money to the king suggested that the courts were unlikely to be sympathetic to efforts to recover property seized in lieu of tonnage and poundage.[7] Charles's financial needs virtually insured that, having failed to get subsidies from Parliament, he would try to raise money by other means. Projectors, their appetites whetted, offered their assistance, and newswriters entertained their clients with tales of the latest schemes.[8] Desire for profit and curiosity about what might happen only partially veiled anxieties about the impact of prospective measures for revenue upon liberty and property. Estimates of the protection afforded by the Petition of Right had already proved unrealistic.[9]

People had also learned that Parliament's proceedings against Arminian clergy could be rendered meaningless by royal action. To Richard Montagu whom the Commons had impeached in the spring of 1628 and Roger Manwaring whom they had censured during the same session Charles had offered pardon and preferment.[10] On 2 March along with those who collected or paid nonparliamentary taxes, the Lower House condemned those who encouraged or allowed innovations in religion, but until Parliament met again, the king would determine whether innovators were punished or rewarded.[11]

The disturbance in the House of Commons on 2 March dramatized the differences that history revealed between the ending of Charles I's third Parliament and the conclusions of its predecessors. The disputes in that Parliament disappointed those who had hoped that the assassination in August 1628 of the Duke of Buckingham would introduce an era of good feelings. Instead divisions seemed to become more serious after the removal of the favourite who had been the focus of previous parliamentary quarrels. Although some members of both Houses had expressed surprise and sorrow in 1625 and 1626 when they were sent home, none had used force in an effort to prevent or delay the execution of the king's order as that group of MPs did in 1628/9.[12]

The prompt arrest of nine men, including Sir John Eliot and John Selden, added to the sensation caused by the incident in the Commons and figured prominently in newsletters and other reports of the end of the session. Walter Yonge accompanied his note of the arrests with one of the grotesque designs that he had used to mark the commitment of the Five Knights imprisoned for refusing the Forced Loan and denied habeas corpus.[13] Although both James I and Charles I had ordered MPs to be taken into custody, neither had arrested so many men at once or had so openly attacked speeches made in Parliament.[14] In his 27 March proclamation against 'false rumours touching parliaments' Charles denounced Eliot, although not by name, as 'an outlawed man, desperate in mind and fortune' who had made a 'scandalous and seditious proposition in the House of Commons'.[15]

The prominence of Eliot, who had attracted attention for his opposition to the Duke of Buckingham in 1626, and that of common lawyer John Selden, who had been involved in the prosecution of Buckingham and in 1628 had managed precedents in conferences with the Lords about the Petition of Right, added to the impact of the MPs' arrests.[16] The other seven 'parliament prisoners', included two, William Coryton and Sir Peter Heyman who had sat in several parliaments and had been imprisoned for resistance to lending money to the crown.[17] Denzil Holles, William Strode and Walter Long had also been in Parliament previously and had voiced opposition to royal policy.[18] Sir Miles Hobart and Benjamin Valentine, on the other hand, had made little mark on political history prior to their participation in the events of 2 March 1628/9.[19]

News of the events of 2 March and the succeeding days spread rapidly. On 2 March Sir Thomas Barrington wrote his mother to say that the fears he had reported earlier were materializing. Apologizing for being 'a messinger of evell tideings', he explained, 'my desyres are so greate to informe you with the occurents of the times as that I will rather make any truth my subject then be silent'. His words suggest that he himself was trying to decide how to assess the situation. On the one hand he thought there was 'a verie greate cause to blesse God that we concluded the day withoute any greater business', yet he noted, 'tis farr more easy to speake bravely then to be magnanimous in suffring'. Anyone whose heart did not bleed at the 'threates of theise times' was 'stupid'. He concluded by praying God to 'send us better grounds of comfort'.[20]

To people like Barrington who worried about 'innovations' in religion the disagreements between King Charles I and Parliament were cause for anxiety. Eager for means of weighing the significance of what had happened, they read the king's speech at the dissolution and looked for other indications of his mood. That speech, his declaration concerning the reasons for the dissolution, and the proclamation of 27 March suppressing 'false rumours touching parliaments', offered little hope that another Parliament would meet soon.[21] Dorchester citizen, William Whiteway, observed that the king had dissolved the Parliament 'in great anger' while Suffolk clergyman, John Rous, described the king's proclamation of 27 March as one 'prohibiting talk of parliaments, etc.'.[22] Rous also recorded a prognostication that the times would be full of dire weather and that '3 greate princes shall die'. He suspected that it had been 'sent abroad ... to busy the heades of the vulgar in this troublesome time, and to hinder theire talk of state matters'.[23] Devonshire diarist, Walter Yonge, noted a rumour that Bishop Laud of London would become Lord Chancellor in place of Lord Keeper Coventry.[24] That change, if it were to occur, would mark a harder line at court.

Some of the libels that appeared during the weeks that followed the dissolution attacked Laud.[25] Libels offered observers another means of gauging the significance of what had happened and predicting what might ensue. Walter Yonge copied into his diary one set of verses against the House of Commons and later entered, with a cross reference, another set responding to the first.[26] In the lines that circulated in writing and in the words of individuals prosecuted for their indiscretions debate about public policies and about the ending of the Parliament continued. One libel found at Paul's Cross in May warned those in power not to persist in their 'stubborness and obstinacy against God and country', their 'breaking of one parliament after another, and their imprisoning and punishing those who wanted to purge the commonwealth of idolatry'.[27] The same issues appear in the remarks for which Christian Cowper, a servant to a Northamptonshire mercer, was examined by Attorney General Heath. Cowper allegedly said that the king was 'well-inclined' to Parliament but had changed his mind after spending the night with the queen.[28] In Shropshire Stephen ap Evan was accused of having responded to the news of the dissolution by saying 'That the King would lose the hearts of his subjects by reason of charging them so deepe with loanmoney and subsidies ... and that the end of it would bee that hee would be hunted out of the land and that the Pallgrave would be crowned in his stead'.[29]

Dominating the attention of political observers in the weeks following the dissolution of Parliament were two sets of rebels against royal authority: the MPs arrested for their conduct on 2 March and the merchants who were refusing to pay tonnage and poundage. From the stances of these men and from that of the crown in dealing with them people estimated the severity of the divisions within the kingdom.

For eleven months uncertainty about the disposition of the cases of the imprisoned MPs provided a potential source of news. Two of them, Coryton and Heyman, quickly made their peace with the king, but the others remained in custody over the summer.[30] During April, May and June, several developments attracted attention. The attorney general asked the judges a series of questions. He also initiated proceedings against the MPs in Star Chamber. The prisoners who, with the exception of Eliot, had appealed for habeas corpus responded by challenging the jurisdiction of the Star Chamber. The crown again sought opinions from the judges, and by various means a ruling on the request for bail was postponed until autumn, after the long vacation. The very delays and apparent manoeuvrings by the crown prompted speculation.[31]

In September as the new legal term approached, reports of popular petitions on the prisoners' behalf helped renew interest in handling of their cases. After hearing rumours that they would be released and a new Parliament called, Thomas Scott began to solicit electoral support among his neighbours at Canterbury.[32] The continued determination of both king and MPs soon showed that hopes of conciliation were illusory. The majority of the MPs stood firm and refused the crown's offer of bail on condition of their submission. Long acceded but quickly changed his mind.[33] Holles who alone gave security for his appearance and obtained freedom drew much notice. Although negotiation and submission were the ordinary means whereby individuals sought restoration to royal favour, Holles's conduct seemed too subservient to some observers, including his father, the earl of Clare. Clare, himself a vocal opponent of the court, was uneasy when he heard about the arrangements that his son had made for bail.[34] William Masham, who had sat in the Parliament, was dismayed. He worried about the implications of Holles's action. Since one of the prisoners had acknowledged royal authority, the rest would probably have to meet the crown's demands before they too could be released.[35]

The events that followed proved Masham's pessimism to be well founded. Although dropping proceedings in Star Chamber, the crown put an information against the MPs in King's Bench and successfully obtained judicial confirmation of that court's authority in the case. In February the court imposed fines upon Eliot, Holles and Valentine for their conduct during the preceding spring.[36] Those who had not previously submitted were to remain in prison until they had given security for good behaviour.[37] Selden, Long and Hobart yielded soon afterward, but Eliot, Valentine and Strode refused. To their friends their confinement continued to be an important issue, but once the cases had been resolved, public attention turned elsewhere. Only occasionally did the fate of the imprisoned MPs draw notice. Eliot's unsuccessful pleas for consideration during his illness in 1632 and his death in November of that year created a stir but prompted no significant efforts on behalf of Valentine and Strode.[38] Charles I released them in an apparent gesture of conciliation just prior to the meeting of Parliament in 1640.[39]

Many of the letters that testify to contemporaries' undeniable interest in the saga of the 'parliament prisoners' refrain from approval or disapproval of the proceedings. The complex legal questions that the cases raised may have made people especially hesitant to talk about matters that were so politically sensitive. Those close to the MPs were less restrained. Walter Long's relatives demonstrated their displeasure at his imprisonment by their scornful treatment of a royal messenger, Jasper Heily. Heily complained that they had refused him diet and lodging at their inn and also had thrown a chamber pot of filth at him.[40] The Longs' desire for revenge may have been political as well as personal. Both considerations seem to have motivated Holles's father and some other sympathizers.[41]

During the summer reports of protests came from the west country where several of the MPs had connections. When there was trouble at the musters in Cornwall, the home of Eliot and Coryton and the site of Valentine's constituency, Sir Bernard Grenville was quick to blame 'sondry ill dispositions poysoned by that malevolent faction of Elliot'.[42] The Chief Baron who was on circuit in the west that summer found trouble in the 'business of arms' in Somerset and Cornwall although he did not explicitly associate the difficulties with the dissolution of Parliament.[43] Other sources noted problems at the musters in Devonshire where Strode lived. Rumours circulated that in both Devonshire and Cornwall protesters were petitioning on behalf of the MPs. Late in September Sir Martin Stuteville in Cambridge had word that the 'whole county of Cornwall' had presented such a petition to the king.[44] About the same time the earl of Clare heard rumblings of a similar petition from Devonshire.[45]

Actual protests resulting from the proceedings against the MPs never matched the rumours.[46] Many people, sharing the king's distaste for the turbulence that had occurred in the House of Commons on 2 March, believed that Eliot and his associates had acted improperly. Oliver Viscount Grandison had little sympathy when they failed to obtain habeas corpus. He hoped they might learn a lesson about the limited benefits of looking to the people instead of the king.[47] After sitting in that Parliament Sir John Lowther confessed in his autobiography that he would 'never with my good will desier to be their again'. Instead of working for 'the generall good or generall favor' most members put their energy toward 'private bills factions aboute elections and labour[ed] to pull doune great officers for the private splene of some leaders, the Multitude glorieing in distruction'.[48] D'Ewes likewise condemned the 'fiery spirits' who had disrupted Parliament, yet he was also uneasy about the king's adjournment and dissolution which had prevented redress of grievances.[49]

The second group of men who captured public attention for their defiance of the crown in the aftermath of Parliament were the merchants who refused to pay tonnage and poundage. Although for more than a century parliaments had granted tonnage and poundage to monarchs at their accession, Charles I's parliaments failed to do so, and a number of merchants resisted when he tried to collect it anyway.[50] He denied the Commons' contention in their Remonstrance of June 1628 that the 'receiving of tunnage and poundage' was contrary to the Petition of Right.[51] These claims and counterclaims continued in Parliament in January 1628/9 where merchants also complained about the conduct of customs' officers. Several individuals, including Richard Chambers, himself imprisoned, and John Rolle, MP for the Cornish borough of Callington, whose goods were seized for resistance to tonnage and poundage appealed to the Commons for help. The House was in the midst of investigating their cases at the time of adjournment.[52]

While having failed to provide relief for aggrieved merchants such as Chambers and Rolle, the Commons had in their resolutions of 2 March reasserted the principle that tonnage and poundage could not be imposed without Parliament.[53] Observers watched after the dissolution to see how many merchants would defy the king and risk imprisonment and loss of their goods. Chambers remained in prison. When tried in the Star Chamber in May, he refused to take back his earlier remark to the council that English merchants had less access to justice than did their Turkish counterparts.[54] His continued adherence to his position amazed contemporaries as the months passed. Having heard in December 1630 that Chambers had told the warden of the Fleet that, whatever was done to him, he would not acknowledge the sentence against him, Joseph Meade commented, 'What stomachs have some men!'[55]

People believed that most merchants had neither Chambers's persistence nor his preoccupation with justice. One of the sets of verses circulating in the weeks following the dissolution of Parliament asserted that the merchants had political motives. They resisted tonnage and poundage as a 'tricke to tame' the 'pride' of the 'Blinde Bishops' who were blocking religious reform.[56] Secretary of State Dorchester suspected that the merchants hoped that 'a little standing off would make some new resolution about parliament be taken at court'.[57] The king may have shared these suspicions, for he sought to emphasize that the denial of tonnage and poundage was both futile and wrong.[58]

Charles's insistence upon compliance with his authority appealed to people's taste for drama and encouraged them to impose political interpretations upon the merchants' conduct. West country Puritans, Yonge and Whiteway, both linked resistance to Parliament's action.[59] Merchants reportedly feared repercussions in Parliament if they should comply with the crown. William Lake told Sir Henry Vane that because they were 'terrified' by the Commons' resolutions, 'Sir John Eliots *brutum fulmen*', 'few or none' paid and those who did used 'other mens names'.[60]

However unlikely another Parliament may have been, parliamentary proceedings during the 1620s had had an impact. Merchants thought twice about ignoring Parliament and paying tonnage and poundage, yet they hesitated too to take steps whereby they would not only disobey their king but also disrupt their business. Anxiety bred antagonism among those who chose a different course of action. Whiteway described the non-resisting merchants as being 'much hated and hardly spoken of by the rest of their neighbors'.[61] Tales circulated too of violence between merchants and customs officers. Emanuel Downing, whose wife was Lucy Winthrop, had heard at Charing Cross that the 'customers of Lynn were beaten out of the Customs House'.[62]

The emotions stirred by the parliamentary disputes led people to connect other incidents to those disagreements. Anger about the shipment of grain rather than resistance to tonnage and poundage probably accounts for the trouble at Lynn.[63] That was certainly the case at Maldon in Essex although the merchants' refusal to pay duties aggravated the depression in the cloth trade under which the area had been suffering for some time.[64] Rioters there in March boarded a ship and took some of the grain that was about to be exported.[65] Clothworkers from the neighbouring villages of Braintree and Bocking played a leading role in a second protest against the shipment of food from Maldon in May.[66] Weavers of these villages who in April were seeing a real deterioration in their trade had followed the JPs from place to place demanding action in response to their petitions for relief.[67] Early in May the weavers petitioned the Privy Council directly.[68]

Emphasizing the legitimacy of the weavers' complaints, the JPs had sent the petition they received in April to the council. They warned that the situation was especially volatile. Unless the board provided 'speedie relief' for the 'want and famine ... some thing may happen which may disturb the Peace of the Countrie'. The magistrates feared that mass meetings of the discontented and trouble between weavers and clothiers might disrupt the calm they had achieved by promising to appeal to the council.[69] Although the petitioners noted that the dissolution of Parliament had disappointed their hopes for help from that source, neither they nor the justices suggested that they sought to convince the king to call a new Parliament.[70] The second petition, though still cautious, ventured farther into the political realm. It asked for relief 'until such time as it shall please God and his Majesty that there be a Parliament' to make a law to reform the problem.[71]

At least some of the JPs may have seen that the discontent that grew from lack of food and work could serve their own political purposes. Puritans were well represented on the commission of the peace for Essex. Among them were William Masham who had been imprisoned for refusing the Forced Loan and his brother-in-law Sir Thomas Barrington.[72] The Lord Lieutenant of the county, the earl of Warwick, had likewise opposed royal policy on a number of occasions.[73] While these leaders performed their obligations and saw that the rioters were punished, they also participated in various efforts to provide remedies for the needy.[74] They had an interest in establishing peace and order, but they had their own ideas about the policies by which Church and commonwealth should be run. Their reputations may have led observers to give greater political weight to the demonstrations of discontent. William Lake cited disturbances in the cloth villages of Essex when he remarked in April that the 'venom' of obstinacy exhibited by the merchants was moving 'in every small vein through the kingdom'.[75]

The Essex clothiers who petitioned the council in May to clear themselves of responsibility for the weavers' ills pointed to another connection between the general disruption of trade and their local problems. Warehouses were filled with stock, and none had been sold. Until the merchants resumed operations, the clothiers could do nothing.[76] The practical economic ramifications of the merchants' stoppage also attracted the attention of people like Walter Yonge who were interested in the political struggle it represented.[77] Bishop Williams thought that the merchants' desire for income would quickly bring them to compliance. He told Secretary Dorchester early in May that he was not surprised that they had abandoned 'this newe habit of statesmen'.[78]

If few people voiced similar sentiments, they seemed to have shared the bishop's expectation that the council would reach an agreement with the principal group of cloth merchants, the Merchant Adventurers. The interplay nevertheless afforded observers both entertainment and a means of taking the political temperature. Sir George Gresley wrote to Sir Thomas Puckering late in May that 'the courtiers brag more of the merchants condescending to trade than is cause: for though some have shipped away cloths that did lie upon their hands, yet it is said some of the same men deny to buy or send away more until the judges have delivered thier opinions of the lawfulness thereof'.[79] A month later Dr Benjamin Laney told John Cosin that 'the merchants cannot be brought to trade so freely as they were wont. Moneys come in slowly'.[80]

For most people living outside the cloth country the decisions of the merchants as to whether to pay tonnage and poundage were, like the fate of the imprisoned MPs, a matter of speculative interest rather than one of everyday life. Royal servants – customs officers – not gentlemen or citizens, were responsible for making the collection and, in contrast to the shipmoney levies of the 1630s, merchants rather than the general population were those upon whom the charges fell directly.[81]

People recognized that so long as England's wars with France and Spain continued, the king needed revenue from tonnage and poundage and also wanted to avoid domestic disorders. Walter Yonge suspected that the reports of peace with France that he heard in April might have been circulated to encourage merchants to trade.[82] The rumours of a treaty were soon proved true, and on 14 April peace was proclaimed. The public greeted that news with no more enthusiasm than it had displayed for the war. Charles issued no official orders for bonfires, and few were made.[83] Reactions were similar a year and a half later when the king concluded the war with Spain.[84]

People concerned about preserving the English Church from Popery found it difficult to be enthusiastic about ending war with the Catholic power of France. William Greenhill reported to Lady Barrington that the peace concluded with France provided that a bishop sent by the pope and eight priests were to come to England.[85]

In the same letter he mentioned several godly ministers who were being questioned. Others whose letters from that spring have survived also watched nervously to see whether the fears about the security of religion that had been expressed in Parliament were materializing.[86]

Chelmsford in Essex became the scene of one widely publicized confrontation over religion when the ecclesiastical authorities attempted to silence popular lecturer Thomas Hooker. Fellow minister Samuel Collins claimed Hooker's fate was drawing as much attention 'as the greate question of tonnage and poundage', occupying 'all mens heads, tongues, ears' outside the county as well as in, and causing debate pro and con at Cambridge.[87] Although Collins may have exaggerated his warnings about the strong feelings of the community in order to ingratiate himself both with Bishop Laud and with Hooker's supporters, other ministers chose to incur their diocesan's displeasure rather than lecture at Chelmsford and 'undergo the giers of that people' who wanted to hear Hooker.[88] Some of Hooker's followers left the town in his wake, but others, whatever their feelings may have been, accepted the new combined lecture that Laud and his subordinates established.[89] The anticipated conflicts did not occur.

At the summer assizes in Durham contemporaries could see another heated battle over what the Commons' resolution had described as 'innovations in religion'. At the assizes, cathedral prebendary Peter Smart was once more attempting to secure an indictment against those responsible for the 'susperstitious vanities' he had seen introduced at Durham.[90] Since his sermon of the previous July denouncing innovations there, Smart's questions about religion had become a *cause célèbre* involving proceedings in the Court of High Commission, charges at the assizes in 1628, and discussion in Parliament.[91] Prebend John Cosin whom Smart held responsible for the changes at Durham was one of the clergymen whose views had prompted MPs and others to worry about preserving the Church from Arminianism.[92] In Smart, Cosin had an opponent who like himself did not flinch from controversy and whose sense of outrage and determination kept the issue of enforcement of the laws concerning religion before the public. Even though the imprisonment that Smart incurred might – like that of Richard Chambers or the MPs – be ascribed to injudiciousness, his failure to bring the ecclesiastical innovators to justice reminded his contemporaries of the threats to English Protestantism.[93]

Pessimism about the prospects for a Protestant Church in England helped bring John Winthrop to decide in 1629 to join those who were seeking to establish in the New World the godly common-wealth they could not set up at home. Robert Ryece agreed that the times were 'dangerous', but he rejected the contention that the imminence of Judgement justified migration. 'The Church and common welthe heere at home, hathe more neede of your beste abyllytie ... than any remote plantation', he wrote to Winthrop in August.[94] The following spring eleven ships with about 700 passengers set out for New England. Not all of these were going for religious or political reasons but some, like Winthrop, were.[95]

When 5 November brought the occasion for the annual commemoration of the discovery of the Gunpowder Plot, it was hardly surprising that people in 1629 thought about Parliament as the protector of Protestantism. For the sermon he preached in the cathedral at Norwich that day Thomas Reeve, minister of Coleby, Norfolk, took for his text, Nehemiah 4:11: 'and our adversaries said, they shall not know, neither see till we come in the midst among them, and slay them, and cause the work to cease'. Arguing that 'great men must be promoters of religion', he went on to note, 'if we know not where the strength of our land lay, our Adversaries can shew us, where but in the parliament? and not in this openly to assault, but secretly to blow up'.[96]

Just days after 5 November, when people were still talking of how the imprisoned MPs had responded to the king's offer of bail, another set of arrests brought attention to Parliament's role in providing revenue for the crown. Taken into custody and questioned about a tract which set forth ways the king could obtain money without Parliament were Sir Robert Cotton and his librarian Richard James, Oliver St John, and the earls of Bedford, Somerset, and Clare, individuals who were pillars of the establishment and also defenders of law and liberty.[97] Although the dimensions of the cause quickly diminished when the Elizabethan origins of the tract became known, the initial arrests and subsequent inquiry prompted political speculation.[98] What did the proceedings portend? Was this a scheme of Lord Treasurer Weston who was reported to be both very powerful and an enemy to Parliament?[99] Was the real cause of royal anger, as one newsletter postulated, the gentlemen's circulation of the tract without informing the crown of its potentially explosive content.[100]

Charles's action offended and confounded the men who had not consciously challenged his authority. Clare, already angry about the king's treatment of his younger son and the other MPs taken into custody in March, expressed his annoyance about his own arrest to his heir, Lord Haughton. Early in December he wrote that he could not predict what would follow. The king would be dishonoured if the group were not punished 'and such honour is to be preferred before our innocence'. Yet both 'town' and lawyers claimed that nothing could be done against them by law.[101] For Cotton the most disturbing aspect of the arrest was the closing of his library. Shortly before he passed away a year and a half later in May 1631, it was reported that he had sent a message to king and court, that the 'long detaining of his books' would be the cause of his death.[102]

The fame of Cotton and his library added to the public interest stirred by the arrests and made it difficult for people to regard the proceedings solely as court intrigue.[103] They were uncertain what to expect, especially after they learned about the origins of the tract and about its circulation. 'I dare not say that this matter will shrinke into nothing, but some are of that opinion', one newswriter commented on 16 November.[104] Attention gradually turned to the kinds of terms that the individuals involved were likely to make with the crown. Bedford, whose connections at court were good, was expected to come out well.[105] As it happened, all of those arrested, except Cotton whose study was kept under surveillance, avoided further punishment.[106] On 29 May, the day for their hearing in the Star Chamber, Queen Henrietta Maria gave birth to a son. The birth was announced, they were allowed to depart, and the paper was ordered to be burned.[107]

What had seemed, in the preceding November, as if it might be the beginning of a campaign to eliminate opposition to the crown, seemed much less significant when it ended six months later. Charles I's dissolution of Parliament, his imprisonment of the MPs, his insistence that merchants pay tonnage and poundage, and his religious policies made it possible for people to believe that he might arrest more individuals.[108] The volatility of political emotions in the aftermath of Parliament meant that incidents were likely to trigger responses which subsequently seemed disproportionate to the occasion and that observers tended to make unwarranted assumptions about the significance of particular events or developments.

The musters held during the summer of 1629 gave men who had political or other grievances an opportunity to vent their frustrations by refusing to comply with orders they received. The musters that year provided an especially good source of ammunition for disputes because neither session of the Parliament of 1628–9 had been able to pass legislation clarifying military obligations and because the powers of deputy lieutenants had been the topic of such wide-ranging debate.[109] Sir Bernard Grenville certainly believed that the troubles that he complained of in Cornwall owed something to parliamentary politics.[110] The deputies in Norfolk in July 1629 told the earl of Arundel, their Lord Lieutenant, that resistance was so great that they could not hold the musters until they had received additional instructions from him. 'Soe manye are the Captaynes both of horse and foote that have given over their charges and such [is] the absolute refusall of such as we hold fitt to be appointed to supplye them'.[111] Elsewhere, as we shall see in Chapter 3, people questioned the levying of rates to pay the muster masters.

The resistance displayed during 1629 worried Charles I and his ministers and disturbed other people who regardless of their political opinions did not wish to see the disorders of Parliament followed by revolt or disturbance in the country itself. Anxiety frequently led to pessimism and panic at the initial reports of incidents which ultimately proved to be far less serious. The fears that individuals expressed do not tell us the actual state of the kingdom, but they are important indicators of beliefs and values. The concerns that appear in letters and diaries from 1629 show that many persons had notions about law, liberty, and the role of Parliament that Charles's concern about preventing disorders and his conduct of government challenged.

If few were prepared to defy Charles I during the months following his dissolution of his third Parliament, more were uneasy about the course of affairs. Those who had themselves been arrested or questioned had, even if they were ultimately released, faced dishonour, worry, inconvenience, expense, and difficult decisions about their course of action. The very unpredictability of their fate added to their burdens. The effects of their experiences cannot be measured easily because for the most part we can see them make no immediate or radical changes in their conduct. Only in accumulated

evidence about individuals and in their continuing observation of the
state of the English Church and commonwealth can we find hints
that their opinions altered. When people looked back upon 1629
from 1640, they saw the dissolution and its aftermath as important
grievances. Their perspective was different and their hopes of
obtaining redress greater. Behind their apparent acquiescence in the
eleven years of personal rule by Charles I was a consciousness of
tension between the nature of that government and the ideas of law,
liberty, and religion expressed in the Petition of Right of 1628 and
the Commons' resolutions of 2 March 1628/9.

By March 1629/30, a year after the turbulent scene in the House
of Commons, the cases of the MPs imprisoned as a result of their
conduct on 2 March had been disposed of and all but three had come
to terms with the government. The intense disappointment and
shock that men had felt at the end of that Parliament had faded as
the months passed, and the resistance to tonnage and poundage had
waned. Secretary Dorchester thus had good reason in March 1629/
30 to write to Oliver Fleming, the ambassador in Switzerland, that
'time has bread no small alteration, all to the better in settling the
disquiet of men's minds after the heats kindled by the disorders of
the last parliament'.[112] The immediate post-parliamentary period
had ended.

If most people had, after a year, accepted the fact of Charles I's
dissolution of his third Parliament and turned to deal with more
immediate problems, they believed that the king would summon
another Parliament when his affairs seemed to demand one.
Parliament's history and the continuity of its institutional structure
encouraged expectations of future meetings and at the same time
kept alive memories of past sessions, particularly those of 1628 and
1629.[113] Individuals assessed and reassessed the events that had
occurred then. Sir Roger Twysden noticed this in February 1636/7
when the judges responded to the king's question about shipmoney.
Some thought Charles should have consulted Parliament 'in a case of
this weight ... They confessed ye last Parliaments had beene much
to blame in their caryages towards hys Matie but ye goodness of
Monarchs had formerly forgot as great Errors'.[114] Later the same
year D'Ewes looked back upon the dissolution of March 1628/9 as

the most gloomy, sad, and dismal day for England that happened in five hundred years last past, the present session of Parliament being suddenly and in a tumultuary manner dissolved in the morning; since which time this poor kingdom, for above eight years and five months' continuance hath never yet enjoyed the benefit and comfort of that great council again, and God only knows when it shall: but the sad effects it hath since wrought in church and commonwealth may more easily be lamented and deplored than recounted.[115]

A few bold individuals defied restrictions upon speaking and writing to point to Parliament as the answer to the evils they saw in Church and state during the 1630s. Prominent among these daring souls were the anti-Arminian pamphleteers who denounced the prelates for dividing the king from his subjects and turning Charles against parliaments. Parliament was the rightful preserver and defender of the Church because the Parliaments of Henry VIII and Elizabeth had laid foundations for the Church of England.[116]

Expressing a similar attitude toward Parliament but taking a broader focus was *The Practise of Princes*.[117] The author, who signed himself as A. Ar., asked whether it was worse to have the king's prerogative infringed by Parliament or to have a continuation of evil practices.[118] He defended Parliament's refusal to vote Charles tonnage and poundage prior to the reformation of 'som things ... which did eat at the roote of religion and state'. If money were given first, 'they should never be once suffered to speake of much lesse to question and sift out' these grievances.[119] Treachery would prevail and men would fear to say what they knew unless God granted prayers that the king in a free Parliament might hear complaints, including those against evil ministers.[120]

The crown was uncompromising in condemning such works and, when possible, prosecuting the authors. Officials at times took their defence of royal authority one step further and issued or encouraged 'correct' views, but the most extensive and the most extreme effort to demonstrate that Parliament was a 'flower of the crown' was apparently neither officially commissioned nor widely circulated.[121] This tract, 'A true presentation of fore-past parliaments', although never printed, survives in several manuscript copies. It was composed between 1628 and 1631 by the Shropshire antiquary, Sir Francis Kynaston, who had some court connections.[122] Despite his disclaimer of any desire for his work to be read, he may have written with the idea of seeking favour and of aiding the royal cause.[123] Sir Francis Windebanke obtained a copy and made notes of some salient points.[124]

In 'A true presentation', Kynaston attempted to answer *The Priviledges and Practice of Parliaments*, a tract which troubled him by its claims that Parliament was the 'onely means to rectifie and remedie matters in Church and commonwealth much amisse'.[125] Kynaston drew upon his classical, literary and legal knowledge to argue that Parliament was instead a body in which subjects could demonstrate their love for the king and thus one by which royal honour and power could be magnified. In Parliament the king and Lords had the principal roles; the Commons were clearly subordinate.[126]

Most of the references to Parliament in sources from the 1630s appear not in polemics like Kynaston's or the diatribes of the anti-Arminians but in routine correspondence or incidentally in legal, historical and literary works. Although few authors focused their attention upon Parliament – no history of it appeared – Parliament was so much a part of the English heritage that people were unwilling, if not unable, to excise it from their lives. Historians recounting the reigns of previous monarchs mentioned parliaments in the course of relating the rulers' achievements and failures at home and abroad, in peace and war. William Habington tells us in his history of Edward IV, that when Edward came to the throne he called a Parliament so that 'no circumstance of sovereigntie might be wanting'.[127] Parliament was a source of men and money for military campaigns, a resolver of grievances, and a maker of statutes. Scholars whose work was published during the 1630s showed particular interest in the statutes of the Reformation, but otherwise they seem to have accepted the dictum of John Hayward, that statutes should not be recited in books of history.[128]

The English thinking about parliaments is also evident in the descriptions of foreign states that circulated in the kingdom during the 1630s. Admiration for Swedish King Gustavus Adolphus and his leadership of the Protestant cause in Europe gave people an especial interest in that country's government.[129] From *The Survey of Sweden* (1632) they could learn how in Sweden 'country' people like any other had a voice in Parliament. In that Parliament too were the clergy who had continued to sit after the Reformation even though they dealt only with church affairs.[130] The Polish experience impressed Sir Thomas Roe who was there on diplomatic business. Roe sent some observations on the court of Poland to Oliver Viscount Grandison who found 'the opposition of that free people in their parliaments and the advantages that a wise king hath made through patience and giving way to the violence and distemper of their humours ... very remarkable'.[131]

Works on other topics, such as religion, war or trade, likewise include references to the role of Parliament. Robert Powell's *Depopulation Arraigned*, a tract printed in 1636, discussed not only the problems of depopulation itself but also those of trying to correct it. Having asserted that 'The wisdome of a Parliament or a State may foresee an insuing evill and they may enact a prohibiting of it', Powell cited a statute of Philip and Mary.[132] For preachers and poets Parliament could be both the scene of great events such as the Gunpowder Plot and a source of illustrations and allusions.[133] Samuel Smith sought to give his congregation some sense of the majesty of the day of judgement by telling them that, compared with it, 'earthly princes attended with pompe going to Parliaments' were nothing.[134] Another author tried to describe London Bridge by saying that the arches, like judges in parliament, were placed on woolsacks.[135] Statutes frequently provided useful images. William Chillingworth resorted to his readers' knowledge about statutes to explain the validity of scripture. 'As a statute though pen'd by some one man, yet being ratified by Parliament is called the Act, not of man but of the Parliament', so, he maintained, although texts of scripture were written by one man, they too have authority.[136] Bishop Thomas Morton of Durham invoked statutes to elucidate royal power. 'Acts of Parliament whilest they are but voted, are but only Consents, but after they have the King's royall assent they become statutes.'[137]

Judges, lawyers and others with business in courts of law referred to statutes in a far more concrete way. So did those responsible for local governance. Statutes, enacted by Parliament, were part of the framework in which such people functioned.[138] Debates and investigations which occurred in Parliament also had an impact upon law and administration after the particular Parliament had ceased to sit. George Long won dismissal of a case brought before the Court of High Commission by his defence that he had been questioned in Parliament and had recovered damages at law.[139]

People occasionally claimed that the absence of parliaments

created particular legal problems for them. Those affected by the trade in Spanish cloth argued that because the trade had largely developed since Parliament had last acted in regard to cloth, the Spanish trade was virtually unregulated.[140] In his tract about depopulation Robert Powell dared to wonder whether 'there be any refuge either for the interpretation or moderation of positive laws (in the vacancy and cessation of the great Court of Parliament) but unto this Court where Kings themselves have often vouchsafed to sit in person'.[141] Although some business required a private or public Act of Parliament, other remedies were available for many matters, and people in positions of responsibility sought to use these during the 1630s. In 1633 when the king visited York, city officials presented his Majesty with a cause they had long promoted in Parliament and elsewhere – the case for making the River Ouse navigable. Perhaps understandably, they made no reference to Parliament in making their presentation.[142] The quantity of private business brought to sitting parliaments does not provide a sound basis for judging people's practical need for frequent parliaments.[143] Neither the complaints of individuals nor other evidence will support the contention that the lack of access to legislation was a serious issue between 1629 and 1640.

Parliament was more than the architect of statutes; it was a great legitimizing force, which by acting or by failing to act expressed collective public opinion about what should or should not be. Petitioners thought they could strengthen their pleas by noting that no objections had been made when their concerns had been considered in Parliament.[144] The author of a *Discourse Concerning the Drayning of the Fennes* listed many previous statutes to prove that his enterprise was one which would lead to profit and honour of king and commonwealth.[145] Some individuals who resisted military charges or opposed Arminian practices justified their conduct by citing questions raised in Parliament. Both rulers and ruled acted during the 1630s as if they believed that officials might be called upon to answer in Parliament.[146]

People also regarded parliaments as means of resolving differences between crown and subject. For individuals with governmental responsibilities in the country the resolution of such conflicts was especially important. Henry Elsyng who had been Clerk of the Parliaments since 1621 and thus had both personal interest and expertise in the matter, reports that how the king might regain the love of his people was a topic of dinner conversation at the earl of Danby's in March 1629/30. Elsyng who was present at the time suggested a Parliament and cited precedents to support his suggestion.[147] He subsequently put his ideas into writing but seems not to have communicated them to the king.

Charles may nevertheless have heard some of Elsyng's thoughts about the way to restore good relations between king and subjects when several years later in December 1636 the earl of Danby appealed for a Parliament to be summoned. Danby maintained that people were objecting not to assisting the king but to the way monies were being levied. If Charles would summon a Parliament, the English would express their love by supplying his needs.[148] A month later the earl of Warwick, who was then engaged in a struggle with the crown over shipmoney, went to the king with similar concerns and similar promises. He asserted that in Parliament the English would support their monarch in war or peace.[149] His own hope that Charles would undertake a war against Spain gave him added reason for offering assurance that Parliament would be co-operative. Like many of his contemporaries, Warwick assumed that the king would call Parliament if he went to war. Although the Venetian ambassador's dispatches furnish the sole report of these lords' pleas, other sources provide evidence that the discontent of that winter was bringing people to search for solutions to the problems of Church and commonwealth.[150]

Danby and Warwick were among those who had sat in Parliament and hoped to sit there again. For such individuals and to a lesser extent for their relatives, friends, and neighbours, Parliament was a part of personal experience. George Garrard who sent Wentworth regular accounts of current events invoked memories of his parliamentary past in many of his letters. On one occasion he compared himself to old George More who was known in Parliament for 'rising late and repeating all that had been said that day'. In the same letter Garrard reported the death of one Weston, whom he identified as not the Baron but 'a red-faced fellow, I knew him in Parliament'.[151] Former and would-be MPs speculated about the possibility of a Parliament as they noted events at court or other developments. If the king were to issue writs, they would want to begin negotiating with their neighbours about the selection of members.[152]

In talking of Parliament prospective MPs and others used a

multitude of images, ranging from the idealized to the disparaging. We hear of an alehouse belonging to one Jephson, which the locals called the 'parliamenthouse of Jephson'.[153] An incident there led to proceedings in the Star Chamber, but the epithet for the alehouse was not at issue.[154] The turbulence of Parliament and its meddlesomeness were proverbial in some circles.[155] When George Garrard related to Wentworth how Sir Henry Anderson had schemed to obtain an audience with the king and had spoken out 'disliking the ways they went in these times, dissuading the king wholly from further taking the shipmonies, and moving his Majesty to return to the old way by Parliaments', he described Anderson's remarks as a 'most parliamentary speech'.[156] For other individuals Parliament was a physician or the Roman Senate.[157] The images at times conflict, but from all quarters comes recognition, tacit if not overt, that Parliament was deeply embedded in the English heritage.

Even when the 'disquiet' of 1629 had settled, the English continued to think of Parliament as an important factor in their lives, institutions and laws. They knew that the absence of a sitting Parliament did not necessarily mean the end of parliaments – that was inconceivable – but many were also aware of differences of opinion about Parliament's role in the kingdom. The traditions, which had instituted Parliament in the subjects' hearts and minds, informed them that the king summoned and dissolved parliaments and that king, Lords and Commons must agree for parliaments to accomplish business. Although hesitant to step out of place and make public statements about the governance of the kingdom and the absence of parliaments, people found events and issues prompting them to think about Parliament. The appeals from the earls of Danby and Warwick in the winter of 1636–7 came at a time when, as we shall see in subsequent chapters, the English had been feeling burdens of plague, shipmoney, and Laudianism. War with Spain seemed likely. The prospect of war with the Scots in 1638–9 brought renewed petitions for Parliament, and the impact of that war added a note of desperation to those appeals. When Charles I summoned a Parliament in 1640, people responded with a combination of disbelief, joy, and nervous anticipation, emotions nourished by memories of previous parliaments and especially by the aftermath of the Parliament dissolved in March 1628/9.[158] If some corporations searched the records to determine election procedures in 1640, people felt little need for research about what Parliament should do.[159] Unfinished business from the session eleven years earlier and the events of the intervening era gave MPs a full agenda.

NOTES

1   Cope and Coates, p. 139; cf. his speech 22 March 1627/8: 'If we pursue (the King to draw one way and the parliament another) the commonwealth must sink in the midst' (*CD 1628* Vol. 2), p. 59.

2   *CD 1629*, p. 101. They had adjourned themselves for two days first.

3   *Barrington Family Letters, 1628–1632*, ed. A. Searle, Camden Fourth Series, vol. 28 (1983), no. 32; also see C. Russell, *Parliaments and English Politics 1621–1629* (Oxford: Oxford University Press, 1979), pp. 413–16.

4   See I. H. C. Fraser, 'Agitation in the Commons, 2 March 1629, and the interrogation of the leaders of the anti-court group', *BIHR*, vol. 30, no. 81 (1957), pp. 86–95.

5   For accounts of the events of 2 March see *CD 1629*, pp. 101–6, 170–2, 239–44, 252–67.

6   *CD 1629*, p. 102.

7   Concerning the Forced Loan see R. Cust, 'The Forced Loan and English politics, 1626–8', PhD thesis, University of London, 1984.

8   Walter Yonge's diary is dotted with reports about sources of revenue for the crown (Yonge, ff. 27v–30); also see *CSPVen. 1628–9*, no. 805; Birch, Vol. 2, pp. 19–21. Concerning Yonge, see G. Roberts (ed.), *Diary of Walter Yonge, Esq.*, Camden Society, vol. 41 (1848), pp. x–xi.

9   *CD 1629*, pp. 4–6, 245.

10 Montagu was made bishop of Chichester; Manwaring was given a living in Essex in addition to his London parish (H. Schwartz, 'Arminianism and the English Parliament, 1624–29', *JBS*, vol. 12, no. 2 (1973), pp. 41–68; see also *CD 1629*, pp. 37, 100).

11 *CD 1629*, pp. 101–2.

12 Lord Montagu described the final moments of all three Parliaments in his diaries (HMC, *Report on the Manuscripts of the Duke of Buccleuch and Queensberry preserved at Montagu House*, Vol. 3 (1926), pp. 252, 302–3, 341–2).

13 See his diary, ff. 5v, 30v, 31.

14 cf. declarations following previous dissolutions: (1621), STC 9241; (1626), STC 9246; Sir Edwin Sandys and the earl of Southampton had been imprisoned in June 1621, and Sir Edward Coke, Sir Robert Phelips, and William Mallory were held for eight months after the dissolution of Parliament in 1621 (R. Zaller, *The Parliament of 1621* (Berkeley, Calif.: University of California Press, 1971), pp. 139–41, 184, 188–9). There were arrests on other occasions, including those of Eliot and Sir Dudley Digges during the session in 1626 (J. N. Ball, 'Sir John Eliot and Parliament,

1624–1629', in *Faction and Parliament*, ed. K. Sharpe (Oxford: Oxford University Press, 1978), p. 191; also Russell, *Politics*, p. 306).

15 Proclamation (1629), STC 8916

16 Concerning Eliot, see Ball, 'Eliot', pp. 173–207; H. Hulme, *The Life of Sir John Eliot* (London: Allen & Unwin, 1957). For Selden, see *DNB*; also R. Tuck, ' "The Ancient Law of Freedom": John Selden and the Civil War', *Reactions to the English Civil War 1642–1649*, ed. J. S. Morrill (New York: St Martin's, 1982), pp. 137–61.

17 Coryton was a friend of Eliot's and a 'Pembroke man' (Ball, 'Eliot', p. 184; Russell, *Politics*, p. 289; *DNB*). For Heyman, see *DNB*.

18 Denzil Holles was son of the earl of Clare and brother-in-law to Sir Thomas Wentworth (P. Crawford, *Denzil Holles, 1598–1680: a Study of his Political Career* (London: Royal Historical Society, 1979). For Walter Long, see *DNB* and Keeler, pp. 256–7; for Strode, see *DNB*.

19 For Hobart and Valentine, see *DNB*.

20 *Barrington Family Letters*, no. 33; also see no. 34 and BL, Egerton MS 2716, f. 67 (Yale film). Barrington's comments should probably be considered in the perspective of what Hunt describes as Barrington's 'impulsiveness and his tendency to dither and lose heart' (W. Hunt, *The Puritan Moment: The Coming of Revolution in an English County* (Cambridge, Mass.: Harvard University Press, 1983), p. 229). The Barrington MSS include a copy of the king's speech at the breakup of the Parliament (HMC, *Seventh Report*, app., p. 576). Also see L. J. Reeve, 'Sir Thomas Roe's prophecy of 1629', *BIHR*, vol. 56, no. 133, pp. 115–21.

21 *Journals of the House of Lords*, Vol. 4, p. 43 (speech); *His Majesties Declaration to all His Loving Subjects of the Causes Which Moved Him to Dissolve the Last Parliament* (1628), STC 9249 Proclamation (1628), STC 8916. Lord Montagu wanted to get a copy of the speech (HMC, *Buccleuch*, Vol. 3, p. 342). The State Papers include several suggestions from subjects as to how the king could re-establish good relations with his people (SP 16/138/46; 16/142/45 and below).

22 BL, Egerton MS 784, f. 73v (Yale film). Concerning Whiteway, see W. Barnes, 'The Diary of William Whiteway', *Proceedings of the Dorset Natural History and Archaeological Society*, vol. 13 (1957–8), pp. 57–8. Rous, p. 39 and pp. v–xii. Also see R. Cust, 'The opposition to the Loan: I. News and opinion in the 1620s', an unpublished paper. I owe Dr Cust thanks for sending me this.

23 Rous, pp. 36–7.

24 Yonge, f. 28. See above concerning Yonge's notes about measures considered by the crown for raising money.

25 Laud, *Works*, Vol. 3, p. 210.

26 Yonge, ff. 28, 30v. Also see Rous, pp. 42–3.

27 SP 16/142/92.

28 Cowper had gone on to make further remarks about the queen (SP 16/140/44).

29 SP 16/147/17. Conrad Russell has reminded me that Evan was complain-

ing generally about taxation, but the context of those remarks is important. Evan objected to taxation especially in the absence of Parliament.

30 For proceedings against the parliament prisoners, see *ST*, Vol. 3, pp. 234–335; also S. R. Gardiner, *History of England* (London: Longmans, Green, 1884), Vol. 7, pp. 87–97, 108–22.

31 e.g. Knyvett, no. 25; also El 6477; Birch, Vol. 2, pp. 15–23 *passim*. Similar comments come from the autumn too, e.g. *Barrington Family Letters*, no. 83.

32 P. Clark, 'Thomas Scott and the growth of urban opposition to the early Stuart regime', *Historical Journal*, vol. 21, no. 1 (1978), pp. 23–4. (I owe thanks to Peter Clark for reminding me of this reference.)

33 Birch, Vol. 2, pp. 27–33.

34 Holles, no. 157. See also Clare's letter to his eldest son and heir, Lord Haughton, where he maintained that the king 'must looke about him reconcyle to ye people and prefer his own kingdomes good before other mens pryvat for *privat incommodium* hathe its *destruxit publicum*' (Holles, no. 152).

35 *Barrington Family Letters*, no. 73. Masham had been imprisoned for resisting the Forced Loan (Keeler, pp. 268–9). Concerning Holles's release, see Whiteway, f. 77; HMC, *Seventh Report*, app., p. 257.

36 Whiteway, f. 78.

37 *ST*, Vol. 3, p. 310.

38 e.g. PRO, C.115/M.35/8416, 8418–9, 8423 (Scudamore Letters, Duchess of Norfolk's Deeds).

39 See below. Thomas Permenter had suggested associating the release of the prisoners with the assembly of a Parliament in a memo which he sent to Laud on 7 March 1628 before Parliament had been dissolved. He also proposed four statutes to be introduced in the Parliament (SP 16/138/46).

40 SP 16/215/26.

41 See above. The earl of Pembroke supported Coryton's continuance as vice-warden of the Stannaries. See *CSPDom. 1629–31*, pp. 249, 456.

42 The two men were rivals. Grenville complained to his friend Sir James Bagg, who was a close associate of the Lord Treasurer, 'Our deputy Leiftenants ar ether fearefull to execute or unwilling to do their duties commanded from ye Councell board'. Twelve days later Grenville reported his dilemma when confronted by an incident at the muster in which he was publicly given a petition by one Arscott, a 'great sider' with 'busey-headed Parliamentmen', followed by a 'thrunge of people ... demanding answer', SP 16/147/14 and 16/147/46. Concerning Grenville, see R. Granville, *The King's General in the West* (London, 1908), pp. 11–14. Concerning Bagg, see M. Alexander, *Charles I's Lord Treasurer* (Chapel Hill, NC: University of North Carolina Press, 1975), pp. 137, 199–200. Concerning earlier troubles in Cornwall, see L. Boynton, 'Martial law and the Petition of Right', *EHR*, vol. 79, no. 311 (1964), p. 276.

43 He told the Lord Keeper that he had given it 'publiequely in charge' (SP 16/150/47).

44   Birch, Vol. 2, pp. 27–9; J. Forster, *Sir John Eliot*, 2nd edn (London: Chapman, 1872), vol. 2, bk xi.v.

45   Holles, no. 154. For reports of the musters in Devonshire see SP 16/145/31; 16/150/43; 16/150/76.

46   Although some observers associated the riots in Fleet Street in July with the divisions evident in the dissolution of the Parliament, there seems to be no direct link between the two. See SP 16/147/74; also Holles, no. 152.

47   SP 16/147/74.

48   C. B. Phillips (ed.), *Lowther Family Estate Books, 1617–1675*, Surtees Society, vol. 191 (1976–7), app., i, p. 229. cf. Twysden's remarks (Kent Archives Office, U47/47 Z1, p. 108) and also Viscount Conway's comment to his son-in-law Sir Robert Harley late in July 1629: 'I have no news because I know that you ... having been so long verst in parliamentary affaires cannot but long after the contingent things to it' (HMC, *Fourteenth Report*, app., ii, p. 26.

49   S. D'Ewes, *Autobiography and Correspondence*, ed, by J. O. Halliwell (London: Richard Bentley, 1845), Vol. 1, pp. 402, 403, 405, 407.

50   In 1625 Parliament prepared but did not conclude action to grant Charles tonnage and poundage for only one year.

51   S. R. Gardiner, *The Constitutional Documents of the Puritan Revolution 1625–1660*, 3rd edn (Oxford: Clarendon Press, 1906), pp. 70–3 (Remonstrance), 73–4 (speech).

52   *CD 1629*, pp. 112, 196–7.

53   *CD 1629*, p. 102.

54   *ST*, Vol. 3, pp. 373–84; also SP 16/142/28; El 7901.

55   Birch, Vol. 2, p. 88. The earl of Clare who commented on Chambers's situation in October 1629 thought his offence may have been 'soundness in our religion' (Holles, no. 157). The treatment of Chambers and other resisting merchants was raised as a grievance in Parliament in 1640. See below.

56   These verses and a response to them appear in many sources, e.g. Rous, pp. 42–3. See also above.

57   SP 16/140/24. Merchants at Colchester claimed they would only pay what king and Parliament 'shall agree on' (SP 16/139/41).

58   He had countered the Commons' action on 2 March by ordering five days later that those who resisted were to be imprisoned and argued in his proclamation of 27 March that the House itself had not actually approved the condemnation of tonnage and poundage. In the same proclamation he also promised 'encouragement' to 'such as cheerfully go on with their trade' and sought to dash any expectations that he might be convinced to summon another Parliament in the near future. *Acts of the Privy Council of England 1628–1629* (London: HMSO, 1958), no. 1117 (order); STC 8921 (proclamation). Charles contended that none of the resolutions had been approved by the whole House.

59   Yonge, f. 29. Whiteway, ff. 74v–75; see also SP 16/139/41.

60   SP 16/141/16. Statements about how many merchants resisted conflict. See below.

61 Whiteway, ff. 74v–5.
62 *WP*, Vol. 2, pp. 74–5; see *DNB*, 'George Downing'.
63 Merchants had petitioned the Privy Council in September and November 1628 for permission to export grain to Europe (*Acts of the Privy Council 1628–1629*, nos 433, 680).
64 See J. D. Walter, 'Grain riots and popular attitudes to the law: Maldon and the crisis of 1629', in *An Ungovernable People: The English and their Law in the Seventeenth and Eighteenth Centuries*, eds J. Brewer and J. Styles (New Brunswick, NJ: Rutgers University Press, 1980), pp. 47–84, a reference I owe to Conrad Russell.
65 Walter, pp. 53–4.
66 Walter, p. 71. Concerning the state of the cloth trade, see B. Supple, *Commercial Crisis and Change in England, 1600–1642* (Cambridge: Cambridge University Press, 1959), pp. 102 ff. See also B. Sharp, pp. 27 ff.
67 Calendar of Essex Quarter Sessions Rolls (Q./SR 266) (Harvard film), 16 April 1629. Bodl., MS Firth, c.4, p. 484. See also Hunt, *Puritan Moment*, pp. 239–42.
68 Cal. Essex Q.S. (Q./SR 266), 8 May 1629.
69 Bodl., MS Firth, c.4, p. 484.
70 cf. Hunt's interpretation, *Puritan Moment*, pp. 240, 247.
71 Cal. Essex Q.S. (Q./SR 266), 8 May 1629.
72 Hunt, *Puritan Moment*, pp. 195, 224–31.
73 Warwick had just been reinstated in his lieutenancy after being removed for opposition to the loan. See *DNB*; also Hunt, *Puritan Moment*, pp. 213, 215–16.
74 Walter, pp. 76–80.
75 SP 16/141/16. Lake talks of 'clothiers', but he may be using the word loosely. Although both weavers and clothiers presented petitions at the quarter sessions, the weavers' complaints were those which the JPs emphasized in their report to the council (SP 16/141/1). It was 'clothiers' in the technical sense of middlemen against whom the weavers complained in their petition.
76 Bodl. MS Firth, c.4, pp. 486–7; also see p. 497.
77 He included in his diary many notes about both the merchants' conduct and the want and disorders in Essex (Yonge, ff. 29–31 *passim*). See also PRO, C.115/N.2, no. 8534.
78 SP 16/142/19. Conrad Russell brought this to my attention.
79 Birch, Vol. 2, p. 15. See also the comments of the Venetian ambassador who may have exaggerated the importance of the merchants' resistance (*CSPVen. 1629–32*, no. 44, p. 29 and no. 98, p. 67).
80 Birch, Vol. 2, pp. 19–21.
81 I am grateful to Linda Popofsky who allowed me to read her paper on 'Legal leadership and strategies in the House of Commons in 1628–29' which brought this point to my attention.
82 Yonge, f. 29. See also Supple, *Commercial Crisis*, pp. 104 ff.
83 The Venetian ambassador was apparently the principal celebrant (Birch,

Vol. 2, p. 13); see also his comment, *CSPVen. 1629–32*, no. 99. The articles of the peace were printed (STC 9250).

84   See Chapter 3.

85   Essex Record Office, Barrington MSS, D/DBa F/4 (Yale film), f. 6.

86   e.g. Yonge, f. 27v, 29v; Rous, pp. 37–9. The bishops received little public credit for their orders warning ministers to preach obedience and to avoid issues which might be divisive (SP 16/140/37).

87   SP 16/144/36; also 16/142/113; see *DNB*. There were petitions from groups of clergy both supporting and opposing Hooker (SP 16/151/45; 16/152/4). See also Chapter 2.

88   SP 16/160/66.

89   Hooker fled to Holland in 1629 and went to New England in 1633 (C. E. Banks, *The Planters of the Commonwealth* (Baltimore, Md: Genealogical Society, 1961), p. 19). Concerning the new lecture, see SP 16/161/54; 16/163/45.

90   Smart attacked these in *A Sermon Preached in the Cathedrall Church of Durham July 7, 1628* (Edinburgh, 1628), STC 22640; see *DNB*. Concerning the assizes in 1629, see *CSPDom. 1629–31*, pp. 15, 19, 20.

91   See *CSPDom. 1628–9*, pp. 243, 259, 266; *CD 1629*, pp. 97–101; also pp. 36–7.

92   Cosin's *A Collection of Private Devotions* (1627) had been written at the king's request for the English ladies at the queen's court (*The Correspondence of John Cosin*, ed. G. Ornsby, part 1, Surtees Society, vol. 52 (1869), pp. 284–5. It prompted replies from both Prynne and Burton in 1628 (see *A Collection of Private Devotions*, ed. P. G. Stanwood (Oxford: Oxford University Press, 1967), esp. p. xxvi). Smart did not name Cosin in the sermon. He dated changes from the death of the last bishop, eleven years earlier and says (*Sermon Preached in … Durham*, p. 35) that the changes occurred before the new bishop (Neile) came. See J. G. Hoffman, 'Another side of "Thorough": John Cosin and administration, discipline, and finance in the Church of England, 1622–44', *Albion*, vol. 12, no. 4 (1981), pp. 347–63.

93   Smart was sentenced by the High Commission at York and subsequently degraded. SP 16/112/8; 16/113/65; 16/147/15, 42; Birch, Vol. 2, p. 21; Cosin, *Correspondence*, no. 90. Among the papers of Sir Robert Harley is a copy of the sentence of Smart. On it is written, 'God's blessing or his vengeance light upon Harsnet [archbishop of York] and his venerable rabble of "rakhell" censurers according to the justice or wrong they have done to me Peter Smart' (HMC, *Fourteenth Report*, app., ii, p. 28). Once imprisoned, Smart seems to have bided his time, and when another Parliament met in the spring of 1640, he poured out his grievances in a petition. His claim in 1640 that he had succeeded in indicting his opponents is not true. For his petition, see Cope and Coates, pp. 280–2.

94   WP, Vol. 2, pp. 105–6. See also 'General Considerations for the Plantation in New-England' (1629) in A. Young (ed.), *Chronicles of the First Planters of the Colony of Massachusetts Bay from 1623 to 1636* (Williamstown, Mass.: Corner House, reprint of 1846 edn), ch. 13. The planters argued that

the task before them required skill so that the very best ministers and magistrates not merely the young and unskilled should go. To claims that like other generations of the godly they would find that the Judgement they expected would not come, they cited the example of what happened at La Rochelle and in the Palatinate.

95 Among other reasons for immediate migration the 'General Considerations' cited decline of trade, poverty, corruption of schools of learning and religion. The statistics are from Winthrop's journal (*WP*, Vol. 2, p. 225 and note). See also, T. H. Breen, 'Moving to the New World: the character of early Massachusetts immigration', *William and Mary Quarterly*, Third Series, vol. 30, no. 2 (1973), pp. 189–222.

96 *The Churches Hazzard* (London, 1632), STC 20832, p. 12; see also, Hildersham's sermon, 4 October 1629, urging his congregation to prepare for death (*Doctrine of Fasting* (London, 1633), STC 13459).

97 Gilbert Barell was also implicated in this business as was John Selden who was already in custody as a result of the events of 2 March. Concerning Cotton, see K. Sharpe, *Sir Robert Cotton, 1586–1631* (Oxford: Oxford University Press, 1979). For St John, see *DNB*; Bedford, *DNB*; Somerset, *DNB*; John Holles, second earl of Clare, P. Seddon (ed.), *Letters of John Holles, 1587–1637*, Thoroton Society, Record Series, vol. 31 (1975), Vol. 1, introduction.

98 A number of copies of the tract have survived (e.g. SP 14/77/65). Since the tract had circulated previously, it is difficult to determine whether the arrest of these gentlemen increased interest in it and stirred people to make copies.

99 Holles, nos 156, 158; *CSP Ven.* 1629–32, no. 257; *The Private Correspondence of Jane Lady Cornwallis, 1613–1644* (London, 1842), no. 136; also Gardiner, *History of England*, Vol. 7, p. 138.

100 SP 16/151/81; Sharpe thinks the tract was a pretext for action against court opponents (Sharpe, *Cotton*, pp. 80–1, 144–6, 214).

101 Holles, no. 158.

102 Birch, Vol. 2, p. 112; Sharpe, *Cotton*, p. 81. Cotton apparently did not expect to live.

103 The earl of Manchester told his brother, Lord Montagu, in a letter of 12 November that he was 'sure' the examination of Cotton and others 'makes a great noise in the country' (Montagu MS 6.53).

104 SP 16/151/81.

105 SP 16/158/55; 16/158/9. Archbishop Harsnett of York, who had little sympathy for any of those involved except Bedford, noted that only Bedford and Cotton were grateful when they were released from custody to await further proceedings (SP 16/151/80).

106 Sharpe suggests Arundel intervened in their behalf (*Cotton*, p. 214), but Pembroke sought Vane's help as an intermediary (SP 16/158/9; also 16/158/55).

107 *ST*, Vol. 3, p. 397; Gardiner, *History of England*, Vol. 7, pp. 140–1.

108 See, for example, PRO, C.115/M.30, no. 8066; C.115/M.24, no. 7757; Essex Record Office, Barrington MSS, D/DBa F/4, f. 15.

109 See Chapter 3 below.

110   See above.
111   W. Rye (ed.), *State Papers Relating to Musters, Beacons, Shipmoney, etc. in Norfolk*, Norfolk and Norwich Archaeological Society (1907), p. 157.
112   SP 16/162/198. He did not mention religion in his letter.
113   Charles had not dismissed the clerks or taken other steps to dismantle or abolish Parliament. See M. F. Bond, 'Clerks of the parliaments, 1509–1953', *EHR*, vol. 73, no. 286 (1958), pp. 78–85, esp. p. 81. The House of Commons was without a clerk from 1633 until 1639; see S. Lambert, 'The clerks and records of the House of Commons, 1600–40', *BIHR*, vol. 43, no. 108 (1970), pp. 217–18.
114   Kent Archives Office, U47/47 Z1, p. 108; cf. Hutton's comments in Hampden's case: 'There was seen too much of the ambitious humour of some in the last parliament, that stirred up nothing but confusion and discontentment, as we now feel it to our great prejudice' (*ST*, Vol. 3, p. 1196, a reference I owe to Conrad Russell). Conrad Russell also brought Twysden's notes to my attention and put me in touch with Kenneth Fincham who shared his references to the Twysden MSS with me. Since then he has edited them in 'The judges' decision on ship money in February 1637: the reaction of Kent', *BIHR*, vol. 67, no. 137 (1984), pp. 230–7. Miss P. D. Rowsby of the Kent Archives Office was especially generous with her time in identifying and photocopying those references for me.
115   Halliwell (ed.), *D'Ewes*, p. 402.
116   Prynne and Burton both wrote on these themes before and after 1628. See, for example, Burton, *For God and the King* (1636), STC 4141; Prynne, *Anti-Arminianism* (1630), STC 20458.
117   (1630), STC 722. See also Eliot's *Monarchy of Man*, which circulated in manuscript among his friends in 1631 (Forster, *Eliot*, Vol. 2, bk xii, iii–v, pp. 379–81, 391–2, 411 ff., 455). I am grateful to Paul Hardacre for this reference.
118   *The Practise of Princes*, p. 15.
119   ibid., p. 7.
120   ibid., p. 22.
121   e.g. Finch in Hampden's case (*ST*, Vol. 3, pp. 1226, 1235); Heylyn's *A Briefe and Moderate Answer to the Seditious Challenges of Henry Burton*, bound with *A Coale from the Altar* (1636), STC 13270 (Folger copy).
122   I first encountered this at the Folger (MS V.b.189) where I discussed it with Derek Hirst. The attribution on that copy to Mr Henry Bromley is clearly in error. Both internal evidence and Windebanke's notes (SP 16/233/51) point to Kynaston's authorship. Among other copies are: Bodl., MS Ashmole 1149; BL, Lansdowne MS 213; Edinburgh, National Library of Scotland, Advocates MS 16.2.23 (attributed to John Dodderidge), HMC, *Second Report*, Vol. 3, Bedford MSS. See also *DNB*, 'Kynaston' and E. Evans, 'Of the antiquity of parliaments in England', *History*, vol. 23, no. 91 (1938), pp. 206–21, a reference I owe to Elizabeth Foster. Moshi Feingold helped me with Kynaston's background.
123   Preface.

124 SP 16/233/51. I have found no evidence that the secretary used the arguments.

125 (1628), STC 7749. I am grateful to William Bidwell for the information that the printed edition of the tract followed several manuscript versions which had been updated as they appeared. Parts of *The Priviledges and Practice of Parliaments* came from Richard Crompton's *L'Authoritie et Jurisdiction de la Majestie de la Roynge* (orig. 1594). Kynaston's tract against it is virtually the only indication that *The Priviledges and Practice* caused controversy.

126 'A true presentation', ch. 7.

127 William Habington, *The Historie of Edward the Fourth, King of England* (1640), p. 19 (STC 12586). Concerning Habington see *DNB*.

128 John Hayward, *The Life and Raigne of King Edward the Sixt* (1630), p. 47 (STC 12998). But see F. Bacon's *The History of the Reign of King Henry the Seventh* (orig. 1622) which took greater note of statutes. I owe this reference to Elizabeth Foster. Concerning Hayward, see *DNB*.

129 See Chapter 3 below.

130 *Survey of the Kingdom of Sweden*. First written in Dutch and sent to England to a person of note and quality who thought it ought to be translated and published (1632), STC 23518. See also *The Present Estate of Spayne* (1630), STC 24929.

131 SP 16/161/56. Concerning Roe see *DNB*.

132 R. Powell, *Depopulation Arraigned: Convicted and Condemned by the Laws of God and Man* (1636), p. 96; see also pp. 104–5 (STC 20160); SP 16/178/1, tract concerning trade.

133 See Thomas Reeve's sermon quoted earlier in this chapter, and also William Chillingworth, *The Religion of Protestants* (1638), p. 312 (STC 5138).

134 'The Great Assize', the first of four sermons in *A Fold for Christ's Sheep* (1638), STC 22849.3.

135 D. Lupton, *London and the Countrey. Carbonadoed and Quartered into Several Characters* (1632), p. 17 (STC 16944).

136 Chillingworth, op. cit., p. 171.

137 Thomas Morton, *Sermon Preached Before the Kings Majesty, 5 May 1639* (1639), STC 18196; see also Ed. Turges, *The Christian Souldier* (1639), p. 235 (STC 24331.2).

138 Concerning statute-making, see below.

139 S. R. Gardiner (ed.), *Reports of Cases in the Court of Star Chamber and High Commission*, Camden Society, New Series, vol. 39 (1876), pp. 286 ff.

140 SP16/240/23.

141 Powell, *Depopulation*, p. 105.

142 York City Archives, House Books, Vol. 35, ff. 201 ff. *passim*. A bill had been introduced in 1621 (W. Notestein, F. H. Relf, and H. Simpson (eds), *Commons Debates, 1621* (New Haven, Conn.: Yale University Press, 1935), Vol. 5, p. 136. See also, P. M. Tillott, *The City of York* (Victoria County History, 1961), p. 169. Also see Harvard University Library, Microfilm, Exeter Letters, f. 361 (8 May 1634). The petition of the Essex weavers who while expressing hope that Parliament could deal with their

problem asked for immediate aid, see Harvard Microfilm, Calendar of Essex Quarter Sessions Rolls, Chelmsford, 16 April 1629; also Bodl. MS Firth, c.4, p. 505; *WP*, Vol. 3, pp. 91–3.

143   Concerning the quantity of private business, see E. R. Foster, *The House of Lords, 1603–1649* (Chapel Hill, NC: University of North Carolina Press, 1983), pp. 201–2; also G. R. Elton, 'Tudor government: the points of contact: 1. Parliament', *TRHS*, Fifth Series, vol. 24 (1974), p. 195; S. Lambert, 'Procedure in the House of Commons in the early Stuart period', *EHR*, vol. 95, no. 376 (1980), pp. 758–9. Among the uses of private acts were naturalization, breaking entails, reversing decrees in Chancery.

144   e.g. SP 16/142/5; 16/154/46; 16/232/71; 16/267/54.

145   (1629), STC 4270.

146   Somerset Record Office, Phelips MSS, DDPH 221/33; Laud, *Works*, Vol. 7, pp. 505 ff.; HMC, *Twelfth Report*, app., i, Cowper, Vol. 2, p. 186; SP 16/204/107; *CSPVen. 1629–32*, no. 257.

147   Henry Elsyng, 'Memorandum for the earl of Danby', in E. R. Foster, *The Painful Labour of Mr. Elsyng*, American Philosophical Society, Transactions, New Series, vol. 62, no. 8 (1972), p. 64. Elsyng, however, was anxious about applying his history 'to the present times' (p. 63). See also Moseley's proposals (SP 16/174/112; 16/175/27, 77; 16/176/24). Cf. Heath's memo to the king which pointed out the need to stop the advance of Popery and proposed the reconfirmation of the Petition of Right. This may have come from about the same time (SP 16/178/3, a reference I owe to Conrad Russell).

148   *CSPVen. 1636–9*, no. 122.

149   *CSPVen. 1636–9*, no. 139; also see V. A. Rowe, 'Robert, second earl of Warwick and the payment of shipmoney in Essex', in *Transactions of the Essex Archaeological Society*, vol. 1, pt. 2, Third Series (1964–5), pp. 160–3; and below.

150   See, e.g. C1 C 27 and C1 C 202 and below.

151   Knowler, Vol. 1, pp. 175–8; see also HMC, *Fourteenth Report*, app., ii, pp. 26, 45. Henry Peacham recommended that young gentlemen study parliamentary speeches as a part of their education, in *The Complete Gentleman*, ed. V. Hetzel (Folger Shakespeare Library, 1962). See also Davenport's comment about Sir Roger Townshend in *Letters of John Davenport*, ed. I. M. Calder (New Haven, Conn.: Yale University Press, 1937), p. 64; H. Ellis (ed.), *Original Letters, Illustrative of English History*, (London: Harding and Lepard, 1827), 2nd series, Vol. 3, p. 266.

152   e.g. Knowler, Vol. 1, pp. 418–19; HMC, *Seventh Report*, app., pp. 547–8; Birch, Vol. 2, p. 61; HMC, *Ninth Report*, app., p. 496 (Woodforde's diary). Concerning Thomas Scott's solicitation of support, see above. Lowther, who declared he had had enough of being an MP after 1629, is an exception (see above). See also, Forster, *Eliot*, Vol. 2, pp. 361–2, 445–8.

153   Harvard MS Eng. 1074, f. 1.

154   See also J. Stephens, *Satyrical Essayes* (1631; orig. 1615), STC 23251.

155   While not charging the parliaments of his own day with being turbulent, Francis Godwin noted that in Henry VIII's day the crown had dominated

Parliament. 'Parliaments were not then so rigid but that they could flatter the Prince and condescend to his demands, though unjust in some cases', F. Godwin, *Annales of England* (1630), p. 143. See also SP 16/162/18.

156 Knowler, Vol. 2, pp. 55–9. Probably the Sir Henry Anderson who had been an MP for Newcastle upon Tyne in the 1620s (Keeler, pp. 86–7).

157 Physician: e.g. W. Prynne, *Anti-Arminianism* (1630), STC 20458. Senate: e.g. H. Burton, *Apology of an Appeal* (1636), STC 4134.

158 See below.

159 See D. Hirst, *Representative of the People?* (Cambridge: Cambridge University Press, 1975), pp. 19–20. The pamphlet which Hirst cites in note 40, *The Priviledges and Practice of Parliaments in England*, was first printed in 1628 and cannot be used to argue his point. See also above.

2

Religion

The House of Commons resolved on 27 January 1628/9 that 'the Matter of Religion shall have the Precedencie over all other Business'.[1] Their decision was procedural and tactical; it also reflected the priorities of MPs and of many others. Having begun the session on 21 January with questions about violations of the Petition of Right and exaction of tonnage and poundage and having provoked the king to warn them against judging 'ill' of him, the House yielded on the 27th to those members who urged them to give priority to religion, to rights of 'an higher nature' as Francis Rous put it.[2]

MPs linked their personal salvation and national strength with the fate of religion. While God had delivered England from its enemies in the past, they were fearful that he would not do so again. The threat to Protestantism was greater than ever. 'Two sects', Sir Robert Phelips declared, 'are dangerously crept in to undermine King and Kingdom, if not now prevented, the one ancient Popery, the other new Arminianism'.[3] The Commons had heard complaints about Arminianism in previous sessions, and in their remonstrance to the king in June 1628 they had mentioned not only Popery but also Arminianism which they described as 'but a cunning way to bring in Popery'.[4] Between June and January more people had become convinced of the gravity of the Arminian 'disease'.[5]

Despite these worries and the members' consequent decision to emphasize religion, the Commons did not concentrate their attention upon that to the exclusion of all else. They attempted to investigate alleged violations of other rights and found themselves adjourned by the king before they were able to do more than collect a list of religious grievances.[6] In the first of the resolutions passed on 2 March, as the Speaker was being held in the chair, the House echoed the words members had used a month before to argue that the Commons should turn their attention to religion. They protested that anyone who brought in 'innovation in Religion' or sought 'to extend or introduce Popery or Arminianism or other opinions disagreeing from the true and orthodox Church' would be regarded as a 'capital enemy' to the 'Kingdom and Commonwealth'.[7]

The Commons were in effect declaring war on innovators whether these were Papists who in the eyes of the law were already foes of the English Church or whether they were Arminians or others who had not been the subject of explicit statutory penalties. Their proceedings drew attention to disunity within the Church and prompted fears about its ability to withstand attack. Anxiety about the very fact of disagreements regarding religious beliefs and practices and ecclesiastical government thus added to the intensity with which people debated these issues during the 1630s. Opinions that in any way resembled those of the 'old' popish antagonist seemed particularly pernicious.

Many of the English in 1629 had parents or grandparents who had been Papists. For them the Roman religion was an immediate, not a distant, phenomenon. They could not be confident that Protestantism was firmly established in England. At the time that Charles dissolved his third Parliament, popish forces were assaulting Protestants in Germany where almost a decade earlier they had succeeded in ousting King Charles's sister, Elizabeth, and her husband Frederick, the Elector of the Palatine, from the Bohemian throne. The indignities suffered by the 'Queen of Bohemia' gave her English friends personal reasons for considering the German wars as one campaign in a universal religious conflict.[8] England's own war with Catholic Spain kept alive memories of the way that papist demands for toleration had interfered with the negotiations for a marriage between Charles and the Spanish Infanta.[9] The French princess, Henrietta Maria, whom he married, magnified the popish problem for the English by her own firm commitment to Catholicism and her support for fellow Catholics.[10] Charles's futile effort to aid French Protestants at La Rochelle added to the doubts his marriage had raised about his softness on Popery, and the peace agreement he made with the French in April 1629 brought no assurance that France would not be party to a popish plot against the English Church and commonwealth.[11] His treaty with the Spanish a year and a half later in November 1630 likewise inspired little confidence among English Protestants. Two aspects of that settlement caught the attention of one puritan correspondent: the 'verie great feast' for the ambassador (he estimated the cost at £7000); and the intrinsically suspicious fact that the articles were 'kept so close' that he could not obtain copies.[12] When Catholics were involved, people were prepared to assume the worst.

The activities of Henrietta Maria kept people's attention focused on Popery at court. Most worried about her influence over Charles and her devotion to her faith and, in contrast to Prynne, disregarded her love of dancing or her participation in a play.[13] The fact that she had courtier friends, like the earl of Holland, whose associations were puritan, not papist, did not diminish fears prompted by reports that many English were going to mass at her chapel.[14] Whereas her role in the factional politics of the court required her opponents to make appropriate countermoves, her role in the machinations of international Popery was more difficult to combat.[15]

The series of papal envoys – Panzani in 1634, George Con 1636–9, and Rossetti in 1639 – who came to England drew attention to the queen and other Papists at court.[16] Their presence made credible rumours such as that about the arrival of a cardinal's hat that reached Brilliana Harley in November 1639.[17] The visibility of the Romanists also gave people added reason to note conversions to that faith and to question whether the English lords and gentlemen who professed Catholicism placed greater weight on their obligations to the pope than on those to the king.[18] The news in 1635 that courtier Wat Montagu, son of the earl of Manchester, himself a staunch Protestant, had been converted caused quite a stir.[19] Religion, politics, and sheer human interest all contributed to the talk about Montagu and the desire to know how king, queen, Manchester, and others at court would receive him in the spring of 1637 when he returned to England from France where he had been at the time of his conversion. Lord Scudamore's correspondent noted in a letter of 12 April that 'many of the great court lords', including Holland and Dorset, were feasting Montagu and seeing him daily but that the reactions of the king and Manchester remained in question.[20] Although Charles eventually yielded and received

Montagu, he did so, the reporter noted carefully, with little warmth.[21]

The king's stance with regard to religion puzzled many individuals who were seeking reassurance about the security of Protestantism. Charles at times imposed restrictions upon the Papists.[22] He did not always yield to Henrietta Maria, yet he never took firm action to close the door on Popery. In 1638 he allowed his mother-in-law, Marie de Medici, the French queen mother, to come to England.[23] Upon her arrival she, unlike the pope's emissary, was greeted with public ceremonies. Despite their antipathy toward her and their fears that she would be maintained at the public charge, people participated dutifully in the official welcome.[24] However much they disliked having another foreign Papist at court, the English were not prepared to resist her coming.

Like Catholics at court, those in the country, many of whom were lords or gentlemen, made the English uneasy.[25] Although people had resigned themselves to the continuing presence of Catholics in England, they remained vigilant for any signs that adherents to the Roman religion were increasing. Religious differences aggravated quarrels over other matters, and incidents led neighbours to demand rigorous enforcements of the penal laws.[26] The panics and searches for arms caused by rumours that the Papists were about to rise in revolt illustrate the fears that lay just beneath attitudes that often appear more relaxed.[27] Aware of the power and influence of Papists at court, the English were quick to complain if they thought Catholics were receiving any special benefits.[28] The political dimensions of what they regarded as the popish problem were not merely local.

Popular concern about Popery in England reveals the myopia in the advice that papal agent Panzani claimed he received in 1634 from Richard Montagu, then bishop of Chichester. Montagu told the nuncio not to take too seriously 'the aversion [to union with Rome] ... in our sermons and printed books'. That was a matter 'of form, chiefly to humour the populace, and not to be much regarded'.[29] If Montagu believed that the public was appeased by routine attacks on Rome, he was mistaken. Neither words nor the deeds of those with authority in Church and commonwealth convinced the English that they need not worry about tolerance of Catholics, Catholicism at court, or a popish plot to take over the kingdom.

Popery threatened to replace law and government in England with tyranny, and religion with superstition and ignorance. The language of sermons and books that Montagu dismissed had for two generations instructed people about the errors of the Papists. The pope was anti-Christ, the veneration of saints idolatry, and the ritual of the mass a means of deluding the faithful whose instruction was neglected by a lack of concern about preaching. Catholics consequently failed to practise piety in their daily lives. They violated the sabbath with games and other unsuitable recreations. The English believed that their own salvation depended upon rooting this dangerous and false religion out of the kingdom.[30]

Fear of Popery lurked behind the Commons' denunciation of Arminianism and 'innovations' in religion in the resolution of 2 March 1629 and continued to arouse suspicion of changes in ecclesiastical policies and practices during the 1630s. Illustrative of this anxiety is a rhyme which John Rous says was one of many circulating in 1634 and 1635. 'The new churchman', it declared, was 'he [who] will be no Protestant but a Christian and comes out Catholike the next edition'.[31] Signs of difference between the leaders of the English Church and Popery brought comment. When William Chillingworth, who had put his pen to Archbishop Laud's service, published a new book against the Papists in 1637, Viscount Conway wrote to his brother-in-law, Sir Robert Harley, 'Soe it seemes we are not goeing to Romne, wheither soever else we are going, it may be we shall make somme new discovery'.[32]

Arminianism, strictly speaking a belief in salvation by free will, was thus at issue with the Calvinist tenet of predestination.[33] Compounding the doctrinal concerns aroused by Arminianism were the emphasis that some Arminians and some others placed upon ceremonies and the boldness with which clergy of various views asserted their own authority, even to the point of claiming that their powers came directly from God.[34] Charles I, who wanted a Church free from corruption and laxness and who personally found the rituals of religion appealing, appointed as bishops men who would vigorously endeavour to mould the Church of England along these lines. He supported prelates like William Laud whom he moved from St Davids to London in 1628 and then made archbishop of Canterbury in 1633. Laud, though not an Arminian, espoused views that many people thought too much like Popery and did much to aggravate the religious controversies of the 1630s.[35]

People who wanted the Church of England to move farther from rather than closer to Rome responded to the apparent growth of Arminianism and Popery during the 1620s with their own efforts to prevent 'innovations' and to bring the Church in accord with scripture.[36] Known to their opponents as Puritans, they were Calvinists, adherents of predestination rather than free will who wanted more preaching, fewer ceremonies, stricter observance of the sabbath, and more reliance upon scripture and statute than upon bishops. Some wanted to make church government presbyterian rather than episcopal. No longer able after 1629 to look to Parliament for religious reform, Puritans found their options limited. They were confronted by a king and increasingly by bishops who seemed unsympathetic to their worries about Popery or about innovations leading in that direction. Like those they opposed, the Puritans disagreed among themselves about what to do and how to do it.[37]

Many sources from the 1630s report acrimonious quarrels between Puritans and Arminians and/or Laudians.[38] The stories that circulated and the instances of emotional exchanges and name-calling make the lines of battle seem longer, clearer and straighter than was the case. Caricatures of persons and ideas overpowered actuality, and individuals judged each other's religious sympathies on the basis of hearsay or observations of conduct rather than careful study of opinions. Beliefs were not always evident to observers.[39] The relatively few people who flung epithets and doggedly defended their positions attracted more attention than the far greater numbers, who were moderate or indifferent in their opinions and could not be described as Puritans, Arminians, or Laudians.[40] Contemporaries realized this and yet, concerned as they were about divisions within the English Church and commonwealth and about the points at issue, they could not dismiss the disputes as rhetorical exercises. The controversies about ceremonies, the sabbath, preaching, and church governance that I shall examine in the remainder of this chapter were serious matters to those who lived through them. At stake was both their own salvation and the strength and honour of England.

Charles I's reign saw a renewal of the controversies about ceremonies that had raged periodically since England's separation from the Roman Church. The centrality of ceremonies in divine services and their visibility made them a significant point in debate between adherents of differing religious practices. Prelates who were zealous in their administrative ambitions saw that by insisting on compliance in this sphere they could impress others with their authority, and people used ceremonies as a convenient basis for judging a whole range of religious attitudes. The position of the communion table, even more than bowing at the name of Jesus or kneeling at the rail to receive the Eucharist, could serve as an indicator of local views. At a glance observers could determine whether a parish had placed its table altarwise in conformity with Laudian dictates.[41] The location of the table also assumed importance because it was related to the general arrangement of a church and its seating pattern. Requirements that necessitated rearrangement could set off dissension among parishioners about their social precedence. Like some supporters of collegiate football teams in twentieth-century USA, parishioners regarded their seats as property and were prepared to defend them by litigation. Few of the disputes that erupted about ceremonies during the 1630s were so clearly theological or as boldly undertaken as that which Durham prebend Peter Smart undertook against John Cosin in 1628.[42]

Stirring up the disputes in many instances were orders or injunctions from ecclesiastical authorities that parishes place their communion tables 'altarwise'. With support from the king, the bishops were able to amend the policy that had been in effect since 1566 and had been confirmed by the canons of 1604 to direct that tables should be at the east end of churches.[43] The king's declaration of December 1628 sought to discourage either clergy or laity from raising questions like the vicar of Grantham's in the previous year about where the table should be.[44] Those bishops, including Laud and Neile, who wanted the tables altarwise made conformity one object of their visitations.

At St Gregory's, London, parishioners appealed the directive of Dean and Chapter of St Paul's that their table be placed altarwise to the Court of Arches, but before the case came to a hearing, the Privy Council intervened with a ruling against them.[45] The council's action, the parish's location in London, and the timing of the case in 1633, just after Laud's move to Canterbury, may all have helped to give St Gregory's publicity and make it a notorious example of official promotion of innovations.[46] In his diary Walter Yonge juxtaposed the board's order for St Gregory's with the letter the bishop of Lincoln had written to the vicar of Grantham on the same subject the preceding year.[47]

Bishop John Williams's originally private and unsigned letter became a focal point in the disputes that followed the council's action at St Gregory's.[48] Although Williams's reputation as a congenial courtier-politician might seem to disqualify him from championing the anti-ceremonial campaign, his prominence probably helped to draw attention to his views.[49] The letter's reasoned argument, based on respected sources of church history and practice and its authorship by a bishop, made it appealing to opponents of ceremonies. Copies circulated, and people cited it to justify their claims that the old way set forth in the canons was acceptable.[50] The letter also served the purposes of Laudian Peter Heylyn who was searching for evidence to use against Williams and particularly for a way of removing him from the deanery of Westminster.[51] Neither Heylyn's efforts to refute the bishop's statements nor Laud's accusation that Williams was piqued by the king's unwillingness to 'take him off from the Star Chamber' prevented a controversy on paper which ran parallel to the disputes in the parishes about tables and altars.[52]

Just after arriving in London at the beginning of May 1637, Robert Leeke wrote to Sir Gervase Clifton, 'All the doings I hear of is the civill warres amongst the clergy whose pennes are their pikes and so they fight dayly between the Table and the Alter, whose severall battayles are set forth in diverse books which Mr Hodges hath undertaken and promised to send you'.[53] Heylyn virtually invited participation in the debate by including a copy of Williams's letter in the appendix to *A Coale from the Altar*, his refutation of the same.[54] Professing a deep-seated concern about accurate and proper interpretation of history, law, and religion, he claimed that he was printing the letter to allow his readers to judge for themselves the fairness of his statements.[55] Williams promptly defended both the intent and content of his letter. He too drew upon law and history and argued that the articles for the metropolitan's visitation of the diocese of Lincoln in 1634 allowed the meaning which he (Williams) had attributed to them.[56] Others joined the fray.[57] A few days after Leeke's letter to Clifton, Heylyn obtained a licence for his *Antidotum Lincolniense* in which he tried to paint the bishop as a radical Puritan, an associate of Prynne, Burton and Bastwick, who were imprisoned and awaiting trial for their attacks on the church.[58] Their trial in June 1637 set the scene for that of Williams a month later even though the charges against him did not include his views about ceremonies.[59] Some observers who recognized that the legal points at issue were different nevertheless suspected that the bishop's mistake was his independence.[60] The situation was complex and confusing. Leeke who was usually able to obtain information told Clifton that he neither knew nor could discover the reason for the sentence against Williams.[61] John Burgh whose sources and/or understanding surpassed Leeke's in this instance reported to Lord Scudamore that Williams had behaved 'strangely'. Not only had he refused submission but in one speech he had asserted that his right to his see was as good as the king's to the crown.[62] The bishop's conduct was not always above question on either political or ethical grounds, but people liked him, appreciated his pastoral care, and noted his benefactions.[63] While few saw him as a fourth martyr in the campaign against innovations, more realized that his case raised questions about the goals and procedures of the Laudian ecclesiastical regime.

Adding to public interest in what Lord Conway referred to as the *'Bellum Grammaticale'* about ceremonies were the efforts of another bishop, Matthew Wren.[64] Upon his translation late in 1635 from Hereford to Norwich, Wren began to take steps to discipline the previously 'troublesome' diocese.[65] Following the instructions issued in 1629 and the example of Laud, he prepared articles for a visitation.[66] These articles, decidedly longer and more explicit than was customary, required the churchwardens in each parish to indicate directly whether the table 'doth ... ordinarily stand up at the East end of the chancell where the altar in former times stood'.[67] The results, as Rous recorded them, were that 'many were troubled and suspended about the ceremonies enquired of'.[68] Wren's campaign for conformity achieved additional notoriety in January 1636/7 with the appearance of the anonymous tract *Newes from Ipswich*.[69]

While many parishes escaped from conflicts over ceremonies, the emotions generated where disputes did erupt troubled conscientious people. The table–altar disputes left those who were churchwardens torn between obedience to episcopal mandates and compliance with pressure from neighbours. Robert Woodforde, the puritan steward of Northampton, in the diocese of Peterborough, kept a running account in his diary of the conflict over the table in his parish. In December 1637 the churchwardens were sent for and 'injoyned to rayle in and fix the table at the east end of the chancel, but they both refused and answered ... boldly'. Two weeks later when they brought down the table 'from the top, and set it long wise in the body of the chancell', they were excommunicated.[70]

When faced with excommunication most churchwardens submitted. Wheeler, of St Botolph's, Colchester, who defended his conduct by claiming that moving the table was against the king's laws and contrary to the rubric in the Common Prayer Book, was an exception. He cited Magna Carta, a series of statutes, the *King's Declaration* concerning the dissolution of the last Parliament, Bishop Jewell, and other authors who, he believed, proved turning tables to altars was popish.[71] Another Colchester man, Samuel Burroughs, attempted, as Peter Smart had, to bring indictments at the assizes against clergy who observed ceremonies.[72] The churchwardens who went furthest in their resistance were probably those of Beckington, Somerset, who were not only excommunicated but also gaoled as a result of their stance with regard to the communion table. Like Wheeler, they invoked the law. Without an injunction from the king or an Act of Parliament, they thought they would be on shaky ground to answer if subsequently questioned in Parliament.[73]

The conflict over ceremonies at Beckington was one of those that was not merely verbal. Such disturbances gave people who were not themselves committed to either side and those who were defenders of the Laudian position grounds for condemning the opponents of change as extremists. Somerset gentleman Sir Robert Phelips whose interest in ingratiating himself with the court was greater than his concern about religious affairs blamed the disturbances at Beckington upon one John Ashe, a man he said was 'held to be both in opinion and faction a puritan'. Ashe, a clothier who was also allegedly distributing dangerous tracts, including *Newes from Ipswich*, had stirred up 'a most violent opposition' to the removal of the table and 'some fowle ryots in the church itself'.[74]

Although violence was exceptional, it was unsettling because it provided people with a perspective for interpreting their questions about the practice of religion and bred worries about the approach of Judgement. Efforts to attribute disorder to individual trouble-makers or to ignorance may have satisfied some persons, but evidence of the clash of opinions was difficult to deny by the summer of 1637 when Prynne, Burton, and Bastwick were tried.[75] The punishment of persons who exemplified undesirable conduct and awareness that beliefs about what was right were in conflict may have encouraged those whose views or conduct was challenged by ecclesiastical authorities to submit. On the other hand differences of opinion could lend support to those who found law and custom contrary to their diocesan's injunctions. In places, such as Towcester, Northampton, or Colchester, where Puritanism was strong, people could find reinforcement and reassurance within the community. At St Peter's, Nottingham, where the churchwardens were excommunicated some forty parishioners, including the mayor, were presented for refusing to take communion at the rail.[76]

The tale of gradual acceptance of conformity told in Laud's annual reports of the state of his province must be weighed against the evidence of resistance and the continuance of questions about ceremonies that appear both on paper and in the parishes. Some people maintained that ceremonies were things indifferent and thus arguments about them academic.[77] Others worried about what was right. Dr John Young, Dean of Winchester, expressed his uncertainty about standing 'at the Creeds' to Laud's Vicar-General, Nathaniel Brent, during the visitation in June 1635.[78] John Andrewes, rector of Beaconsfield, Buckinghamshire, told Laud of a fellow, a gardener, who had asked about the authority on which people were enjoined to bow at the name of Jesus and had even raised the possibility that the governors of the church might 'prescribe orders contrary to Gods law'.[79] In addition to the scriptural texts upon which some ministers justified their attacks on the prescribed ceremonies, the English could find evidence of different practices in historical sources such as the writings of Elizabethan Archbishop Whitgift whose record as an opponent of the Puritans and an upholder of order within the Church could scarcely be criticized.[80] Outbreaks of plague and other calamities gave both clergy and laity reason to wonder whether God was angry with the state of religion in England.[81]

The steps that people took to avoid confrontation or to accommodate themselves to Laudianism reveal sensitivity to the ceremonial conflicts. As Henry Jacie wrote to Winthrop, 'good men [who] cannot abide these ceremonies, and . . . would never use them' if they had choice did so occasionally to preserve themselves from the 'persecution of the bishops'.[82] Some clergymen gave communion both to those who did not meet Laudian requirements and to those who did.[83] Some substituted 'he' for 'Jesus' each time they came to it so they could conceal their reluctance to bow at the name.[84] Members of the laity who continued to attend church manifested their opinions by arriving too late for anything but the sermon, remaining seated at particular times in the service, by refusing to go to the rail for communion, or by deserting their own parishes for others.[85]

Those who compromised did not escape problems or criticism. Some individuals thought a violation of conviction, even for purposes of continuing in the ministry, a serious fault. Woodforde took a stern view of the decision of the curate of St Giles, Northampton, late in life, to deny the 'Sacrament to those that refused to come up to the rayles'.[86] Muriel Gurdon likewise was sorry when 'many that seemed to be zeleous doe yeld obedience to the inventions of men'.[87] She thought that 'wors' than 'that in so short a time so many of Gods faithfull ministers should be silenced'. To Sir Walter Earle it was important that the 'kings conformable clerk' not be given a benefice.[88]

The loss or gain of income from a living was not the only financial consideration involved in decisions about ceremonial conformity. The Laudian programme emphasized the repair and furnishing of churches. Dilapidated buildings without proper ornaments and clergy who had no vestments interfered with the 'beauty of holiness', but remedies were costly. The grand jury at the Lent assizes in Northampton in 1633 presented the 'burden of an extraordinary charge ... imposed ... by the Lord Bishops officers of the Diocese whoe commaunding the clergie to read divine service in their hoods according to their degrees have alsoe injoyned the same to be provided at the charge of their severall parishes ... the wch amounteth to the somme of £700 and upwards and being more to some smale parishes than a subsedy and alsoe agt law ... by reason that those hoods are ornaments of dignity mearely for distinction of degrees and are not expressed in the canon to be provided at the charge of their parishes'.[89]

The Laudian projects gave people legal questions with which to garb their perennial dislike of rates or other charges and set off battles over church seats. Resistance was not necessarily a matter of opposition to the improving of the setting for worship.[90] Some communities engaged in church beautification during the 1630s, and numerous individuals contributed toward the repair of St Paul's. The latter campaign in which Laud took a special interest never accomplished what he hoped it would. The gentlemen commissioned to solicit funds for the campaign cited various reasons, including local church renovation and burdens of plague, poverty, and taxation, for their meagre collections.[91] They themselves had other and greater demands on their time and energy. Dislike of Laud and the ecclesiastical dignitaries with whom St Paul's was associated may also have deterred contributions. The church was remote, not an object of local pride.

If some contemporaries are to be believed, popular irreligion and disrespect for Church, clergy, and religion may have been as important as rampant differences in belief in creating opposition to Laudian orders for ceremonies and for the provision of appropriate settings for them. Dr John Andrewes seems to have felt this was the case in his own parish in Buckinghamshire.[92] The proverbial churchwarden who returned *omnia bene* was another manifestation of the same attitude.[93] Balancing apathy, resentment of authority, and inertia were the deep convictions of those who waged the battles over ceremonies. Their partisan rhetoric and their physical efforts to insure that services were conducted properly in their parishes informed many of their more passive contemporaries about the points at issue and created an atmosphere in which the conduct of even the disengaged could assume political significance. The struggle that was occurring attracted attention disproportionate to the numbers of its participants, and its dimensions concerned people like Lincolnshire clergyman Dr Sanderson who himself believed ceremonies were indifferent yet should be used as a matter of obedience. He attacked those who made trouble over such matters in the sermon he preached at Paul's Cross in May 1632.[94] Although the concerns for Church and commonwealth that the ceremonial controversy aroused undoubtedly exaggerate its immediate threat, the dispute, as Sanderson and others realized, could become serious. It was only part of a larger disagreement about the religion of the Church of England.

Differences of opinion about the proper observation of the sabbath represented another area of religious conflict during the 1630s. In October 1633, shortly after Laud went to Canterbury, King Charles reissued his father's *Declaration to His Subjects Concerning lawful*

Sports to be used. With that unequivocal announcement of his views Charles addressed a topic that had drawn some communities into bitter quarrels and from time to time had been debated in sermons, tracts, and parliamentary speeches.[95] For people like Exeter citizen Ignatius Jordain the appearance of the king's book was distressing. Jordain who believed that sports were inappropriate on Sundays asked his bishop, Joseph Hall, who was then in London to request that Charles recall the declaration.[96]

Illustrating the depth of feelings about use of the sabbath and helping to arouse interest in the king's publication was the dispute about church ales which had occurred in Somerset only a few months before.[97] The controversy erupted when at the Lent assizes in 1633 Judge Richardson failed to follow royal instructions and revoke orders made in previous years against the feasting, dancing, music, and sports on Sunday evenings that parishes used to raise money. Church ales, opponents maintained, all too often led to disorder. They encouraged immorality and, even worse in the eyes of some, interfered with lectures. Other people had little patience with the strict sabbatarianism that hindered parish conviviality and the collection of funds for the upkeep of the church. Aware that Richardson had defied the king's order, they appealed to Laud who, though still bishop of London, they knew would be sympathetic. By the time of the summer assizes the affair had become a heated personal and political contest in addition to an ideological quarrel.[98] Both Richardson and Sir Robert Phelips who made himself the crown's spokesman overstated the case, and people beyond the borders of Somerset learned about the conflict.[99]

Phelips reiterated his defence of the king's stance in his enthusiastic endorsement of the 'book of sports', as the declaration was popularly called.[100] He denied that it constrained worship. The king, he wrote, 'hath no thought ... to have the certeyn and religious dutyes' of the sabbath 'to be omytted or contemned'. The aim of the declaration was instead to 'prevent yt judaycall strictness' which some put upon the law. He glossed over the concerns of some JPs about the permission of activities that could get out of hand and about legal ambiguities. He denounced instead 'distempored sheryffs [who] seeme to disslyke and mutter agaynst' the declaration and were in effect disturbing 'the publicke peace and quiett' by their failure to obey the 'mandates' of their 'superyers'.[101]

Phelips was not alone in commenting about the king's book.

Rather than ending controversy, it became itself the focus of debate.[102] Local officials argued about what activities were permissible. Some doubted that the king's declaration could be legal in view of two statutes enacted since his accession. The first of these, 1 Car. I, c. 1, forbade people from going out of their parishes for recreation on Sundays and prohibited even within parishes any bearbaiting, bullbaiting, interludes or common plays 'or other unlawful exercises or pastimes'. The second, 3 Car. I, c. 2, declared illegal various forms of carting and droving on the sabbath and also butchers' killing or selling victuals on that day. These statutes, which were less restrictive than some MPs would have liked, had themselves left room for conflicting interpretations about what was lawful. The declaration compounded the grounds for disagreement and aroused considerable anxiety by its allowance of maypoles, a perennial source of trouble in many parishes. The paganism associated with Maytime revelries made them a particularly dangerous violation of the sabbath to Puritans like Whiteway.[103] When a maypole in Glastonbury fell upon those who were erecting it, he believed that divine judgement had intervened.[104]

The central role of the king's declaration in the dispute about sabbatarianism gave that controversy a form different from that of the conflict about ceremonies. Those whose consciences led them to oppose his book had either to leave the problem in the hands of God or to risk challenging the crown even though they took their stance on a religious basis. Few JPs, regardless of their own views, went so far as Mr Cole who announced at the sessions in Bury St Edmunds that he would indict anyone who used the authorized sports.[105] Some justices prosecuted violators of the sabbath on other grounds. Even that failed to prevent a bitter controversy between Northamptonshire justices John Crew and Dr Robert Sibthorpe who took different sides on the issue. While Sibthorpe was away, Crew cited two glovers who were also musicians as vagrants and ordered them to leave Brackley. Convinced that Crew and the 'zelot', a puritan minister who had probably instigated the action, feared that the glover-musicians would encourage parishioners to take the 'libertyes' allowed by the king's book, Sibthorpe used his own magisterial authority to stay the order for departure. That annoyed Crew and added questions of honour and pride to their existing differences.[106] Similar issues seem to have been involved in a dispute at Maidstone where some young men who had got into trouble for their sabbath-breaking with puritan borough officials appealed to the JPs of the county in hopes of relief. The justices referred the case to the Privy Council who summoned the mayor and magistrates of the town. Peace was made after the latter explained that the true cause of the men's commitment had not been their Sunday recreations and submitted to the council's authority.[107]

Lay persons who practised sabbatarianism in their own lives outnumber by far the justices who in their official capacity challenged Charles's book. Families, such as the Harleys or the Temples of Stow not only abstained from the authorized recreations but also refrained from most other nondevotional activity on Sundays.[108] Woodforde, who specially marked the sabbaths in his diary, ordinarily attended services both morning and afternoon. If he did anything else besides pray, he failed to keep a record.[109] However much the sabbath-breaking of others may have troubled these people, the declaration did not require them to alter their own activities.[110]

The requirement that clergy read Charles's orders to their parishioners forced them, unlike the laity, to confront the issue of Sunday sports directly and publicly. They could either comply or risk showing disobedience and lack of respect for a statement that came from the king himself. Some nevertheless attempted in this case, as they did with other innovations, to find a way to salve their consciences and at the same time appease the authorities. Thus, although reading, they tried to indicate that they were not endorsing the views in their text. Sir John Lambe alleged that Thomas Valentine, of Chalfont St Giles, Bucks., whose conduct had been under scrutiny by the ecclesiastical authorities for some time had read the book only to show people 'how ill yt was'.[111]

The ministers who, according to one report, in their 'Cartwrightian uncanonical prayers' prior to sermons 'do pasquil and libel' it may have been following the letter of their instructions, but they were certainly not abiding by the spirit of those directives.[112] Several clergy openly refused to read the book. Mr Spenser of Scaldwell, Northamptonshire, stated firmly that he would not read it for a great sum of money.[113] John White, rector of Holy Trinity, Dorchester, and a member of the Massachusetts Bay Company, took a similar stance. He resisted the pleas of the bishop and chancellor of the diocese that he read the book before the archbishop's visitation. When he discovered that the churchwardens, probably with a hope of protecting him from the visitors, had gotten Mr Holliday to read it on a Friday morning when nobody was at church, White became very angry.[114]

Letters and diaries enumerating conscientious clergy who were disciplined for failing to read the book corroborate the testimony in ecclesiastical sources about the importance that the king, Church, and people attributed to declaration and its enforcement.[115] Charles, by asking Francis White, bishop of Ely and an experienced theological controversialist, to write a tract against sabbatarianism, encouraged a battle of books that complemented disputes in the parishes. Although written as an attack upon the views of Theophilus Brabourne, with whom White had previously argued on the issue, the bishop's work, *A Treatise of the Sabbath-Day*, as contemporaries recognized, was meant to prove that strict observance of the sabbath had no basis in Christian theology.[116]

White's 'bytter' book that Robert Ryece thought 'dyd overthrowe the tenents [*sic*] of the church of England' prompted answers.[117] Ryece mentioned specifically and then summarized for John Winthrop 'a very lytle treatise of 16 leaves in 4to entyteled a briefe answere to a late treatise of the Sabbath daye, digested dialogue wyse betweene 2 divines A and B, withowte the name of any awthor'.[118] Published without authority, the Answer responded both to White and to Peter Heylyn whose discussion of historical questions about the sabbath had been published soon after White's.[119] The bishop replied and many others joined in the debate.[120]

Because both the sabbatarians and their opponents regarded the point at issue as not merely what people should do on Sundays but as how religion should be practised and who should determine that, their emotions flared in arguments relating to the king's declaration. Most of those who were unhappy about its provisions and about the prosecutions of ministers who refused to read it, did not persist in public demonstrations of their convictions. Beneath their outward submission they had reservations about royal ecclesiastical policy that prevented them from giving the book their whole-hearted support. It appeared to be yet another indication that England was moving through innovations and Arminianism towards Rome.

The conflicts about the sabbath and those about ceremonies both touched upon preaching which was itself a third major topic of debate during the 1630s.[121] Since the Reformation spiritual and temporal leaders had been working towards establishing a preaching ministry resident in the parishes throughout England. To assist in achieving this goal people individually and in groups, and in some towns the corporations, had instituted lectures.[122] By 1629 Arminianism, Laudianism, and other innovations in religion seemed to be jeopardizing the considerable progress that had been achieved over the preceding three-quarters of a century. The articles for improving church government that the crown authorized in December of that year directed that catechizing replace afternoon sermons in parishes 'when and wheresoever there is no great cause apparent to break this ancient and profitable order'. In addition they stipulated that each lecturer 'read divine service according to the liturgy printed by authority, in his surplice and hood before the lecture'; that lectures in market towns were to be 'read' by 'grave and orthodox divines' who preached in gowns, not cloaks, and were beneficed nearby within the same diocese; that no one be permitted to lecture in a town who was not willing to accept a living in that town.[123] By seeking to insure that participating ministers would be conformable to the innovations authorized by the king and bishops the articles imposed real restrictions on lectures.

News of these articles caused 'greate talke'.[124] People in the parishes in the archdeaconry of Norfolk received a printed, half-sheet version of them at the sessions at Swaffham. Rous who entered them in his diary commented that they had been printed 'we knowe not where, seeme to come from the King, in what sorte we knowe not; only this is knowne, that they want the ordinary ratification', that is they did not state that they had been issued 'by the King'.[125] Yonge who like Rous worried about restrictions upon preaching did not raise legalistic questions about the articles. He understood that they had come from Archbishop Abbot on the king's 'direction'.[126]

The response to the instructions testifies to the importance that sermons had in contemporary life. People whose preferences in preachers and styles of preaching differed recognized that a minister's words wielded considerable influence.[127] Personal ties often intensified interest in measures concerning ministers. The role and position of the clergy virtually guaranteed that those who were questioned for their beliefs or conduct had support from patrons, parishioners, friends, or colleagues. They were also likely to have enemies in the local community. Disagreements about the content and practice of religion and about disciplinary procedures during the 1630s aggravated and were aggravated by conflicts arising on personal or political grounds, and under the vigorous administration of the Laudians passions flared to extremes that were rare in the Jacobean period. When Bishop Wren made new orders about the reading of prayers in August 1637, riots broke out in Ipswich.[128]

Letters and diaries of Puritans tell tales of the trials and tribulations of conscientious ministers that illustrate and supplement evidence about policies restricting sermons and lectures. The sagas convey an impression of episcopal harassment.[129] Robert Ryece implies that the orders Bishop Corbet got from Laud regarding Dedham lecturer John Rogers may have distressed that man to the point of death.[130] When Muriel Gurdon saw Wren's visitation articles in 1636, she anticipated that several ministers who thought themselves 'very conformable' would be 'put by'.[131]

The clergy themselves at times encouraged the notion that they were being persecuted. Francis Cheynell complained to his friend and patron Sir Gervase Clifton that 'being often called to Oxford and too often to Sir John Lambe's agents', he was 'seldom at home'.[132] John Davenport's letters to Lady Vere similarly include detailed accounts of his sufferings at the hands of ecclesiastical authorities.[133] By relating such information ministers were at once confiding in people from whom they might obtain both spiritual and material support and also fulfilling their responsibilities as instructors of the laity.

Their efforts were not in vain. People came to their rescue with offers of sanctuary, pensions, and other forms of assistance.[134] With help from both clergy and lay persons Thomas Shepard was able to remain in England for more than four years after Laud silenced him at Earls Colne.[135] When Dr Stoughton and Mr Workman went before the Court of High Commission, Sir Robert Harley accompanied them and earned the 'frowns' of the archbishop for his efforts.[136] City officials in Gloucester who granted Workman an annuity after he had been questioned by the bishop for 'dangerous doctrine and refractory carriage to the canons and established government of the Church' were called before the Privy Council.[137]

Supporting clergy who had fallen foul of the authorities had risks, and most individuals and corporations who defended ministers did so cautiously. The mayor and jurats of Rye sprang to deny the truth of some of the allegations against their curate, Mr Blackwood. Concerning a churchwarden's charge they explained that although he often read the litany and ten commandments, 'yet sometymes he doth omytt the reading thereof through weaknes of body as he saith and we truly believe'. It is 'altogether false' to charge him of preaching two hours, 'for the mostly he keepse himself to his howre and sometymes preacheth less than an howre'.[138] Rather than argue about how religion should be practised, they sought to show that Blackwood for the most part complied with the current standards.

In some instances people expressed their support for ministers in petitions. A group of Essex clergymen petitioned Laud on behalf of Chelmsford lecturer, Thomas Hooker, in 1629. They claimed that Hooker was 'for doctryne orthodoxe and life and conversation honest, and for his disposition peaceable, no wayes turbulent or factious'.[139] Their litany of virtues seems calculated to impress even though it lacked *conformable*, the one that mattered most to Laud and to the king.[140] Although in defending ministers on the basis of their lifestyles, they may have been evading contentious issues, they were nevertheless discussing qualifications that they deemed important.[141]

When efforts to protect clergy failed, most people did not persist. They believed that their ability to alter decisions of a bishop, archbishop or the High Commission was limited. Some followed favourite preachers to New England.[142] Others deserted their own parishes on Sundays so that they could hear men whose preaching was more to their taste, but many rejected the notion that an orthodox minister's words must be discounted.[143] Francis Cheynell's hopes for a living were disappointed when he found that 'my Lo. Say and Mr Ball of Northampton, an Apollo at least, thought mee not right for their toothe because I say it was an happy thinge for a man to bee constantly orthodox and not basely popular'.[144] The majority of the English would have agreed with him. Even Wooodforde seems to have listened to whatever preacher was available. His notes about the sermons he heard indicate that he did not avoid ministers whom he knew held views different from his.[145]

Most people placed more emphasis upon having sermons than upon having particular kinds of sermons. To insure access to preaching individuals at times compromised and at times challenged the ecclesiastical authorities. Sir Henry Slingsby who had been unsuccessful in efforts to have his chapel consecrated admitted that despite the 'inhibition [on preaching in unconsecrated places] we venture to have sermons in our Chaple now and yn altho' we incur some danger if it were complain'd off'. He did not deny the prelacy's claim that chapels would lead to conventicles, but he grumbled about the emphasis being placed upon consecration. 'It is not amiss to have a place concecrat'd for Devotion, as our Churches are, thereby to separate ym for yt use: but we cannot stay our self here, but must attribute a sanctity to ye very walls and stones of ye Church; and herein we do of late draw near to ye superstition of ye Church of rome'.146

People could not always circumvent policies in the way that Slingsby had. Because the Laudian efforts to insure that preachers were orthodox effectively reduced the numbers of sermons available, they brought complaints. The most vocal puritan proponents of preaching noticed the godly and learned ministers who were prevented from delivering their messages and the lectures that were suppressed rather than any steps bishops took to provide sermons. Protests greeted the orders of 1636 that some lectures and sermons be omitted in the time of plague. *The Forme of Common Prayer, together with an Order of Fasting: for the averting of Gods Heavie visitation* stipulated that the minister 'who is not a preacher' tell the congregation that homilies, though 'by a misunderstanding conceit ... not acceptable with many' were nevertheless epistles or declarations on the word of God and meant to teach.147 Where sermons rather than homilies were allowed, 'there [was to] bee but one ... at Morning Prayer, and the same not above an houre and not above one at Evening Prayer of the same length'. Individuals must not in any case go out of their parishes to hear sermons.148 To those who believed that sermons were an essential part of religion, the orders seemed designed to bring judgements upon England that were far worse than the extreme weather and plagues it was then suffering. Ryece wrote to John Winthrop, Jr, in September 1636 lamenting that 'In all these calamyties wee never went to God publickly by fasting and prayer, which was deemed as hateful as conventicles'.149 *Newes from Ipswich* likewise decried the suppression of lectures and the silencing of preachers as unprecedented and likely to 'draw downe more plagues and judgments on us'.150

Beneath the emotional outcry over the disciplining of popular preachers and the angry accusations that the prelates were depriving the people of sermons in times of crisis was also a debate about how the clergy should preach. The theological discord and disagreements about the necessity of disciplinary and ceremonial conformity that magnified differences in opinion about the part sermons should have in divine service were complicated by questions of form and style in preaching. The English held various views about what constituted a good sermon and debated the relative merits of reading from the Book of Homilies or from personally prepared texts, and speaking *ex tempore*.[151]

Henry Burton epitomized many of the worst kinds of preaching in the eyes of the Laudians. Speaking at the censure of Prynne, Burton, and Bastwick, the archbishop characterized Burton's sermons as 'fitter ... to stir up sedition' than to do good.[152] Burton's offences included dealing with affairs of state, attacking ceremonies, and going on for too long.[153] Lengthy extemporaneous praying was as bad as that kind of preaching.[154] Both sermons or prayers which were 'particularized', that is pointed toward individual sins or sinners, were likewise condemned.[155] Ministers found that orthodox doctrine was not enough to protect them from summons to the High Commission; they also had to deliver their message in an appropriate way.[156]

Puritans too cared about form. They believed that the best sermon was not one of the homilies from the authorized book but a work in which the minister embodied his own spiritual teachings. In his second sermon on *The Preacher's Charge and People's Duty: About Preaching and Hearing of the Word* at Lownd in Suffolk, John Brinsley asserted that while reading was preaching, preaching properly meant performing a ministerial function.[157] Like heralds who made announcements not in their own names but in the name of the king, preachers did not speak for themselves. They spoke for God. Samuel Ward of Ipswich addressed this issue more explicitly when answering the articles of the ecclesiastical commissioners. He denied charges that he believed it unlawful to read prayers or homilies, but he confessed that he conceived that there might be more life in a sermon delivered *viva voce* than in one read even if the latter were more elegantly penned.[158] The concern for spiritual vitality which Ward thought was also necessary in prayer may have been behind Lord Saye and Mr Ball's criticism that Cheynell preached 'in too high a straine'.[159] Either too much learning or set forms that, as Ward noted, even a parrot could be taught to repeat took away the essence of religion.[160]

Contributing to the arguments about preaching were personal jealousies, disputes about property, and concerns about unruly

crowds and divisions within communities.[161] Sir Robert Phelips
wrote to the bishop of Bath and Wells in 1631 to reiterate his
complaint against Spratt, a lecturer at Ilchester, who had been guilty
not only of indiscretion tending to 'schism and faction' but also of
'scantye carraydge' toward Phelips.[162] Parish clergy who resented
lecturers' drawing a larger audience than they likewise furnished
evidence that assisted ecclesiastical officials in disciplining such
preachers.[163] Even when the incumbent of the parish was a party to
agreements for the institution of a lecture, quarrels could occur.[164]
Rivalry was one of the issues in the dispute in Ashford, Kent, in 1629
and seems to have been a factor too in the troubles at St Botolph's
without Aldgate in the same year.[165] After being questioned about
who paid him, Thomas Edwards, the lecturer at St Botolph's, was
allowed to continue on condition that he preached a sermon of
obedience to superiors in the Church and sent a copy of it to the
bishop.

The habit of obedience, fear of disorder and desire, if possible, to
avoid confrontation encouraged people to seek ways of moderating
the sharpest edges of the constraints upon preaching that they
attributed to Popery, Arminianism and the Laudians. While some
individuals who spoke for compromise may, like Samuel Collins,
have been more interested in self-promotion, others had no wish to
put themselves in a situation where there was contention.[166] The
'silent majority' of Caroline England were those who preferred
conscientious ministers of good character to those with any
particular view of religion.[167] Such men, especially if they had the
active support of a patron, could escape difficulties with Laudian
authorities.[168] The administrative zeal of some prelates nevertheless
disrupted the *modus vivendi* established in many parishes and in so
doing brought questions of church government into the centre of
debate.

For long the most visible and readily available targets for people
discontented with religion or worried about wealth and materialism
in the Church, the bishops during the 1630s came under attack for
their policies, procedures and claims of authority. The House of
Commons in their remonstrance of June 1628 concerning religion
named two prelates, Laud and Neile, whom they believed were
instrumental in paving the way for Arminianism and Popery.[169] The
Commons cited that allegation in February 1628/9 and noted the

power that the pair who were also Privy Councillors exercised in advising the king and promoting clergy of similar views.[170] The appointment of Richard Montagu as bishop of Chichester was a particular grievance at the time.[171] In the years that followed as more and more clergy of the stamp of Laud and Neile came to fill the ranks of the episcopate, concerns about the policies and power of the prelates grew.

The movements of bishops were recorded just as were those of other dignitaries. The prelates sat in the House of Lords when a Parliament met, some of them were Privy Councillors, and some members of the High Commission. As diocesans they exercised authority that people encountered in making presentations to benefices and in participating in religious activities in their own parishes. The Laudian emphasis upon conformity and discipline provided a stern setting for contacts between bishops and lower clergy or laity during the 1630s.

Regular visitations brought the prelates or their representatives to the parishes and, like the coming of secular officials, required that inhabitants provide entertainment. The ecclesiastical inspection also forced parishes to respond to the questions about local conditions and practices which the bishops published in the articles that heralded their appearance.[172] Those prelates who were committed to the ideals of order cherished by Laud and the king approached visitations with an ardour that disrupted routines in which churchwardens had automatically answered *omnia bene* to articles that remained the same year after year. People began to pay heed to the content of the articles and worry about what would happen when the visitors actually appeared. The length and contents of those Wren issued in 1636 just after his translation to Norwich attracted considerable attention and stirred fears that they would lead to wholesale suspensions.[173] When some gentlemen in Northamptonshire saw the 'unusuall' articles that came out for their bishop's visitation in the summer of 1639, they prepared an appeal to him for moderation.[174]

Although churchwardens who were themselves united and determined to resist the visitors' pressure to tell all could prevent the assembling of evidence to substantiate official suspicions about local practices, personal quarrels as well as differences of opinion about religion eased the task of those who were seeking data. Woodforde was realistic in his anxiety about how the churchwardens would respond in August 1637. 'Oh Lord', he wrote, 'it is an evill time and the prudent hold their peace'.[175] The apparent prudence of those in a number of puritan villages in Ely in 1639 was exceptional.[176]

Although individuals seeking a bishop's support in connection with presentation to a benefice were not being judged in quite the same way that ministers and people in a parish were during visitation, the situation nevertheless allowed the prelate power over a person's livelihood. Influence could sometimes affect episcopal decisions, but contemporaries could not be confident that the assistance of powerful friends would alter the outcome of their suits.[177] Francis Cheynell's disbelief when he got the approval of the High Commission for a vicarage reveals his expectations that he would be unsuccessful. He reported to Clifton:

> I have obtained so much favour from his Grace that hee did in open Court declare himselfe for my Admission whereupon they are all concurred, and Sir Nathaniel Brent was commanded by the court to give mee his testimoniall and to signify that approbation of the Court to the Bishop of Peterburgh and his Lordship hath admitted mee. It is admired by some who know mee well that the High Commissioners should be my patrones, nor did I beleeve it till I received the kings advocates testimony from a friend of mine wch was sent me to give more ample satisfaction to his lop of Peterborough.[178]

Though relieved at the outcome, Cheynell seems to have had no notion about the grounds for it and thus no way of determining whether he would continue to enjoy such favour. He would remain at the mercy of his superiors.

The practices of the Church courts and the High Commission in enforcing conformity also left those summoned to answer for their conduct uncertain about how their cases would be determined. Their procedures, especially their use of the oath *ex officio* by which defendants swore to answer the charges against them without knowing what those charges were, had long been a source of complaint.[179] Because the High Commission like the Star Chamber and Privy Council was an instrument of the prerogative, it served Laud, even more than the ecclesiastical courts, as an engine to force obedience to episcopal authority and in so doing acquired a fearsome reputation. This image was not softened by the commission's preference for extracting offenders' compliance instead of punishing them. The fines and imprisonment it imposed when it did penalize the guilty also prompted protests.[180] John Hayward who thought both the archbishop and his man, Mr Baker, were 'very strongly' against him wrote to Sir Richard Buller of much trouble in that court 'by my Lo. of Canterbury'. 'Other business', he added, 'there is a course of law and courts of Justice for: but as for that Court, – I dare write nothing of it, least my letter should miscarie'.[181] Some clergymen fled rather than appear before the court.[182] Others took the course adopted in 1631 by three ministers of Braintree who when threatened with proceedings there decided to submit.[183] Those who were able negotiators might be able to convince the court of their good intentions and be released only to face another summons when their deceit was discovered.[184] Sensational cases, though a minority of those heard by the High Commission, gave the court and its ecclesiastical personnel who enforced controversial policies and practices, notoriety.

From what they heard about the proceedings of the High Commission, from stories about the difficulties of patrons in bestowal of livings, from tales of ministers seeking appointments, from reports of confrontations between episcopal visitors and parishes, and from their own experiences, men developed pictures of the Caroline prelates that despite their distortions were compelling. The power of the bishops could not be ignored, and people followed death or translation of one prelate and the selection of his successor in the knowledge that the change could have a significant effect upon worship in the parishes under his jurisdiction. Although most interested in their own areas, individuals also watched appointments over the country to get a sense of the direction of religious policy. In June 1631 Sir Thomas Barrington reported to his mother the deaths of three prelates. Although none was his bishop, Barrington cared about who would replace them. 'Owr prayers to God are and ought to be', he wrote, 'that the next scene may be better performed'.[185] Priscilla Paynter who in Exeter under Bishop Hall still in April 1637 'injoy[ed] the ordinance of god, the true means of grace in a most powerful and plentyfull maner' knew that 'in some parts of our land' people were not so fortunate as she.[186]

William Laud whose views the Commons had denounced in June 1628 came to be the chief villain for those concerned about the growth of Popery and Arminianism. Support from the king who had called upon him to preach at the coronation and on other state occasions had enabled him to exercise power beyond that represented by his growing collection of important offices.[187] In the diocese of London where he was bishop from 1628 until 1633 when he succeeded Abbot as archbishop of Canterbury his active administration showed clergy and laity alike that he would discipline those who failed to conform.[188] Humourless himself, his lack of endearing personal characteristics gave opponents little opportunity for appreciating his sincerity or seeking to understand his opinions and goals.

Laud may easily have been the most frequent target of libels during the 1630s. Referred to by the earl of Clare in 1629 as 'ye criminous head of ye clargy', he attracted more attention with his efforts to secure election as chancellor of Oxford in 1630.[189] Whiteway claimed the bishop had achieved this by 'some secret practices'.[190] The speed with which Laud replaced Abbot at Canterbury in 1633 also caused comment. As Lord Montagu heard the news, 'old George of Canterbury stepped aside and laid down to sleep, and upstarted the Bishop of good London and put on his cloathes before we were sure he [Abbot] was fast asleep and key cold. I hope', the correspondent added, 'the propinquity of water at Lambeth will cool immoderate heat'.[191] Not long after that tales circulated about a man who, having gone to Reading to see the house where Laud was born, noticed the stocks, pillory and whipping post in front of the house. The following week the mayor of Reading received an order to put them somewhere else.[192] Whiteway who entered that incident in his diary noted in a postscript that the next term a gentleman was fined £2000 for saying that the archbishop was an Arminian.[193] Such stories illustrate the image of dogmatism and intolerance that Laud furnished for his contemporaries. Apparently preferring outward observance to inward beliefs and Popery to Protestantism, he became at once epitome and caricature of episcopacy.

Attacked by the Commons in 1628 along with Laud was Richard Neile, successively bishop of Rochester, Lichfield, Lincoln, Durham, Winchester, and from 1632 until his death in 1640, archbishop of York.[194] Neile's notoriety dated from long before. In 1614 he had caused a stir in Parliament by accusing the Lower House of trouble-making and attacking the king's prerogative. Among his protégés he counted not only Laud but others including Richard Montagu and John Cosin whose views became the centre of controversy. When

Neile became archbishop of York, he and Cosin worked together in facilitating the spread of Arminianism in the northern province. Henry Jacie who enumerated the changes they instituted for the benefit of Winthrop in New England suggests they were also responsible for the notable increase of Popery in Yorkshire, Durham, and Northumberland.[195] If Neile had not died in October 1640, he surely would have been impeached during the Long Parliament.

Other bishops and some of those who served as their deputies also gave contemporaries reason to be fearful of episcopal leadership in the Church. The list of those impeached in the Long Parliament is long and Prynne's enumeration of Laud's instruments even longer.[196] Richard Montagu whose Arminian tracts and notions of episcopal authority had played an important role in raising these issues in Parliament during the 1620s seemed to be especially dangerous to many observers during the 1630s.[197] Matthew Wren, whose efforts to rid the diocese of Norwich of nonconformity in 1636 had inspired the blistering attack on the prelates in *Newes from Ipswich*, was also notorious.[198] Perhaps the best known of the episcopal agents was Sir John Lambe who was not only a close associate of Laud and from 1633 Dean of the Arches but also the commissary general in the diocese of Lincoln and as such a very significant figure during Bishop Williams's difficulties.[199] The very fact that he was not himself a bishop may have made contemporaries dislike him more when he confronted them in his efforts to enforce Laudianism.

Newes from Ipswich which appeared in January 1636/7 portrays the bishops and their aides as corrupt criminals who threatened Protestantism and law in England.[200] Professing to reveal the truth, the tract summoned evidence from recent developments and particularly from Wren's visitation of the Norwich diocese the preceding summer to demonstrate to its popular audience the outrages to which they had been victim. Word of its contents circulated widely and rapidly although relatively few people probably had an opportunity to see or read it for themselves.[201] Adding to interest in it were reports that its author was Henry Burton, the preacher of St Matthew's, Friday Street, who was already in trouble with the authorities for his anti-Arminian and anti-prelatical writings and sermons.[202] Efforts to suppress it and to prosecute those associated with it gave it even more fame.

Other lesser known tracts present a similar picture of the bishops and their subordinates. In March 1636/7 soon after the publication of *Newes from Ipswich* Ryece described for Winthrop a work, 'Certayne Questions propownded to Archbishops, bishops, Archdeacons and commysaryes, Chawncellers Officials and other audacious usurpers upon his Maties Royall prerogatyve lawes and his loyall subjects lawfull liberties, woorthie thare awnswere and all mens knowledge', whose title says much about its content.[203] Clifton's correspondent who had promised him a copy of 'those sharpe invectives against ye Bishopps' early in 1636 ended up sending 'onely ye venom of it' which he had obtained from a friend who was one of the bishop of London's chaplains. This venom was a list of about 40 terms or phrases applied to the bishops. These *Episcoporum Epitheta*, as they were called, ranged from 'vermin', 'Tigers', and 'Vipers' to 'Bloodsuckers', 'Romish Prelates and wicked Bishops', 'cruel stepfathers of the church', 'enormous and egregious malefactors', 'Tyrants', and 'not God's Bishops but ordained by ye Divell'.[204]

The cases of some of the boldest critics of Popery, Arminianism and Laudianism, like these tracts, reflected and at the same time gave currency to an image of episcopacy that raised questions that less radical individuals found troubling. Alexander Leighton whose book, *An Appeal to Parliament, or Sion's Plea Against the prelacie*, had arrived too late for use in Parliament, became the focus of attention after his arrest, prosecution in the Star Chamber, escape from prison and capture.[205] Arguing as Leighton did 'against the Bishops', Rous noted with some cynicism, was a 'mistake' if one wanted to avoid trouble, yet his theme was one that kept recurring.[206]

Unlike Leighton Henry Sherfield did not directly attack the bishops. He and others of the puritan faction in Salisbury were on friendly terms with their bishop, Davenant, who had himself been in trouble for preaching predestination and was engaged in a struggle with members of the cathedral chapter. Sherfield shocked his contemporaries by his violent destruction of the painted window at St Edmund's church in the city. For this anti-idolatry and rash intervention in complex local conflicts he attained some fame.[207] Prosecuted in the Star Chamber where Laud, still bishop of London, denounced him for attacking the authority of the Church and king, Sherfield was fined £1000.[208] The heavy sentence – Secretary Coke had proposed only an admonishment to conform – demonstrated emphatically who would exercise control in the Church.[209]

Yonge saw the same issue in the Exchequer decree of February 1632/3 against the Feoffees for Impropriations, the dozen Puritans who had been purchasing benefices in order to support 'learned and godly ministers'. Technically charged with not being chartered as a corporation and thus acting beyond their power in making ordinances, the Feoffees by taking control of the revenue from livings could control incumbents. They were in fact threatening the power of the 'ecclesiasticall state'.[210] At Laud's instigation the king asked Noy to proceed against them.[211]

The proceedings that did most during the 1630s to publicize questions concerning the authority of bishops were those in the Star Chamber in June 1637 against Prynne, Burton, and Bastwick, three well-known polemicists in the cause of religion who were veterans of confrontations with the authorities. Instead of desisting or retreating when penalized, they became even more strident and more penetrating in their criticism of the prelates' conduct and policies. They were particularly concerned by episcopal claims to hold power *jure divino*. This was, they argued, a direct attack on the royal prerogative.[212]

Their trial and sentencing provided a dramatic spectacle that publicized a politico-religious conflict greater than any since the dissolution of Parliament in March 1628/9. Anticipation grew as reports circulated that the three defendents had defied custom and prepared a defence which was five closely-written skins of parchment in length and instead of responding to the charges was 'a justification full of citations of scripture and writers' that their counsel refused to sign.[213] The battle of the books then raging over the position of the communion table and the preparations for proceedings against Bishop Williams added to interest in the trial.[214] Laud himself characteristically contributed to the clash with a tirade against the trio that was subsequently printed by royal command.[215] Denouncing them as reviling schismatics, he defended ceremonial practices and episcopal authority which he asserted was indeed *jure divino*.[216]

Emotions ran high among the multitudes who attended. As John Finet told Lord Scudamore, they were moved by the court's sentence 'to compassion, spite, and almost to comotion after their several unsettled dispositions and affections'.[217] People unable to attend were eager for reports of what happened.[218] Copies of Laud's speech, when it came out, were snatched up so quickly that newswriter

Rossingham found none available.[219] The fate of the three continued
to be news during the weeks that followed as the sentence was
executed and crowds turned out to watch the prisoners being taken
to places of custody far from London.[220]

Prynne, Burton, and Bastwick gained much attention but
contrary to the prediction of Finet who had described them before
the trial as 'desperate madd factious fellowes' who 'covett[ed] a
kinde of puritanicall martirdom', they did not achieve that kind of
personal stature.[221] Their blatant exaggerations and fear-mongering
fed appetites hungry for sensation, and the official reaction provided
drama and entertainment. Most of the English thought of them as
fanatics or extremists.[222] Rather than making martyrs of Prynne,
Burton, and Bastwick the case raised in more compelling form than
previously telling questions about the direction of the Church of
England. It showed Archbishop Laud in his most defensive and
authoritarian stance. Like the men he condemned, he exhibited an
excess of devotion to a cause that few of his countrymen could
accept. His lack of moderation troubled people more because he used
it to protect his own power.[223] The impact of this trial and that of
Bishop Williams, which followed it by a few weeks, may have been
evident in the libels that Laud noted as appearing against him in
August.[224] If the majority refrained from libellous or other direct
acts in defiance of ecclesiastical officials, they had seen reason for
their fears about the advance of Popery, Arminianism, and other
innovations in religion.

The experiences of the summer of 1637 made it hard for the
English to ignore either the divisions among them with regard to
religion or the determination of their king and archbishop to
suppress opposition. Disagreements and tension disrupted the
conduct of business within communities, among the clergy, between
clergy and laity, and among the laity. Law, petitions, and
negotiations could do little to resolve conflicts when episcopal
officials insisted on conformity. Many people thought the situation
called for prayer. The country must be cleansed of the sins that had
brought it to such a state, but the leaders of the Church seemed to
be promoting idolatry, ignorance, and superstition instead of
godliness. When King Charles with the support of the bishops set
out to bring the Scots to obedience, the religious dilemma reached a
critical point.

The cries of protest against innovations in religion which MPs raised in 1628/9 set the stage for the politics of religion during the 1630s. The Laudians' persistence in pursuing their goals, their association with Arminians, and their suspicion of those who seemed reluctant to co-operate with their programme moved a few individuals to risk punishment and challenge them openly. Law and tradition offered one basis of attack as well as a means of defence for people called to answer for resisting ecclesiastical authority. They cited scripture, Magna Carta, the Petition of Right, Reformation statutes, as well as canons, royal declarations, and statements by prominent legal and ecclesiastical figures. Although these arguments won few concessions, they continued to have an appeal.

The weight of customary procedures, social status, personal and local bonds, bureaucratic inertia, and political realism tempered many clashes. Church officials, though determined to punish the contemptuous and convinced that they themselves were ultimately answerable only to a higher law, followed established courses in many respects.[225] Laud himself was not blind to the laws governing the Church and recognized that arguments could not change the minds of some individuals.[226] Neither he nor Bishop Wren could uncover nonconformity when churchwardens failed to present it.[227] People were reluctant to censure or inform against their social superiors and especially unlikely to act against 'great men'.[228] Slingsby was able to have sermons in his unconsecrated chapel because no one reported him.[229] Sibthorpe who had boldly preached on behalf of contributions to the Forced Loan in 1627 and had worked vigorously for Church and king in his county found that the puritan lords and gentlemen of Northamptonshire posed obstacles to the imposition of Laudian conformity. He did not want to spend money on suits and knew what kinds of charges and evidence would be necessary for proceedings in the Ecclesiastical Commission.[230]

Whether or not they felt the bishops' claims were warranted, people saw that the prelates were in power, that episcopal authority had royal support, and that the situation was unlikely to change at the moment.[231] Thomas Scott of Canterbury was by 1632 distressed by the Laudians' opposition to lectures and by their insistence on kneeling at communion, but he was not prepared 'to flie unto unlawfull meanes'.[232] Sir Thomas Wroth, who also expressed deep concern about 'the sad condition of these times', believed that true Christians would have to suffer, perhaps die to preserve their faith.[233] They were not unique. Those called before the High Commission hesitated to defy its authority and incur the burdens consequent upon its punishment. Individuals bowed to orders even when charging that these were illegal. It was far easier and safer to invoke the law than to institute legal proceedings. Clergy and laity needed to work together to conduct routine business in parish, village, division, and county, and gentlemen with patronage in the Church wanted the bishop to approve their nominees. Rather than petitioning for answers to questions of jurisdiction or authority people could do as the Northamptonshire gentlemen did in 1639 and ask their prelate for immediate relief.[234]

The means by which the discontented could attempt to exercise political influence over religion without risk were severely limited when no Parliament was meeting, but people used those private and informal as well as public and formal tactics that were at their disposal. Religious differences entered into conflicts between clergy and laity over jurisdiction or assessment for shipmoney and military charges.[235] Ministers took advantage of opportunities available to them in sermons, in responses to inquiries, and in relations with patrons and parishioners to attempt to influence the direction of Church and community. Members of the laity, depending upon their position and inclinations, supported and encouraged the clergy, wrote letters, petitioned and engaged in legal proceedings. Some people from both groups who were most disturbed by religious developments sailed for Europe or New England and thus avoided the dilemma of how far to challenge authority and act upon their convictions.

Many individuals turned more fervently to God. In so doing they were in one sense giving up politics but in another they were reinforcing the convictions that brought them to oppose the leadership in the Church of England and preparing the way for what would become religious war.[236] As the practice of religion became more urgent, the burdens imposed by Laudianism became heavier, and the numbers of its opponents grew.[237] The Bishops' War against the Scots in 1639 gave people a new perspective upon their situation, and when the summoning of Parliament in 1640 provided an opportunity to express grievances, people complained about Popery, Arminianism, and innovations. They attacked the bishops and episcopacy and demanded far-reaching reforms to protect and preserve the Church.

NOTES

1 *Commons' Journals*, Vol. 1, p. 922; cf. *CD 1629*, pp. 21, 112.
2 The king spoke on 24 January (*CD 1629*, p. 11); Rous spoke on 26 January (pp. 12–14); see also pp. 14–21.
3 *CD 1629*, p. 16.
4 The remonstrance is printed in J. Rushworth, *Historical Collections* (London, 1659), Vol. 1, pp. 619 ff.
5 *CD 1629*, p. 20. See also Russell, *Politics*, pp. 29–32; and H. Schwartz, 'Arminianism', pp. 41–68.
6 See Chapter 1.
7 *CD 1629*, pp. 101–2.
8 S. Adams, 'The Protestant cause: religious alliance with the West European Calvinist communities as a political issue in England 1585–1630', PhD thesis, Oxford University, 1972.
9 Concerning the marriage negotiations, see R. Lockyer, *Buckingham* (London: Longman, 1981), ch. 5.
10 I am using Catholic to refer either to Papists, people loyal to Rome, or to recusants, those who refused to attend the Anglican Church. (Although contemporaries did not always admit this, recusants might be but were not necessarily Papists. Because my sources sometimes blur the distinction I have been unable to observe it rigorously.) See C. Hibbard, 'Early Stuart Catholicism: revisions and re-revisions', *Journal of Modern History*, vol. 52, no. 1 (1980), pp. 1–34; C. Hibbard, *Charles I and the Popish Plot* (Chapel Hill, NC: University of North Carolina Press, 1983); also see M. Havran, *The Catholics in Caroline England* (Stanford, Calif.: Stanford University Press, 1962). I am grateful to Caroline Hibbard for discussing a number of points about Catholicism with me. Conrad Russell has also provided assistance.
11 Concerning Charles and Henrietta Maria, see Lockyer, *Buckingham*, p. 243; also Q. Bone, *Henrietta Maria Queen of the Cavaliers* (Urbana, Ill.: 1972). Concerning the peace, see Chapter 1.
12 *WP*, Vol. 2, pp. 322–3. The articles were printed in due course (STC 9251).
13 *Histrio Mastix* (1633), STC 20464, was not merely an attack on the queen but a tract denouncing certain kinds of conduct as immoral. See the proceedings against him for the book in *ST*, Vol. 3, pp. 561–86; also Whiteway, ff. 91, 99; Yonge, f. 56v; S. Foster, *Notes from the Caroline Underground*, (Hamden, Conn.: Archon, 1978) p. 41; W. Lamont, *Marginal Prynne* (London: Routledge & Kegan Paul, 1963), pp. 28 ff. Prynne also found the queen's religion offensive.
14 M. Smuts, 'The puritan followers of Henrietta Maria in the 1630s', *EHR*, vol. 93, no. 366 (1978), pp. 26–45. Concerning Holland, see below. For comments about her religion, see Rous, pp. 49–50. See also Birch, Vol. 2, p. 225; SP 16/140/44; 16/142/28.
15 For reports of her apparent influence at court see, for example, El 7818, 7820, 7823. Also see Sharpe, 'Faction at the court', pp. 44–6 and Hibbard, *Popish Plot*.

16   Concerning Panzani's mission, see G. Albion, *Charles I and the Court of Rome* (London: Burns, Oates & Washbourne, 1935); also Joseph Berington (ed.), *The Memoirs of Gregorio Panzani* (Birmingham: Swinney & Walker, 1793; 1970 reprint). Also see Yonge, f. 64v. Concerning Papists at court, see Hibbard, *Popish Plot*, esp. pp. 40–2; also Prynne, *The Jesuits Looking-glasse* (1636) in *The Popish Royall Favourite* (1643), STC W P4039.

17   *Harley Letters*, p. 10. She took note of the fact that no one would claim it.

18   Lady Newport's conversion also caused a stir. See HMC, *Sixth Report*, app., p. 283; also Cl C 389; Birch, Vol. 2, p. 158; HEH, Hastings MSS, HA9597; SP 16/171/37. Libels alleged that the Catholics who were close to the king were perverting both religion and government (e.g. Hibbard, *Popish Plot*, p. 20).

19   His statement about his conversion appears in SP 16/302/50. See also HMC, *Thirteenth Report*, app., p. 125; Yonge, f, 64v; *CSPVen. 1632–6*, no. 585; *DeL'Isle*, p. 99; Knowler, Vol. 1, pp. 489, 505.

20   PRO, C. 115/N.4, no. 8612.

21   PRO, C. 115/N.4, no. 8613, 8615.

22   See, e.g. W. R. Trimble, 'The Embassy Chapel question, 1625–1660', *Journal of Modern History*, vol. 18, no. 2 (1946), pp. 97–107; also Yonge, ff. 36, 66v; Whiteway, f. 87.

23   Laud was one who worried about this (Laud, *Works*, Vol. 7, p. 496, a reference I owe to Caroline Hibbard). Marie de Medici had a reputation for intrigue. See, for example, *The Remonstrance made by the Queene-Mother of France to the King* (1619), tr. from the French, STC 17555; *Declaration de la Reyne Mer du Roy tres-Chretien Contenant les raisons de sa sortie des pais-bas* (1638), STC 17553.

24   Ipswich, which was hardly sympathetic to Popery, contributed to the queen mother's entertainment at the request of Sir Henry Vane. See W. H. Richardson (ed.), *The Annals of Ipswich*, by N. Bacon (Ipswich: S. H. Cowell, 1844), pp. 518–19; also HMC, *Sixth Report*, app., p. 284; D. Bergeron, *English Civic Pageantry, 1558–1642* (London: Edward Arnold, 1971), pp. 117–18; Woodforde, p. 497; *Harley Letters*, pp. 9–10; HMC, *Report on the MSS of the Gawdy Family*, pp. 169–70; Prynne, *Hidden Workes of Darknes* (1645), STC W P3973, pp. 189, 196. In her paper, '*La Belle-Mere*: Marie de Medici at the court of Charles I', Caroline Hibbard cites some of the contemporary comments about the queen mother's arrival. Very little of this comment was favourable. I am grateful to Professor Hibbard for sharing this paper with me. It was a Frenchman who memorialized the occasion of Marie de Medici's entry into London, Jean Puget de la Serre, *Histoire de l'Entrée de la Reyne Mere dans La Grande Bretaigne* (1639), STC 20488; cf. *The arrivall and intertainements of the embassador from the Emperor of Morocco* (1637), STC 18165.

25   e.g. WP, Vol. 3, pp. 386–8. See J. Bossy, *The English Catholic Community 1570–1850* (London: Darton, Longman & Todd, 1975). Some worried that religious differences weakened the kingdom and could lead to war. See, for example, D. Parsons (ed.), *The Diary of Sir Henry Slingsby of Scriven,*

bart (London, 1836), pp. 10–11. Barbara Donagan alerted me to concern about this issue.

26   e.g. SP 16/195/12; but some people criticized the commissions established to enforce statutes against recusancy, not on the grounds that these were inefficient, but because the commissioners themselves might profit from vigorously exercising their commissions (see T. S. Smith, 'The persecution of Staffordshire Roman Catholic recusants: 1625–1660', *Journal of Ecclesiastical History*, vol. 30, no. 3 (1979), pp. 330–1; Birch, Vol. 2, p. 195; also Knowler, Vol. 1, p. 51; Havran, *Catholics*, pp. 92–9).

27   See R. Clifton, 'The popular fear of Catholics during the English revolution', *Past and Present*, no. 52 (1971), pp. 23–55. See below concerning the anti-popish panic in Kettering, Northamptonshire, in 1639. Also see PC 2/46, p. 64.

28   Birch, Vol. 2, pp. 170–1; Phelips MS DDPH 221/24. See also protests against Catholics as sheriff (SP 16/225/77); against favouritism in subsidy collection (SP 16/185/43; 16/229/32). The Catholic contributions for the war against the Scots in 1639 also caused resentment. See Chapter 5.

29   Berington, *Panzani*, p. 248. Concerning Montagu, see Chapter 1. The depth of conviction behind the officially sanctioned rhetoric of Gunpowder Plot sermons is hard to judge, but even the most formal of the preachers' condemnations of Popery reminded those who heard them that adherence to Popery set some Englishmen apart. See, for example, J. Taylor, *A Sermon preached in Saint Maries Church in Oxford* (1638), STC 23724; T. Reeve, quoted in Chapter 1; T. B., *A Preservative* (1629), STC 1071; also El 6873; Birch, Vol. 2, pp. 213–14.

30   See R. Clifton, 'Fear of Popery', in C. Russell (ed.), *The Origins of the English Civil War* (London: Macmillan, 1973), pp. 144–67.

31   Rous, pp. 78–9.

32   HMC, *Fourteenth Report*, app., ii, p. 50; probably *The Religion of Protestants* (1638), STC 5138. For Chillingworth, see *DNB*.

33   N. Tyacke, 'Puritanism, Arminianism, and counter revolution', in Russell, *Origins*, p. 119. Conrad Russell stimulated my thinking about Arminianism.

34   See W. Lamont, *Godly Rule, Politics, and Religion, 1603–1660* (London: Macmillan, 1969).

35   I am grateful to Sears McGee for sharing with me prior to its publication his paper, 'William Laud and the outward face of religion' in R. L. DeMolen (ed.), *Leaders of the Reformation* (Selinsgrove, Pa: Susquehanna University Press, 1984), pp. 318–44. cf. K. Sharpe, 'Archbishop Laud', *History Today*, vol. 33 (1983), pp. 26–30 and Tyacke, 'Puritanism'. The Commons named Laud and Bishop Neile as Arminians in their remonstrance of June 1628 (Rushworth, Vol. 1, p. 621). See also below.

36   See Tyacke, 'Puritanism'.

37   Bishop Davenant of Salisbury complained, 'Why that should now be esteemed Puritan doctrine, which those held who have done our Church the greatest service in beating down Puritanism, or why men should be restrained from teaching that doctrine hereafter, which hitherto has been

generally and publicly maintained, (wiser men perhaps may) but I cannot understand' (quoted by Tyacke, 'Puritanism', p. 139). Concerning the definition of Puritanism see P. Collinson, 'A comment: concerning the name Puritan', *Journal of Ecclesiastical History*, vol. 31, no. 4 (1980), pp. 483–8; B. Hall, 'Puritanism: the problem of definition', *Studies in Church History*, vol. 2, (1965), pp. 283–96, esp. p. 294; C. H. George, 'Puritanism as history and historiography', *Past and Present*, no. 41 (1968), pp. 77–104; W. Lamont, 'Puritanism as history and historiography: some further thoughts', *Past and Present*, no. 44 (1969), pp. 133–46. Also see Thomas Pierson (*Harley Letters*, pp. xvi–xvii); Lord Herbert, who allegedly loved a 'puritan' but not a 'predestinator' (HMC, *Fourteenth Report*, app., ii, p. 30); J. Newton, 'The Yorkshire puritan movement, 1603–40', *Transactions of the Congregational Historical Society*, vol. 19 (1960), p. 4.

38   Although the term Laudian was not used during the 1630s, I shall employ it to refer to Laud's policies or followers.

39   e.g. Michthelwaite's (W. Prest, *The Inns of Court* (London: Longman, 1972), pp. 200–1).

40   I shall not discuss those Protestant sects who wanted to separate from the Church of England and despite their small numbers were a cause of considerable anxiety to contemporaries, e.g. Kent Archives Office, Dering MSS, U350/C2/54.

41   Even in cases where the table was moved during services, its position in either instance could be more easily discerned.

42   See Chapter 1.

43   In his introduction to a new printing of the Thirty-Nine Articles in December 1628 Charles had emphasized the role of the clergy in settling questions about religious policy (Gardiner, *Constitutional Documents*, pp. 75–6). The Commons debated the king's declaration as a grievance (*CD 1629*, pp. 116–22).

44   The bishop of Lincoln's response to the vicar's question became controversial. See below.

45   PC 2/43, pp. 304–5.

46   e.g. H. Burton, *For God and the King* (1636), STC 4142, p. 33. It was one of the cases cited at Laud's trial (SP 16/499/42).

47   Yonge, ff. 54v–56.

48   The letter is printed in P. Heylyn's *A Coale from the Altar* (1636), STC 13270, pp. 67–78. Williams had reiterated his position concerning tables in a letter of June 1633 about St Martin's, Leicester (SP 16/241/18).

49   Williams had challenged Laud's right to conduct a visitation of his diocese, but he did not have close bonds with puritan leaders. Concerning Williams see J. Hacket's apologia, *Scrinia Reserata* (London, 1693); B. D. Roberts, *Mitre and Musket* (Oxford: Oxford University Press, 1938); and below.

50   C. Holmes, *Seventeenth-century Lincolnshire* (Lincoln: History of Lincolnshire Committee, 1980), pp. 115–16.

51   See G. Vernon, *The Life of the Learned and Reverend Dr. Peter Heylyn* (London, 1682), pp. 41–2, 67 ff. Heylyn was a prebendary of Westminster and a leader in the prebends' petition against Williams in 1635. See *DNB*;

also Roberts, *Mitre*, p. 132. But Heylyn claims that when he discovered copies of Williams's letter circulating, he decided to refute it in order to end the disturbance it was causing to the church (*A Coale*, title and introduction). Vernon (p. 89) says the Dean of Peterborough brought the letter to Heylyn's attention. Also see SP 16/263/35.

52 Laud, *Works*, Vol. 7, p. 337; also see *DeL'Isle*, p. 96. See, for example, Dr John Burges, *The Lawfulness of Kneeling in the Act of Receiving the Lord's Supper* (London, 1631), STC 4114; T. Paybody, *A Just Apologie for the Gesture of Kneeling in the Act of Receiving the Lord's Supper* (London, 1629), STC 19488; also see A. Cade, *A Sermon Necessary for These Times* (1636), preached at Leicester, 11 October 1631, visitation, STC 4329a; and G. Cuming, 'The life and works of Anthony Cade, B.D., vicar of Billesdon, 1599–1639', *Transactions of the Leicestershire Archaeological and Historical Society*, vol. 45 (1969–70), pp. 47 ff.

53 Cl C 309; cf. *DeL'Isle*, pp. 95, 108; also BL, Loan MS 29/172, f. 139. There were also publications about bowing, e.g. 'Certayne Queres propownded to the Bowers to the names of Jesus and to the Patrons thereof, wherein the auct[orities] and reasons alledged by Bishop Andrewes and his followers in defense of this ceremony are breefely examined and refuted' (*WP*, Vol. 3, p. 357; BL, 873.e.9 (Huntington photocopy), attributed to Prynne).

54 pp. 67–78.

55 Introduction. Heylyn seems to have made a distinction between *bona fide* controversy and what he thought was unwise response to criticism. See below, Chapter 4. See also *WP*, Vol. 3, pp. 302–5.

56 His response was *The Holy Table* (STC 25726) which he licensed for publication himself but did not sign. The date of the book's licence is 30 November 1636. See *Holy Table*, p. 83; also Rous, p. 80; *DeL'Isle*, p. 95; PRO, C.115/N.4, no. 8612.

57 e.g. Lincoln prebendary Dr John Pocklington's *Altare Christianum*, a second edition of which he said had been enlarged to respond to *The Holy Table* (2nd ed 1637), STC 20076. Also see *DeL'Isle*, p. 102.

58 STC 13267 (1637); it was licensed 10 May 1637. See also, *DeL'Isle*, p. 109. For their trial see below.

59 For his trial, see *ST*, Vol. 3, pp. 770–804; his sentence, SP 16/364/42.

60 e.g. BL, Loan MS 29/172, f. 139; also K. Weber, *Lucius Cary. Second Viscount Falkland* (New York: Columbia University Press, 1940), pp. 70–1.

61 Cl C 314; cf. Windebanke's comment, HMC, *Sixth Report*, app., p. 282.

62 PRO, C.115/N.4, no. 8616; cf. C.115/N.8, no. 8806.

63 *The Fairfax Correspondence*, ed. G. W. Johnson (London: Richard Bentley, 1848), Vol. 1, pp. 337–9. The earl of Clare sympathetically followed Williams's difficulties (e.g. Holles, nos 197, 216, 234, 248, 250). Also see Holmes, *Lincolnshire*, p. 117.

64 BL, Loan MS 29/172, f. 139.

65 See Laud's account of his province for 1635 (Laud, *Works*, Vol. 5, pt. 2, p. 334). See also *DNB*, 'Wren'.

66   See SP 16/153/100; also P. King, 'Bishop Wren and the suppression of the
     Norwich lecturers', *Historical Journal*, vol. 11, no. 2 (1968), pp. 237–54.
67   Wren's articles (STC 10298); cf. Laud's articles (Laud, *Works*, Vol. 5, pt.
     2, pp. 419 ff.), metropolitan visitation of Winchester, 1635; (pp. 435 ff.),
     deanery of Shoreham. The Huntington's copy of Wren's articles (HN
     381080) has these key phrases underlined and little else so delineated.
     Conrad Russell notes the possible significance of Wren's use of the word
     table. Although the writers of tracts in the ceremonial controversy had
     chosen the terms *table* and *altar* to indicate conflicting views, official
     statements had talked in terms of placing tables *altarwise*. See, for example,
     canon 7 of 1640 (*Constitutions and Canons Ecclesiastical Agreed upon at
     London and York* (1640), STC 10080). Also see Laud, *Works*, Vol. 5, pp.
     405, 421.
68   Rous, p. 80. See also *WP*, Vol. 3, p. 261.
69   See below.
70   Woodforde, p. 496. The churchwardens successfully appealed to the Court
     of Delegates (HMC, *Fourth Report*, app., p. 47, a reference I owe to Conrad
     Russell).
71   SP 16/314/130. Jewell was one of the authors cited as an authority for the
     Church of England by the House of Commons in February 1628/9 (*CD
     1629*, p. 99). Wheeler's widow petitioned the House of Lords for redress for
     her husband's sufferings in February 1640/1 (HMC, *Fourth Report*, app., i,
     p. 49.
72   W. Hunt, 'The godly and the vulgar: Puritanism and social change in
     seventeenth-century Essex, England', PhD thesis, Harvard University, 1974,
     pp. 492–3); also see Yonge, f. 73v.
73   SP 16/375/84.
74   Somerset Record Office, Phelips MSS, DDPH/221/25v; also DDPH/221/
     26; *WP*, Vol. 3, pp. 400–1. Concerning Phelips, see T. G. Barnes, *Somerset,
     1625–1640* (Cambridge, Mass.: Harvard University Press, 1961).
75   Sibthorpe ascribed the refusal of 80 to 100 parishioners in Towcester,
     Northamptonshire, to go to the altar and kneel in order to receive
     communion to infection from a lecturer 'who had been supported by the
     Londoners' (presumably the Feoffees for Impropriations) but had left for
     New England (SP 16/393/75); see also, 16/393/15.
76   G. F. Nuttall, 'Peterborough ordinations 1612–1630 and early nonconfor-
     mity', *Journal of Ecclesiastical History*, vol. 30, no. 2 (1979), p. 240. R.
     Marchant, *The Puritans and the Church Courts in the Diocese of York*
     (London: Longman, 1960), pp. 194 ff.; Marchant, 'The restoration of
     Nottinghamshire churches, 1635–40', *Transactions of the Thoroton
     Society*, vol. 45 (1961), p. 79. Concerning parishioners who moved the table
     back from the east end, see W. C. Renshaw (ed.), 'Notes from the Act Books
     of the archdeacon's court of Lewes', *Sussex Archaeological Society
     Collections*, vol. 49 (1906), pp. 63–4.
77   See, for example, Ward's answer (*CSPDom. 1635–6*, pp. xxxix–xliv; R. C.
     Richardson, *Puritanism in North-West England* (Manchester: Manchester
     University Press, 1972), pp. 35–6, 82; Mr Castell reportedly objected to

'new tricks' and said he could live as well in New England (SP 16/366/17); Newton, 'Yorkshire Puritan', p. 4; Williams, *Holy Table*. For moderate statements, see J. Dyke, *A Worthy Communicant* (1636), STC 7429, which with its emphasis on the moral preparation of the individual could be regarded as an attempt to divert attention from quarrels about exterior things; A. Cade's *A Sermon Necessary for These Times*, preached at the visitation at Leicester (1636), STC 4329a; J. Mede, *The Name Altar* (1637), STC 17768.

78 *The Diary of John Young S.T.P. Dean of Winchester*, ed. F. R. Goodman (London: SPCK, 1928), pp. 105–10. The two had some discussion of other ceremonial practices. Young professed himself willing to comply with orders from his superior since 'it wes not fit for anie man under the ranke of a Bishop to innovat anie thing in the Church' (p. 109).

79 SP 16/326/18.

80 e.g. SP 16/322/32; *CSPDom. 1635*, p. xxxviii; *Diary of John Young*, p. 126. Common lawyer Edward Bagshaw referred a client in trouble for failing to bow to Whitgift (SP 16/267/90).

81 e.g. SP 16/350/54. Jennison did this in his works on plague (see below).

82 *WP*, Vol. 3, p. 59; see also SP 16/399/80; cf. Cl C 78.

83 e.g. *CSPDom. 1635*, p. xxxii; SP 16/286/86; 16/339/53; Laud, *Works*, Vol. 5, pt. 2, p. 360. Ministers may have been reluctant to antagonize the laity. See below.

84 e.g. SP 16/308/52; Richardson, *Puritanism*, p. 34; SP 16/388/35.

85 See, for example, SP 16/308/52; STT 1891. Many of the comments about the conduct of laymen come in connection with statements about clergy.

86 Woodforde, pp. 496–7. See also Cheynell's comments (quoted below) about the views of Lord Saye and Mr Ball concerning ministerial conformity.

87 *WP*, Vol. 3, p. 243.

88 SP 16/222/28, a reference I owe to Conrad Russell.

89 Bedfordshire Record Office, St John of Bletsoe MSS, no. 1331; also Hunt, *The Puritan Moment*, p. 261; SP 16/375/73; I. Green, 'Career prospects and clerical conformity in the early Stuart church', *Past and Present*, no. 90 (1981), p. 113 and note.

90 Concerning local disputes about beautification, see York, City Library, House Books, Vol. 36, ff. 186v, 218–19; E. R. C. Brinkworth, 'The Laudian Church in Buckinghamshire', *University of Birmingham Historical Journal*, vol. 5 (1955), pp. 45–6; Marchant, 'Nottinghamshire churches', pp. 65, 66, 72; STT, Manorial Box 3, several items concerning seats at Boycott; W. L. Sachse (ed.), *Minutes of the Norwich Court of Mayoralty, 1632–35*, Norfolk Record Society, vol. 36 (1936), p. 97. Rye protested against a churchwarden's charge that the corporation stored artillery in the chancel. This, they said, was done for the king's service and with episcopal authority (East Sussex Record Office, Rye Correspondence, 47/123, January 26, 1636/7; see also Fletcher, *County Community*, pp. 82–3.

91 See also, SP 16/378/73; El 7409, 7412, 7414, 7418; also R. Ashton, *The City and the Court, 1603–1643* (Cambridge: Cambridge University Press,

1979), pp. 197–8 (a reference I owe to Fred Lock); STT 2340. Marchant, 'Nottinghamshire churches'; SP 16/304/35; 16/371/14.

92   SP 16/269/36; also 16/286/86; H. Sydenham, *Sermons Upon Solemne Occasions* (1637), STC 23573.

93   e.g. R. Bernard, *Christian See to Thy Conscience* (1631), STC 1928; Marchant, *Puritans and Church Courts*, p. 199; Fletcher, *County Community*, pp. 83–4. Concerning visitations, see below.

94   W. Jacobson (ed.), *The Works of Robert Sanderson* (Oxford: Oxford University Press, 1854), Vol. 4, sermon vii.

95   STC 9257; see P. Collinson, 'The beginnings of English sabbatarianism', *Studies in Church History*, Vol. 1 (1964), pp. 207–21. For early debates, see, for example, W. Notestein, H. Relf, and H. Simpson, *Commons Debates, 1621* (New Haven, Conn.: Yale University Press, 1935), Vol. 2, pp. 82–4; the work of Nicholas and Richard Byfield printed in 1630 and 1631, N. Byfield, *Mr. Byfield's Answer with Mr. Brerewoods Reply* (1630), STC 3622; R. Byfield, *Doctrine of the Sabbath Vindicated* (1631), STC 4238; T. Brabourne, *Defence ... of the Sabbath* (1632), STC 3473. See also SP 16/211/87; P. Heylyn, *The History of the Sabbath* (2nd edn, rev., 1636), STC 13275, pp. 249 ff.; J. Bentham, *The Societie of the Saints* (n.d.), STC 1889, which probably appeared before this, takes pains to defend strict observation of the sabbath. See Cope, *Montagu*, p. 142 n.

96   Hall did this, but he also sharply reproved Jordain (Knowler, Vol. 1, pp. 165–7; Whiteway, f. 96v). Jordain's biographer claims that Jordain had enclosed a letter to the king in his letter to Hall (*The Life and Death of Mr. Ignatius Jurdain* (London, 1654), To the Reader).

97   T. G. Barnes, 'County politics and a Puritan *cause célèbre*: Somerset church ales, 1633', *TRHS*, Fifth Series, vol. 9 (1959), pp. 103–22.

98   Barnes, 'Church ales'; also SP 16/238/4; 16/255/39.

99   e.g. Whiteway, f. 94. See also *WP*, Vol. 3, p. 358.

100   Phelips expressed his opinion in a paper where he discussed statutes concerning 'religious dutyes', among which he included not only the two Caroline statutes cited below but also the Elizabethan Act of Uniformity (1 Eliz. 1, c.2) which imposed a penalty upon those who did not attend church, and the Jacobean statute 'agaynst profane cursing and swearing' (21 and 22 Jac. I, c.20); DDPH 221/15.

101   DDPH 221/15; cf. F. White, *A Treatise of the Sabbath-Day* (2nd edn, 1635), STC 25384, p. 254.

102   e.g. SP 16/279/14; 16/296/45.

103   See, for example, the order of the Devonshire justices in July 1631 (Devon Record Office, Quarter Sessions Order Book, 1625– pasche 1633, p. 356). Also see Woodforde, p. 496.

104   Whiteway, f. 102v. This is one of the cases Burton cites in his *Divine Tragedie* (1636), STC 20459, p. 15. Also see Yonge, f. 59v; P. Seaver, *Wallington's World* (Stanford, Calif.: Stanford University Press, 1985), pp. 56–7.

105   Birch, Vol. 2, pp. 277–81. Cole claimed also that he would indict any minister who refused to give communion to people who would not kneel.

106 STT 1880. John Crew, 1598–1679 (*DNB*). Concerning his sabbatarianism, see J. T. Cliffe, *The Puritan Gentry* (London: Routledge & Kegan Paul, 1984), p. 41; concerning his patronage of ministers, see also below. Sibthorpe had earlier antagonized many of his Northamptonshire neighbours with his sermon in support of the Forced Loan. See *DNB*.

107 PC 2/44, pp. 198–272; also SP 16/362/96; 16/267/6.

108 e.g. *Harley Letters*, pp. 8, 14, 28; STT 181, 2326; also Cl C 669; Cope, *Montagu*, pp. 79–83, 102–3, 114, 127. See also Cliffe, *Puritan Gentry*, pp. 40–1.

109 New College MS Archive 9502, e.g. entries for 20 or 27 August 1637. Richard Cust and Conrad Russell told me that the original diary was at New College. Caroline Dalton, assistant archivist at New College, helped to arrange for me to obtain a microfilm of the diary.

110 The substitution of catechizing for lectures on Sunday afternoon troubled them more. See below.

111 SP 16/335/19; see also 16/337/74; 16/395/37; 16/326/18. There were a number of reports that clergy had preached against the book (e.g. SP 16/265/14; 16/267/6; 16/397/91; see also Yonge, f. 64).

112 SP 16/326/18. See also the charge against the vicar of Ledbury that he had made some irreverent remarks about the book in his catechizing (SP 16/375/78).

113 SP 16/308/52; also 16/266/54. Concerning W. Spenser, see *Alum. Cant.*

114 Whiteway, f. 104v. As a citizen of Dorchester and a Puritan, Whiteway was in a good position to report the incident. Also see Yonge, f. 64. Concerning White see *DNB*; also F. Rose-Troup, *John White: The Patriarch of Dorchester and the Founder of Massachusetts, 1575–1648* (London: G. P. Putnam, 1930).

115 Yonge, ff. 56v, 60, 64, 72; Whiteway, f. 104v; SP 16/278/45; 16/388/27; 16/337/74; 16/397/91; PRO, C. 115/M.36.

116 The book was published in 1635, STC 25384. White claimed Brabourne had taken his ideas from the Puritans. See esp. its introduction. See Yonge, f. 64; also *DNB*, for White and Brabourne. Brabourne was on trial in the Court of High Commission in 1635.

117 *WP*, Vol. 3, p. 298; cf. *DeL'Isle*, pp. 86–7.

118 *WP*, Vol. 3, pp. 299–302. The Answer has been attributed both to Prynne (BL 4355.b.7 (HEH photocopy)) and to Richard Byfield who had previously written about the sabbath (Byfield, *Doctrine of the Sabbath Vindicated* (1631), STC 4238; see *DNB*).

119 P. Heylyn, *The History of the Sabbath in two Bookes* (1635), STC 13275. See *WP*, Vol. 3, pp. 303, 358–61. In the second of these references, six months after the first, Ryece tells Winthrop that at the end of the Answer was inserted 'the history of Mr. Prynne pursewed by Mr. Noy a greate favourer of Sabbathe recreations and pollutions', a history which dealt with Noy's prosecution of Prynne for *Histrio Mastix*.

120 *An Examination and Confutation of a Lawless Pamphlet, Intituled a Brief Answer to a late Treatise of the Sabbath Day* (1637), STC 25379. See also, Burton's *Divine Tragedie*; Pocklington's sermon, *Sunday, No Sabbath*,

preached 17 August 1635, and printed in 1636 (STC 2077); David Primerose, *A Treatise of the Sabbath* (1636), STC 20387, which claims to have been written prior to White's but was held and not published till afterwards; *A Discourse of the Sabbath and the Lord's Day*, by Christopher Dow (1636), STC 7088.

121 I am using preaching to include the giving of sermons, whether in a lecture or in a parish pulpit.

122 See P. Collinson, *The Religion of Protestants* (Oxford: Clarendon Press, 1982), esp. ch. 3. Also see P. Collinson, 'Lectures by combination', *BIHR*, vol. 48, no. 18 (1975), pp. 182–213. P. Seaver, *The Puritan Lectureships* (Stanford: Stanford University Press, 1970).

123 Rushworth, Vol. 2, pt. 2, pp. 7–8. These orders which were reissued in 1634 were presaged by James I's instructions in 1622 (E. Cardwell, *Documentary Annals of the Reformed Church of England*, Vol. 2 (Oxford: Oxford University Press, 1844), p. cxxxii).

124 Rous, p. 47.

125 Rous, pp. 51–3.

126 Yonge, f. 37; see also f. 36; and Barrington MSS (Essex Record Office, D/DBa F/4, f. 19 (Yale film)); SP 16/153/100–5.

127 Concerning preaching, see H. Davies, *Worship and Theology: From Andrewes to Baxter and Fox* (Princeton, NJ: Princeton University Press, 1975), ch. 4.

128 HMC, *Ninth Report*, app., i, p. 261.

129 This impression distorts reality. See J. Morrill, 'The religious context of the English Civil War', *TRHS*, Fifth Series, vol. 34 (1984), p. 164.

130 *WP*, Vol. 3, pp. 355–63. Concerning Rogers, see *DNB*. For other references to ministers in trouble see e.g. Yonge, ff. 45–45v, 52v.

131 *WP*, Vol. 3, pp. 258–9.

132 Cl C 78.

133 e.g. BL, Add. MS 4275, f. 166; also *Barrington Family Letters*, nos 75, 76.

134 See e.g. B. Donagan, 'The clerical patronage of Robert Rich, 2nd earl of Warwick, 1619–1642', *Proceedings of the American Philosophical Society*, vol. 120 (1976), pp. 407–8. Also see, HMC, *Fourteenth Report*, app., ii, p. 34; Newton, 'Yorkshire puritan movement', p. 16.

135 He moved from place to place, and his life was not without vicissitude. See his account (Ch. 24 in A. Young, *Chronicles*), a reference I owe to Barbara Donagan.

136 The minister who reports this does not say whether Harley spoke in their defence or whether it was merely his presence which provoked that reaction (*Harley Letters*, p. xxiv). Concerning Stoughton, see SP 16/300/2; 16/297/39; 16/302/63; *CSPDom. 1635–6*, pp. 470–8.

137 See Birch, Vol. 2, pp. 228–32; PC 2/43, p. 405; P. Clark, ' "The Ramoth–Gilead of the Good": urban change and political radicalism at Gloucester, 1540–1640', in *The English Commonwealth*, eds P. Clark, A. G. R. Smith, and N. Tyacke (Leicester: Leicester University Press, 1979), p. 186; J. N. Langston, 'John Workman, puritan lecturer', *Transactions of the*

Bristol and Gloucestershire Archaeological Society, vol. 66 (1945), pp. 219–32.

138 There were other allegations concerning the storage of ordnance and artillery in the church that may have made officials especially eager to reply. The letter was written by the deputy mayor since, as he explained, the mayor was out of town (Rye Correspondence, 47/123, 25 January 1636/7). Two years earlier Rye officials had appealed to the earl of Dorset for a larger allowance for their vicar (Rye Correspondence, 47/119, 27 January 1634/5). See also Fletcher, *County Community*, pp. 71, 73; cf. HMC, *Gawdy*, p. 161, and concerning Ipswich and Mr Ward, see P. King, 'Bishop Wren and the suppression of the Norwich lecturers', *Historical Journal*, vol. 11, no. 2 (1968), p. 253.

139 SP 16/151/45. Similar phrases were employed in defence of other preachers who were in trouble (e.g. SP 16/344/37; 16/196/61; 16/154/98–99; 16/167/23.

140 Laud at the same time received a petition from a second group of Essex clergymen. These ministers who called themselves *conformable* urged without mentioning Hooker that 'those irregulars' be forced to conform (SP 16/152/4).

141 See B. Donagan, 'Puritan ministers and laymen: professional claims and social constraints in seventeenth-century England', *Huntington Library Quarterly*, vol. 47, no. 2 (1984), pp. 81–111. I am grateful to her for allowing me to see a copy of this paper prior to its publication.

142 See Chapter 1.

143 Laud, *Works*, Vol. 5, pt. 2, pp. 321, 325; SP 16/271/82; STT 1891; SP 16/311/33.

144 Cl C 84. There was also an objection to Cheynell's style of preaching (see below). Two years later at the visitation he found himself in trouble because he objected to doing reverence to the altar until there were some public instructions or ecclesiastical injunctions (SP 16/399/80). Also see DNB. Thomas Ball of All Saints, Northampton, was a well-known puritan preacher (*DNB*).

145 See New College MS Archive 9502, e.g. 20 August 1637. He heard Dr Turner preach in London 2 February 1637/8. The first baron Montagu reputedly was so eager to hear sermons that he did not care by whom they were delivered. See Cope, *Montagu*, pp. 162, also 154–5.

146 Slingsby, *Diary*, pp. 19–20. Slingsby's chapel had the table altarwise at the east end. It also had painted windows (pp. 3–4).

147 (1636), STC 16553a.

148 The orders declared that St Paul's epistles were designed 'to be read by the ministers especially in the Publike Congregations'.

149 *WP*, Vol. 3, pp. 298–306.

150 (1636), STC 20469. See also Robert Jennison, *The Cites Safetie* (1630), STC 14489 and *Newcastles Call to her Neighbour and Sister Townes and Cities throughout the land to take Warning by her Sins and Sorrowes* (1637), STC 14492.

151 *Certayne Sermons or Homilies*, orig. 1547 (STC 13639) and in many

subsequent editions. Concerning views of preaching, see e.g. Laud's speech
at the censure of Prynne, Burton, and Bastwick, where he admitted that 'the
preaching of God's word, where it is performed according to His ordinance,
be a great means of many good effects in the souls of men'. He maintained,
however, that sermons were not the 'only means to humble men' as *Newes
from Ipswich* had asserted (*A Speech delivered in the Starr-Chamber on
Wednesday, the xiv of June mdcxxxvii at the Censure of John Bastwick,
Henry Burton, and William Prinn*, Laud, *Works*, Vol. 6 pt. 1, p. 47; cf. p.
57. Also see Collinson, 'Combination', pp. 202–13; Collinson, *Religion*,
pp. 48–51.

152   Laud, *Works*, Vol. 6, pt. 2, p. 47.

153   See also STT 1891; SP 16/383/46; 16/280/54; 16/140/37; 16/308/52;
16/311/33.

154   SP 16/280/71; 16/326/18; 16/311/33; 16/308/52.

155   SP 16/308/52; 16/326/18; STT 1880; S. R. Gardiner (ed.), *Reports of
Cases in the Courts of Star Chamber and High Commission*, Camden
Society, New Series, vol. 39 (1886), pp. 199, 213, 241 ff; SP 16/197/59;
STT, Manorial Box 3 and STT, Legal, Misc. Papers.

156   e.g. Gardiner, *Star Chamber and High Commission*, pp. 181–6.

157   (1631), STC 3790. Brinsley (1600–65) had been removed from his position
at Great Yarmouth by the High Commission in 1627 (*DNB*).

158   *CSPDom. 1635–6*, pp. xxxix ff., answers to articles 6, 8, 7, and 10 in thta
order. I am grateful to Barbara Donagan for help on this point.

159   Cl C 84. They probably meant that the sermons contained too many flowers
of learning. See, for example, his letters Cl C 73, 75, 80. His preaching,
however, suited Mr Crew who, Cheynell said, 'is accounted a strict man
amongst gallants', though Saye 'takes him to be the remisse' (Cl C 84). The
letter hints at other differences between Saye and Crew.

160   *CSPDom. 1635–6*, pp. xxxix ff., answer to article 10.

161   Laud mentions crowds as a reason for restricting lectures during the plague,
in his speech at the censure of Prynne, Burton, and Bastwick (Laud, *Works*,
Vol. 6, pt. 2, p. 46). Rosemary O'Day suggests that the frequent quarrels
between clergymen and laymen about tithes are, for the most part, distinct
from disputes about preaching, ceremonies, and sabbatarianism (*The
English Clergy: The Emergence and Consolidation of a Profession
1558–1642* (Leicester: Leicester University Press, 1979), pp. 191–200 ff.).

162   Phelips Mss, DDPH 221/22.

163   The bishops worried especially about controlling lecturers who had benefices
outside the diocese or had none at all. See Laud, *Works*, Vol. 5, pt. 2, p. 319;
also see SP 16/168/6; 16/169/23; 16/531/135.

164   See the negotiations concerning the lecture at Coventry in Coventry Council
Minute Book, ff. 318–319v (Yale film); also see SP 16/339/53.

165   SP 16/164/14; 16/145/67; 16/146/3; 16/152/32.

166   SP 16/142/113; 16/144/36; also see *DNB*, 'Collins'. SP 16/160/66; 16/
269/36.

167   For complaints about ministers who did not meet standards, see *WP*, Vol.

3, pp. 386–8; Gardiner, *Star Chamber and High Commission*, pp. 271–3; also Green, 'Career prospects'.

168 e.g. Lord Montagu's appointees (Cope, *Montagu*, pp. 154–5). See also the account of Thomas Smyth's efforts to learn about a clergyman before offering him a benefice, in *Calendar of the Correspondence of the Smyth Family of Ashton Court 1548–1642*, ed. J. H. Bettey, Bristol Record Society, vol. 35 (1982), no. 301, 317.

169 Rushworth, Vol. 1, p. 621.

170 *CD 1629*, pp. 34–5.

171 See also above.

172 For descriptions of visitations see e.g. Whiteway, f. 105; Exeter City Archives, Act Books, Vol. 8, ff. 5–5v (Harvard film); Young, *Diary*, pp. 105–10. Also see Fletcher, *County Community*, pp. 83–4.

173 STC 10298 (the articles); see HMC, *Gawdy*, p. 158; WP, Vol. 3, pp. 261, 355–63; Rous, p. 80; Yonge, f. 66v. See above concerning underlinings of passages known to be controversial in a Huntington copy of Wren's articles; see also *Articles to Be inquired of in the Archdeaconrie of Salop, within the Diocese of Hereford, in the yeare 1639* (STC 10217; HN 289939). Laud's well-publicized visitations of his London diocese set the pattern and tone for visitations during the 1630s (see, for example, WP, Vol. 3, pp. 57–61).

174 Bedfordshire Record Office, St John of Bletsoe MSS, no. 1361; see also Chapter 5.

175 Woodforde, p. 496. Anticipated evil did not always occur. Clarke says that Herbert Palmer had resolved 'rather to lose all and suffer anything' than to read the Book of Sports or bow to the altar but when he went to the archbishop's visitation held by Sir John Lambe, 'he found beyond expectation, rather a connivance at him, then an enforcement thereof'. (S. Clarke, *The Lives of Two and Twenty English Divines* (London, 1660), p. 239).

176 M. Spufford, 'The quest for heretical laity in the visitation records of Ely in the late sixteenth and early seventeenth centuries', *Studies in Church History*, vol. 9 (1972), pp. 223–30.

177 See John Shaw's note of the difference he believed the fact that he was a chaplain to the earl of Pembroke made to an official of Archbishop Neile of York in 'The life of Master John Shaw', *Yorkshire Diaries and Autobiographies in the Seventeenth and Eighteenth Centuries*, Surtees Society, vol. 65 (1875) p. 129.

178 Cl C 600. It is not clear exactly what the situation was. Concerning patronage, see R. O'Day, 'The law of patronage in early modern England', *Journal of Ecclesiastical History*, vol. 26, no. 2 (1975), pp. 247–60. I am grateful to Rosemary O'Day for responding to my questions about patronage.

179 SP 16/373/3; see also Burton, *Apology of an Appeal*, pp. 11 ff. Concerning the oath see M. Maguire, 'The attack of the common lawyers on the oath *ex officio* as administered in the ecclesiastical courts in England', in *Essays in History and Political Theory in Honor of Charles Howard McIlwain* (Cambridge, Mass: Harvard University Press, 1936), pp. 199–229.

180   See R. G. Usher, *The Rise and Fall of the High Commission* (Oxford: Oxford University Press, 1913). The Church courts could not fine and imprison. Burton and Bastwick who had firsthand experience with the commission attacked it bitterly. See below.

181   Cornish Record Office, Buller Papers, BC 24/4/49. It is not clear what was the nature of Hayward's business in the court.

182   Hunt, *Puritan Moment*, pp. 259–60. Holmes, *Lincolnshire*, pp. 118–19.

183   *WP*, Vol. 3, pp. 57–61.

184   e.g. Thomas Valentine of Chalfont St Giles (SP 16/337/74; 16/395/37).

185   *Barrington Family Letters*, no. 186. The three he names as deceased were York, Ely, and Worcester. He was wrong about the last. In a subsequent letter (no. 187) he reported what he had heard about replacements. The two livings the Barringtons had were in the diocese of York (p. 194 n.). See also Yonge, ff. 47, 65; Whiteway, f. 83v; DeL'Isle, p. 131.

186   *WP*, Vol. 3, pp. 395–6. Concerning Hall see *DNB*; also T. Kinloch, *The Life and Works of Joseph Hall* (London: Staples Press, 1951).

187   See S. McGee, 'Laud'. Also H. R. Trevor-Roper, *Archbishop Laud, 1573–1645*, 2nd edn (New York: St Martin's, 1965).

188   Holles, no. 154; *WP*, Vol. 3, pp. 57 ff.; Yonge, f. 45v.

189   Holles, no. 154.

190   Whiteway, f. 78v; also Yonge, f. 37.

191   HMC, *Report on the MSS of the Duke of Buccleuch and Queensberry* (Montagu House), Vol. 1, pp. 273–4; also Yonge, f. 52v; Birch, Vol. 2, pp. 227–8.

192   Whiteway, f. 95; see also *Fairfax Correspondence*, Vol. 1, pp. lxxvii–lxxviii.

193   Whiteway, f. 95; see also Yonge, f. 73. For other libels see e.g. SP 16/250/59; 16/248/93; 16/254/50; 16/258/50; 16/260/79; Laud, *Works*, Vol. 3, p. 229.

194   An anonymous complaint which was sent to Laud in 1629 also implicated Neile in the promotion of Arminianism (SP 16/161/39). Concerning Neile, A. Foster, 'The function of a bishop: the career of Richard Neile, 1562–1640', in *Continuity and Change: Personnel and Administration of the Church of England 1500–1642*, eds R. O'Day and F. Heal (Leicester: Leicester University Press, 1976), pp. 38–53. Also see *DNB*; Marchant, *Church Courts*, pp. 53 ff.

195   *WP*, Vol. 3, pp. 126–8; Shepard, p. 527 in Young, *Chronicles*.

196   For the proceedings against the bishops see *ST*, Vol. 4; W. Prynne, *Canterburies Doom* (1646).

197   Montagu was bishop of Chichester from 1628–38 and then bishop of Norwich. See *DNB*; also Collinson, 'Combination', p. 206.

198   He was translated to Norwich from Hereford in 1635 and moved to Ely in 1638. Concerning Wren see *DNB*. He was attacked in *The Wrens Nest Defiled* (1640), STC 26016. Also see King, 'Bishop Wren'. The city of Norwich petitioned the king and Laud about him in 1636 (J. Evans, *Seventeenth-Century Norwich* (Oxford: Oxford University Press, 1979), pp. 86–94).

199   See *DNB* 'Lambe'; also B. Levack, *The Civil Lawyers in England*,

1603–1641: A Political Study (Oxford: Clarendon Press, 1973), pp. 246–7. Among other well-known episcopal agents were Sir Nathaniel Brent, Laud's vicar general who conducted his metropolitical visitations, and the diocesan chancellors such as Duck, Farmery, Easdall, and Mottershed. See Levack, pp. 212–13, 225–6, 229, 227, 257; R. Marchant, *Church Courts*, pp. 48 ff., 250.

200 STC 20469 (1636); see S. Foster, *Underground*, pp. 73–4.

201 Cl C 27, Birch, Vol. 2, pp. 259–63; Yonge, f. 67; also SP 16/344/108.

202 See *DNB* and below.

203 *WP*, Vol. 3, p. 357.

204 Cl C 616. The source for the epithets was probably Prynne, *A Looking-Glasse for all Lordly Prelates* (1636), STC 20466. Rous quotes from some attacks on the bishops in his diary, e.g. pp. 42–3, 78–9. Concerning anti-episcopal libels, see also Phelips, DDPH 221/25.

205 See S. Foster, *Underground*, pp. 25–6; S. R. Gardiner (ed.), 'Speech of Sir Robert Heath, attorney general in the case of Alexander Leighton in the Star Chamber, 4 June 1630', *Camden Miscellany*, Vol. 7, Camden Society New Series, vol. 14 (1875). Also see Yonge, f. 38.

206 Rous, p. 53.

207 SP 16/211/20; *ST*, Vol. 3, pp. 519–62; P. Slack discusses the complex issues in the case in 'Religious protest and urban authority: the case of Henry Sherfield, iconoclast, 1633', *Studies in Church History*, vol, 9 (1972), pp. 295–302. See also Rous, p. 70; Yonge, ff. 51, 52v; *CSPDom. 1631–3*, p. 571.

208 *ST*, Vol. 3, pp. 548–53.

209 *ST*, Vol. 3, pp. 546–7. Dorset agreed (pp. 554–5). Chief Justices Heath and Richardson proposed a fine of £500 (pp. 541–6).

210 Yonge, f. 51.

211 See E. W. Kirby, 'The Lay Feoffees: a study in militant Puritanism', *Journal of Modern History*, vol. 14, no. 1 (1942), pp. 1–25. Also see *Activities of the Puritan Faction of the Church of England 1625–33*, ed. I. M. Calder (London, 1957). Concerning a group of lay feoffees in Norwich, see Evans, *Norwich*, p. 87.

212 For the proceedings against them see *ST*, Vol. 3, pp. 711–70. Five books were involved: Bastwick's *Apology* (1636), STC 1576; his *Letany* (1636), STC 1572; Burton's *Apology of an Appeal* (1636), STC 4134, with the two sermons, *For God and the King: Newes from Ipswich*, and *The Divine Tragedie* (*ST*, Vol. 3, p. 718). See also *DNB*, 'Prynne'; 'Burton'; 'Bastwick'.

213 PRO, C. 115/N.4, no. 8614.

214 See above.

215 STC 15306. The speech also appears in Laud, *Works*, Vol. 6, pt. 1, pp. 35–70.

216 He ignores the fact that the defendants had charged that he was claiming power from God.

217 PRO, C.115/N.8, no. 8806. Also see *CSPVen. 1636–9*, no. 261.

218 The pages of contemporary letters and diaries are filled with reports, e.g. *DeL'Isle*, pp. 84 ff. *passim*; Yonge, f. 67; Rous, p. 82.

219 SP 16/362/76.

220 SP 16/363/42; 16/363/119; also WP, Vol. 3, pp. 484–8; SP 16/368/14; 16/375/82; DeL'Isle, pp. 112, 114, 115, 120; Woodforde, p. 496.

221 PRO, C. 115/N.4, no. 8615; cf. the comments of Sir Robert Phelips (DDPH 221/20); see also T. Fuller, *Church History of Britain* (1655), Eleventh Book, p. 155.

222 There were exceptions, of course. Among these was Nehemiah Wallington. See P. Seaver, *Wallington's World*, pp. 3, 150, 159–60.

223 There were at least two publications which gave the defendants' view of the trial: STC 1570, *A Briefe Relation of Certaine speciall and most materiall passages and speeches in the Starre-Chamber, Occasioned and delivered the 14th day of June 1637* (1637), giving the defendants' answers and statements of their difficulties in getting a fair trial as they conceived it; and STC 15309, *Divine and Politike Observations Newly Translated out of the Dutch language wherein they were lately divulged. Upon Some Lines in the speech of the ArchB of Canterbury, pronounced in the Starre-Chamber upon June 1637* (1638), attacking the printing of the speech and Laud for reflecting upon royal authority in the way that he accused the defendants. It argues that the bishops are acting in unlawful and dangerous ways.

224 Laud, *Works*, Vol. 3, pp. 228–30.

225 O. Kalu, 'Continuity in change: bishops of London and religious dissent in early Stuart England', *JBS*, vol. 18, no. 1 (1978), pp. 28–45; also Green, 'Conformity'; Fletcher, *County Community*, pp. 83–4.

226 Laud, *Works*, Vol. 6, pt. 1, p. 310; Vol. 7, pp. 87–8. I owe this point to Sears McGee.

227 See above.

228 e.g. SP 16/286/86.

229 See above.

230 STT 1880, 1882; see also SP 16/260/17. Sir Nathaniel Brent who conducted visitations for Archbishop Laud lamented in March 1636/7 that although Stephen Marshall's heart was inconformable, yet nothing could be proved against him concerning deviation from the Church's ceremonies. SP 16/351/100; see also *CSPDom. 1635*, p. xxxiv.

231 Lord Montagu was distressed by the bishop of Peterborough's suppression of the lecture at Kettering; he let his sorrow at that action be known and bowed to the bishop's authority (Cope, *Montagu*, pp. 151–2). See also Donagan, 'Warwick' pp. 407–10; Green, 'Conformity'.

232 Peter Clark, 'Thomas Scott and the growth of urban opposition to the early Stuart regime', *Historical Journal*, vol. 21, no. 1 (1978), p. 24. Barbara Donagan discusses factors restricting ministers' freedom of action and in some instances their willingness to take a strong stand in 'Puritan ministers'.

233 *CSPDom. 1635*, pp. 377–8, a reference I owe to Conrad Russell.

234 See above.

235 e.g. assessment for shipmoney and military charges jurisdiction, see below; also A. Fletcher, 'Factionalism in town and countryside: the significance of Puritanism and Arminianism', *Studies in Church History*, vol. 16 (1979) pp. 297–9.

236 John Sym, *Lifes Preservative Against Self-Killing* (1637), STC 23584,

pp. 134–5, 147–8. I am grateful to Barbara Donagan for sharing with me her article on 'Godly choice: puritan decision-making in seventeenth-century England', prior to its publication in the *Harvard Theological Review*. As a result of that article, I read John Sym. See also J. Morrill, 'Sir William Brereton and England's wars of religion', *JBS*, vol. 24, no. 3 (1985), pp. 311–32.

237 See Fletcher, 'Factionalism', pp. 291–300; also M. Schwarz, 'Lay Anglicanism and the crisis of the English Church in the early seventeenth century', *Albion*, vol. 14, no. 1 (1982), pp. 1–19.

3

Defence

Defence assumed a new importance for the English in the 1620s. The struggles in Germany, where King James's daughter Elizabeth and her husband the Elector of the Palatine were fighting against imperial and papist forces, stirred interest in foreign affairs and reminded people of the dangers that foreign enemies posed.[1] Some urged the king to intervene in the continental war; some advocated a naval campaign against Spain. In 1624 after the negotiations for a Spanish marriage for Prince Charles had collapsed, Parliament asked James to break the treaties that had governed relations between the two nations since 1604.[2] His death left Charles to face the war that soon followed.

With the actual experience of war the enthusiasm of those who had urged that England should undertake a Protestant crusade waned. Not since Queen Elizabeth had rallied the nation against the Spanish Armada had a monarch asked the country to devote so many of its resources to military purposes as Charles I did during the early years of his reign. Unable to get support from Parliament in 1625 or 1626, he ignored the lessons of history and sought to draw upon other resources – benevolences, loans, and shipmoney. The magnitude of the task he had set for himself increased in 1627 with the outbreak of war against France.

England's militia, organized in the Elizabethan era under great peers appointed as Lords Lieutenants by the monarch and the lesser nobles and the prominent gentlemen who were their deputies, like other parts of local government depended heavily upon the energy of those in positions of responsibility, co-operation among them, and their ability to command respect from the constables and the people of the community.[3] To the deputies fell the real task of executing the orders the lords sent them from the king and Privy Council. Deputies called musters of horse and foot where men between the ages of 16 and 60 were to show arms appropriate for their status, they held exercises for those in the trained bands, they appointed muster masters to supervise training, they saw that the county beacons, powder, and defences were maintained, and when necessary they imposed rates for these purposes.[4] The demands of war placed a severe strain upon these arrangements which, since 1604 when the statute for the militia had been repealed, had no authority but custom and the royal prerogative.[5] The council expected that obligations be enforced with rigour and issued orders that required additional men and money for coats and conduct, billeting, and supplies.

Charles reaped a harvest of bitterness when he summoned a third Parliament in 1628. MPs complained about the costs of the war and its management. The Duke of Buckingham whom they had attempted to impeach in 1626 remained at the helm of the enterprise. His presence gave his enemies added reason for criticizing the unsuccessful campaigns, the fiscal and military measures that had evoked such an outcry in the country, and the religious policies that made them suspicious of the crown's commitment to fighting Popery. Convinced that they needed to act to prevent a recurrence of the grievances they had felt, MPs debated how best to achieve their goals and eventually decided to proceed by petition. They concentrated upon formulating that and obtaining the approval of the Lords and the king for it although they also investigated some specific instances of alleged wrongdoing and began work on a new statute for the militia.[6]

Copies of speeches and accounts of proceedings circulated through the kingdom to inform individuals everywhere what Parliament was doing and to remind them of the wartime grievances they shared. When King Charles finally gave his approval to the Petition of Right, people celebrated with bonfires and bellringing.[7] He had acknowledged that they should be free from forced loans, arbitrary imprisonment, martial law, and the billeting of troops. People knew too that Parliament had debated the powers of the deputy lieutenants and talked about other issues including militia rates, coat and conduct money, and impressment of soldiers. The session had reaffirmed the tradition that the English monarch did not undertake war without Parliament.[8] It informed the English about military matters and gave them an additional perspective for viewing their wartime experiences.

Memories of what was said and done in Parliament affected the conduct of war and the management of defence during the following period. People cited the Petition of Right. They had been alerted to the sensitive legal and political issues concerning their military obligations and the power of deputy lieutenants. The failure of parliamentary efforts to place these upon a statutory basis presented difficulties for all concerned with military matters on the local level. In the face of increased pressure from the king and council to end the laxity that had frequently characterized England's defensive preparations, heightened awareness of uncertainties about what could be enforced brought endemic disputes about what was due to epidemic proportions.

In challenging the demands made of them for defence during the 1630s people were for the most part making specific objections even when raising legal points. They questioned procedure, resented expense, disliked particular individuals involved in local administration, or had various other personal reasons for not wanting to comply. Few became isolationist, antiwar, or pacificist. Properly conducted, war could be a glorious enterprise. The contests between foreign powers not only gave people a chance to observe history and men an opportunity to gain military experience, but also had at stake the future of England and Christendom.

The English remained during the 1630s intensely interested in continental developments and particularly in the fate of fellow Protestants. When relatives and friends who were abroad could not supply accounts of the latest engagements between the armies in Germany, reports about the movement of the fleets, word of the fate of the Huguenots in France, or news from the European courts, they looked to newswriters or to the printed sheets.[9] They treasured the pamphlets recounting the achievements of Swedish King Gustavus Adolphus whose military successes had brought hope to the anti-Imperialists. When he died in battle in November 1632, many English mourned.[10] Walter Yonge devoted more than a page in his diary to notes about this king who was so different from Charles I. Gustavus, Yonge noted, spoke eight languages besides Swedish, kept his own intelligence, could instruct his troops, had ministers in his army, selected his officers on ability rather than birth, called his soldiers brothers, and gave one who complained of hunger half a biscuit from his own pocket.[11]

Popular fascination with military manoeuvres, weapons, and heroes added to English interest in European wars during the period.[12] Books and pamphlets, official and unofficial, fed appetites hungry for detailed descriptions of the art of warfare.[13] Corporations worked to establish artillery yards and appealed for the right to muster and train their own men.[14] Young men, eager for adventure, went off to serve in the armies of foreign princes.[15] Naval action also appealed to a generation bred on the tales of the Elizabethan sea dogs.[16]

Observation and study of both historic and contemporary military engagements and growing concern about dangers to the Church at home made the English somewhat more hesitant about advocating that their king should take up arms during the 1630s than they had been ten years earlier.[17] People were suspicious of the courtiers and councillors they thought sympathetic to the French or Spanish and worried that Charles might be convinced by them to make an alliance that would jeopardize England's religion and liberty.[18] However much they welcomed the end of war with France in May 1629 and that with Spain in November of the following year, they showed little enthusiasm upon hearing that treaties with those popish powers had been concluded.[19]

The poets who praised the king for bringing the benefits of peace to England tended to gloss over the political and religious factors that worried some observers. Like the court masques that emphasized what Charles had done for Britian, poems took advantage of contrasts between his reign and less happy eras or the war-torn states of Germany.[20] Preachers applauded peace too but often qualified their praise with reminders about the importance of looking to God. Richard Bernard, puritan cleric of Batcombe, Somerset, thought a just war better than an unjust peace. Warning that it was 'an evil quality to delight in war', he denounced unruly soldiers and some of the destruction associated with battles, but he did not denounce war *per se*.[21]

Not until 1639 when Charles asked his English subjects to embark upon a campaign against the Scots did the question of peace or war become a major issue. During the 1630s debates focused instead upon his insistence that they perform their military obligations and contribute to defence. Notions about duty, habits of obedience, and belief in the necessity of protection against attack or invasion encouraged compliance, but the weight of these demands, misgivings about the direction of the kingdom, and memories of the experience of the 1620s made people slow to co-operate. The first part of this chapter will discuss the controversies that arose over various aspects of the authority of the Lord Lieutenants and their deputies, including the levying of fees for muster masters. A second section will treat the disputes about writs of shipmoney which the king issued to coastal areas in 1634 and extended to the entire kingdom in the following years.

MPs in 1628 had few doubts that people had suffered from abuses by soldiers and from the way that some deputy lieutenants had used their authority during the preceding years. Time and again members talked of the importance of passing legislation to deal with these problems, but they disagreed about what a statute should provide.[22] Several of the deputies who sat in the Commons rose to point out the dilemmas that they had encountered in trying to execute their responsibilities. As Sir Edward Rodney said, necessity and royal power forced them to act.[23] Their need for authority to imprison men who refused to contribute to the musters led the earl of Dorset to object to the Petition of Right when it came before the Upper House.[24] He proposed at one point that a provision be added to the Petition concerning martial law and the musters.[25] A number of Lords, like the Commons, believed that the deputies were hampered by the absence of a statute for the militia and urged that a bill be drafted.[26]

The questions raised during that session gave deputies one basis for explaining their failure to respond to orders that their lords passed on to them from the Privy Council during the following years.[27] With or without invoking the parliamentary debates of 1628 the deputies could also point to the resistance of constables upon whom they depended for enforcement of their commands and the unwillingness of people to obey.[28] Some individuals did not maintain arms appropriate for their status, and some failed to attend the musters. Much more frequent was opposition to the rates deputies imposed for military purposes and particularly for payment of the muster masters.

Although the English acknowledged an obligation to keep arms and to show them at the musters, they did not always perform these duties. When charged with default, most, whether they believed themselves wrongly accused or whether through oversight or personal or political circumstances they had been remiss, attempted to justify their conduct. Standard excuses included having moved from the county, poverty, illness, and erroneous or inequitable summons.

Sir Thomas Temple, who like many gentlemen tried to avoid any unnecessary expenses, took exception to a warrant from a Warwickshire constable concerning his appearance at musters in 1635. Whether wishing to intimidate the constable, make a legitimate procedural query, or to employ all possible arguments in his behalf, Temple not only claimed to be liable in Buckinghamshire where he was a JP and therefore exempt in Warwickshire but also challenged the wording and contents of the warrant.[29] Thus without contesting the fundamental obligation, he sought to escape from service.

Some defaulters, after being reported by local officers and deputies, were cited to appear before the Privy Council. Although they could ordinarily expect to be discharged upon submission and promise of conformity, they had been selected as examples from among the greater numbers who were in default and had been put to the expense and inconvenience of a journey to Westminster.[30] Special complaints from the lords or deputies can explain the council's sending for individuals like Thomas Flowers of Nottinghamshire whom the earl of Newcastle described as saucy.[31] The rivalry between Somerset deputies Sir Robert Phelips and Lord Poulett which disrupted the musters there over a period of years caused the case of one Roman Spracklin whom Poulett charged with default to come to the board's attention. Phelips sprang to Spracklin's defence, appealed to Pembroke, the Lord Lieutenant, and to the king. Protesting against what he alleged were the improper practices of his fellow deputies, Phelips complained of their unjust maligning of him, their imputing that he was interfering with his Majesty's service, and their holding the muster at Kingsmoor in his division without so much as letting him know.[32] The issue quickly became the conduct of the deputies rather than whether Spracklin had fulfilled his obligation.

One Cornish case that came to the council involved both friction between deputies and between a captain in the militia, Robert Rous, and John Roberts, a man he had accused of refractoriness at the muster – incitement to faction and failure to yield to authority.[33]

Rous's excommunication by the consistory court at Exeter left him embittered against Roberts who was a churchwarden. Rous complained of Roberts not to deputy Sir Richard Edgcumb in whose division the incident had occurred but to Sir Reginald Mohun and Sir Bernard Grenville who lived outside that area. When Edgcumb discovered this, he was picqued and stayed the execution of the warrant against Roberts.[34] Soon the council became involved.

Those who were involved in disputes in their communities were among the most frequent to appear at the board as a result of their conduct at the musters. The close links between local military organization and society itself meant that the musters became one of the stages upon which individuals waged personal battles. Default allowed those who wished to demonstrate their resentment against the deputies or against the council itself a way of doing so. A second major group of those called to answer may have been summoned because they had a reputation for political and/or religious opposition. Northamptonshire Puritans Richard Knightley and Sir Christopher Yelverton were among those who appeared for default in 1635 when the orders for the musters were marked with greater stringency.[35]

Although individuals like Knightley and Yelverton may have chosen to absent themselves from the musters in order to express their discontent about other military, political, or religious issues, in general disputes about default during the 1630s seem little different than they had in earlier decades. The impact of the events of the 1620s is evident to a far greater extent in the intensified conflicts over military charges and rates. People had long contested rates by questioning whether assessment was equitable or raising jurisdictional points. On occasion some had challenged the legality of military rates.[36] After 1628 a number of deputies confessed their hesitancy to impose rates in the face of local opposition.

Rates imposed for the purpose of paying muster masters, the professional officers employed to train and exercise the militia, aroused specially vigorous protests. The council's efforts to enforce earlier directives that counties pay their muster masters not only hit nerves already sensitive on the subject of taxation but also pushed areas that had not paid their muster masters or done so by different means to change their customary practices.[37] The board's action in addition fed long-standing resentment of some holders of that post whose principal qualification seemed to be their willingness to buy it or their favour from the Lord Lieutenant whose appointee they were.[38] Muster masters who campaigned to obtain their pay from a reluctant populace often exacerbated ill-feeling.[39]

The disputes about muster masters' fees that attracted the most attention at the time involved many of the same issues that arose in discussions about other military rates. When responding to the board's questions about payment, deputies – as they did in other instances – raised legal, political and financial points. Most presented doubts about the legality of rating not as their own but as those of their neighbours or of the last Parliament. The Northamptonshire deputies explained in July 1629 that because money for officers of the muster 'hath of late bene soe publiquely impeached', they had 'forborne to make mention thereof'. Rather than cause controversy and perhaps in consequence collect little, they would await the council's advice about 'some such other coorse as yo Lops in yo wisedome shall thinke most convenient'.[40] A year later the Suffolk deputies claimed that they were afraid to levy fees for muster masters lest they be questioned in Parliament. They suggested that men who were not parliament men should do it.[41]

In explaining why they could not collect monies to fulfil their responsibilities, deputies at times blamed other officials, including sheriffs and constables. In the year that he was sheriff of Northamptonshire Sir Robert Bannister refused to sign their warrants.[42] Several years earlier the county's Lord Lieutenant, the earl of Exeter, had complained about the conduct of William Waters, chief constable of Towcester, who had levied the money but would not pay it.[43] Constables in Shropshire were also thought to be delinquent in doing their duties in this regard.[44] Those who were being sued by people who had not been repaid for expenses incurred in billeting may have been particularly reluctant to ask for additional sums.[45]

Some individuals were less cautious than the deputies about expressing their views. Sir Arthur Haselrig directly challenged the levying of muster masters' fees. Haselrig, a Leicestershire man, showed little reluctance to oppose policies and practices which he believed were wrong. During his hearing before the council he allegedly turned to deputy lieutenant Sir John Skeffington and told him that things had reached a sorry state when men such as he took money for musters from the country.[46]

Complaints by deputies, muster masters, and grand juries indicate that some people in the country were denouncing the fees on legal grounds, but often other issues also contributed to their unwillingness to pay. In Dorset the deputies had inquired about overdue billeting charges in 1629 when they informed their Lord Lieutenant that the muster master had not been paid.⁴⁷ Taking up his own cause in a petition to the council the following year, the muster master complained that despite letters from the Lord Lieutenant he had had no pay for two and a half years, ' the countrey only alledging that there is no lawe for any such taxation'.⁴⁸ A decision by the corporation of Weymouth and Melcombe Regis two years later in July 1632 suggests that he was still trying to obtain money. The corporation agreed by 'general consent' that if he sued, the town would bear the costs of answering.⁴⁹

After considering various means of protesting against rating for payment of the muster masters, the Hertfordshire grand jury at the summer assizes in 1629 opted for political and thus public rather than legal and closed action. Instead of indicting the constables who had sent out the warrants for the fees, they rejected that course and read a petition.⁵⁰ Prosecuting the constables might have deterred them or others from executing the orders in the future, but it would probably have done little to communicate to the crown the dislike of the royal policy which called for professional muster masters paid by county rates. The jury seemed determined to make this point. They persisted in petitioning despite the efforts of the earl of Salisbury, their Lord Lieutenant, to convince them that the charge was small and the importance of the muster master's service to the king great.⁵¹

In April 1635 six years after the Hertfordshire grand jury had petitioned, a grand jury at the quarter sessions in Shropshire presented the imposition of charges for fees for the muster master 'as a greate greevance and oppression' of all from whom these are 'demanded or extorted'.⁵² They suggested that the muster master was an unnecessary officer.⁵³ When two JPs, Sir Richard Newport and Timothy Tourneur, both with connections with the earl of Bridgewater, the Lord Lieutenant, took some exception to the presentment, a third, Sir John Corbet, intervened in the jury's defence. He called for the statute book, turned to the Petition of Right and asked the clerk to read it. This the clerk did. Corbet then attacked Tourneur for telling the jury that they were 'too busy', an allegation sometimes made of MPs.⁵⁴ Tourneur replied that he was only doing his duty, telling the jury that there were other grievances which they had not mentioned which were a greater burden and that the muster master was a necessary official.[55] Sir John and the rest of the justices coughed to protest but only one, Mr Charlton, spoke to support Sir John by saying that the office had been denied once previously in the time of Lord Zouch.[56]

Sir John Corbet of Stoke-upon-Terne and Adderley had served as sheriff in 1628 and had been active in local affairs.[57] Apart from a dispute in the Court of Arches involving his rights as patron of a chapel, he had left little mark on records until the quarter sessions of April 1635.[58] Tourneur charged that Corbet had plotted with the foreman of the grand jury whose wife was Corbet's kinswoman to make the presentment.[59] This may be true, but other JPs recalled that 'the same hath beene in divers of ye predecessors times lds lieutenants oppunged and presented as a grievance at the assize', and once by a grand jury which included Edward Burton, the present muster master.[60] Although none of the principals invoked evidence from other counties, they might have done so, for many had reported to the council in 1629 that they did not levy rates to pay their muster masters.[61]

People in Shropshire were showing their unwillingness to pay the fees. Burton reported to Bridgewater later in April that five hundreds had paid him, six had requested and had been granted more time, and three had 'absolutely denied payment'.[62] A month later the clerk of the peace told Bridgewater that 'the fee itselfe is generally distasted, and yr truest friends (for so I may be bold to call them whom I know to be so) disgust it utterly'.[63] Although Burton had apparently received full payment by late July, problems persisted. Two years later in 1637 Bridgewater was still concerned about the way in which the muster master was paid.[64]

The grand jury's petition of April 1635 seems to have been a direct result of the deputies' issuance of warrants for collection of the fee the preceding November.[65] Burton's complaints that even if he received what was due to him for the current year, his work for the two previous years had gone unremunerated, may also have aroused people's resentment.[66] Although he was apparently a local man, not an outsider, and although none of the papers which survive from the affair suggest that there was any open criticism of his qualifications for the place, he may have obtained the post because he was Bridgewater's servant. If Burton's countrymen saw him as one of the time-serving profiteers that Markham says too many Lord Lieutenants were appointing, their unhappiness about rates may have increased.[67]

Neither Burton nor any of those who opposed rates for his pay indicate whether fees for this purpose were unprecedented in the county. George Betts, who had been muster master in Caernarvonshire, Merioneth, and Flintshire when Bridgewater was appointed Lord President of Wales, complained that he had not been paid in preceding years.[68] The deputies in Hereford may have refrained from taking steps for payment of muster masters even longer than those in Shropshire did.[69] By relenting and issuing warrants the Salopian deputies removed pressure to comply with the council's orders from their shoulders to those of the people in the shire. In their presentment the grand jury responded to this burden.

The presentment simply declared the imposition of the fees a grievance. It did not challenge the legality of the fees and in fact argued that the king's service 'hath not at all nor is like to be neglected by the defect of such an officer'.[70] Tourneur who in relating the incident to Bridgewater was eager to show his own zeal in defending authority claimed that he 'had reprehended the Jurie making the presentment being a thing not given in charge nor any Article of our inquiry' and thus in effect invoked law.[71] In response to this, Tourneur testifies, Corbet rose to the defence 'and said he mervayled that I was so touchie in that busines for it was a thing so complayned of in the Petition of Right'. Whether or not Corbet had planned to cite the Petition, his doing so even in a general way and without gloss, served to transform the proceedings.[72]

The Petition of Right from its inception was a symbol of liberty, a worthy companion to Magna Carta. Londoners celebrated with bonfires Charles's agreement to give a second, more satisfactory answer to it, and in January 1628/9 the Commons had reacted angrily to evidence of alterations in the copy printed in the book of statutes from the Parliament.[73] Tourneur, like Corbet, knew this. He claimed to have admitted to his adversary that the Petition was 'a thing to the People wondrous, plausible' and one 'I liked it well as having my share in it, but yet to be urged with warynesse'.[74] His history was better than Corbet's, and it also served both his avowed purpose of defending the royal prerogative to 'leavie soldiers' and what may also have been his goal, the discrediting of the jury's action.[75]

News of the proceedings at the Shropshire sessions travelled quickly. Bridgewater who was in London heard 'a Flying reporte' before he had direct information from the clerk of the peace or anyone who had been there.[76] He complained of 'a greate noyse of ye Bussines about the towne before I was able to give any answer'.[77] The council's summoning of the jury, the two constables who according to some were behind the presentment, and Justices Corbet and Charlton who had defended the jury's action, and Corbet's six-months' imprisonment in the Fleet added to the publicity afforded the incident.[78] Even without the drama of conciliar prosecutions, the opposition to the fees was a protest with which people elsewhere could identify.

The Shropshire deputy lieutenants kept a low profile during the proceedings. Bridgewater wrote to them expressing his surprise that they had not informed him what had happened. Sir Andrew Corbet, not a kinsman of Sir John, excused himself on the grounds that he had not been present at the sessions and had not known about the incident.[79] Pointing out in the same letter that, unless there were more deputies, the service could not be performed, he urged Bridgewater to be conciliatory toward the jurors who had not intended to be undutiful but were only following precedents. Whether Corbet's remarks were inspired by self-interested desire to lighten his burdens as a deputy or by a public-spirited or politically-motivated hope to relieve his countrymen, he preferred peace to controversy. He and his fellow deputies nevertheless continued to issue warrants for muster masters' fees.[80]

Most deputies did likewise. Having informed their Lord Lieuten-ant and through him the council about the unpopularity of orders and the consequent likelihood that the county's record might be less than perfect, they made some efforts to do their duty. They were conscious of constitutional issues, but in their action they tended to play politics. Truly unpopular measures were virtually impossible for them or for the constables upon whom they depended in this to enforce. Typically, they answered queries from the lords and council, sought advice, and offered their own suggestions and observations about military administration in their area. Likewise, few who resisted payment of rates for muster masters persisted when they faced sanctions. Most did what those in Shropshire did – submit and pay their money. Both those in authority and those desiring to challenge it indulged in rhetorical excess to make their point. Rarely did they accompany their words with equally vigorous action. Sir

Arthur Haselrig refused when asked to repeat publicly to the Privy Council his angry remarks to Sir John Skeffington. He promised the council he would conform.[81] Sir John Corbet's six months in the Fleet and removal from the commission of the peace were unusual and stemmed not from unwillingness to pay the fees but from his conduct at the quarter sessions.[82]

Because the crown was, for the most part, willing to accept submission from offenders and because it could not enforce military obligations rigorously if local leaders and communities would not co-operate, serious political conflict was averted. When in 1639 Charles began to insist upon performance of military obligations so that he could pursue his war with the Scots, he revived memories of the burdens of the wars of the 1620s and strained the loyalty of people who, though they acknowledged the need for defence and their duties to him, disliked spending money and perceived a discrepancy between his demands and the spirit of law and tradition.

Charles I's issuance of writs for shipmoney to coastal areas in 1634 and to the entire country the following year added to the military charges imposed on his subjects. Few denied the need for naval defence. The defeat of the Spanish Armada had demonstrated the utility of a strong fleet, and people knew that trade and fishing were important for their livelihoods and for the kingdom's prosperity. Those with interests in shipping appealed to the council time and time again for protection against pirates or foreign competitors, but belief in a navy was not equivalent to willingness to pay the necessary costs.[83]

In 1628 MPs were vociferous in their demands that the seas be guarded and were outraged about what they believed had been lapses in coastal protection during the preceding years. In both their remonstrance concerning Buckingham and in that against tonnage and poundage they complained about shipping losses.[84] Thanks to the duke's ineffectiveness as a naval leader, the sums taken from the merchants for the as yet unauthorized tonnage and poundage and the contributions asked of coastal areas for shipping seemed to bring few benefits.[85] Although some London citizens petitioned Parliament 'about assessing of men for setting out of ships', the Commons did not make a major issue out of Charles's efforts in 1626 and 1627 to do as Queen Elizabeth had in 1596 and collect shipmoney from maritime areas.[86]

When the king had requested assistance from the ports, they had replied by enumerating the burdens they already bore. The costs of the vessels and men previously pressed into service and the billeting of troops had left them with few resources to contribute. Some were able to convince the council to order neighbouring areas to assist, but in some instances the board sharply reproved those who sought to challenge the levies.[87] If Charles and his advisers had not abandoned the plans to impose shipmoney on the entire country in 1628, resistance might have reached serious proportions.[88]

In 1634 they altered the directions for assessment and collection of shipmoney. Instead of basing shipmoney upon the subsidies as in the past or involving the deputy lieutenants and using the procedures that had been followed for other military rates the king and council placed primarily responsibility upon the sheriffs and called for a parochial rating system.[89] This change created initial consternation, especially in 1635, when by a second departure from custom, writs were sent to the entire kingdom, not just the coastal areas. People complained about strangeness and raised a host of questions about what to do. Although their suspicion and concern about how to handle shipmoney, had no noticeable effect on what was a very high rate of payments in these early years, their introduction to the levy was hardly one that endeared it to them. To the many other innovations they were experiencing, the English by 1635 could add shipmoney. Sir Roger Twysden declared, 'The first tyme (at least in our memory) it was layd on ye subject' was 1634.[90]

The council itself added to the unpopularity of shipmoney as it came to devote more and more energy to enforcement. Sheriffs who had to continue responding to the board's queries and collecting unpaid sums after their year in office resented the prolongation and further expense of what was already an undesirable post. In subjecting over one hundred and fifty gentlemen over a four-year period to the unpleasant chores of shipmoney, the crown incurred political costs that reduced its fiscal advantages from the methods of administration. Although only a fraction of these men were to fight against Charles in the civil war, far more of them thought themselves ill-rewarded for their loyal service.

Memories of the financial exactions of the late 1620s, particularly the Forced Loan, were still strong in the mid 1630s when Charles embarked upon his plans to provide for England's defence by means of shipmoney. Although the crown had been far more vigorous in attempting to persuade or frighten people to give in 1626 than in confronting refusers, its presentation of payment as a fundamental matter of loyalty and its summons of the non-compliant and requirement that they attend every few days had embittered those involved.[91] The imprisonment of a much smaller number of resisters and the judges' denial of bail to the Five Knights had become central issues in Parliament in 1628.[92] People knew that the Petition of Rights should protect them from a recurrence of extra-parliamentary taxation and arbitrary imprisonment. With their consciousness raised by recent history, they scrutinized proceedings in connection with shipmoney.

As word that the king had issued writs for shipmoney reached people in various parts of the country, they wondered whether this meant that he would go to war. They sought additional information about his plans, about the ways that the monies he requested would be assessed and collected, and about reactions to this news in other areas.[93] Eager to avoid any expenditures that they could, many questioned the proceedings. They drew upon experience in contesting military charges and other rates. By invoking not only jurisdictional points, custom and equity but also the impartiality and disinterestedness of sheriffs and constables, they could oppose shipmoney without explicitly defying the crown.

The sheriffs who were at the centre of activity concerning shipmoney had, like the deputy lieutenants in dealing with military obligations, little need to express their own opinions. Responsible for performing the duties of their office, they concentrated on the factors that affected their ability to execute the orders they received. The sheer quantity of the letters exchanged between them and Edward Nicholas, clerk of the council in ordinary and secretary of the admiralty, that appear among the State Papers or are entered in the Registers of the Privy Council provides some indication of the task sheriffs faced and the toll shipmoney took from them. Individual sheriffs, such as Sir Thomas Danby or Sir Peter Temple, whose papers have survived have likewise left evidence of the all-consuming nature of dealing with the levy.[94] Danby spent £100 on shipmoney between 28 November 1637 and 2 January 1638 when he was sheriff of Yorkshire. In addition he travelled to London at a cost of £60 and had other expenses in connection with the assizes.[95] Some sheriffs were still trying to collect arrears and to satisfy the Privy Council long after their terms were over.[96]

While discovering that the board expected them to surmount any obstacles and being eager to prove their zeal, sheriffs confessed themselves at times unable to extract monies from the constables or the people of their counties. The sheriff of Staffordshire said in February 1636/7 that his countrymen were so angered that the county's allotment had been increased that they claimed they would petition and not pay until they were answered. He believed that he could accomplish little if he bound them all. If he were to die for his neglect, he could do no more.[97]

Sheriffs struggled to collect without antagonizing other gentry in their county. The sheriff of Shropshire told Nicholas in December 1635 that he had not returned the names of some 'refractory' gentlemen because he was still hoping to convince them to pay without taking that step.[98] Even moderation had pitfalls. Sir Roger Twysden criticized Sir George Sandes, sheriff of Kent in 1636–7, for having 'a desire to great of contenting all men'. Because Sandes 'harken[ed] to all complaynts', he issued contradictory orders.[99] More frequent were accusations that sheriffs showed partiality in rating.[100] Shropshire's clerk of the peace told the earl of Bridgewater in 1635 that the 'highmynded, selfwilled, ignorant and transcendantly malicious' sheriff had been so indiscreet in showing his love to his friends and followers and his 'unlimited power' to his adversaries 'that it is generally thought the Lords shall have many a complaynt of his unequall dealing both with the clergy and layitye'.[101] Many people did go to the Privy Council with formal allegations that their sheriffs, the constables or collectors had been unfair in making assessments.[102]

When, as happened in Northamptonshire and Oxfordshire, resistance was strong, attempts to enforce payment or to distrain property in lieu thereof could lead to violence. Woodforde tells us that when the sheriff's bailiffs came to one Northamptonshire town to distrain, 'the women assembled and some men and affrighted them, there was much running with forkes and cowle staves, etc.'[103] Sheriffs also faced special problems when prominent individuals such as Denzil Holles who as one of those MPs imprisoned in March 1628/9 had a reputation as a defender of liberty or Lord Saye who was known as a bold leader of the Puritans refused to pay.[104] Threats of litigation against both sheriffs and other officials associated with shipmoney had to be taken seriously. Sir Robert Phelips replied to charges that he had threatened at a public meeting to sue the bailiff of Ilchester for shipmoney he had collected by admitting that he had probably made the statement although he did not remember doing so.[105] Constables were less willing than sheriffs to risk offending lords or gentlemen, and tenants bowed to pressure from landlords.[106] Without the constables the sheriffs could do little.

Sheriffs, whether or not they were personally involved in local disputes and rivalries, found that these also added to the obstacles they faced in handling shipmoney. Quarrels in parts of Somerset, Essex, and Northamptonshire meant that successive sheriffs of those areas encountered opposition to almost any decision they made.[107] To his discomfort, Shropshire sheriff Harris noted that the controversy about preachers that was virtually monopolizing the attention of the citizens of Shrewsbury in 1637 had made his task harder.[108] Although the lines of division that formed over shipmoney in Newcastle upon Tyne differed from those on other issues, they nevertheless were strong enough to impede collections.[109]

The council accused some sheriffs of insufficient diligence in performing their duties, but it chose its rhetoric to goad the reluctant or frighten the timid into action. All took their posts seriously enough to make some effort to obey the shipmoney writs. Even men such as Sir Marmaduke Langdale who was sheriff of Yorkshire in 1639, Sir Anthony Irby, Sir Alexander Denton, or Sir Robert Poyntz who in 1637 were respectively sheriffs of Lincolnshire, Buckinghamshire and Gloucestershire tried to meet the quotas assigned to their counties.[110] The responsibilities of the shrievalty gave men access to means of dissent but at the same time limited the ways in which they could use that dissent. They delayed and negotiated, expressed understanding for those of their countrymen who protested the levy, but collected the monies due.

The complaints about shipmoney that gave sheriffs good reason for finding their experiences in office distasteful also serve to illustrate how the repeated levies reduced Charles's political capital among the population as a whole. When people cited assessments in violation of custom and equity, they were noting departures not only from commonly acknowledged grounds of procedure but also from the bases for assessment specified in the king's directions.

The multitude of possible definitions for custom and equity allowed those who wished to contest their ratings ample grounds for doing so. Many petitioners whether individuals or local officials compared their own ratings to those of others and then compared abilities to pay. 'The great noblemen of our shire lie on his [the sheriff's] side, far more of our towns are forest than theirs and besides the losses from drought and flood common to both parts of the county, we have suffered much by plague', JPs in the southern division of Nottinghamshire argued.[111] Gervase Markham similarly claimed that he was oppressed since Lord Chaworth and Sir Gervase Clifton, who he thought were worth more, were assessed less.[112] Their countryman the earl of Clare, who was also dissatisfied, declared to his son in October 1635, 'I am more cruelly cessed to this shipping than any man of my estate in England'.[113] The laity complained that the clergy received preference.[114] Despite the exaggerations of those who were eager to obtain relief, discontent was real. The earl of Bridgewater worried that 'unles some course be taken for more equal proportional assessments', there would be trouble. Too many of the aggrieved had got no redress.[115]

Petitioners sometimes argued that their assessments violated custom. To make their cases they presented evidence about past practices and, on occasion, also argued that the sheriff was not well-enough acquainted with the shire.[116] They decried departures from custom that might cause inequities, create precedents and thereby affect proceedings far into the future. In protesting a £50 addition to its assessment in violation of custom Barnstaple reminded the council that it was 'much decayed' in contrast to Exeter which had at the same time obtained a reduction of that amount. By the customary 'hundred rate' Barnstaple should pay only £85 instead of either the £100 it was originally charged or the £150 assessed after the adjustment.[117] To support their claim that the two divisions of Northamptonshire should have the same quotas the JPs from the east argued that the two areas were equally rated for the trained bands of horse and foot, for provisions for the king's household, for gaols, hospitals, and houses of correction, for children born in gaol, and for pardons for reprieved prisoners. Because the subsidy was charged on a person only where he lived and shipmoney was 'chargeable upon all in every place where they hold anything', it was not an appropriate model.[118] Coventry made the same point in challenging the sheriff of Warwickshire who had assigned it $\frac{1}{8}$, an amount close to that of the subsidies, rather than the $\frac{1}{15}$ that it traditionally bore in military charges.[119]

Both individuals and communities also contested shipmoney assessments as they did other unwanted rates by disputing jurisdiction. At Cambridge where the university and town had a long-standing quarrel, the vice chancellor and heads of houses declared that they were prepared to pay shipmoney if that was necessary in order to preserve their exemption from the town's jurisdiction.[120] In many episcopal cities the battles between corporate officials and cathedral clergy regarding authority over persons in the close took on new life in the form of conflicts about the assessment of shipmoney.[121] In some instances counties, interested in diminishing the amounts they were charged, joined too. Cheshire contended that the bishop not only did not reside in the city 'nor did he ever acknowledge the house in Chester to be within the jurisdiction of the city'.[122] Claiming that the sheriff of Yorkshire had increased their quota because of villages York had annexed by its charter of 1632 and that he was at the same time trying to assess the area himself, the city found its efforts to collect opposed too by the Dean and Chapter who were lords of part of the annexed territory.[123] Corporations elsewhere faced similar challenges to their assertions of jurisdiction. The inhabitants of Hunton in the Weald of Kent complained that the mayor of Maidstone had issued a warrant for levying £7 shipmoney there although 'they have never been taxed till now in any payments with or by Maidstone'.[124]

Procedural questions were another common ingredient of the public's response to the king's shipmoney writs. These like those concerning equity, custom and jurisdiction, could be argued more safely than could either political or constitutional issues. Accustomed to taking procedure seriously, the English paid attention to minute points in the assessing and collection of shipmoney. Several towns in Devon complained to the board in 1634–5 that they had not received duplicates of writs until the time allowed for assessments had almost expired.[125] They did not believe that they should consequently be penalized and forced to accept the sheriff's rating instead of doing it themselves. Colchester which was assessed by the sheriff that year protested that they had not had enough time to rate themselves.[126] Coventry was more interested in showing that the sheriff of Warwickshire kept his mind closed to revisions in their rate than in proving outright violations of procedure, but they described for the Privy Council exactly how how he had informed them by letter of their assessment, how he had subsequently agreed at their request to hold a meeting and how he had conducted that meeting. Just as the bailiff of Birmingham was about to speak, the sheriff 'stood up and began with threats and by looks to saie take heed, beware lest you be £50 more'.[127]

Procedural arguments were not a monopoly of corporations. Sir Robert Phelips was a master of this. He was one of the individuals who claimed to have received no notice of shipmoney assessments until he was distrained for nonpayment.[128] To defend himself from the accusation that he had interfered with the shipmoney process at Ilchester for his own advantage, he provided a long and detailed statement of exactly what had occurred there from the moment when sheriff Henry Hodges sent warrants to the constable for assessing the hundred.[129] Another Somerset man, William Strode, also made procedural points a central part of his protests about shipmoney. Having argued with the constable over the rating of the tithing of Barrington, he continued the quarrel when the constable seized his cow in distraint and went on to complain to the council. He accompanied his saga of personal grievances with assurances that he had done his utmost not to retard the service. At the conclusion of his statement he placed a list of four practices which he thought were 'impediments' to the king's service in collection of shipmoney.[130]

Both individuals and communities exhibited zeal and persistence in seeking relief for their grievances concerning shipmoney. 'The Book of Matters Touching Shipmoney', prepared by Humfrey Burton, clerk of the council in Coventry, gave a detailed account of events concerning shipmoney beginning with the receipt of the writ on 24 August 1635 in order to prove for posterity that that corporation should be rated 'but at a $\frac{1}{15}$ part of Warwick[shire] in all levies, assessments, and taxations wherein the said city joyneth with the County of Warwick'.[131] Burton who took advantage of his position as clerk to insert into his narrative the texts of relevant writs, letters, and petitions also made the most of his opportunities for observation when he served in the delegations sent to the sheriff, to the bishop, and to the Privy Council.[132] Determined to persuade anyone who saw his evidence of the legitimacy of Coventry's cause, he recorded his judgement of the sheriff's 'peremptorines' and wilfulness along with other evidence.[133]

While Burton's book may be a unique survival, the town's commitment and political sophistication were not unusual. Individuals and communities studied records concerning jurisdiction and rating and scrutinized the council's estimates of the actual costs involved in furnishing a ship.[134] Sir Francis Knollys who was in his mid-eighties by 1636 drew upon his own experience in naval affairs to criticize the rates proposed by the sheriff of Berkshire and to suggest that the ship the county had furnished the previous year might serve again.[135] For sending letters, travelling to meetings, and dealing with administrative problems concerning shipmoney in various other ways, the Chamberlains Accounts for the city of York show expenditures of £49 14s 10d in 1634.[136]

Appeals to patrons provide additional illustrations of the efforts that people put forth in regard to limiting the burdens they incurred from shipmoney. The citizens who took Coventry's petition to London were punctilious about giving gifts, providing entertainment, and following protocol. They even took pains to cultivate the clerks of the council.[137] Upon their arrival they went first to the Lord Keeper for 'his direction', and at his suggestion they revised their petition before submitting it to the council.[138] Having discovered that the Lord Privy Seal was acting as an advocate for the sheriff of Warwickshire, they sought to learn how this had happened.[139] Preventing powerful opposition was as important as cultivating influential support.

Choice of a patron depended very much on particular circumstances. Exeter looked to their steward 'high Chamberlain' Pembroke rather than to the earl of Bedford who was Lord Lieutenant and their aide in many matters.[140] Although the Lord Lieutenants had no technical responsibility in regard to shipmoney, some communities nevertheless addressed them. The earl of Warwick, one of the Lord Lieutenants for Essex and one who had himself resisted payment of shipmoney until threatened with the loss of office, informed the council in April 1637 of the reasons why many of the gentry of the county were 'backward'.[141] Several Somerset communities relied on Phelips who used his connections in their behalf instead of going directly to the Lord Lieutenant or another great man.[142] Lord Montagu's connections with the court through his brother, the earl of Manchester who was Lord Privy Seal and a Privy Councillor enhanced his value as an intermediary to his Northamptonshire neighbours.[143]

Most of the letters or petitions to the Privy Council, threats of litigation, resorts to violence, and verbal protests about shipmoney sought to reduce assessments rather than to deny them or raise legal questions. Contemporaries monitored the way that both their neighbours and those in other counties responded. They knew that some people – Twysden's mother was one – did not pay.[144] People were also aware that some who paid did not necessarily do so immediately. Twysden reports that although no one in Kent refused the 1635 writ 'peremptoryly', Mr Richard Spencer, younger son of Lord Spencer of Northamptonshire, 'did long stand out, being sick or one some other excuses styll put of ye undersherif who was sent to him ... tyll not long before Christmas 1636 a friend of hys dyd pay ye money ... both wth out hys [Spencer's] will and knowledge'.[145] Some expressed their discontent by withholding payments until they were faced with distraint.[146] Some chose to lose property rather than pay; others submitted after attempting to intimidate the officers charged with making the seizures.[147]

Stories circulated about demonstrations against shipmoney that did not involve withholding monies assessed. Robert Ryece told John Winthrop that the king 'was exceedinge angry for his badde entertaynement' during the summer progress of 1636. A sheriff (Ryece thought in Shropshire) 'had but 10 men and never a gentleman with hym, but every gentleman was from his howse, and in all places where the K[ing] shoolde lodge the goodman gone, none at home but the wyfe, with abondance of all sortes of victualls and servants. Heere formerly was Benevolences and shipmoney denyed, which some construed was the cawse of every mans generall absence'.[148] Shipmoney was an issue of sufficient significance that gentlemen might wish to communicate their unhappiness about it to the king. The amounts that ultimately reached the Treasurer of the Navy do not provide an accurate indication of popular response to the levy.

The rhetoric with which some individuals accompanied their resistance is likewise deceptive since many of the most biting attacks on the levy came in the heat of confrontation with a sheriff, bailiff or constable or among a congenial and disrespectful crowd in the local alehouse. Libellous statements like that of the Gloucester woman and her son who complained of shipmoney and wished the king were dead if he must have all and the Northumbrian man who claimed that the king was no better than a beggar expressed discontent without seeking to obtain relief.[149] Apart from notorious troublemakers few people accompanied fearlessly voiced views with similarly daring conduct, but not all who did not pay explained their action. Correspondents reported the remarks they heard just as they noted cases of nonpayment. Like some of the battles over religious conformity, proceedings regarding shipmoney became a prime topic of discussion.

The English paid particular attention to questions about the lawfulness of the levy. After hearing some doubts about its legality, Charles in December 1635 only a few months after he had issued writs to extend shipmoney to the entire kingdom asked the judges to attest to his authority to ask for the funds. A little more than a year later, citing his desire to remove any grounds for resistance, he requested that they deliver a formal opinion on the matter. One consideration prompting him to act may been a tract, circulating in manuscript that maintained that shipmoney was contrary to Magna Carta, the Petition of Right, various statutes and common law in addition to being a cause of the decay of trade, decline of rents, and burdens to the subjects.[150]

Charles was also angry about opposition to shipmoney among the nobility. Lord Saye was challenging the crown's proceedings in court through a well-publicized suit against the sheriff of Lincolnshire and a constable there who had distrained his property.[151] In January the earl of Warwick had personally appealed to the king to call a Parliament and in so doing had implicitly if not explicitly posed questions about the legitimacy of shipmoney.[152] Although the earl of Danby had not mentioned shipmoney a month earlier when he had urged the summoning of Parliament, his plea and the rumours that other nobles were also disturbed by the absence of parliaments and the continuation of extra-parliamentary levies for defence seemed to challenge shipmoney.[153]

Charles, having asked the judges for an opinion, took care to see that their response was widely publicized. Lord Keeper Coventry reminded them just prior to their going on circuit in February that they should take special care at the assizes to exhort people to pay shipmoney.[154] Observers followed these proceedings closely and obtained copies of the king's queries, the judges' answer and the statements made at the assizes.[155] Francis Cheynell, who expected that Sir Gervase Clifton had already 'received exact information of my L. Keepers speech concerninge the payment of shippemoney', sent an account of Judge Jones's remarks that was as long and detailed as his memory could provide and as, he thought, the 'state of the businesse doth require'. He reported that Jones 'did runne over ye heads of my Lord Keepers speech and make divers additions of his owne'.[156]

Some observers found that the judicial opinion satisfied their doubts, but for some that statement stirred new financial and political anxieties.[157] Twysden knew of people who thought that the king should have taken the question of shipmoney to Parliament since 'this was ye greatest cause according to ye general opynion of the world was ever herd out of Parlyament in England'.[158] In his commonplace book where he noted these views, he entered his prediction that the 'common sort of people' who felt loss of money far more than any other loss of liberty would have much to say in the next months. He believed that lawyers 'who were agaynst ye writ made considerations of far greater consequence'.[159]

Twysden's observations proved true the following autumn when the crown prosecuted Buckinghamshire gentleman John Hampden in the Exchequer for refusing to pay 20s in shipmoney. The trial which may have resulted from negotiations with Lord Saye who was pressing for a hearing of the issue came at a time when shipmoney was no longer a novelty. Hampden, like Saye, a Puritan and a director of the Providence Island Company, had been returned at the top of a list of delinquents by sheriff Sir Peter Temple who was Saye's nephew.[160] By initiating proceedings against Hampden, the crown pre-empted Saye and had its way in defining the question and determining circumstances of the trial. Yet balancing the advantages of resolving legal questions concerning shipmoney were the disadvantages attendant upon the airing of debate about it.

Like the proceedings against Prynne, Burton, and Bastwick five months before, Hampden's case captured public attention in London. 'The busines nowe talkt on in towne is all about the Question of the shipp monye', wrote Sir Thomas Knyvett on 11 November 1637, a week after the trial had begun.[161] So many people wanted to see what happened that space in the court was at a premium. As Knyvett ruefully told his wife, he had missed 'the first in the kings part ... Although I was up by peepe of the day to that purpose, I was so farre from getting into the roome that I could not get neer the doore by 2 or 3 yards, the crowd was so great'.[162] Hampden's lawyers also attracted multitudes. Woodforde noted that he 'gott into the Cheqr Chamber though with some danger in the crowd' to hear the second day of St John's argument.[163]

Those in London who were able to attend or to obtain accounts of the trial reported the latest developments to friends and relatives throughout the country. Although St John addressed his arguments to the judges, not the crowd, he made points that the public appreciated. After defining the difficult question which the king's shipmoney writ raised by 'altering of the Property of the subjects Goods without their consent', yet doing this 'for a thing so necessary as the defence of the kingdom both at land and sea', St John cited statute after statute to show why the money could not be laid without consent of the subjects in Parliament.[164] Knyvett who had not heard him in person described him as having 'argued for the subject very bould[ly] and bravely'.[165] At the opening, according to Woodforde's sources, the barrister 'was much applauded and hummed by the bystanders, though my Lord [Chief Justice of Common Pleas] Finch signified his displeasure for it'.[166] By 30 November Hawkins who was sending the earl of Leicester accounts of the proceedings speculated that if Holborne did as well as St John in defending Hampden and if the attorney did no better than the solicitor had for the king, the question would be left 'more doubtfull then it was at first'.[167] Observers, he said, disagreed in predicting how the judges might rule.[168]

Only two weeks before the proceedings in the Exchequer began, John Burgh wrote to Lord Scudamore that people 'for the most part submitt' to 'the strong currant of the present tyme'. Despite the sums being required and the English being unaccustomed to such payments, 'they onely privately breathe out a little discontented humor and lay downe theire purses'. Burgh thought that 'the great tax of the shipp money is so well digested (the honor of the busines sinking now into apprehension and amongst most wynning an affection to it)' that shipmoney would become 'perpetuall'. Anyone who compared the burden from shipmoney with what people paid elsewhere should, he noted, have little complaint.[169] Like the king and some of his councillors and judges, Burgh failed to understand the difference in perspective between rulers and ruled. To those who are taxed the knowledge that others are taxed more is irrelevant. Beneath compliance with commands grumbling and resentment can fester so that a regime's stability can be more apparent than real.

Hampden's trial revealed some of the political costs of shipmoney. As questions about the legitimacy of the levy were raised, collections sagged. Sheriffs found that people were hesitant to pay while the case was pending. With this, like local disputes, they wanted to wait until a decision had been reached.[170] St John offered legal grounds for justifying resistance, and rumours circulated that the judges would not be unanimous.[171] The release of the opinions one or two at a time between February and May added to talk and kept the issue in the public eye.[172] Partisans rejoiced or lamented according to their preferences as the judges announced their views. In contrast to 'Judge Jones [who] fluttered in his argument, meteor like hunge between heaven and earth and yet in the end concluded against Mr Hampden', Woodforde noted that Hutton was 'a man of courage' who 'delivered his opinion freely and playnely against the businesse, shewing it contrary to the lawes of the Realme, and answered the argument brought on the other side with much applause of the people.'[173] Correspondents tried to obtain copies of these and other documents from Hampden's case just as they did speeches from Parliament and state occasions.[174] Dugdale told Sir Simon Archer that Croke's opinion which may have been especially sought after since he, like Hutton, had found for Hampden was selling at 10s.[175]

When all the opinions had been delivered, Hutton and Croke were in the minority. The majority ruled unequivocally for the crown.[176] Charles took advantage of that to insist upon payment. The matter was presumably settled, but contemporaries were not sure. Although the king had 'won' the case, his judges had not been unanimous. Sheriffs reported in May that some individuals were citing the opinions of Croke and Hutton as reasons for not paying.[177] Burgh who had been confident before the trial that shipmoney was on the way to becoming perpetual told Scudamore in June when new writs were issued that he did not 'dare' to guess what reaction there would be.[178] The proceedings against Hampden made people conscious that the levy raised questions beyond those of equity and jurisdiction that had dominated much of the discussion about it on the local level. The outcome seemed to jeopardize the protection that people thought they had obtained with the king's assent to the Petition of Right a decade earlier. Property was not sacrosanct if the king could take it to provide for the defence of the kingdom.[179] Hampden, Saye, and their friends had added these legal grievances to those political and religious charges they already held against a regime they believed was leading the English Church to Rome and ruin. Although set apart from most of their contemporaries by their anger and their commitment to working to prevent a course of developments that they feared, this small group played an important role in offering an interpretation of events different from that coming from the royal court.[180]

The decision that upheld the shipmoney writs removed ambiguities about those obligations. Individuals could not defy that ruling without also disobeying law and betraying their loyalty to the king, yet the burden of shipmoney was as great as ever. It became no lighter because it was legitimate. The unbending attitude of councillors and their supporters itself caused antagonism. Dr Sibthorpe believed that he had incurred the animosity of his Northamptonshire neighbours in part through his vigorous advocacy of shipmoney.[181] The earl of Strafford, perhaps unknowingly, reaped the same reward for seeing to it that his fellow Yorkshireman, Sir Hugh Cholmley, was brought to answer for 'refusing to pay shipmoney' which, Cholmley noted, carried 'the whole liberty of Whitby Strand after' him. Cholmley resented this and seems as a result to have become more determined to stand up for rights which he felt were being threatened.[182] Neither those who were responsible for collection nor those from whom money was due were convinced that Charles and his advisers realized what shipmoney cost the subjects. Although both sheriffs and the council used compromise in the settlement of disputes, the parties involved were not always able to appreciate the extent to which the crown was yielding.[183] Some people seemed more able to win abatement of their rates than did others.[184] Apparent instances of unfairness aroused a sense of grievance.

Charles's request for reduced amounts in 1638 brought some relief, but in 1639 when he asked for sums equivalent to those of earlier years, more withheld payment.[185] Uneasiness about his war against the Scots and the additional charges associated with that enterprise gave them added reason for limiting their contributions to shipmoney at that time. The extent to which people paid even in 1639 suggests that their protests exaggerate their complaints, but considered in isolation from other evidence neither payments nor protests can provide a reliable measure of political opinion. The earl of Warwick who had begun by challenging shipmoney on principle and had incorporated his opposition to the policy in his appeal for a Parliament in January 1636/7 had, when the council confronted him later that spring, modified his stand and turned to raising questions about rating and administration. Under pressure he thought it expedient to change his conduct though he had not revised his views.[186] People of lesser status and courage were not prepared to incur the risks incumbent upon speaking freely. Sir Robert Phelips avoided the problem. Adopting the rhetoric of obedience and service to the crown, he championed custom, equity, and aggrieved neighbours in ways that obstructed collection if they did not actually deny payments.[187] Twysden who was outwardly compliant confessed that he did not reveal his true opinion about shipmoney to Sir Henry Vane.[188]

Shipmoney may have moved few individuals to revolution, but it gave greater numbers reasons for disliking if not distrusting the policies promulgated by Charles and his council. Their passive submission to royal authority became more grudging as they saw the majority of the judges rule against Hampden and found themselves facing annual writs for shipmoney. Their resentment of shipmoney reached a critical point when the king went to war against the Scots in 1639 without calling Parliament and began to prosecute sheriffs more vigorously for failing to collect their county's quota from an increasingly reluctant public.[189]

For his efforts to improve England's defences during the 1630s King Charles paid a political price that was only partially evident at the time. His people did not challenge the need for defence, but they were uneasy about the king's hesitance to oppose Popery at home and abroad, reluctant to pay shipmoney and other military charges, resentful of inequitable assessments, disturbed by procedures that did not always respect local custom, and conscious that the king's efforts touched legal questions about their rights and royal power that had been raised in Parliament in 1628.

The rhetoric of the king's councillors and judges informed people that if they did not obey his orders, they were disloyal and would pay the appropriate penalties. In defining the choice as one between obedience and disobedience, the crown appeared to ignore the grievances that individuals experienced and for which they wanted relief. Not wanting to defy royal authority, they were at times bitter about the difficulties of obtaining resolution for their problems. Although both local officials and the board itself did hear and redress many complaints, they also treated some persons with severity and denounced some harshly.

Those who resisted shipmoney and military obligations often had personal reasons for doing so. Rivalries and disputes within and between communities played an important part in both the administration and response to the demands of defence. The expected consequences of open opposition meant that people sometimes used indirect rather than direct means of questioning the king's right to their money or service. Most who did raise legal points submitted when confronted, but a few persisted and in so doing kept these issues in the public eye. The crown's prosecution of John Hampden for his refusal to pay shipmoney made that levy a national issue. Even though the majority of the judges ruled for the king, the dissenting opinions and the arguments of Hampden's defenders gave the English an alternative view of law and justice. The immediate impact of the case was limited, but it added to Charles's difficulties when he went to war against the Scots in 1639. By assuming that money was more important than principle and heeding rhetoric more than action, he underestimated the opposition to military charges and overestimated that to shipmoney in 1640. He failed to understand that his subjects were not convinced by his explanations of the necessity of defence. They perceived that he was putting his interests ahead of theirs. Although most had complied with his demands during the 1630s, many had been loath to do so.

NOTES

1   See S. Adams, 'Foreign policy and the Parliaments of 1621 and 1624', in Sharpe, *Faction*, pp. 139–71.

2   R. Ruigh, *The Parliament of 1624: Politics and Foreign Policy* (Cambridge, Mass.: Harvard University Press, 1971).

3   See L. Boynton, *The Elizabethan Militia* (London: Routledge & Kegan Paul, 1967).

4   Contemporaries were not precise in their usage of the term 'muster' and I shall use it here to include both the muster proper, the inspection of arms, and the training or exercises. See Boynton, *Militia*, p. 13.

5   See A. Hassell Smith, 'Militia rates and militia statutes, 1558–1603', in *The English Commonwealth*, eds P. Clark, A. G. R. Smith, and N. Tyacke (Leicester: Leicester University Press, 1979), pp. 93–110; also R. Ashton, *The English Civil War: Conservatism and Revolution, 1603–1649* (London: Weidenfeld & Nicolson, 1978), pp. 54–5.

6   See C. Russell, *Parliaments and Politics*, ch. 6. Also see *CD 1628*.

7   See E. R. Foster, 'Petitions and the Petition of Right', *JBS*, vol. 14. no. 1 (1974), p. 22.

8   Concerning the traditional association of Parliament with war see Russell, 'Nature of Parliament', p. 129.

9   e.g. PRO, C.115/N.30; Phelips MSS, DDPH 212/8; C1 C 27; C1 C 188, which in addition to the news it contains, says that *The Swedish Intelligencer* is being sent (1632) STC 23522; HA 9598; *Numb. Primo. The Principall Passages of Germany, Italy, France and other places* (1636), STC 4293; *Diatelesma Nu. E. The Moderne History of the World, expressing the principall Passages of the Christian Countries* (1637), STC 4292.

10 See A. Gill, *The New Starr of the North* (1632), STC 11875; F. Schloer, *The Death of the two Renowned Kings of Sweden and Bohemia*, a sermon preached at the Hague (London, 1633), STC 21819; J. Russell, *The Two Famous Pitcht Battels of Lypsich and Lutzen* (Cambridge, 1634), STC 21460; *The Great and Famous Battel of Lutzen* (1633, trans. out of the French), STC 12534. Also see Birch, Vol. 2, pp. 200, 203, 208–12, 225–6; C1 C 638; M. Breslow, *A Mirror of England* (Cambridge, Mass.: Harvard University Press, 1970), ch. 6.

11 Yonge, ff. 48–50.

12 Boynton, *Militia*, pp. 263 ff.

13 e.g. W. Bariffe, *Military Discipline* (1635), STC 1506; HEH, MS HM 27514, G. M. [Gervase Markham?], 'The Muster-master' (a small quarto MS of 38 leaves). This tract has been edited by C. L. Hamilton in *Camden Miscellany*, Vol. xxvi, Camden Fourth Series, vol. 14 (1975), pp. 49–76; *Instructions for Musters and Armes, and the Use thereof*. By Order from his Majesties most honourable Privie Council (27 July 1631), STC 7684.

14 SP 16/303/5; 16/311/59; PC 2/45, p. 284; Whiteway, f. 77v.

15 e.g. W. C. Trevelyan (ed.), *Trevelyan Papers*, part 3, Camden Society, vol. 105 (1872), pp. 191 ff; *Barrington Family Letters*, no. 50.

16 See e.g. *Two Famous Sea-Fights* (London, 1639), STC 22132; T. Heywood, *A True Description of his majesties Royall Ship* (London, 1637), STC 13367; C. D. Penn, *The Navy under the Early Stuarts* (Leighton Buzzard: The Faith Press, 1913).

17 There were exceptions, e.g. the earl of Warwick.

18 See S. Adams, 'Spain or the Netherlands? The dilemmas of early Stuart foreign policy', in Tomlinson (ed.), *Before the Civil War*, pp. 91, 100–1; K. Sharpe, 'Faction at the court', pp. 44–6.

19 See above.

20 e.g. R. Fanshawe, 'An Ode upon the occasion of His Majesties Proclamation in the year 1630', quoted in C. V. Wedgwood, *Poetry and Politics under the Stuarts* (Cambridge: Cambridge University Press, 1961), p. 41; T. Carew, *Coleum Britanicum* (1634); STC 4618; J. Shirley, *The Triumph of Peace* (1633), STC 2249; cf. T. Heywood, *Royall Ship*, and T. Heywood, *The Royall King and the Loyall Subject* (London, 1637), STC 13364. Also see Anselment, 'Clarendon'.

21 *The Bible-Battells or the Sacret Art Military For the rightly wageing of warre according to Holy Writ* (1629), STC 1926. See also *The converted Mans New Birth* (1629), STC 565; S. Bachiler, *The Camp Royall* (1629), STC 1107; John Davenport, *A Royall Edict for Military Exercises. Published in*

a Sermon preached to Captaines and Gentlemen that Exercise armes in the Artillery Garden (London, 1629), STC 6313; also John Randol, *Noble Blastus. The Honor of a Lord Chamberlaine and a Good Bedchamberman or the Courtier justified in Conditions of Peace.* Sermon preached 27 March 1631 before Sir Lucius Cary at Burford Church, Oxon. (1633); STC 20684; Thos. Palmer, *Bristolls Military Garden*, a sermon (London, 1635), STC 19155.

22   e.g. *CD 1628*, Vol. 2, pp. 80, 87; Vol. 3, pp. 327, 373, 629; Vol. 4, pp. 290, 293.

23   *CD 1628*, Vol. 2, p. 254; cf. p. 80.

24   F. H. Relf (ed.), *Notes of Debates in the Lords ... 1621, 1625, and 1628*, Camden Third Series, vol. 42 (1929), p. 203. Concerning the importance of the issue of arbitrary imprisonment see J. Guy, 'The origins of the Petition of Right reconsidered', *Historical Journal*, vol. 25, no. 2 (1982), pp. 289–312.

25   Relf, *Lords Debates 1628*, pp. 174–5. Conrad Russell brought this reference to my attention.

26   Relf, *Lords Debates 1628*, pp. 82–3, 178–9.

27   In addition to the notes and letters in the Privy Council Registers there are many copies of correspondence concerning musters in manuscript collections from the period (e.g. the Letter Book of Thomas Howard, first earl of Suffolk (Phillips MS 3863) (Yale film); Hastings Correspondence (Huntingon Library), e.g. HA 13021; HA 9726; HA 10620).

28   Concerning the constables see T. G. Barnes, *Somerset 1625–1640* (Cambridge, Mass.: Harvard University Press), p. 121.

29   STT 2315; cf. the resistance of gentry at Salford in D. P. Carter, 'The "Exact Militia" in Lancashire, 1625–1640', *Northern History*, vol. 11 (1975), p. 94. (Anthony Fletcher brought this article to my attention.) Also see A. Hassell Smith, 'Rates', p. 96.

30   e.g. PC 2/42, pp. 425, 426, 460; PC 2/44, pp. 291, 294.

31   SP 16/250/33 and PC 2/44, p. 49; also SP 16/181/4; 16/150/61; 6/145/31; Clark, 'Thomas Scott', pp. 23–4.

32   Phelips, MSS, DDPH 221/23; see also DDPH 212/5. Barnes, *Somerset*, pp. 103–4, 122, 266–71.

33   SP 16/166/52; 16/181/57.

34   SP 16/181/57. Concerning Grenville, see above. See also the case of Sir William Faunt and his grievance against the earl of Huntingdon, HA 3150; HA 5541; HA 2296 (several years earlier Faunt had been returned for refusing to pay muster masters' fees, SP 16/225/67).

35   Knightley (SP 16/302/13); the description fits either father or son, both of whom were Richard Knightley (Keeler, p. 243; *DNB*). Yelverton (SP 16/301/43 and below). Also see Boynton, *Militia*, pp. 257 ff.

36   See Ashton, *Civil War*, p. 57; also see Hassell Smith, 'Rates'.

37   Following its inquiries in December 1629, the Privy Council received reports indicating that practices varied considerably from county to county, for example, SP 16/160/10; 16/160/11; 16/161/5; 16/161/7; 16/161/20.

38   Concerning previous complaints see Ashton, *Civil War*, p. 58. There were

also debates about the necessity of having a professional, an outsider, to train local forces. See Gervase Markham's tract of 1630, 'The Muster-master'.

39 See below.

40 SP 16/147/40.

41 SP 16/531/65. See also Lord Poulett's description of the situation in Somerset (SP 16/170/19; 16/184/80).

42 SP 16/340/45.

43 SP 16/211/85.

44 Concerning Shropshire see below. Also see Shropshire Record Office, Ludlow MSS, Box 293, nos 251, 139. There was opposition to charges in a number of towns. See e.g. M. G. Hobson and H. E. Salter (eds), *Oxford Council Acts, 1626–1665*, Oxford Historical Society, vol. 95 (1933), pp. 38–9; SP 16/215/84; 16/161/7.

45 SP 16/161/27; 16/176/19; 16/281/14.

46 SP 16/225/67. This was one of a number of incidents in which Haselrig (d. 1661) was involved. See also SP 16/231/59; 16/305/57; 16/351/91; HA 8538; *DNB*. He was brought before the High Commission in 1634/5. (The cause is not clear. See e.g. SP 16/261/154; 16/261/211; 16/261/271b). See also his later complaint against Laud (*CSPDom. 1641–3*, p. 547).

47 They also noted that there were castles in need of repair and furnishings (SP 16/151/61).

48 SP 16/181/11.

49 M. Weinstock (ed.), *Weymouth and Melcombe Regis Minute Book, 1625–1660*, Dorset Record Society Publications, vol. 1 (1964), 9 July 1632.

50 SP 16/148/17. Concerning grand juries, see J. Morrill, *The Cheshire Grand Jury, 1625–1649, a Social and Administrative Study* (Leicester, Department of English Local History, Occasional Papers, Third Series, no. 1 (1976); J. Cockburn, *A History of English Assizes* (Cambridge: Cambridge University Press, 1972), pp. 111–14.

51 SP 16/148/17.

52 El 7631. The Privy Council's letters concerning the musters appeared just after the presentment was made (PC 2/44/536–8); cf. Rye, *Norfolk*, pp. 194–7, 199–203. For background to the presentment, see below. My account of this incident appeared in 'Politics without Parliament: the dispute about muster masters' fees in Shropshire in the 1630s', *Huntington Library Quarterly*, vol. 45, no. 4, (1982), pp. 271–84. See also C. Hamilton, 'The Shropshire muster-master's fee', *Albion*, vol. 2, no. 1 (1970), pp. 26–34.

53 El 7631.

54 cf. Grenville's comment about his Cornish opponents in 1629 (SP 16/147/46). Laud used similar terms to describe undesirable clergymen (Laud, *Works*, Vol. 7, p. 26).

55 The presentment had referred to him as unnecessary.

56 This was during the reign of James I. This account of the proceedings comes from that sent to the earl of Bridgewater by Richard Harris, clerk of the peace (El 7632); see T. G. Barnes, *The Clerk of the Peace in Caroline Somerset* (Leicester, Occasional Paper, no. 14, 1961).

57 *List of Sheriffs for England and Wales from the earliest times to A.D. 1831* (PRO, Lists and Indexes, no. 9, 1898, p. 119; Keeler, p. 142). He was not the Sir John Corbet who was imprisoned for resisting the Forced Loan. See also *DNB.*

58 SP 16/230/4.

59 El 7647.

60 El 7646.

61 See above.

62 El 7637; concerning Ludlow's arrears, Corporation MSS, Box 293, nos. 251, 139.

63 El 7649.

64 El 7673; 7679–80.

65 El 7624, 7625.

66 El 7625; 7651; 7673; Ludlow, Box 293, no. 251; cf. how Weymouth and Melcombe Regis reacted to possible pressure (see above).

67 Lord Lieutenants, Markham said, were appointing as muster masters men who wanted profit rather than the most worthy of the captains who would be men 'of faire vertue, good Birthe, temperate, and myld Nature of great skill, highe valor, and deepe Judgement'. By this means the lieutenants were making the position worthless (Markham, 'Muster-master', p. 61).

68 El 7094; also 7081, 7082.

69 El 7674; also PC 2/43, pp. 398–9.

70 El 7631.

71 El 7658; cf. J. T. Cliffe, *The Yorkshire Gentry: From the Reformation to the Civil War* (London: Athlone Press, 1696), p. 303; SP 16/247/26. If Stapleton had invoked Magna Carta in his refusal to pay muster masters' fees, the testimony of the constable does not report this. Lord Lieutenant Wentworth, however, denounced Stapleton as being 'as arrant a saucy Magna Charta man as all in the Country' (Cliffe, *Yorkshire*, p. 303).

72 The clerk of the peace, who wrote to Bridgewater much sooner after the sessions than Tourneur did, does not indicate if or how Corbet related the Petition of Right which he had read to the issue at hand; El 7632.

73 See E. R. Foster, 'Printing the Petition of Right', *Huntington Library Quarterly*, vol. 38, no. 1 (1974), pp. 81–3; E. R. Foster, 'Petitions and the Petition of Right', *JBS*, vol. 14, no. 1 (1974), pp. 21–45, esp. pp. 21–3; also *CD 1629*, pp. 4–6. The city of York purchased three copies of the book of statutes that included the Petition (STC 9510) in 1633 (City Library, Chamberlains Accounts, 1633).

74 El 7647; also 7658. This sounds as if Tourneur had been an MP in 1628, but there is no evidence that he was.

75 El 7647.

76 El 7638.

77 El 7644.

78 El 7628–30, 7634–6, 7643–4, 7645, 7652, 7664–9; see also Corbet's petition to the House of Commons in 1640 (El 7670).

79 El 7656, 7639.

80 El 7671, 7680.

81 SP 16/225/67. See above.

82 El 7676.

83 e.g. PC 2/42, p. 550; 2/43, p. 46; 2/43, p. 333; also SP 16/328/62; also see C. D. Penn, *The Navy*. Fletcher says that awareness of need limited resistance to shipmoney in Sussex (*County Community*, p. 208).

84 *CD 1628*, Vol. 4, pp. 200–4, 316–18, 470–1.

85 *CD 1628*, Vol. 2, p. 249–50; see also Fletcher, *County Community*, p. 189.

86 *CD 1628*, Vol. 2, p. 144. See A. H. Lewis, *A Study of Elizabethan Shipmoney 1558–1603* (Philadelphia, Pa: University of Pennsylvania, 1928).

87 See Boynton, *Militia*, p. 166; Barnes, *Somerset*, p. 204; Gardiner, *History of England*, Vol. 6, pp. 132–3.

88 The crown recalled its letters for shipmoney in 1628 immediately after issuing them. See R. Swales, 'The ship money levy of 1628', *BIHR*, vol. 50, no. 122 (1977), pp. 164–76.

89 See Hassell Smith, 'Rates', pp. 106–8. Concerning shipmoney see, P. Lake, 'The collection of ship money in Cheshire during the sixteen-thirties: a case study of relations between central and local government', *Northern History*, vol. 17 (1981), pp. 44–71. I read this article after having written the bulk of this chapter but found its argument and information both reconfirming and stimulating my own. See also, E. Marcotte, 'Shrieval administration of ship money in Cheshire, 1637: limitations of early Stuart governance', *Bulletin of the John Rylands Library*, vol. 58 (1975–6), pp. 137–72, who de-emphasizes the political significance of opposition. M. D. Gordon, 'The collection of ship-money in the reign of Charles I', *TRHS*, Third Series, vol. 4 (1910), pp. 141–62; Gordon's figures have recently been challenged.

90 Kent Archives Office, U 47/47 Z1, p. 189.

91 See R. Cust, 'The Forced Loan and English politics, 1626–8', PhD thesis, University of London, 1984; also Cust, 'Charles I, the Privy Council, and the Forced Loan', *JBS*, vol. 24, no. 2 (1985), pp. 208–35.

92 See Guy, 'Origins'.

93 C1 C 307, 387, and 201; Whiteway, ff. 109v–110; HMC, *Gawdy*, p. 150, 156; Coventry, MS A.35, Book of Matters touching shipmoney (Yale film), f. 15. Conrad Russell brought this book to my attention.

94 HEH, Stowe-Temple, Shipmoney Papers. A selection of these manuscripts has been printed, *Ship Money Papers and Richard Grenville's Notebook*, eds Carol G. Bonsey and J. G. Jenkins, Bucks Record Society, vol. 13 (1965). The printed collection omits sections from the MSS without so indicating. Others of Sir Peter's shipmoney papers are among the Temple Correspondence, STT Box 10. Concerning the papers of Sir Thomas Cholmondley, sheriff of Cheshire 1637–8, see E. Marcotte, 'Cheshire'.

95 Cliffe, *Yorkshire*, p. 253.

96 e.g. STT 913, 2059.

97 SP 16/346/108; cf. 16/311/30; 16/331/26.

98 SP 16/303/371; see also 16/386/52; 16/282/14.

99 Kent Archives Office, U 47/47 Z1, p. 194, also pp. 195–6. See also SP 16/301/76; 16/347/23; 16/357/2.

100   Those sheriffs who were relative strangers to their shires at the time of their
          appointment were at a disadvantage in this and many other aspects of
          their jobs.
101   El 6976. See above concerning Harris's part in the muster master
          controversy. He also attacked the high constable, who was the principal
          assessor in this area.
102   e.g. SP 16/317/94; 16/306/63; 16/312/37; see also 16/370/41; also see
          Twysden's remarks about inequities (Kent Archives Office U47/47 Z1, pp.
          197–8). In Hallingbury Magna, in Essex, parishioners who may have been
          tenants of the Barringtons claimed that collector John Stacey had not only
          threatened those who would not join him that he would rate them higher
          than before but that he had actually executed his threat (SP 16/321/24;
          Barrington Family Letters, p. 4)
103   Woodforde, p. 497; also SP 16/346/107; 16/371/65; 16/367/7.
104   Holles: SP 16/341/38 and also above. Saye: Rous, p. 85; SP 16/362/31;
          16/362/76; Birch, Vol. 2 278; Yonge, ff. 64, 71. See N. Bard, 'The ship
          money case and William Fiennes, Viscount Saye and Sele', *BIHR*, vol. 50,
          no. 122 (1977), pp. 177–84. Also see W. Willcox, *Gloucestershire: A Study
          in Local Government, 1590–1640* (New Haven, Conn.: Yale University
          Press, 1940), pp. 128–30, a reference I owe to Conrad Russell. See also SP
          16/332/6; 16/331/40; 16/331/45.
105   Phelips MSS, DDPH 223/56; DDPH 223/58.
106   The dependency of bailiffs and constables upon men who were disinclined
          to co-operate made the sheriff's work especially difficult. SP 16/395/59;
          also see 16/318/6; 16/336/78; 16/417/52.
107   SP 16/357/139 and 140; 16/319/29; 16/320/18; 16/321/24; 16/325/4;
          16/342/72; 16/317/46; 16/318/6; 16/417/47.
108   SP 16/354/48; 16/366/5. This is Sir Paul Harris, not Richard Harris, clerk
          of the peace, mentioned above (see *List of Sheriffs*, p. 120).
109   R. Howell, *Newcastle upon Tyne and the Puritan Revolution* (Oxford:
          Oxford University Press, 1967), pp. 61–2, 115–17.
110   In 1638 the council heard charges that the sheriffs of Essex, Oxfordshire,
          Northamptonshire, Gloucestershire, and especially Buckinghamshire were
          associated with men who were 'hollow-hearted' to the king (SP 16/386/
          88). Concerning Langdale see Cliffe, *Yorkshire*, p. 315; Irby, see Holmes,
          Lincolnshire, pp. 131 ff.; Denton, see Keeler, pp. 154–5; Poyntz, see SP 16/
          355/79, 90, 105.
111   SP 16/374/1; 16/378/78; cf. the appeal of JPs from the eastern division of
          Northamptonshire, Montague MS 27 (HMC, *Buccleuch*, Vol. 3, pp.
          375–6); also SP 16/300/39; 16/301/98; also petitions from Essex (SP 16/
          357/2) and Chester (16/370/67). See Twysden's remarks about London
          (Kent Archives Office U47/47 Z1, p. 83). Wigan was among the towns
          which mentioned severe outbreaks of plague as a further reason why they
          should pay less shipmoney (SP 16/363/53).
112   SP 16/306/62. Markham, an invalid, was inclined to be contentious (e.g.
          SP 16/312/43; 16/313/50; also 16/149/24 and *DNB*).
113   Holles, no. 228.

114 See below.

115 E1 7239.

116 e.g. in Warwick in 1635–6 (Coventry, f. 15). For other cases see SP 16/304/ 34; 16/357/107; PC 2/46, p. 430; SP 16/381/42; 16/336/17.

117 SP 16/306/57.

118 Montagu MS 27 (HMC, *Buccleuch*, Vol. 3, pp. 375–6); cf. the statement of the Nottinghamshire JPS (SP 16/374/61).

119 Coventry, ff. 19, 24v; also see arguments about purveyance, e.g. SP 16/350/ 37, 16/350/38, 16/351/63.

120 SP 16/297/23 and 16/298/29. Conrad Russell reminded me about this dispute.

121 SP 16/300/67–8.

122 SP 16/370/67; see also Lake, 'Shipmoney'.

123 York City Library, House Books, Vol. 36, ff. 164, 169v, 242v, 289–94v; PC 2/46, p. 247.

124 PC 2/44, p. 347; also SP 16/299/56; 16/371/78.

125 PC 2/44, p. 293; see also p. 295.

126 PC 2/44, p. 327; also SP 16/282/51; PC 2/44, pp, 387–8; SP 16/311/62.

127 Coventry, f. 14v. They recited how he had made direct threats to Coventry but removed the passage from their petition to the Council on the advice of the Lord Keeper and the clerk of the Council who may have feared that the phrases would divert attention from the legal questions in the petition to those of the city's attitude toward the sheriff (ff. 16v–17v).

128 Phelips MSS, DDPH 228/33; also see SP 16/299/57; 16/303/63.

129 Phelips MSS, DDPH 228/31–4; cf. SP 16/380/5.

130 SP 16/345/33; also 16/365/8.

131 Coventry, f. 1; cf. *Oxford Council Acts*, p. 79; also Yonge, ff. 61–61v; SP 16/282/51.

132 Coventry, ff. 12v, 13v, 15v, 21, 22v, 27v.

133 He later described the sheriff as 'much discontented' (Coventry, ff. 14v, 22v, 34).

134 W. L. Sachse (ed.), *Minutes of the Norwich Court of Mayoralty, 1632–35*, Norfolk Record Society, vol. 36 (1967), pp. 189–90; York, House Books, Vol. 36, pp. 257v–9v; also Yonge, ff. 71v.

135 SP 16/341/50. The considerable respect which Knollys enjoyed among his countrymen gave his remarks weight and worried those who believed that the subjects should respond without question to the king's writs.

136 York, Chamberlains Accounts, 1634, f. 36v. It is not always possible to separate shipmoney costs from those the city incurred in other connections.

137 Coventry, ff. 16v, 27v, 30v, 34; cf. York, Chamberlains Accounts, 1634–9.

138 Coventry, ff. 14v, 16v.

139 Coventry, f. 43. They also attempted to ensure that Lord Cottington who at one point spoke against their cause would not 'meddle further' (Coventry, ff. 25v–7v, 42v).

140 Exeter, Act Books, Vol. 8, ff. 18, 22, 82 (Harvard film).

141 PC 2/47, p. 330; Rowe, 'Warwick and shipmoney', pp. 160–3; also below. The Northamptonshire JPs of the eastern division sent a copy of their

petition of October 1635 to their Lord Lieutenant, the earl of Exeter (Montagu MS 27 (HMC, *Buccleuch*, Vol. 3, pp, 375–6).

142   SP 16/333/1.

143   SP 16/350/37; also 16/301/78; 16/347/31; 16/299/1.

144   Twysden says that he persuaded her to pay once for London and once for the country, but 'more than those two tymes she never did' (BL, Add. MS 34163, ff. 79–80v).

145   Kent Archives Office, U47/47 Z1, p. 189, cf. p. 83.

146   SP 16/333/2; 16/350/39.

147   See SP 16/333/2; 16/379/132; 16/337/27; 16/321/76. The sheriff of Norfolk complained that people were putting their property in the names of others so that distraint would be difficult (SP 16/385/1).

148   *WP*, Vol. 3, p. 355. See also Rowe, 'Warwick and shipmoney'; Yonge, f. 64; SP 16/299/1; 16/298/47; 16/317/16; 16/395/40.

149   SP 16/387/64; 16/317/16.

150   Written by Prynne, the tract was printed later, *An Humble Remonstrance to His Majesty against the Tax of Ship-money* (1641), HN 58925, pp. 27–8. The 1643 edition (HN 90816) contains a letter to the reader relating the story of the tract. Internal evidence suggests that the tract may have been composed in the winter of 1636–7; see Lamont, *Prynne*, pp. 23–4.

151   Bard, 'Saye and Sele'; also see above.

152   *CSPVen. 1636–9*, no. 139; also see Rowe, 'Warwick and shipmoney'; and Chapter 1.

153   *CSPVen. 1636–9*, no. 122.

154   *ST*, Vol. 3. pp. 839–46; Coventry had also talked about shipmoney in a similar address in June 1635 (p. 837).

155   Copies survive in a number of manuscript collections, e.g. Phelips MSS, DDPH 212/11; HMC, *Third Report*, p. 74; DeL'Isle, pp. 87, 89. See also Twysden (Kent Archives Office, U47/47 Z1, pp. 102, 105, 106; and Fincham, 'Judges'.

156   C1 C77.

157   e.g. Edward Hyde (HMC, *Sixth Report*, app., p. 281; also A. P. Newton, *The Colonizing Activities of the English Puritans* (New Haven, Conn.: Yale University Press, 1914), pp. 241–3).

158   Twysden (Kent Archives Office, U47/47, Z1, pp. 107, 110; also pp. 199–200); Fincham, 'Judges'. Also F. Jessup, *Sir Roger Twysden, 1597–1672* (New York: Barnes and Noble, 1967; orig. 1965), p. 38 and above.

159   Twysden (Kent Archives Office, U47/47, Z1, p. 110).

160   Bard, 'Saye and Sele', pp. 182–3; also Twysden (Kent Archives Office, U47/47. Z1, pp. 106–7, 197 ff. Concerning Hampden, see *DNB*; P. Zagorin, *The Court and the Country* (New York: Atheneum, 1970), pp. 100–3; HMC, *Gawdy*, p. 164.

161   Knyvett, p. 91, no. 40.

162   ibid.

163   Woodforde, p. 496.

164   *ST*, Vol. 3, p. 864.

165 Knyvett, p. 91, no. 40.

166 Woodforde, p. 496; cf. *DeL'Isle*, p. 132, which describes St John's argument as much as 'expected'.

167 *DeL'Isle*, p. 136.

168 ibid., p. 139; HMC, *Gawdy*, p. 166.

169 PRO, C.115/N.4, no. 8617.

170 SP 16/398/51.

171 e.g. SP 16/386/88; 16/389/124.

172 e.g. PRO, C.115/N.4, nos. 8622–5.

173 Woodforde thanked God for Hutton's courage (p. 497). See also HMC, *Gawdy*, p. 168.

174 Among the earl of Bridgewater's manuscripts are several collections, e.g. El 6977, major opinions, Bramston's placed first, then Finch, but includes Croke and Hutton as well as those judges who found for the king; El 6978, St John's speech; El 7877A, fairly complete with attornies' arguments as well as judges' opinions. See also HM 728, which is fairly full and includes arguments of St John and Littleton; Northumberland MSS, Alnwick Castle (Yale film), Vol. 14, f. 166, brief of Justice Croke's argument; see also HMC, *First Report*, app., pp. 14, 31; *Second Report*, app., pp. 3, 98; *Third Report*, app., pp. 75, 121, 365; also SP 16/413/120.

175 W. Dugdale, *The Life, Diary, and Correspondence of Sir William Dugdale*, ed. Wm. Hamper (London, 1827), no. 23. Dugdale sent a copy borrowed from one of the judge's kinsmen. He thought he might be able to get one cheaper than 10s.

176 See C. Russell, 'The shipmoney judgements of Bramston and Davenport', *EHR*, vol. 77, no. 303 (1962), pp. 312–18; also *ST*, Vol. 3, pp. 1125–251.

177 SP 16/390/116; 16/390/157; see also Knowler, Vol. 2, pp. 169–71; Cockburn, *Assizes*, p. 236.

178 PRO, C.115/N.4, no. 8626.

179 Concerning the impact of the case see also Herbert's objections to Massinger's play, *The King and Subject* in P. Edwards and C. Gibson (eds), *The Plays and Poems of Philip Massinger* (Oxford: Oxford University Press, 1976), Vol. 1, p. xxxix; also J. Adams (ed.), *The Dramatic Revels of Sir Henry Herbert* (New Haven, Conn.: Yale University Press, 1917), p. 22; M. Heineman, *Puritanism and Theatre: Thomas Middleton and Opposition Drama under the Early Stuarts* (Cambridge University Press, 1980), p. 221.

180 Newton, *Puritans*, pp. 242–4. The evidence he cites does not warrant the conclusions he draws.

181 STT 1884.

182 *The Memoirs of Sir Hugh Cholmley* (London: privately printed, 1787), pp. 60–1.

183 See Lake, 'Shipmoney'; also C1 C 202. See Marcotte, 'Cheshire', pp. 159–60.

184 Twysden noted that his mother who was not in London had a disadvantage (Kent Archives Office, U47/47 Z1, p. 83).

185 Gordon, 'Shipmoney'.

186 Rowe, 'Warwick and shipmoney'; also *CSPVen. 1636–9*, no. 139. Also

C. Holmes, 'The county community in Stuart historiography', *JBS*, vol. 19, (1980), p. 66.

187   Barnes, *Somerset*, pp. 216 ff., 242; e.g. Phelips MSS, DDPH 223/58; 223/70–1; also SP 16/365/8.

188   Jessup, *Twysden*, pp. 36–7.

189   See Chapter 5.

4

Projects, Prosecutions and Pompousness

Members of Parliament cited a myriad of projects and procedures in their speeches and petitions about grievances during the parliaments of the 1620s. Over the preceding century with the aid of royal protection inventors or undertakers had developed countless enterprises which reaped profits for them and for the crown while meeting growing consumer demands.[1] The public had mixed feelings about these. Likewise coming under criticism were some official efforts to expand the role of government to maintain social and economic order. People complained not only to Parliament but also to king and council, to the courts, to patrons, and to their neighbours about personal affronts by projectors or royal servants, grants believed unjust or illegal, and abuses or corruption arising from both inaction and action. Many of the items, they noted, had continued in the face of persistent and repeated protests. The Commons asked Charles in 1625 in his first Parliament to respond to the grievances they had presented to his father the year before. In answering he promised to amend grants that were unlawful and suggested that Parliament make reforms where appropriate. Although he defended some patents and practices, he declared that he would try to make modifications where he could.[2] Time would soon prove that instead of remedies his reign would bring more problems.

During the parliaments of the 1620s some of the members had concluded that their grievances were interconnected.[3] Many who did not, recognized the need to be continually vigilant against those who were seeking profit at the expense of others or of the kingdom itself. They did not hesitate to make repeated appeals about procedures they did not like or to seek exemptions from orders or regulations. Through their investigations and impeachments of both projectors and officials the Commons had themselves sought to curtail wrongdoing and provide relief against oppression.[4] Their achievements were limited. Despite their efforts the duke of Buckingham remained in office. His use of his extensive patronage and royal favour disappointed many hopeful of preferment and embittered others who believed themselves victims of his beneficiaries.[5] Only a few of the bills they proposed had become statutes. The most important of these, the Act of Monopolies of 1624, had limited its prohibition to certain kinds of grants. Corporations were exempt.[6] Whether from king, Parliament, council, courts, or elsewhere relief for grievances was more often temporary than permanent and more likely promised than achieved.

When John Felton's knife killed the duke of Buckingham in August 1628, people hoped that a new era in politics would begin.[7] Prominent in their wishes was ending the domination of money in the distribution of favours. The system associated with Buckingham had been characterized by a lack of respect for status, qualifications, and justice that jeopardized the relationships and standards of conduct that had been customary. The king's court was tarnished by disreputable people who behaved in ways that threatened order and decency if not law, liberty, and religion.[8]

Although no one person came to hold the position that Buckingham had held, people soon discovered that money had not lost its sway. The king's strong sense of his own honour and his impatience with criticism meant that he supported councillors who were prepared to strike hard against individuals who appeared to challenge his authority. Thus both those who held high office and those who were far removed from the seats of power might find themselves suffering unnecessarily. Plague, dearth, and unemployment which had periodically troubled the country added to their burdens during these years. Their difficulties in communicating their plight or obtaining sympathy meant that issues which may seem minor in comparison to questions of religion or defence assumed a greater significance than they otherwise might have. Their frustration mounted during the 1630s, and their pleas took on a more serious tone. The king seemed not to understand the causes of their distress. This chapter will discuss such issues. The first section will treat some of the projects by which Charles sought to increase his revenue during the 1630s. The second part will deal with officials, institutions, and practices associated with his government that evoked complaints from those who encountered them.

Charles's dissolution of his third Parliament in March 1628/9 meant that he would have to raise the funds that he needed from other sources. The five subsidies voted by the first session of that Parliament would not last long. People expected that he would continue to collect tonnage and poundage even though Parliament had not acted upon that, and they watched to see what other schemes for filling his coffers would follow.[9]

Before winter had come, they discovered that one of these would be distraint of knighthood. The council dusted and put into effect the plans it had made but not used in 1627 to proceed against those who had failed to respond to the summons to become knights at the king's coronation.[10] Because James I had not enforced similar orders, memories of what had been tradition were faint, and complaints arose soon after the crown began demanding answers from men who had not appeared. As Secretary Dorchester noted, people did not challenge the legality of the proceedings. They instead cited reasons why they should not be fined for delinquency.[11]

Individuals continued to point out why they were not liable for knighthood even after the council altered its tactics and replaced the commission of its own members with separate commissions of local lords and gentlemen for each county.[12] Whiteway concluded that the commissioners had 'raised little money' when they sat in Dorchester on 15 September 1630 'for most men made excuses'.[13] Many objected that they were either under age at the time of the coronation or did not have the requisite amount of land for knighthood.[14] Others pleaded that they were in royal service at the time.[15] The crown won few friends by its errors or oversights. Even if individuals knew that they had evidence to prove they were not delinquent as charged, they nevertheless had to take responsibility for convincing the commissioners that their stand was legitimate.

Those who had unknowingly neglected to become knights likewise had reason to be unhappy.[16] They were annoyed at the notion that they should be fined for oversights committed some years earlier. Lord Montagu, a commissioner in Northamptonshire, doubted the king's wisdom in insisting on collecting revenue rather than considering the intentions and loyalty of those to be distrained. 'I find that many gentlemen that were forward in the loan and privy seals troubled that no more respect is had of them than of those that refused. I can say little to it', Montagu wrote to his brother, 'but I would it might be well considered of'.[17] Others agreed that some individuals deserved to be relieved from penalties in this instance. Clothier Christopher Potticary thought he was one. He explained that he kept 1000 people in work and had paid the loans 'being 5 subsidies'.[18]

People objected not only to the fact of the fined but also to their amounts. Walter Yonge who was not himself named as a delinquent declared them 'grevances [rather] than fynes'. 'I conceive', he wrote, 'that his Matie is not damnified £20 by any subjecte for his not attending to take the honor of knighthoode'. In some instances Yonge thought that the fines exceeded the amounts for which the land in question could be sold. He also disliked the lack of correlation between how much someone was fined and the extent of his lands.[19] JPs whose fines were to be a minimum of £25 felt they were particularly heavily burdened. Rather than pay, Humphrey Walcott of Shropshire asked to be removed from the bench.[20] Reports that Catholic lords were compounding for only twice what they paid in subsidies while others were charged with three or more times that amount gave those fined added grounds for bitterness.[21]

Like those accused of delinquency, those lords and gentlemen who were named to their county's commission for distraint of knighthood found that the execution of the king's orders was burdensome. Their instructions required them to assume a power that ordinarily belonged to the sheriff and to summon those of their neighbours who had not become knights. This troubled not only those like Lord Montagu who placed much weight upon adherence to proper procedure but also disrupted relationships among the local gentry. Montagu's concerns may explain why the Northamptonshire commissioners seem to have departed from the directions.[22] The earl of Exeter, the county's Lord Lieutenant, told Clifton that while elsewhere 'sum proceede according to there instructions but here as the[y] say according to the statute for the sheriff summons all'.[23]

The papers concerning knighthood which survive among the manuscripts of some commissioners suggest that even when the sheriff summoned delinquents, the service was demanding.[24] The council pressed for action, and individuals delayed in responding. Sir Edward Hales wrote to Sir Edward Dering in March 1631 to propose that they ask the Lord Treasurer to clarify their instructions. Hales saw little point in summoning again those who had refused to compound, stood on their pleas, or claimed they were not liable. He worried too about their lack of time in view of their other responsibilities, including the forthcoming assizes, the sessions, and care more for the poor.[25]

The king's efforts to distrain for knighthood came at a time when local leaders in many areas faced problems arising from dearth, disease, and poverty. By late March of 1630 plague in London, though not a 'major epidemic', was severe enough to warrant warnings against concourse of people, and it persisted through the summer and autumn.[26] Cambridge, claiming that their weekly charge to keep the population in order, to save them from danger of sickness and secure the surrounding country was £200, solicited contributions from elsewhere. They had over 4000 would-be receivers of relief and only 100 able to give.[27] Poor harvests in 1630 meant that grain, already in short supply in some parts of England, would be scarcer. JPs had to worry about providing food for people in their counties and preventing attacks on those suspected of transporting grain to make a profit.[28] The Elizabethan orders for dearth which the council re-issued late in September required justices to meet with constables and arrange to obtain data about the amounts of grain available and its price. The board also wanted the JPs to attend markets and to report on their findings.[29] In January 1630/1 the Book of Orders made further additions to their responsibilities.[30]

Despite the considerable burdens that the king's orders for distraint of knighthood imposed upon the commissioners most confined their protests to grumbling. With a few exceptions both they and those named as delinquents realized that the proceedings, however distasteful, were legitimate. When upon one man's plea in the Exchequer the judges upheld the king's right to the fines, Charles nevertheless publicized that.[31] His insistence upon payments and the relative co-operation of the commissioners insured that he eventually collected considerable revenue.[32] For that he had to pay by appearing to weigh outward forms more heavily than substance and to care more for money than loyalty and service.

A second source of income that Charles tapped during the 1630s was the royal forests. Following in his father's footsteps he had begun at his accession selling woodland rights to lords and gentlemen eager to extend their estates. For them the frustrations of competing with each other for grants and negotiating terms with him were an annoying but necessary part of the price of improving their holdings. To people of lower status disafforestation brought little to compensate for the loss of rights of common.[33] Although they demonstrated their dissatisfaction with riots in the Forest of Dean and in Gillingham forest between 1629 and 1631 and also made formal protests, they obtained no relief.[34] The king and council had no sympathy for rioters. Local authorities who did not want to antagonize the board or threaten their own interests tried to enforce order and punish offenders.

When Charles decided in 1634 to revive forest law, both those who had benefited and those who had suffered from disafforestation found it necessary to defend their property. At the general eyre which began in the summer of 1634 in the Forest of Dean, moved into Waltham in Essex in October, and went to Northamptonshire the following year the chief justice in eyre, the earl of Holland, announced that the boundaries of the forests were those of Henry II's time not those of the perambulation of Edward I. Thus people who had thought themselves outside the forest were subject to its law and liable to be fined for violations.[35] By uncovering wrongdoing in the Forest of Dean Holland apparently hoped to win a round in his quarrel with Lord Treasurer Portland who had clients there.[36] Assisting him was the newly appointed chief justice, Sir John Finch, who did not hesitate to lecture those accused of violations about the king's authority and their own obligations of obedience. He rather than Holland came to bear much of the onus for the eyre's proceedings.[37]

By suddenly changing the bounds of the forest, the eyre angered individuals and towns who consequently found themselves subject to its law. Sir Basil Brooke appealed to the king about some 'aspersions' in the proceedings of the justice seat for the Forest of Dean.[38] People in Essex sought to counter the action at Waltham through their quarter sessions. Claiming that they would be 'greatly prejudiced by the introduction of forest law', a group petitioned the JPs that the sessions, along with other lords and gentlemen of the county, consider the matter before the eyre reconvened and do what 'shall seem best to their judgements that the country under his Majesties laws and gracious favour may hold their lands and inheritances with such freedom and immunities as have been enjoyed this many hundred years'. They proposed that the county bear the charge for the undertaking through a general contribution.[39] Holland's brother, the earl of Warwick, who was Lord Lieutenant of Essex and one whose lands the new boundaries affected took offence at not receiving a personal warning that bounds were being extended. 'If', he maintained, 'I had had the spirit of divination what Mr. Attorney would have been at by enlarging the bounds of the Forest, myself and many of the Lords and freeholders of the county would have been there with their evidences and charters, to have given satisfaction to that court not to extend their bounds farther than they were'.[40] Although he surely knew what had happened at Gloucester, he believed that he should have been informed officially, a courtesy customarily accorded to one of his rank. In its absence his honour was impugned, his ability to protect his neighbours undermined, and his annoyance evident.

Reports of the proceedings in Essex bred fear in Northampton-shire. Lord Montagu who had land and rights in Rockingham forest and was praying that the eyre would not penalize him and his countrymen too heavily confessed his anxieties to his brother, the Lord Privy Seal. He asked too for some word of when to expect the court.[41]. People were preparing to entertain the dignitaries. The last minute postponement of the visitation meant that those efforts went for naught and the inhabitants of Northamptonshire had yet another reason to complain about the forest business.[42]

Until the eyre arrived people worried about what its redefinition of the forests would mean to them. After it came, they faced the necessity of defending property they believed was theirs and paying fines in order to secure and protect rights that they had in some instances purchased very recently. As with distraint of knighthood, the amounts violators of the forests were fined shocked both those who were themselves liable and others. At Northamptonshire penalties came to a total of some £80,000, with the heaviest going to the earl of Westmorland. 'The sheriff', Clifton's son noted, 'has all remitted by £500 and generally they doe report nobly of my Lord of Holland's temper for hee gave leave to any of the country to bring in their evidences to have them read against the King'.[43] Being granted the opportunity to argue and negotiate mitigated the pain of the proceedings, and contemporaries hoped to reduce their fines still further afterwards. The process nevertheless meant that they had to present their cases and appeal for mercy. All this took time and in many instances remained unsettled in 1640.[44]

Relatively few individuals did more than complain about the inconveniences and losses they incurred as a result of the forest business. Most realized that their chances of winning a legal battle over the bounds of the forest were limited. The rhetoric of Chief Justice Finch and the crown's summoning petitioner Sir Basil Brooke to the Star Chamber emphasized that any who challenged the eyre would be regarded as questioning royal authority.[45] Here again Charles collected revenue, but in so doing he lost affection.

People objected even more vehemently to some of the other measures by which Charles attempted to make money during the 1630s because while burdening the public, these brought benefits to private persons. The passage of the statute against monopolies in 1624 had restricted but not prevented royal grants. People still proposed enterprises to the crown, some obtained approval, and some previously established projects continued to cause controversy. Fishermen who depended upon salt raised outcries at monopolistic arrangements that interfered with their work and raised prices.[46] Official grants of licences to export grain were likewise the focus of protest and in some instances violence.[47] Many of the most vociferous complaints came from competitors. Merchants from London and the outports vied for protection of trading rights, and rival soap companies clamoured for recognition.[48] During the bitter and prolonged dispute between the independent soapmakers and the newly established company, the role of Catholics in the company and its support from Lord Treasurer Portland added to criticism of the business.[49]

Those who profited at the public expense also brought criticism against the plans for draining the fens. The crown had approved several projects for that purpose over the preceding half century.[50] In the course of these projectors, commissioners of the sewers and inhabitants quarrelled about their respective authority or rights. With Charles's grants to the earl of Bedford beginning in 1630 and to the earl of Lindsey in 1636 drainage became a much bigger business.[51] Disputes likewise grew. Commoners rioted to defend their means of livelihood.[52] Gentlemen who had other grievances against the drainers encouraged and at times even joined them.[53]

Advocates on both sides presented petitions and wrote tracts. When in 1638 the king responded to some complaints by removing Bedford as undertaker and putting himself in that position, he added another individual, one significant because of his status and involvement in politics, to the list of those antagonized by these schemes.[54]

Other projects which directly affected property aroused similarly intense and emotional conflicts. John Burgh warned Lord Scudamore in February 1635/6 that commissions were being sent out to inquire into depopulation and that those found guilty –and he believed these would include most landed men – would be dealt with not by the commissioners but by Star Chamber. This would mean larger fines and more income for the crown.[55] While depopulation was a generally recognized evil, and while the dearth and unemployment which struck some parts of the kingdom at the beginning of the decade could justify a search for and punishment of depopulators, the determination of Charles and his councillors to extract money at the expense of fairness and understanding prompted complaints.[56]

The earl of Clare who during the 1630s faced allegations concerning both depopulation and illegal building in London vented his annoyance to his son. 'I must be careful about what I can legally do', he wrote in 1631.[57] Four years later when threatened with proceedings in the Star Chamber, he expected that 'as much shall be done against me as proclamations can be stretched unto and if they goe not as farr as desired, power now termed prerogative shall supply'.[58] He acknowledged the crown's right to prosecute, but he felt that the charges were not entirely valid. In one town, he claimed there was more wealth and more tillage than when he had bought it in the time of Queen Elizabeth.[59] He also resented disregard of his status, 'ye poore respect ye make of ye nobles'. Instead of hearing the charges against him directly from the council, as had once been customary, he learned of them through the sheriff.[60]

The lords and gentlemen whom Charles angered through his investigations of depopulation and buildings in London were also those whose way of life was most directly affected by proclamations against staying in London and against eating flesh during Lent. While these orders imposed relatively minor inconveniences in contrast to those for distraint of knighthood, the forest, or depopulation, they nevertheless required the payment of money in return for privilege. Sir Thomas Knyvett who adopted a light-hearted tone in reporting these to his wife in November 1632 saw that the crown was quite serious about forcing violators to pay. If she failed to 'stricktly observe fasting dayes, with out any kind of Flesh at all, either hot or cold', he would suffer as much as if he were 'Questioned for it, for heer hath been divers sorely fined in the Starr Chamber already'.[61] He went on in the same teasing way to tell her of the prosecution of Palmer, a man from Kent, who was fined one thousand pounds, for remaining in London. 'This is a business much pried into', he noted. 'For my parte I hope this not much concerne me, if I can but keepe my wife at home'.[62] Palmer's case gained much publicity. Observers collected evidence, some that would justify his fate and some that argued he deserved sympathy.[63] Two years later prosecutions in the Star Chamber of 'some offending the proclamation against staying in towne' were causing 'great speech'. Clifton's correspondent who was in London at the time resolved that, in so far as he could, he would try to avoid trouble on that score.[64]

The proclamations provided the English with yet another example of their king's monetary preoccupations. Although most individuals sought to limit their own liability to the fines and fees these involved, and when unable to do so, paid rather than resisted royal authority, they disliked what appeared to be an increasingly fiscal relationship. The traditional ties between ruler and ruled were those of affection and obedience. Charles neglected to cultivate loyalty from which money should naturally flow. At the same time his efforts to inform people about his needs were perfunctory at best. They did not demand more. Most of them, though they were interested in the masques and entertainments at court and the plans for rebuilding of Whitehall, expressed little concern about expenditure for such purposes.[65] Their failure to appreciate the king's financial situation nevertheless meant that more and more they were supporting him not because of love but because duty required it. In the absence of understanding their burdens were heavy. Adding to their distaste for the devices Charles was using to raise revenue were doubts about many of the men and procedures associated therewith.

After Queen Henrietta Maria whose religion made her a *persona non grata* in the eyes of many of the English, those most closely identified with the king in his reign were a group of energetic individuals who through their frequent presence at court, on the Privy Council and in Star Chamber, influenced decisions and sought to advance men of like persuasion to places of power. The public watched them and the shifting power among them.[66] Through newsletters and gossip people all over the kingdom became familiar with details of their personal lives and opinions. Their vigorous defence of the royal prerogative was a commonplace.

Laud, all England knew, not only advocated strict uniformity in religion but also opposed disorder of any sort. Even before he moved from London to Canterbury in 1633, he was actively involved in consideration of policies and administrative measures regarding a wide range of topics. Applying to temporal matters the same zeal and style that he used in governing the Church, he was a formidable force. His dislike of parliaments and impatience with dissent made him a prime target for general as well as specifically religious libels.[67]

Richard, Baron Weston, appointed Lord Treasurer in 1628, was also regarded as an enemy of Parliament.[68] His views and his reputation as a power builder led contemporaries to hold him responsible for some of the policies they did not like. The earl of Clare who was not one of Weston's admirers reported in September 1629 that the Treasurer, 'sayd to govern all', was thought to be behind the harsh stance against the imprisoned MPs.[69] A year later Whiteway attributed distraint of knighthood to him.[70] Exeter acknowledged his sway by choosing him as their High Steward upon the death of the earl of Pembroke in the spring of 1630.[71] Three years later the king made him earl of Portland. Opponents at court, like those in the country, complained about his efforts to promote clients and his apparent personal profits from office. His support for Francis Baron Cottington who as Chancellor of the Exchequer served him as a partner and ally and who like Portland was suspected of Catholic sympathies, profiteering, and opposition to Parliament gave his critics more reason for distrusting him.[72] When he died in 1635, few mourned him.[73] Clerk of the Council Nicholas told his brother that many who had not loved Portland, feared his successor.[74]

A third figure whose energy, ability and heavy-handed tactics came to be synonymous with Charles's rule in the public eye was Sir Thomas Wentworth. Some contemporaries were surprised when the king made him Baron Wentworth just after the end of the parliamentary session of 1628 where he had played a leading role in the preparation of the Petition of Right. Named Lord President of the North in December of the same year and a Privy Councillor in 1629, Wentworth left his Yorkshire neighbours with few doubts about the energy with which he would exercise his authority.[75]

Although his journey to Ireland in 1633 to assume his responsibilities as Lord Deputy removed him from the North and royal court, his administration there and his series of quarrels reverberated in England.[76] People identified him as an ally and friend of Laud and would probably not have been surprised if they had read the letters the two exchanged where they discussed a policy they called 'Thorough'.[77] The earldom of Strafford that Charles granted him in January 1639/40 marked his magnified role in advising the king about dealing with the Scottish crisis. The English watched his conduct closely that spring, and what they saw bred the distrust that inspired his impeachment in the opening days of the Long Parliament later that year.[78]

Two other men, William Noy and Sir John Finch became notorious for using their legal training in defence of unpopular projects and policies. When Charles named the common lawyer and former MP William Noy as attorney general in 1631, contemporaries expected that another Parliament would soon follow.[79] Their disappointment was the greater when they found that Noy was no different from others who, upon becoming servants of the king, placed their talents at their master's disposal. For the three years until his death in 1634 the attorney general devised and defended various money-making projects. Admittedly 'an able minister of great parts and reputation', Noy had through his work upset 'divers sorts of men' who, as one correspondent reported upon his death:

> 'now stick not to expresse a gladnesse that he is gone; and say (by way of ironie) yt now the project of sope will be washed and wiped away, that of buildings will fall, that of tobacco vanish into smoke, That of fuell be pluckt up by ye roots, that of victualls and provisions be unprovided of a patron, That of Taverns have the verie memorie of yt drowned in cupps of wine and that now gentlemen and their ladies (who were driven by him to the solitarie life of the countrie) will be at libertie to returne and reside in the citie at their pleasure.[80]

The puritans who regarded Noy as 'a greate favourer of Sabbathe recreations and pollutions' also shed few tears for him.[81]

Sir John Finch, Speaker of the House of Commons in 1628-9, was, unlike Noy, a *persona non grata* to some MPs when that Parliament ended.[82] By his conduct as Holland's assistant in the general eyre of the forest and during five and a half years as Chief

Justice of Common Pleas he made other enemies.[83] The instructions he issued and the opinions he delivered on the western assize circuit led people who heard them to remark about his imperious manner.[84] In January 1639/40, when King Charles named him Chief Justice Lord Keeper, he reportedly warned Finch that 'the world took notice that he was a passionate man, wch was noe good quality in a judge'.[85] Less than two years later the House of Commons impeached him.

The others who served Charles lacked the drive or the power to do more than occasionally modify the impact of this small group of men whose characters, convictions, and *modus operandi* represented the king's government to the English people. Courtiers like Holland and Carlisle were themselves tainted by the dust of corruption and conniving that people also associated with their opponents, Portland and Cottington.[86] Manchester, Dorchester, and Secretary Coke who were sympathetic to Puritanism were ineffectual in serious disputes. They could not count on royal favour against Laud or others if they questioned the wisdom of policies and procedures that seemed to depart from custom and arouse public opposition.[87] Chief Justice of Common Pleas Heath was dismissed in 1634 reportedly because he inclined toward Puritanism.[88]

The actions of the Privy Council, the Courts of Star Chamber and High Commission, and the other councils and courts of law reinforced the public image of Charles's government propagated by the individuals closest to him. The provision of revenue and the protection of authority seemed to be the paramount concerns. Both dissenters and those who, though loyal had somehow offended, received harsh treatment. Petitioners who sought assistance or mercy were disappointed with the difficulty in obtaining relief.

The Privy Council's close association with the monarch and its broad range of administrative and judicial responsibility meant that whether or not a Parliament was sitting, people looked to it for help. Some, like Captain Henry Bell, appealed time and time again despite repeated failures. In February 1636/7 Bell claimed that during five years in prison he had submitted 104 petitions. By August 1639 his count had climbed to 216.[89] His was an extreme case, but whatever doubts people may have had about the receptivity of the board to their pleas during the 1630s, they continued to address themselves there.[90]

Petitioners knew that they might improve their chances if they had support at court. In trying to promote her husband's case for compensation for loss of his position in the forest, the countess of Huntingdon visited Lord Treasurer Portland, Lord Privy Seal Manchester, the earl of Dorset and Secretary Coke.[91] Cities not only paid agents but presented gifts to officials whose favour they wanted.[92] Mastering the techniques of lobbying and the technicalities of patronage, though part and parcel of public life, could nevertheless impose heavy demands for energy and funds without yielding any benefits. Perhaps because he had invested so much in his case, Captain Bell expressed his outrage at his lack of success in August 1639. Announcing that he believed he had been treated contrary to the word of God, the law of England and the law of nations, he declared that he preferred to live among the Turks if there were to be no parliaments. In Parliament alone he hoped for justice.[93] Few put their discontent with failure in such political terms as he did although others often had much at stake. Exeter merchants vigorously defended their economic privileges against the Londoners.[94] Royal scrutiny of corporate charters forced townspeople to fight for what they thought was theirs against what seemed to be an alliance between neighbouring areas jealous of them and the crown.[95] When disappointed by the board's decisions most reacted with cynicism or resignation and ascribed their lot to tactical errors or insufficiently powerful friends. Their frustration at the council's willingness to deal with projectors and its emphasis upon its own authority must nevertheless be taken seriously.[96] Even those who in one way or another became royal beneficiaries had complaints about their experiences.[97]

Like the king, the council readily bowed before ecclesiastical claims and in so doing angered cities seeking resolution of long-standing quarrels with bishops or cathedral clergy. Shipmoney added to the parties' financial interests in the outcome. For some observers the decision about Archbishop Laud's visitation of the universities revealed how little the board weighed law and custom in contrast to clerical power. After Laud declared that he would visit the universities, representatives of both attended king and council to defend their rights as chartered corporations.[98] Francis Cheynell, himself from Oxford where the archbishop was chancellor, reported the hearing to Clifton. 'Cambridge men', he noted 'were most resolute because they had a chancellor [the earl of Holland] to back them'. To the archbishop's claim to make a metropolitical rather than royal visit, Cambridge advocates responded, 'if your power bee not derived from the King, then it is either concurrent with the king and so equall to the kings power'. They made their case 'so plaine', Cheynell reported, 'that the king himself enterposed and told the archbishop that hee must then write Woolseys style ego et Rex meus ... and therefore the archbishop fell lowe upon his knees and desired the king to beleeve him his humble subject and that hee only desired to curb sedition and so prevailed at wch my Lord of Holland was so moved that he sayd they might proove what they would but the archbishops petition should bee heard sooner then their arguments'.[99] Even those observers who did not know all the details of the encounter realized that Charles and his council had turned deaf ears to the universities' pleas to uphold their charters. What chances did individuals have when such was the fate of great corporations?

The council's seeming departures from traditional notions about just proceedings contradicted the very order which contemporaries valued and it tried to uphold. Those who flocked to trials, eagerly sought copies of libellous or seditious books and desired news about the fate of individuals who boldly expressed opinions about Church or State, had little desire to see their own communities disrupted by people they considered fanatics. Preachers denounced especially those whose greed or dissipation affected others and called upon magistrates to enforce the laws and to alleviate suffering during hard times.[100] JPs acknowledged their role in maintaining order. They did not quarrel with the aims of the *Orders and Directions, together with a commission for the better administration of justice and more perfect Information of his Majestie; how and by whom the lawes and statutes tending the reliefe of the Poore, the well-ordering and training up of youth in Trades and the Reformation of Disorders and Disordered persons, are executed throughout the kingdome* that the king and council issued in January 1630/1.[101] The crown's claims that this so-called Book or Orders, was 'not to diminish the authority, but to stir up the diligence' of the JPs seemed reasonable.[102] The book required justices to enforce the statutes which sought to preserve order in town and country and to report their activities in this regard to the sheriff who would in turn inform the judges.

Less a codification and reorganization of local government than a supplement to other measures, the orders drew from the past and from practices followed in some areas. They nevertheless added to the responsibilities of the already heavily burdened justices who at the time of the book's appearance were struggling to alleviate the problems that dearth and poverty were already causing that winter.[103] Many JPs dutifully complied and submitted returns; others did not. Instead of prosecuting the negligent the council urged co-operation and in 1633 asked for only half-yearly rather than quarterly reports.[104] Although neither the board nor the justices made the orders a major issue, these directions were one example of a number of measures by which the council was attempting to exercise greater, and not always welcome, oversight over local affairs.

The board was more emphatic about the need for strict enforcement of laws in circumstances of poverty, plague, and dearth. At the Star Chamber trial of William Archer for not bringing his corn to market, Laud declared that he agreed with 'Justice Harvy that this last yeares famin was made by man and not by God, solicited by the hard heartednesse of men'.[105] The court sentenced Archer for his offence but, taking cognizance of his charge that the Essex justices had neither visited his barn, nor asked him to sell corn, the council warned JPs that they must not allow the same to be said of them.[106] In response to conciliar demands for action local officials complained about panics caused by transportation of food during times of alleged shortages and the difficulty of providing relief when plague struck[107] Rather than be held responsible for trouble if it occurred in their counties, JPs submitted terse and guarded statements about conditions and at the same time worked to provide remedies.[108]

To justices and to others the council seemed at times to be unnecessarily severe or impatient in dealing with both communities and individuals. Most took its orders seriously and went to some lengths to avoid its displeasure. Being called before the board often necessitated – as it did for Sir Hugh Cholmley – in addition to the initial questioning, the 'further vexation' of being 'commanded for three weeks or a month to attend the Council Table, *de die in diem*'.[109] Depending upon one's circumstances the effect of staying in London and neglecting family and affairs elsewhere could be very serious. Great men or corporate leaders who may have been less inconvenienced by such orders found some of the council's rebukes offensive to their dignity.[110] Correspondents noted the heavy fines assessed against those who violated proclamations and orders, reported the statements made by officials at hearings, and commented about such orders as those concerning books and papers belonging to Sir Robert Cotton and to Sir Edward Coke. These two men, although not always defenders of the royal prerogative, were spokesmen for law and precedent.[111] The council's reputation convinced many that beyond a certain point resistance was not worth the effort.[112]

The regional councils in the North and in Wales had reputations similar to that of the Privy Council. Under Wentworth's leadership the Council of the North's assertion of authority provoked complaints from both country gentlemen and the city of York.[113] They realized that the power of the council and its president to affect their lives placed a premium upon their ability to deal successfully there. The city of York worked to see that Wentworth (or the vice-president) used his influence for the city's benefit.[114] While less powerful than the Council of the North, the Council in the Marches of Wales had a similar relationship with individuals and communities in Wales and in the four neighbouring shires of England.[115] The earl of Bridgewater who became Lord President in 1631 was eager to enjoy the perquisites and powers of his office, but he did not undertake administration with the zeal and commitment which were characteristic of Wentworth. The Council of Wales consequently stirred up far less controversy than did its northern counterpart.[116]

Serving as an arm of the council in enforcing unpopular policy and in punishing offences against the prerogative throughout the kingdom was the Star Chamber.[117] Contemporaries recognized that by following crown cases in the court they could get a sense of the political atmosphere. John Pory apparently relied on information from an officer there to report to Lord Scudamore details of the latest proceedings.[118] While people did not hesitate to use the court for personal business, they knew that when acting as royal watchdog it prosecuted with zeal and penalized with severity.[119] In October 1634 Rossingham noted that some had been sentenced there for laughing at libels.[120] Even without the oath *ex officio* which made people who were charged in the High Commission tremble, being brought into Star Chamber by the crown meant trouble.[121] Its heavy fines were notorious. Although relatively few of these were collected in full, they stirred resentment on grounds of principle and because reduction required negotiation.[122] The trial of Prynne, Burton and

Bastwick dramatically illustrated what might happen to daring opponents of the regime, but there were a host of other proceedings involving both individuals and corporations who had offended or antagonized the king. Charged in the court in connection with its Irish plantations, the city of London was unhappy both about its treatment there and about the fine incurred as a consequence.[123]

While exemplifying for the English the consequences of disobedience, the Star Chamber was not the only forum that gave them an opportunity to see the way the judges supported royal policy. At the half-yearly assizes held in their own counties contemporaries got a closer look at the judges who came to them. There too they could see friends, hear news, and do business. In diaries and letters they recorded the entire experience from sermons to executions and took note of extraordinary incidents. They listened to the addresses with which the visitors traditionally prefaced the proceedings. From that they learned about the current concerns of king and council. The well-informed, having already received reports of the instructions issued by the Lord Keeper prior to the circuits, could see how their judge presented that material.[124]

Although between 1629 and 1639 seven different judges appeared on three of the six circuits (Norfolk, home, and midlands), eight on the western circuit, six on the northern, and four on the Oxford, a number of judges had the same assignment five or more times during the period and thus became familiar figures to local people.[125] Both individuals and communities used the opportunity of the assizes to appeal to the judges to hear particular causes with favour or to use their influence in other ways.[126] These petitions supplemented any formal presentments from grand juries concerning public grievances. A relative lack of evidence about such presentments may mean that for the most part they were routine.[127] Like other public figures and great men, the judges at times won approval for their conduct and gratitude for patronage and on occasions when they seemed vindictive or failed to provide what their clients wanted sparked criticism. Details of their conduct both off and on the bench, similarly fed appetites of the curious and the politically concerned.[128] People understood that dissent could end judicial careers, but they nevertheless expected that judges uphold the law and avoid the vituperative statements that Finch was inclined to make.[129] The most bitter of the complaints in 1640 focused upon him, but others of the judges also came under attack. Only Croke was not impeached.[130]

Political (and religious) complaints, not legal complaints, formed the bulk of the grievances that the English held against Charles I's rule during the 1630s. The men to whom he listened and gave power were individuals who manifested too much interest in their own enrichment, were quick to take offence, had too little respect for customary niceties of conduct, and failed to distinguish between disagreement and disloyalty. In their hands projects, policies and procedures that inconvenienced or annoyed people became more controversial and more burdensome.

Discontent with projects, policies and official pompousness festered because the aggrieved had few means of obtaining satisfaction. Neither practical nor ideological considerations encouraged people to raise legal points and resort to the courts. Relief depended for the most part upon the very persons whose conduct caused the problem. King and council were not entirely deaf to appeals for justice, but the complaints they received and the action they took were limited.[131] Not all recognized ills received remedial attention. Although gentlemen resented currying favour in order to avoid being sheriff and the crown disliked the consequent limiting of candidates for that important office, no changes were instituted.[132] Some promised reforms bore little fruit. In April 1639 Charles issued a royal proclamation calling in twenty-six grants on the grounds that, contrary to advance claims, they had not been profitable to the subject.[133] A year later fourteen of these grants still existed.[134]

Removing officials was difficult, if not virtually impossible.[135] Many had tenure for life. Those few great officers of state and judges who served at royal pleasure enjoyed as a consequence protection from attack in most circumstances. John Felton's knife, not Parliament, succeeded in ending the duke of Buckingham's power in the 1620s. Impeachment worked when the king allowed it to. Without Parliament the English had not even that means of trying to call royal servants to account. They had to convince the monarch that he must do so. Although complaints against minor figures were much less likely to be deflected by the king's intervention, the process of petitioning and the possibility of countermoves meant that anyone desirous of justice had to be prepared to commit considerable resources to the undertaking. Even extensive efforts might achieve little more than harassment. Sir Henry Slingsby tells a story that illustrates how hard it was to curb the power of an unwilling petty functionary. A feodary of the Court of Wards in Yorkshire who, having been 'put out ... for his bad behaviour', nevertheless 'hung about ye court' and caused trouble. Slingsby who believed himself a victim of the fellow brooded in his diary, 'It is an easy matter for one in authority to extend ye power of it to another man's wrong and prejudice, and ye more easy by so much as common practise doth authorise it however reason and nature may condemn it as unjust'.[136] Not only was satisfaction elusive, but in many instances an official's critics suffered more than he did.[137]

People occasionally accused JPs and others who served the crown in the counties, hundreds, and parishes of pursuing their own self-interest at the expense of the public welfare.[138] These allegations lacked the bite of those against officials whose links with the community were more tenuous and dependence upon the court greater. Charges against locally selected urban leaders were similarly moderate. Shrewsbury was one of those towns where factions exchanged accusations of oligarchy and mob rule and invoked corporate charters and Acts of Parliament in justification of their positions.[139] The structure of municipal government provided means of resolving many of these internal squabbles. Only when settlement seemed to require appeal to the crown to revoke one charter and grant a new one did such problems assume broader dimensions and raise the far more difficult questions of obtaining satisfaction from the king.

Because local officials found it hard to resist when pressed by both crown and countrymen, they were less often a source of continuing grievance. When opponents appealed against them to the council or sued in the Star Chamber, they occasionally responded with their own complaints or suits, but they were sensitive to criticism from their neighbours.[140] Most bowed to concerted opposition and acquiesced when faced with remonstrances from the council. Few dared to ignore with impunity inquiries or summons to attend the board.[141]

In contrast to the possibility of resolving conflicts between governors and governed on the local level were the frustrations of seeking relief from actions of those who were more direct servants of the king. Because tradition and political survival both counselled caution in making serious charges against royal officials, complaints expressed in the language of loyalty focused on misunderstandings and sought clarifications. Responses to such had no need to deal with issues that were not raised and thus left unanswered the indirect and implicit questions about justice and morality that came during the 1630s to suppress the affection of the English for Charles I. People applauded the king's concern about enforcement of law on the local level. They shared with him an interest in seeing that England was orderly and prosperous, but they realized that there were discrepancies between what he preached in his frequent invocations of the law and what his servants were doing. Too often the law seemed to be stretched, injustices ignored, officials arrogant, and money valued more than principle. In one way or another communities, groups with special interests and individuals had difficulty in securing protection for what they believed was rightfully theirs.

Many of the grievances which Englishmen felt during the 1630s were of long standing; others resulted from Charles's efforts to rule without Parliament. The incidence of plague, dearth, and unusual weather added to people's burdens and at the same time gave them reason for probing current affairs to determine why the kingdom should be suffering. The king and his ministers told those who were in distress to look towards the court for solutions to their problems, but by insisting upon obedience and refusing to tolerate dissent or criticism, the king undermined his own leadership.

Peter Heylyn may have been thinking of Charles I when he wrote about the Emperor Augustus in 1632, 'It is the misery of the best Princes, even when they do well, to be ill spoken of. And therefore many times such follyes are with more policy dissembled than observed, by the greatest kings'. Heylyn, who used his pen to defend Laudianism, thought that most of such criticism came not from 'malice' but from 'delight in pratling'. People who had freedom of speech were less 'sensible of loss of liberty of state'.[142] Augustus was wise enough to know this.

Neither King Charles nor his associates recognized the lesson of the Augustan example. Upon watching the king's entry into Oxford in August 1636, Francis Cheynell commented, 'The lesse order is kept the more joye is strewen in acclamations'. There was so much formality on that occasion that 'there was not a vivat given as his Majesty passed along; every one expected who would begin and so with intent every man desired to follow, no man began for fear he be thought guilty of singular devotion and allegiance, singularity being the greatest enemy to both'.[143] Charles and his servants too often themselves neglected to show spontaneity and to communicate warmth and understanding. They consequently gave greater offence when they also failed, whether inadvertently or consciously, to live up to the standards they professed. City officials admonished not to carry the signs of office when attending Church and others reproved for neglect of proper respect for higher authorities wondered why the crown refused them an honour which was theirs.[144]

Departures from customary procedures and beliefs troubled people. Although few were prepared to express their concern as clearly as the earl of Clare did in letters to his son and fewer still took any direct action to protest the projects, prosecutions, and procedures they observed, many gave indications that they were uneasy about what seemed to be happening.[145] The moderation with which most conducted themselves should not obscure the depth of their concerns. In some areas of the country at least, politically and legally conscious subjects perceived that grievances were not merely isolated or perennial problems but representations of a course of public affairs about which they had reason to be watchful, if not anxious. This is not to say that there was revolutionary sentiment in the country. There is a long distance between discontent and revolution. The first Bishops' War decreased this distance.

NOTES

1   See J. Thirsk, *Economic Policy and Projects* (Oxford: Clarendon Press, 1978).
2   S. R. Gardiner (ed.), *Debates in the House of Commons in 1625*, Camden Society, New Series, vol. 6 (1873), pp. 37 ff.
3   See Stephen White, *Sir Edward Coke and 'The Grievances of the Commonwealth'* (Chapel Hill, NC: University of North Carolina Press, 1979), pp. 28–9.
4   e.g. the proceedings against Mompesson and others in the spring of 1621. See R. Zaller, *Parliament of 1621.*
5   See Lockyer, *Buckingham;* also L. Peck, "'For the King not to be bountiful were a fault ...'": Perspectives on court patronage in early Stuart England', paper read at the Anglo-American Conference, University of London, July 1985, and to be published in a revised version in the *JBS.*
6   See E. R. Foster, 'The procedure of the House of Commons against patents and monopolies, 1621–1624', in *Conflict in Stuart England*, eds W. A.

Aiken and B. D. Henning (New York: New York University Press, 1960), pp. 59–85.
7 See Lockyer, *Buckingham*, pp. 453, 459.
8 Peck, 'Bountiful'.
9 See Chapter 1.
10 See H. M. Leonard, 'Distraint of knighthood: the last phase, 1625–1641', *History*, vol. 63, no. 207 (1978), pp. 23–37.
11 SP 16/162/18; also *Barrington Family Letters*, no. 113; see Forster, *Eliot*, Vol. 2. pp. 400–1.
12 Leonard, 'Distraint', pp. 24–5.
13 Whiteway, f. 80v; also f. 83; Yonge, f. 42v; Montagu MS 27.
14 e.g. Montagu MS 27; SP 16/173/88; 16/180/24 – 5; PRO, C. 115/M.23, no. 7671.
15 e.g. the earl of Essex (Birch, Vol. 2, pp. 162–3); Richard Knightley, who was sheriff (Cl C 631).
16 e.g. Essex who pointed out that he was actually present at the coronation (Birch, Vol. 2, pp. 162–3).
17 Montagu MS 10.60 (HMC, *Buccleuch*, Vol. 3, p. 352).
18 SP 16/184/65; see also 16/173/88; *Lowther Family Estate Books*, pp. 229–30.
19 Yonge, f. 43. See also the comment of William Davenport who was fined, in J. Morrill, 'William Davenport and the "silent majority" of early Stuart England', *Journal of the Chester Archaeological Society* (1974). p. 121.
20 Leonard, 'Distraint', p. 33.
21 Birch, Vol. 2, pp. 168–73; PRO, C. 115/M.35, no. 8393; concerning other irregularities see Yonge, f. 45v; SP 16/238/83; 16/242/64. Conrad Russell tells me that there is evidence that some people may have been penally assessed.
22 Montagu MS 10.8 (HMC, *Buccleuch*, Vol. 3, p. 353); Cope, *Montagu*, p. 135; Leonard, 'Distraint', p. 27.
23 Cl C 631.
24 Montagu MS 27; Cl C 482; HMC, *MSS of Reginald Rawdon Hastings*, Vol. 4, p. 215.
25 BL, Stowe MS 743, f. 85
26 P. Slack, *The Impact of Plague in Tudor and Stuart England* (London: Routledge & Kegan Paul, 1985), pp. 200, 217–19. Order of 19 March 1629/30 in *Certaine Statutes especially selected and commanded by his Majestie to be carefully put in execution by all Justices and other officers of the Peace* (1630), STC 9342. In April, Exeter's chamber took steps to prevent Londoners from coming to the fair (Exeter, Act Books, Vol. 7, f. 376v (Harvard film). In October the earl and countess of Exeter left London that month because plague was 'so near' them (Cl C 590; see also Cl C 407).
27 One Cambridge appeal went to Exeter (Exeter, Royal Letters and other Letters and Papers, f. 339 (Harvard film); also Slack, *Plague*, p. 220. See Woodforde, p. 497, concerning the solicitation of funds for Northampton in 1638.
28 See below.

29 *Orders ... for the preventing and remedying of the dearth of graine and victuall* (1630), STC 9253.

30 See below.

31 SP 16/191/17; Leonard, 'Distraint', pp. 29–31.

32 Forster, *Eliot*, Vol. 2, p. 411.

33 Sharp, *In Contempt*, p. 86; G. Hammersley, 'The crown woods and their exploitation in the sixteenth and seventeenth centuries', *BIHR*, vol. 30, no. 82 (1957), pp. 136–61; E. Kerridge, 'The revolts in Wiltshire against Charles I', *Wiltshire Archaeological and Natural History Magazine*, vol. 57 (1958), pp. 64–75.

34 See Whiteway, f. 76; Sharp, *In Contempt*, pp. 86 ff.; Willcox, *Gloucestershire*, pp. 194 ff. The crown did take some steps to punish depopulators and enclosers. See below.

35 The first eyre was 1632 in Windsor Forest, but it was handled differently. See G. Hammersley, 'The revival of the forest laws under Charles I',*History*, vol. 45, no. 154 (1960), pp. 85–102; P. A. J. Pettit, 'Charles I and the revival of forest law in Northamptonshire', *Northamptonshire Past and Present*, vol. 3, no. 2 (1961), pp. 54–62.

36 SP 16/236/14; M. Alexander, *Charles I's Lord Treasurer* (Chapel Hill, NC: University of North Carolina Press, 1975) pp. 195 ff., but cf, Hammersley, 'Revival', pp. 92, 97.

37 See Whiteway, f. 105v; Hammersley, 'Revival', p. 102. See below.

38 PRO, C. 115/M.36, no. 8436. As a result of his petition he found himself charged in the Court of Star Chamber. See also SP 16/289/105 and below.

39 The petitioners addressed the earl of Warwick, earl Rivers, Lord Peter, Lord Maynard, Sir Thomas Barrington, Sir Harbottle Grimston, Sir Benjamin Ayliffe, Sir Thomas Wiseman, Sir Thomas Cheeke, Sir Henry Mildmay, and Mr Smyth (Essex Record Office, Calendar of Quarter Sessions Rolls, Q/SR 286 (Harvard film)); also see PRO, C. 115/M.36, no. 8438.

40 *CSPDom. 1634–5*, p. xxxiv; also SP 16/278/3. Essex had two Lord Lieutenants at this time: Portland and Warwick. See J. C. Sainty, *Lieutenants of Counties, 1585–1642, BIHR*, special supplement, no. 8 (1970).

41 Montagu MS 10.26; Cope, *Montagu*, pp. 147–51; see also Yonge, f. 64v; Harvard MS Eng. 1266, v.2, ff. 193v–194, A Note of the Proceedings of the Justice Seat held for the Forest of Dean at Gloucester Castle, 10 July 1634.

42 See Montagu MS 27. Northampton borough had decided to get Lord Holland a gilt cup (Northamptonshire Record Office, Borough Assembly Books 3/2, p. 37).

43 Cl C 537; cf. Birch, Vol. 2, p. 248; El 6514.

44 P. A. J. Pettit, *The Royal Forests of Northamptonshire*, Northamptonshire Record Society, vol. 23 (1968), pp. 87–92; Hammersley, 'Revival', pp. 99, 100, 102; Cope, *Montagu*, pp. 148–9.

45 PRO, C. 115/M.36, no. 8636; Hammersley, 'Revival', pp. 101–2.

46 e.g. Rye 47/129.

47 See Chapter 1. Transportation of food became an issue in times of dearth such as 1630–1. Whiteway (f. 79) tells of a man who was in 'great danger'

and whose house was ruined by the common people' at Calne 'because he transported corn'. See also SP 16/176/35; 16/177/4; and also 16/187/12; 16/190/39; 16/191/3–4.

48 See W. H. Price, *The English Patents of Monopoly* (Boston, Mass.: Houghton, Mifflin, 1906).

49 See M. Alexander, *Lord Treasurer*, pp. 203–5.

50 See M. Kennedy, 'Fenland drainage, the central government, and local interest: Carleton and the gentlemen of South Holland', *Historical Journal*, vol. 26, no. 1 (1983), pp. 15–37.

51 H. C. Darby, *The Draining of the Fens* (Cambridge: Cambridge University Press, 1940), pp. 38–61; also S. Wells, *The History of the Drainage of the Great Level of the Fens*, 2 vols (London, 1830), Vol. 1, pp. 96–129.

52 See K. Lindley, *Fenland Riots and the English Revolution* (London: Heinemann, 1982); SP 16/327/36; 16/330/48.

53 See Holmes, *Lincolnshire*, pp. 121–30. Also see, M. Kennedy, 'Charles I and local government: the drainage of the east and west fens', *Albion*, vol. 15, no. 1 (1983), pp. 19–31.

54 Darby, *Draining*, pp. 57–8.

55 PRO, C. 115/N.4, no. 8606.

56 R. Ashton, *The City*, pp. 167–71; V. Pearl, *London and the Outbreak of the Puritan Revolution* (Oxford: Oxford University Press, 1961), pp. 20–2; Knowler, Vol. 1, pp. 489–90; Yonge, ff. 54–54v, 64v; R. Powell, *Depopulation Arraigned* (1636), STC 20160; Kerridge, 'Revolts'; Sharp, *Contempt*, pp. 144 ff.; SP 16/307/2; Whiteway, f. 88; HA 2296.

57 Holles, no. 177. Clare expressed his anger at the court on other occasions. See Chapter 1. The earl of Bedford also fell foul of the building proclamations, see PRO, C. 115/M.36, no. 8445.

58 Holles, no. 222; see also, nos 245, 246.

59 Holles, no. 246; see also STT 2295; STT 1616.

60 Holles, no. 177; cf. Warwick's response to the eyre for Waltham Forest above; also the treatment of the mayor and aldermen of Oxford in different circumstances (Cl C 84); also SP 16/176/32.

61 Knyvett, no. 27; cf. HMC, *Gawdy*, p. 137.

62 Knyvett, no. 27.

63 BL, Egerton; 2716, f. 94; Birch, Vol. 2, pp. 192, 195; D'Ewes, *Autobiography*, Vol. 2, p. 78; Yonge, f. 51.

64 Cl C 307.

65 People did worry that England would have to support the queen mother when she arrived. See Chapter 2. Concerning masques and rebuilding at Whitehall see e.g. PRO, C.115/N.4, nos 8606, 8619.

66 e.g. Yonge, f. 54; Whiteway, f. 91v; Cl C 376; Alexander, *Lord Treasurer*, p. 194.

67 See Chapter 2; also Trevor-Roper, *Laud*, pp. 167 ff., 211–30.

68 See Alexander, *Lord Treasurer*, esp. pp. 145–7, 151. Laud, *Works*, Vol. 7, p. 118; *CSPVen. 1629–32*, no. 257; We do not have Portland's papers which might shed much more light on his role in the council.

69 Holles, no. 156; also Yonge, ff. 29, 35v.

70   Whiteway, f. 80.
71   Exeter, Act Books, Vol. 7, f. 377 (Harvard film). Weston was from Essex, not from the west country. At his death they replaced him with the next earl of Pembroke.
72   Alexander, *Lord Treasurer*, pp. 188–203.
73   M. Havran, *Caroline Courtier: The Life of Lord Cottington* (London: Macmillan, 1973), esp. pp. 89, 104–13.
74   SP 16/285/11.
75   See C. V. Wedgwood, *Thomas Wentworth, First Earl of Strafford* (New York: Macmillan, 1962); also *DNB; Lowther Family Estate Books*, pp. 229–30; Cholmley, *Memoirs*, pp. 60–4; Cliffe, *Yorkshire*, pp. 297, 300–12.
76   e.g. Smyth letters, no. 264; also see H. Kearney, *Strafford in Ireland, 1633–41* (Manchester: Manchester University Press, 1960).
77   See Knowler, Vol. 1, p. 111; Laud, *Works*, Vol. 6, pt. 2, p. 310; HMC, *Sixth Report*, app., p. 278; Holles, no. 235; Yonge, f. 45v; Birch, Vol. 2, p. 195.
78   See Chapter 5.
79   Yonge, f. 46v; Birch, Vol. 2, pp. 136–8, 140–5; Whiteway, f. 86. Also see *DNB*.
80   Phelips MSS, DDPH 212/12; see also D'Ewes, *Autobiography*, Vol. 2, p. 78.
81   *WP*, Vol. 3, p. 358; also pp. 358–61.
82   See Chapter 5 concerning the investigation of his conduct in 1628/9. Also see Chapter 1.
83   See above; W. J. Jones, *Politics and the Bench* (London: Allen & Unwin, 1971), pp. 20, 139–40; also the charges against him in 1640 (*ST*, Vol. 4, pp. 11–14).
84   e.g. Strode's case, SP 16/427/31; *DeL'Isle*, p. 219; also Woodforde, p. 496.
85   El 7817.
86   Holland's connections with the queen sometimes assisted him. See Smuts, 'Puritan followers'; B. Donagan, 'A courtier's progress: greed and consistency in the life of the earl of Holland', *Historical Journal*, vol. 19, no. 2, (1976), pp. 317–53; also J. Beatty, *Warwick and Holland* (Denver, Colo: Alan Swallow, 1965); R. Schreiber, *The First Carlisle*, Transactions of the American Philosophical Society, vol. 74, pt. 7 (Philadelphia, Pa: 1984), pp. 182–90; also above.
87   See e.g. PRO, C.115/N.4, no. 8612; also Yonge, f. 54; cf. Holmes's comment about Dorset (*Lincolnshire*, p. 118).
88   See PRO, C.115/M.36, nos 8432, 8435; *DNB*; also Jones, *Bench*, p. 143. Heath had had difficulties earlier. See BL, Add. MS 36989, f. 488; cf. the case of Baron Walter (Jones, *Bench*, p. 39).
89   SP 16/427/7; SP 16/346/79; notes concerning many of Bell's petitions appear among the State Papers, Domestic.
90   See e.g. PC 2/41, pp. 163, 308; PC 2/42, p. 277; PC 2/43, pp. 334–6, 467; PC 2/44, pp. 197, 414.
91   HA 4846, 4847, 4851.

92 e.g. Exeter, Act Books, Vol. 8, f. 69 (Harvard film); see Chapter 3 concerning Coventry and shipmoney.

93 SP 16/427/7. He said that if he could not get justice he would be forced to complain so loudly that it would be heard throughout the kingdom and beyond.

94 W. T. MacCaffrey, *Exeter, 1540–1640* (Cambridge, Mass.: Harvard University Press, 2nd edn., 1975) pp. 150 ff.; W. H. Price, *Patents*, pp. 113 ff.

95 See e.g. Pearl, *London*, pp. 23–37, 86–7; Shropshire Record Office, Ludlow Corporation Minute book 356/2/1, ff. 184, 193, 203–205v, 208, 214; Ludlow Corporation, Box 293, no. 249; Exeter, Act Books, Vol. 7, f. 427v; Vol. 8, 28v, 63 (Harvard film); SP 16/251/27; 16/252/8 (Colchester). In 1639 the York Chamberlains Accounts show an expenditure of £153 6s 6d for defence of the city's charter. Accounts in other years do not list such expenses as a separate item. York, House Book, Vol. 35, ff. 95, 104v, 107, 116; Fletcher, *Sussex*, pp. 235–7. Victoria County History, *The City of Leicester* (Leicester, Vol. 4) ed. R. A. McKinley (London: Institute of Historical Research, 1958), pp. 57, 60 ff.

96 See e.g. Rye, Correspondence, 47/129, 47/130; Phelips MSS, DDPH 221/33; Holles, nos 225, 228.

97 See Ashton, *City and Court*, pp. 141–2; Gardiner, *History of England*, Vol. 8, pp. 71–4, 284.

98 See M. H. Curtis, *Oxford and Cambridge in Transition, 1558–1642* (Oxford: Clarendon Press, 1959), pp. 32–4.

99 Cl C 73. Cheynell may have had personal reasons for being critical of Laud.

100 e.g. Robert Bolton, *Two Sermons Preached at Northampton* (1635), STC 3256, and see especially a third sermon (preached at the Lent assizes in Northampton in 1630) which is bound with the two (Folger copy). Bolton and others also regarded troubles as divine warnings to cleanse the kingdom of sin. See, for example, R. Jennison, *The Cities Safetie* (1630), STC 14489; Jennison, *Newcastles Call to her Neighbour and Sister Townes and Cities throughout the land to take Warning by her Sins and Sorrowes* (1637), STC 14492; W. Gouge, *Gods Three Arrows: Plague; Famine; Sword in Three Treatises* (1631), STC 12116; Chas. Fitz-Geffrie, *The Curse of Corne-hoarders with the Blessing of Seasonable Selling* (1631), STC 10938.

101 (1630), STC 9252. Concerning the book, see B. W. Quintrell, 'The making of Charles I's Book of Orders', *EHR*, vol. 95, no. 376 (1980), pp. 553–72; also P. Slack, 'Books of Orders: the making of English social policy, 1577–1631', *THRS*, Fifth Series, vol. 30 (1980), pp. 1–22.

102 Birch, Vol. 2, p. 99; also Yonge, f. 40.

103 See above.

104 Sheriff Edmund Arscott of Devon told the judges in July 1632 that although he had no formal report, he knew the JPs were very active (SP 16/221/40). See Quintrell, 'Book of Orders', p. 567; also SP 16/259/98; PC 2/43, p. 278.

105 Laud 'commended this observation as being made by his Majestie' (Gardiner, *Star Chamber and High Commission*, p. 46).

106   PC 2/41, p. 193.
107   Reports about food shortages prompted attacks upon transporters. Justices in counties near London protested that provisions for the city kept prices high and interfered with supplies. In times of plague the better off fled, trade was disrupted, sometimes by exaggerated fears of infection, and resources for relief were consequently very low when demand for help was at its highest. Wigan sought and obtained an exemption from shipmoney in 1637 on grounds of poverty resulting from severe plague. See SP 16/182/74; 16/186/26, 62; 16/185/19; 16/176/56; 16/177/52, 53, 56; 16/182/7, 20, 81; 16/183/37. Bedfordshire Record Office, St John of Bletsoe MSS, no. 1342; SP 16/334/6; Nottingham Record Office, Portland MSS, DD4P 68/13; *PCR*, Vol. 3, p. 183; SP 16/182/45; T. T. Wildridge (ed.), *The Hull Letters* (Hull, 1886), no. 14; Rye, Correspondence, 47/116; Devon Record office, Quarter Sessions Order Books, 1625–Pasche 1633, pp. 202, 315–16; Order Book, 1633–1640, Bapt. 1639; BL, Lansdowne MS 1098, f. 137; also STT 2151; STT 2277; *Hertfordshire County Records: Calendar to the Sessions Books*, ed. W. Le Hardy (Hertford, 1928), Vol. 5, p. 153. Also see above.
108   See Lord Montagu's advice to Sir Roland St John to report figures for grain supply without comment so as the councillors could draw their own conclusions about adequacy (Bedfordshire Record Office, St John of Bletsoe MSS, no. 1328); see also SP 16/177/26, 29, 43, 52–3, 55; Nottingham Record Office, Portland MSS, DD4P 68/12–14, 102–104; St John of Bletsoe MSS, no. 1342; Exeter, Act Books, Vol. 7, ff. 387v, 390 (Harvard film); Cope, *Montagu*, pp. 136–8.
109   Cholmley, *Memoirs*, p. 61.
110   e.g. SP 16/345/5; Ashton, *City and Court*, p. 173; cf. the earl of Clare's statements in connection with depopulation and building (above); also York, House Books, Vol. 35, ff. 335v–36v, 340–40v, 341v.
111   e.g. PRO, C.115/M.35, nos 8384, 8400.
112   e.g. Ashton, *City and Court*, p. 162
113   See R. Reid, *The King's Council in the North* (London: Longmans, Green, 1921).
114   e.g. York, House Books, Vol. 35, ff. 79, 87v, 111, 186v, 193v, 203, 214, 220v, 307, 328v, 350; Vol. 36, f. 25; York, Chamberlains Accounts, 1629; Cholmley, *Memoirs*, p. 51 (Whitby); also, Reid, *Council*.
115   e.g. Shropshire Record Office, Bridgnorth, Third Great Leet Book, p. 570, but Ludlow's minute book shows little evidence of serious friction with the earl of Bridgewater; see El 7204 and El 6586; see also C. Skeel, *The Council in the Marches of Wales* (London: H. Rees, 1904).
116   e.g. El 7087; 7091; 7104; 7106. Bridgewater took some pains with the appointment of sheriffs and escheators, see e.g. El MSS Vols 98 and 99. But see Worcester County Records, *Calendar of the Quarter Sessions*, Vol. 2, 1591–1643, ed. J. W. Willis Bund, presentment of 14 June 1640, pp. 684–6.
117   See T. G. Barnes, 'Star Chamber mythology', *American Journal of Legal History* (1961), pp. 1–11, and 'Due process and slow process in the late

Elizabethan and early Stuart Star Chamber', *ibid.* (1962), pp. 221–49, 315–46.

118 PRO, C.115/M.35, no. 8419; also nos 8417–18.

119 Sir John Stawell reportedly 'liked better to goe by ye Starre Chamber way first' in settling his dispute with Sir Robert Phelips and was well pleased with the results (SP 16/153/54). The court was a means of bringing enemies to answer and one means by which troublesome officials could be humbled or at least harassed. See Cl C 307; Cl C 692; F. Bamford (ed.), *A Royalist's Notebook: The Commonplace Book of Sir John Oglander* (London: Constable, 1936), pp. 85–6; *CSPDom.* 1637–8, p. 345; SP 16/278/3; HA 9597; HA 5542; SP 16/153/54; also T. G. Barnes, 'Star Chamber litigants and their counsel, 1596–1641', in *Legal Records and the Historian*, ed. J. H. Baker (London: Royal Historical Society, 1978), pp. 7–28.

120 PRO, C.115/M.36, no. 8438. Rossingham may also have had contacts at the court. See nos 8437, 8440–1. The earl of Clare was probably speaking in a spirit of defiance when he said he feared not 'ye Star Chamber' (Holles, no. 230).

121 Concerning the High Commission, see Chapter 2.

122 G. Aylmer, *The King's Servants* (New York: Columbia University Press, 1961), p. 64, notes that the court's revenue actually fell during the 1630s.

123 Ashton, *City and Court*, pp. 159–60; cf. the complaints of Bristol merchants (SP 16/273/1).

124 See J. Cockburn, *Assizes*; BL, Egerton 2716, f. 13; also Chapter 3 concerning their statements at the assizes about shipmoney. Whiteway, Woodforde, and Rous all routinely recorded executions and also commented about assize sermons but were less consistent in reporting the judges' addresses to the court. Executions: Whiteway, e.g. ff. 80, 82; Rous, pp. 48–9, 61; Woodforde, p. 498. Sermons: e.g. Rous, p. 62; also pp. 50–1; Whiteway entered the name of the preacher along with those of the judges in his diary. See also, PC 2/42, p. 59; Verney MSS, Claydon Letters, August 1637 (Yale film); BL, Egerton 2716, f. 48.

125 Jones who first rode the Oxford circuit for the winter assizes of 1626 did so every time subsequently until 1641. Denham's service in the west was only three years shorter. Others with repeated service were Hutton and Croke in the midlands, Finch in the west, Whitlocke in Oxford, and Harvey in Norfolk (Cockburn, *Assizes*, pp. 270–2).

126 See, for example, Knyvett, no. 35; Cl C 657; Birch, Vol. 2, pp. 136–7; Cl C 310.

127 Knyvett, no. 37; also, no. 42; HMC, *Twelfth Report*, app., pt. iv, p. 501; Cl C 310. York bestowed gifts upon Judge Hutton, himself a northerner, even though he consequently was not assigned to that circuit (York, House Books, Vol. 36, ff. 161, 183, 218v, 219v, 230, 277v, 288v). See also *Calendar of Chester City Council Minutes, 1603–1642*, ed. M. J. Goombridge, Record Society of Lancashire and Cheshire, vol. 106 (1956), p. 161; Shropshire Record Office, Ludlow Corporation Minute Book, 356/2/1, ff. 161v, 189v, 199v, where they looked to Sir John Bridgeman, chief justice of Chester.

128 See Bedfordshire Record Office, St John of Bletsoe MSS, no. 1331; T. G. Barnes (ed.), *Somerset Assize Orders, 1629–1640*, Somerset Record Society, vol. 65 (1959), appendix 2, no. 184; SP 16/171/37; 16/148/17; El 7646; Yonge, f. 71; SP 16/427/31; *Barrington Family Letters*, no. 199.
129 See above.
130 Jones, *Politics*, pp. 13–14; also Gardiner, *History of England*, Vol. 9, p. 289. Finch escaped trial by flight.
131 See G. Aylmer, 'Attempts at administrative reform, 1625–1640', *EHR*, vol. 72, no. 283 (1957), pp. 229–59.
132 See, for example, El MSS Vols 97 and 98; Birch, Vol. 2, pp. 253–6; PC 2/46, pp. 370–1.
133 STC 9140.
134 Aylmer, 'Administrative reform', p. 233.
135 Aylmer, *King's Servants*, pp. 106, 179–80.
136 Slingsby, *Diary*, p. 16.
137 Although I have not discovered the outcome of Oxford's quarrel with the king's officers, the Oxford Council Acts make clear the city's initial attitude (*Council Acts*, pp. 67–8); see also the case of Atkinson (B. Whitelocke, *The History of England or Memorials of English Affairs* (London, 1682), p. 13).
138 e.g. in rating disputes. See Chapter 3.
139 PCR, Vol. 2, pp. 369, 390, 407, 631–2; Vol. 3, pp. 22–3, 339; SP 16/366/48; 16/323/115; 16/354/48; 16/361/24. There were factional divisions on other issues within the city. See also P. Clark and P. Slack, *English Towns in Transition, 1500–1700* (Oxford: Oxford University Press, 1976); Whiteway, ff. 84v, 86 (Dorchester).
140 e.g. Bamford, *Oglander*, pp. 85–6; PC 2/41, p. 106; HA 5543; PC 2/44, pp. 170–1.
141 The crown followed complaints or outbreaks of trouble such as the riots at Newcastle in 1633 with investigations (Howell, *Newcastle*, pp. 53–62; PC 2/43, p. 295). See also above.
142 P. Heylyn, *Augustus, or an essay of those meanes and counsels, whereby the Commonwealth of Rome was altered and reduced into a Monarchy* (1632), STC 13268, pp. 148–50. I owe this reference to Michael Mendle.
143 Cl C 84.
144 Cl C 84; SP 16/170/4; PC 2/41, p. 193; D. Bergeron, 'Charles I's royal entries into London', *Guildhall Miscellany*, vol. 3, no. 2 (1970), pp. 91–7.
145 Holles, no. 158, 177; cf., Massinger, *The Emperor of the East*, 1, ii, 238, where Pulcheria says, 'You roare out, All is the Kings, his will above his lawes: and that fit tributes are too gentle yokes for his poore subjects ... Is this the way to make our Emperor happy? Can the groanes of his subjects yeeld him musick?'; cf. also Hyde's letter to Falkland (K. Weber, *Lucius Cary, Second Viscount Falkland* (New York: Columbia University Press, 1940), pp. 70–1).

5

1639: The 'Bishops' War'

When Charles I decided in January 1638/9 to lead an army against
the Scots to force them to accept the Laudian prayer book, he took
a step that was the culmination of a series of errors in his relations
with that kingdom and proved disastrous for his rule of England.
Lacking his father's fondness for his native land and his political
sense, Charles appeared neither to know nor to care to learn much
about that part of his domain. He antagonized some Scots at the
outset of his reign with his revocation and did little to soothe ruffled
feelings when he finally went to Scotland in 1633. While in
Edinburgh he indicated that he intended to continue to reform the
Scottish Church to bring it closer to the English. He persisted in this
policy despite the resistance to the prayer book that brought riots in
July 1637 at its institution and led to the Covenant the following
February.[1]

The English, whose suspicions and fears had prevented James I
from accomplishing his dream of union between the two kingdoms
and had bred some animosity toward the Scots at the Jacobean
court, paid relatively little attention to Scottish affairs.[2] Although
they followed Charles's journey northward in 1633, they began to
notice Scotland only when they heard of the opposition to the new
prayer book. The king who like his father had handled that sphere
of policy without recourse to the ministers or council whom he
consulted in ruling England, did little to inform his people about his
aims or the circumstances there.[3]

Reports that people rioted at St Giles in Edinburgh in July 1637
when the Laudian liturgy was introduced attracted attention in
England where the public were also wrestling with questions about

the power of bishops and the course of religion. Only a month before they had watched the Star Chamber trial of Prynne, Burton, and Bastwick whose efforts to expose the arbitrary and superstitious practices of the Laudian prelates had become notorious. Reports about the proceedings and the punishment of the trio were continuing to fill the pages of correspondence when the Edinburgh riots occurred.[4] The Scottish disturbances provided observers with another case of resistance to the religion imposed by the authorities in Church and state. The prominence of women there heightened the drama.[5]

More people began to seek news of Scottish affairs during the months that followed as it became evident that the beliefs that prompted that Sunday morning disorder were deeply held and widespread. Walter Yonge was one who began to add notes about developments in Scotland to his ever lengthening saga of the sufferings of godliness in England.[6] The Scots themselves, desirous of support, helped feed the growing English appetites for information.[7] By the late autumn of 1638 when the assembly of the Scottish kirk at Glasgow defied the Marquess of Hamilton's order to disperse and proceeded to condemn the recently imposed prayer book and canons, people in England began to talk about the possibility of war.[8] Their worries about innovations in religion at home – the queen mother's arrival that October had raised fears of Popery to a new pitch – seemed to corroborate the evidence of trouble that was coming from the north. On 28 November Woodforde wrote in his diary, 'Its said that warre is concluded against Scotland'.[9]

Those words soon proved true. Charles determined to undertake a military campaign to suppress what he regarded as the Scots' rebellion. Without summoning Parliament as his predecessors had traditionally done on such occasions, he asked his people to aid him. The issue that he, the council and the loyalist clergy emphasized was obedience.[10] Henry Valentine who preached to the king at St Paul's just before Charles left for the campaign declared, 'God is our invisible King, so the king is our visible God'. Those who revolted were erroneously calling his piety, Popery and innovation, and his clemency cruelty and persecution.[11] Good subjects must not only avoid insurgency but aid their ruler in suppressing the risings of others.

For some of the English the conflict in Scotland was not the consequence of rebellion; it was instead *Bellum Episcopale*, the

Bishops' War. They assessed the king's interpretation of the situation against the views they derived from other sources. To many it brought together questions concerning religion and defence and illustrated how difficult it was to obtain justice or redress of grievances in the absence of Parliament. By glossing over these issues and by interpreting the dispute in terms of disobedience to royal authority, the king created a dilemma for those who wished neither to be disloyal nor to participate in a burdensome war for a cause they did not espouse. The first section of this chapter deals with the initial phases of the crisis Charles created by his determination to suppress the Scots' resistance to the prayer book. The second looks at developments during the eleven months when there were some hopes that conditions would improve. The Pacification of Berwick of June 1639 ended the fighting, and in December of the same year Charles announced that a Parliament would meet. Hopes nurtured by those developments withered when he dissolved that assembly in May 1640 after it had sat only three weeks. The intensification of politics in the months following the dissolution is the topic of the final section of the chapter. By September 1640, when the king agreed to call another Parliament, the content and spirit of English politics had been transformed.

In January 1638/9 Charles began the preparations for his northern campaign that meant that the English would no longer be mere spectators of the sectarian hostilities that had ravaged the continent.[12] Questions about liability for military obligations and ability to fulfil them assumed added urgency with the prospect of war. Religious issues likewise took on new meaning. The king's demands for support led the conscientious who were troubled by the advance of Popery and Arminianism to weigh the bonds of allegiance to him with those imposed by God. If they joined his war, they would be fighting on behalf of crown, bishops and – if the rumours were true – papal agents, to enforce innovations in the Scottish Church.[13]

Charles looked to the nobility to play a leading part in his enterprise. With letters dated 26 January he called upon them to meet him at York on 1 April 'with such equipage and horses as your birth, your honor, and your interest in the public safety oblige you unto'. He wanted to know within fifteen days what assistance he could expect. By making a direct and personal appeal to the lords, he was seeking a highly visible demonstration of loyalty. If they did their duty, lesser members of society should presumably follow their example. Explaining that although the Scottish troubles had begun 'upon pretence of religion', they had been 'raised by factious spirits ... fermented by some few ill and traiterously affected persons'. If the English peers failed to acknowledge their duty and contribute to his needs, they too were rebellious.[14]

Contemporaries waited expectantly to see how many lords would comply. Charles had left no doubt about the importance that he placed on this expedition which he himself intended to lead, and the Scots had responded to his decision to confront them in battle by intensifying their efforts to win English support. They expressed their desire for closer bonds between the two kingdoms at the beginning of February in their *Information to all good Christians within the Kingdome of England ... for vindicating their intentions and actions from the unjust callumnies of their enemies.*[15] Denying that they were about to invade England, the Covenanters maintained that they only wanted the redress to which the law entitled them so that they might preserve their Church from the popish and Arminian plots of English clergy. The presence at Charles's court of a papal representative, George Con, who was a Scotsman, seemed to confirm their worst suspicions about the king's plans.[16] They were confident that if a Parliament were to meet in England, that body would 'approve of the[ir] equitie and loyaltie'.[17] They thus identified the Covenanters' complaints with those of the English regarding religion, law, and liberty.

A war of propaganda followed. The king insisted that the issue was obedience, but some who claimed to be speaking in his behalf took up the religious questions that he ignored.[18] Royalist preachers denounced Scottish beliefs such as the 'new-fangled Geneva device' of 'lay presbytery'.[19] Their arguments, despite their intent and Charles's statements, gave greater currency to the notion that the struggle was, as the Covenanters persistently maintained, a holy war. The Scots defended their painstaking answer to the king's charges by voicing the fear that, unless they did so, they would be presumed to concede his points.[20]

Charles sought in vain to prevent circulation of any but his own version of the conflict. News travelled south both by letter and by word of mouth, and people in England obtained copies of 'official' Scottish statements, tracts critical of royal policy, and other reports that tended to confirm the doubts that some had about the war.[21] As the expedition proceeded, reports of participants gave observers more cause for scepticism.[22] In May 1639 Sir Thomas Hutchinson told his Nottinghamshire countryman, Sir Gervase Clifton, that he had concluded that it was 'not possible that such insolent speeches as are reported of him [Lesley] in England can be true'.[23]

The king's declarations and requests for aid thus competed with the Scots' statements for the attention and acceptance of the lords and other Englishmen who had to determine how far they would comply with their respective obligations to support the war. Convention and custom allowed for pleas of hardship when royal commands proved burdensome – peers at times asked to be excused from attending Parliament, the Privy Council, or other royal gatherings.[24] The lords took advantage of that tradition and responded to the request to take up arms against the Covenanters by addressing the nature of their duties as members of the nobility and discussing the ways these might be fulfilled. They acknowledged their duty and affirmed their readiness to serve, but many of them cited factors such as old age, poor health, poverty or other responsibilities, although not political or religious issues, that impeded them. The earl of Nottingham wrote that his heart was loyal but his body weak – he had not yet recovered from his last sickness. Moreover, his estate which was not worth £400 p.a. could hardly maintain his wife and family.[25] The earl of Peterborough apologized that eight of the horses he would bring would be undressed. The warning was short, he had few horses and arms, and three parts of his estate were not yet in his hands.[26] The earl of Clare cited £9000 debt against an estate of £4000, nine children (seven of them daughters), and great law suits, yet he promised he would obey with such equipment as time and availability of provisions would allow.[27]

Public interest in their responses reached an extraordinary level. By mid-February reports of refusals were circulating. Thomas Smith told Sir John Pennington then that 'many of the lords refuse absolutely in person or purse'. Some, he added, including Saye and Brooke were advising the king to call Parliament.[28] Hearing such tales, the earl of Huntingdon wrote to the Earl Marshal ruing the times 'that any of his Majesties nobility of this kingdome should refuse to serve the Kinge his Majestie goinge in his own person'. He described those who would 'make a scruple of it' as being of the 'new stamp'.[29] Far less alarmist and more accurate was the word which

William Montagu passed along to his father. He noted 'very few if any refuse' although there was talk that 'my Lord Sey and my Lord Brooke, and some of that knott' would.[30]

Viscount Saye and Sele and Baron Brooke whose conduct was the source of speculation were widely known for their Puritanism and their open challenges to Charles's policies.[31] With other Puritans in the Providence Island Company they had joined in a scheme to plant a colony, Saybrook, in the New World.[32] Saye who was quite a bit older than Brooke had been more prominent in opposition previously, but on this occasion both originally indicated that they would not participate in the Scottish campaign.[33] Brooke stated that he did not believe himself obliged except by Parliament.[34] Although not actually mentioning Parliament, Saye was similarly firm in denying his liability for the campaign. Ultimately both went to York but continued to make manifest their doubts about the expedition. None of the other lords stood out.

Despite Charles's forceful statements about the peers' duties and the council's collection of precedents from Henry VIII and Elizabeth to support his orders, some lords were excused from joining the expedition.[35] Most leaves to be absent went to individuals whose age, health, or service to the king elsewhere precluded participation, and observers found little reason to comment. Lord Montagu who obtained an excuse had declared himself ready to go despite age and infirmity but at the same time, though not inclined to be over-confident about receiving court favours, had assured his worried children that he had no real intention of carrying out his offer.[36] As on many previous occasions where the success of his suits had been mixed, he relied upon the intercession of his brother, the earl of Manchester who was Lord Privy Seal. Montagu's age and his acknowledgement of the need for some contribution to the expedition probably ensured his escape.[37] Health seems to have been the grounds for excusing the earl of Kingston and several others.[38]

Except in a few cases the crown and the lords devoted more energy to determining exactly what an individual peer would contribute than whether he would attend. Negotiations gave those lords who were uneasy about the purpose of the war or doubtful that it would succeed an opportunity to try to limit their role and the king a chance to press them for support. The high stakes made the bargaining unusually intense. People played for politics and religion, not just for perennial reasons of finance and self-interest. Charles's indecisiveness about what he wanted both lengthened the process and caused nobles to grumble about the way the entire business was being handled. His attempt to fight the war without obtaining support from Parliament was in itself a cause for scepticism.[39] Reports of the strength of Covenanters also led individuals to conclude that the enterprise was dubious. The earl of Kingston told Sir Gervase Clifton at the beginning of March that he did not expect to live 'to heare of a second Flodden Field'.[40] Memories of the embarrassments of the wars of the 1620s may have been another factor in the reluctance of men like Lord Montagu to pour money into a losing cause.[41]

In this case as in others many lords relied upon intermediaries to arrange terms with the crown and to inform them what others were giving.[42] Peers were not only hesitant to make an individual stand in opposition to the king but also concerned to avoid both the embarrassment and expense of an inordinately large contribution and the dishonour of one less than Charles would accept or than others of their rank supplied. Their preoccupation with the part particular nobles would have in the expedition runs through their correspondence during February and March. When the earl of Kingston heard that the lady Arundel had taken a house in York, he thought that meant her lord would be going and passed on the news.[43] The earl of Bridgewater confessed that he was uneasy about responding without knowing what others were doing.[44] He would, no doubt, have been pleased to receive the long list of the numbers of horses contributed by various lords that Lord Montagu received from his son.[45]

Negotiations about contributions dragged on because the king changed his demands and the lords encountered difficulties finding horses and arms. Peers who went to great lengths to meet their obligations were frustrated when their efforts seemed to yield little. The earl of Bridgewater had originally offered money because it was 'extreame hard to gett horses and', he believed, 'impossible to have Armes ready' by the day specified.[46] When he found that Charles instead wanted horses, he nevertheless undertook to procure some, but just at the point that he had made the necessary arrangements, he heard that the king preferred money.[47] He protested to Secretary Coke, 'I can not expende and disburse my moneyes and have them ready lying by me. I have no minte nor spring out of which moneyes may flowe into my purse or cheste'.[48] Yet when the secretary responded, confirming the king's desire for money, Bridgewater despite his complaints complied.[49] Montagu was less willing to conform to what he believed were unreasonable demands, but even he who had reservations about the purpose of the campaign sought to overcome obstacles and procure equipage.[50]

The king forced those peers who actually joined the expedition to weigh their obligations to him once more. At York he put them to swear that they would 'constantly and cherfully oppose all seditions, rebellions, ... and treasons' against him. Saye and Brooke balked. They declared that they would defend England, but they refused to acknowledge a duty to invade a foreign land.[51] According to the earl of Rutland who recorded the proceedings in his diary, they had made a similar statement in his hearing three days earlier. He hints that they were not alone in their concern about the 'ambiguity' of the oath, but he does not elaborate.[52]

A note among Lord Montagu's papers suggests that after swearing, some lord, perhaps Rutland, although Montagu does not name him, began to worry about whether he had done anything prejudicial to the peerage. That lord wrote out what he believed the meaning of the oath to be – that is that he would 'fight under the kings Banner in the kingdome agaynst all such as wer named in the oath so far as law required'. With this interpretation he approached others. 'Some of them subscribed that exposition but some of them though they assented yet thought not good to subscribe.' The next day they went to the king who after a day's interval responded that he understood the oath as they did.[53]

If Charles, as Rutland indicates, emphasized that the lords were bound to fight whether or not he was present in person, he did not address all the points in question.[54] Some sources suggest that the peers were most disturbed by the phrase requiring to risk 'lyfe and fortune' for the monarch.[55] Walter Yonge underlined both that phrase and those concerning circumstances in which the obligation applied when he entered the oath in his diary. Yonge also enumerated objections to it: Why should any who had already taken the oaths of supremacy and allegiance take this? If they held their lands and goods subject to the king's needs, they had lost their propriety. The 'ancient legal way of raising money' was by Parliament. Taking an oath or sustaining a charge illegally violated the Petition of Right.[56]

Charles's explanation of the oath in itself seems to indicate that he feared that if he did not answer, others might follow Saye and Brooke who had refused to swear and had objected that the oath was not authorized by Parliament.[57] Sir Henry Mildmay's report to Windebanke of an incident in camp tells of the earl of Bristol's allegations that a number of peers believed that Parliament should be summoned. Bristol reportedly spoke to the king one evening 'publikely of the grounde of this quarrell and for a Parliament sayinge that most of the lords heere boath concellors and others were resolved to petition his Majesty for one'.[58] The lords' lack of enthusiasm for the king's venture was hardly a secret. Rutland claims that once when volunteers were being sought, 'a witty lord sayd ther was no volunteers for they all came to York against their will'.[59]

The peers, including Saye and Brooke whose refusal to swear to the statement at York led Charles to imprison them, had taken seriously his request that they perform their obligations to him, but they had also made it clear that they expected that he would be equally careful to fulfil his responsibilities among which many counted the summoning of Parliament to prepare for war. Having discussed among themselves the meaning of the oath he proffered, they had sought clarification and then proposed that subjects throughout the kingdom make the same declaration of loyalty. Through the experience of the first Bishops' War they were revitalized as a political community. Prompted by the king, they were asserting themselves in the handling of public affairs and by their passive and limited resistance to his policies they were instructing the English people.

Accounts of the war and the conduct of the peers circulated widely.[60] The king's demand that the lords take the oath and his reaction to Saye and Brooke's refusal attracted much attention. Some observers thought their boldness deserved the punishment they received, but others believed that Charles had erred in handling them. Their reputations virtually guaranteed that the affair would, as Thomas Windebanke worried, gain notice beyond the north, and their willingness to invoke the law might bring a lengthy dispute about military obligations.[61] Sir Edmund Verney who was very conscientious about his own duties to the king commented after Saye was released, 'ther was never soe weake a thing done as the commitment of that man'.[62] Although most nobles had gone to York, had signed the oath, and had denied complicity when confronted by Bristol's claim, their ambivalence not only may have weakened Charles's offensive and given him an incentive to come to terms with the Scots but also raised questions about his proceedings in the minds of others of his people.

Neither Charles nor most observers paid such heed to the conduct of lesser individuals, yet these too manifested doubts about the war. Gentlemen asked to serve in the north adhered to the dictates of custom and, like the nobles, couched their replies in the terms of the request they received.[63] Some sought and obtained excuses from attendance. Francis Cheynell who was advocating that Clifton 'forsake Mars his campe for Venus her tent' told his patron that he might 'safely say that there is a businesse of very great importance which doth nearely concerne your estate and children who called you away very unexpectedly [*sic*]'. He suggested that 'the duke [? Lenox] or my lord Holland can procure your leave to withdraw your person so you leave your artillery'.[64]

Members of the gentry felt some pressure to demonstrate their support for the king's enterprise. Sir Edward Dering told the earl of Thanet that although he was honoured by the summons to York, he was financially embarrassed and physically unable to go to York. To prove his loyalty he cited his 'travaile ... more than any mans in ye kingdome' in the knighthood commissions, his action to prevent shipmoney being 'dashed ... in peeces' and his debts as a result of his being lieutenant at Dover castle.[65] For Dering Charles's request for yet more assistance seemed too much.[66]

Some of those individuals whose official or public responsibilities required that they assist with the king's war effort demonstrated their reservations about it by failing to accord his authority the customary ceremonial respect. When the earl of Arundel, general of the army, came to Northampton, the mayor and aldermen 'fayled to present their service' to him and only did so when ordered by a warrant.[67] In Exeter civic officials kept their hats on when the king's proclamation 'touching the grievous practices of Some in Scotland was read' in the cathedral, 'the rest of the congregation being uncovered'.[68] In response to the Privy Council's subsequent summons they petitioned to be spared attendance on the grounds that they had not been consciously protesting. They claimed that it had been cold, and although they were uncovered at the beginning, they and many others had put on their hats without least thought of irreverence.[69] The board granted their petition but required that they make a written submission to the king and personally present the same to the bishop.[70] Their arguments bore little weight in view of their experience with the formalities of public life.[71] Like nobles and gentlemen, corporate leaders refrained from opposition on the most important occasions. Whatever their feelings about the Scottish campaign, the mayor and aldermen of York dutifully entertained Charles when he came to their city to assemble his forces.[72]

In the provinces the deputy lieutenants bore the brunt of both the popular resistance to the increased military charges resulting from the war and the urgent royal demands for men and arms. The council's orders that trained bands from counties go north and that additional troops be raised sparked far more serious and widespread opposition than had previous efforts to collect rates and enforce obligations. Sir Robert Harley, deputy lieutenant in Herefordshire, found that 'all lusty men' were trying to avoid the press.[73] Tales relating the lengths to which some went to escape or to find substitutes and the ways in which people tried to use the press to exact revenge upon their enemies circulated and created the impression that order had broken down. The Northamptonshire deputies sought to settle an old quarrel with George Plowright, a constable, who had in the course of struggles over shipmoney sued them in the Star Chamber for scandalous words and for abuse of him. According to Plowright and Dr Sibthorpe, the Laudian rector of the parish, who came to his defence, the 'puritan' deputy lieutenants ordered the constable pressed for service in the north just at the point that his Star Chamber suit was coming to trial.[74] Although he paid a man to go in his stead, he went north anyway and was consequently unable to produce witnesses for the Star Chamber case, ordered to pay costs, and on default imprisoned. Sibthorpe hoped that Plowright could be excused and the deputies punished for their vengeful proceedings.

The deputies' task was the harder because few men were enthusiastic about going north to fight. Even with the king's provision that any trained soldier who wanted to stay at home could find a substitute, they had to force people to serve.[75] As the prospect of actual combat increased, so did reluctance to train and exercise. Lady Pelham reported that when her Lincolnshire neighbours observed how concerned their Lord Lieutenant, the earl of Lindsey, was about the quality of forces there, they suspected that fighting would occur and became fearful.[76] Desertions were a serious problem among soldiers travelling towards Scotland.[77]

In addition to their difficulties in providing troops the deputies struggled to collect from the county the sums needed for coat and conduct, horse, wagon, and billeting money. Hindering their efforts were bitter memories of the exactions of the wars of the 1620s and the Petition of Right's assertion of protection against some of the abuses of those years.[78] People who had objected to paying fees for muster masters in time of peace would protest against measures they thought unwarranted. More of those who were challenging payment did so by citing reasons other than the standard professions of poverty, unjust or erroneous assessment although these remained the most frequently used excusses.[79] A few Puritans mentioned that the necessity of providing for the queen mother which aggravated the fiscal problems of the country made it unable to pay military charges.[80]

When the council ordered that trained bands be sent out of the counties, the chorus of complaints grew shrill.[81] Deputies bickered with the board about the costs and arrangements for moving troops and supplies and angrily protested against complying with commands that defied tradition, weakened local defences, and disrupted communities.[82] In Yorkshire the deputy lieutenants and colonels of the trained bands formally addressed the king, acknowledging their duty to serve, but imploring him to consider the condition of their country, their fortunes, their wives and children, and not to withdraw all the forces at once. They rejected the proposal to replace local men with those from elsewhere. That, they argued, would cause insolence and disruption instead of solving the problem.[83] Having learned that pay for their men would not begin as long as the troops were within the county, they were also concerned about the financial ramifications of the orders they had received.[84] Their soldiers might be positioned on the northern edge of the shire, far from their homes, and yet still at the county's charge.

Aggravating the fiscal, military, and political problems that arose in the wake of orders for transportation of trained bands were administrative quagmires and sheer uncertainty about the costs involved.[85] In Devonshire deputies who had seen little point in prosecuting impoverished delinquents and had consequently concentrated their efforts on extracting money due from the able found themselves accused of injustice.[86] The very inequities in charges that arose from the differing locations and situations of counties brought deputies to plead for changes in assessment. Those in Cambridge, a poor and 'thoroughfare' county which had to provide posthorses and other supplies for traffic to the north, felt that they needed some consideration, especially because their countrymen, though heavily rated, had dutifully paid shipmoney. Were there no rewards for loyal service?[87] Sir Henry Slingsby whose appointment as a deputy depended upon a letter from the Lord Lieutenant instead of formal commission took advantage of the fact to bow out after two months. He confided to his diary in January that 'Neither ye one nor ye other can expect to receive advantage by this war where ye remedy will prove worse yn ye disease'.[88]

The council was not prepared to believe that the problems the deputies listed were always as serious as they indicated. To some the board sent warnings against exaggeration. In a few instances local opponents alleged that deputies were not merely less conscientious than they should be but were actually undermining the king's enterprise. The earl of Lindsey who had quarrelled with his Lincolnshire neighbours on various occasions sent to Secretary Windebanke the names of people he suspected of encouraging resistance to having the trained bands leave the county.[89] Sibthorpe similarly charged that lords and gentlemen in Northamptonshire were leading their countrymen in disobedience to the crown. If they were able to continue to 'overbeare meane men', he worried, 'it will be hazardous for inferiors to do hearty service to supreame'.[90]

As the preparations gave way to movement toward Scotland and actual fighting, reports of insolence and outbreaks of disorder followed those of ill-prepared troops and resistence to service. The Harleys heard that soldiers from Hereford had killed one of their conductors.[91] Hardly surprised by the low morale of the poorly provisioned army, contemporaries were nevertheless disturbed by it. Sir Henry Slingsby wrote in his diary that the men were ready to mutiny and consequently had done much damage to the country-side.[92] People living along major routes to the north got a chance to see at first hand both the conduct and condition of the troops.[93] For them the campaign assumed a reality beyond taxation, the possibility of military service, and the disruption of life.

The war became an issue in itself. It sharpened and was sharpened by the pain of other grievances. Fewer people paid their shipmoney assessments in 1639.[94] Sheriffs and constables reported that they could not perform the duties which war imposed and also collect the levy and that individuals who had paid heavy military charges could not or would not pay still more for shipmoney.[95] Opposition to the purpose of the war also prompted resistance. Broadsides, such as *Reasons that Ship and Conduct Money Ought to be paid*, asserted that these levies were financing Popery which, after it had been set up in Scotland, would be established in England.[96] Many who did not meet their assessments offered no excuse or explanation. They simply defied the orders. The growing impatience of king and council seemed at times to impede rather than encourage support of all kinds. When the Common Council of London responded to a royal request for a loan with only £5000 and a petition of grievances, Charles, angered by that token and qualified response, let it be known he would receive neither and found the city reluctant to co-operate when he asked for help again in June.[97]

Because some courtiers and others contributed willingly to the cause and denounced resisters in terms even stronger than those of king and council, acrimony disrupted communities and interfered with smooth relations between local officials and the board. A few royal supporters talked of the situation in England itself in the spring of 1639 as one of rebellion. Denouncing the Covenanters as Puritans, their most outspoken opponents charged that the two groups were connected, if not conspiring against order and authority.[98] In writing to Sir John Lambe early in June 1639 Sibthorpe expressed his fears, 'If *Bellum Episcopale*, as they say some stile it, be not ended, and *Rebellio Puritanica*, for soe I know it may be truely stiled, be not subdued, from which Good Lord Deliver us'.[99] He thought Lambe might be more worried about the machinations of the Puritans if he lived in Northamptonshire where a closely knit group of clergymen and laymen whose number included lords and gentlemen, deputy lieutenants and JPs resisted shipmoney, ecclesiastical government and Charles's efforts to fight the Scots.[100]

Sibthorpe was hardly unbiased in his views, but his appraisal of the strength of religious feelings is not without substance. In the borough of Northampton where the mayor and aldermen were unwilling to show support for the northern campaign, Puritans apparently took it upon themselves that spring to move their communion table from the position in the east end of the church where ecclesiastical authorities had ordered it placed. On Easter day Woodforde rejoiced, 'Our table is still brought downe, blessed be the Lord. Lord keep us still from sinful innovacons'.[101] That same spring one of the anti-popish panics that had swept a number of English communities in the years since 1590 struck the market town of Kettering where Puritanism was also deeply rooted.[102] Sibthorpe reported to Lambe that in response to rumours that Papists would attack on a Sunday while the inhabitants were attending church the townsmen had ordered extra watches and the stationing of men in the steeple and on the battlements during the services. One man who was particularly anxious had allegedly gone to worship attended by six armed guards. All these efforts yielded only three or four horsemen riding toward York whom the townsmen had held briefly and then used to carry letters to relatives in the north.[103]

Puritanism and opposition also erupted in vigorous resistance to shipmoney and to the Scots' war in Essex and Hertford in the spring of 1639, and close connections with Scotland helped breed sympathy for the Covenanters in Newcastle.[104] Those English and Scots who desired to thwart Charles's religious policies were, however, cautious about espousing each other's causes and circumspect about defying royally sanctioned policies.[105] The Northamptonshire Puritans who so alarmed Sibthorpe and the men of Newcastle whom the council was busy investigating professed loyalty to the king and willingness to observe the law. They challenged some orders overtly and others by inaction or circumvention, but they were not prepared to revolt outright.

The boldest criticism of the king's campaign against the Scots came in remarks or papers which the authorities condemned as libels. One found at Ware in Hertfordshire protested against the shedding of innocent blood. Maintaining that innovations in religion were a serious problem, it claimed that people were willing to fight for God and king, but not against the Scots.[106] The bishops who used their authority to impose religious conformity and personified links between religion and political grievances were target of numerous attacks.[107] They insisted upon obedience to their orders and to those of the king who sanctioned their action with his own. One of the most succinct statements of the links between English and Scottish grievances comes in a bill which John Rous tells us was among those given to the preacher by the parish clerk on 1 April. Even though the preacher refused to read it, Rous recorded its contents, 'John Commonwealthsman of Great Britaine, being sicke of the Scottish disease, desires the prayers of this Congregation for a parliament'.[108]

In calling for a Parliament libellers took up an issue that had concerned the nobility in their responses to the king's demands for service and oaths of loyalty and one that others shared. Educated about the role of Parliament through the experiences of the 1620s, people of all ranks believed by 1629 that a monarch should summon Parliament if he were to engage in a war that required their support. Each time since 1630 that war seemed likely, people began to talk of a session of Parliament. Sir Thomas Peyton told Henry Oxinden in November 1638 that he was 'certayne' that the Scottish situation would 'bring forthe a Parliament here in England: for whether the King comply or confronte theire demands, it is thought they will be such as the Kyng will answer with the voyce of the whole kingdome'.[109] When Lord Montagu's son, William, told his father early in February that the king was receiving enough contributions so there would be no need of Parliament, Montagu, an old 'parlia-mentman' and a stickler for precedents, was very uneasy.[110] Later that month the Venetian ambassador reported that the people were becoming 'ever bolder in their cries for Parliament'.[111] Those closer to Charles thought he had no alternative. Cottington reported to Wentworth that no course had been taken for levying money. The king would not 'hear of a Parliament, and he is told by a committee of learned men, there is no other way'.[112] Wentworth who was of the same opinion, especially if war were prolonged, told Northumber-land so the following February.[113]

The advocates of Parliament believed that Charles needed counsel as well as more material support from his people who whether they regarded Scotland as a foreign kingdom or looked upon it in fraternity were hesitant to follow him blindly into war. Neither James I nor his son had consulted Parliament about their Scottish policies, but James had taken his proposal of union between the two kingdoms to the Lords and Commons and had bowed to their views about that. During the 1620s Parliament had taken more and more cognizance over foreign affairs and war. By not summoning Parliament in 1639, Charles lost an opportunity to unite his people behind him. These were circumstances in which Parliament could perform its time-honoured function of giving legitimacy to royal acts.

The Covenanters, whose propaganda was reaching England despite the crown's efforts to suppress it, suggested that an English Parliament would have sympathy for their claims that the king and prelates were violating law and liberty in imposing innovations in religion without the consent of their Parliament and the Assembly of their kirk.[114] That argument paralleled the contentions voiced in England by the bold souls who had insisted repeatedly in the years since 1629 that Parliament must meet if the Babylonian captivity of the English Church were to be ended. Although those who opposed the war on religious grounds were not necessarily those most eager for Parliament, they were in many cases the same persons. Whereas past Parliaments had attacked Laudian and Arminian innovations in religion, during the absence of Parliament those policies had advanced to new-found power. The prospect of the king's using force against the Scots to perpetuate these policies and extend their sway made the need for Parliament to preserve religion greater than ever.

The deep divisions in the kingdom which the war had made manifest were in themselves reason for a Parliament; so were the manifold grievances that the English cited when asked to bear the charges of the campaign. Among Parliament's traditional roles was that of redresser of grievances. Anyone who felt burdened by shipmoney, military charges, monopolies, or the other exactions by which Charles had attempted to supply his needs during the 1630s could look to Parliament for relief. Individuals could hope to accomplish various kinds of personal business there too. More important in the political psychology of the time was the belief, cited on various occasions since 1629, that Parliament was an instrument of reconciliation that could heal differences between ruler and subject.[115]

Because the summoning and dissolution of Parliament was the king's prerogative and because Charles had in 1629 been emphatic that he would fight fiercely for that prerogative, most people, however strongly they believed Parliament should meet, said little about that when they responded to appeals to contribute to the Scottish campaign. The king's failure to summon one nevertheless provided them with yet another reason for dragging their feet instead of joining his cause with enthusiasm.

The slowness with which the English gave Charles their support magnified their divisions and conflicts in regard to the war which in turn caused anxiety and further division. To the king's servants and to his self-appointed defenders all this manifested the disobedience of his people. Some persons both at court and elsewhere talked of the importance of improving management of military affairs, but to other observers the growing crisis was a divine warning to cleanse the kingdom of sin.[116] Despite experiencing threats and then delivery from the Spanish Armada, the Gunpowder Plot, the foreign wars of the 1620s, and recurrent episodes of plague and dearth, England had not repented. The events of 1639 suggested that Judgement might be imminent.

John Napier whose *Plaine Discovery of the whole Revelation of Saint John* had gone through several editions since the original of 1593, had predicted that 1639 would be the beginning of war between good and evil.[117] Repentance and reform seemed essential, but people could not agree whether individuals should be responsible only for their own lives or also for the commonwealth.[118] Puritans who emphasized the importance of unanimity in making decisions found the situation especially troubling.[119] Anxious and uncertain what to do, most people hesitated to take any steps that would openly challenge royal authority. The countess of Westmorland was virtually alone when, convinced of the utter impracticality of the king's conducting a divided nation into a war financed through the prerogative, she addressed an appeal for peace to Secretary Winde-banke in May 1639.[120]

Charles, despite people's reservations about the war, obtained sufficient support to conduct his campaign until he could conclude negotiations with the Scots. Nobles had complained and gone north. Although worried by the oath, they subscribed to it. The deputies had overcome resistance to raise enough men who, however poorly provided for and unwilling, had stayed to fight. The customs farmers had loaned him money when the City of London had refused.[121] For his persistence he had paid a price. By adding to the burdens of his subjects without allowing them an opportunity to communicate to him their concerns and grievances, he and his councillors had failed to show the patience, understanding, or trust that they expected from a monarch. They weighed his arguments about the importance of his cause against the statements of the Covenanters which circulated despite his prohibitions and which voiced complaints not unlike their own. From the Scots too came an example of political action that they might follow as his demands for assistance gave them a renewed stake in public affairs. The impact of the first Bishops' War was evident during the months that followed its conclusion.

*

Charles came to terms with the Scots in mid-June, two and a half months after he had arrived in York to assemble his forces. In the Pacification of Berwick he agreed that an assembly would meet to resolve the current problems and that a Parliament would confirm its action. Both sides promised to withdraw their forces.[122] When word of the treaty reached people in England, they rejoiced.[123] The fact of peace which brought a respite for both king and subject seemed more important than its specific provisions. In the English Church at Rotterdam M. Harris preached a sermon entitled, *Brittaines Hallelujah or a Sermon of Thanksgiving for the Happy Pacification in Brittaine.* He praised Charles for saving England from insurrection which, if it had succeeded, would have been even more serious than a domestic conspiracy such as the Gunpowder Plot. The king deserved to be pictured as a saviour of the Church of England along with Queen Elizabeth who, he believed, had saved the Church from the Spanish Armada.[124]

Before long the hopes stirred by the cessation of hostilities and by relief from some of the wartime burdens waned. It was soon realized that the king and Covenanters had not resolved their differences.[125] A chorus of complaints arose at the summer assizes. Chief Justice Finch reported that he had had to manoeuvre in order to avoid a grand jury presentment against shipmoney at Exeter.[126] Even though the sums due by the writs issued the previous November were only one third what they had been in earlier years, the vehement debates about rating continued, collections lagged, and arrears mounted.[127]

Archbishop Laud persisted in his efforts to impose religious conformity in England, and opponents sought to curtail them. In Essex several ministers were indicated at the assizes.[128] Desirous of making it easier to prevent attacks upon those who refused to give communion to individuals who would not come up to the rails, Charles in December asked the judges whether there was any statute which would permit such indictments.[129]

In Northamptonshire gentry who gathered 'accidentally' at the sheriff's table at their summer assizes drew up a representation to the bishop who was expected at Northampton on his visitation the next week.[130] They appealed to him 'to take such a course in the moderating of his Articles (some whereof were conceived to be very strict and unusuall) that the officers and ministers under him might not make use of them (contrary phaps to his lops intention) to presse new things to be practiced in the worship and service of God wch are not enjoyned by the Rubrick and canons of the Church of England assuring his Lop of a generall readynes in them to conforme to the government of the sd Church and to observe all the rights and ceremonys therof according to the Rubrick and canons and soe to leave it to his Lop consideration'.[131] Taking pains to express their recognition of his authority and that of the Church and attempting to put the best possible construction upon his intentions, they appointed two well-known Laudian clergymen, Dr Clarke and Dr Sibthorpe to deliver their appeal.[132] 'Other gentlemen were alsoe entreated' to speak to the bishop 'as they could gaine opportunity'.[133] Their strategy and wording were designed to obtain relief, not to offend, and yet what they did challenged the repeated claims of prelates that it was the clergy, not the laity, who governed the Church. Perhaps inspired by the Scots, they had acted collectively though, as they pointed out, not officially.

Laud himself refrained from any discussion of the impact of the Scots' war on the Church of England when he wrote his report of the conditions in the province of Canterbury for the year 1639. He complained, however, that in his own diocese, 'Many that were brought to good order for receiving the holy communion, where the rails stand before the table, are now of late fallen off, and refuse to come up thither to receive'.[134] Duppa, bishop of Chichester, who had seen an attempt at the quarter sessions in the autumn to attack the Laudians' stand on altars, said that his diocese was 'not so much troubled with puritan ministers, as with puritan justices of the peace, of which latter there are store [sic]'.[135] The report in general is neither anxious nor pessimistic. Both the bishops who sent returns and the archbishop himself had an interest in convincing the king that they were doing their jobs. The statement they submitted served that end.

The prelates were far more concerned about the situation in Scotland in the autumn of 1639 than that in England. Bishop Hall volunteered to write a response to the Scots' anti-episcopal arguments. Laud, on behalf of the king, encouraged him, and the work appeared in the following spring.[136] People began again to talk of war. Despite the fight which occurred in October between the Hollanders and Dunkirkers in the waters off the Downs, it was events in the north which seemed most likely to erupt in violence.[137] Many Englishmen would have agreed with the newswriter who observed in October, 'The theater for these kingdomes hath nowe for a good while been chiefly placed at Edenbourg'.[138]

When Traquair prorogued the Scottish Parliament on the king's behalf early in November, many English observers thought things could not be worse.[139] Few seem to have expected that Charles would summon a Parliament in England. He had not done so the previous spring when he was making plans for his northern campaign, and since then he had given no indications that his intentions had changed with regard to the Scots or to the oft-repeated complaints of the English about religion, shipmoney, military charges, or other grievances. Although people were resigned and unhappy, they were no longer as restive as they had been during the fighting.

They therefore greeted tidings that a Parliament would assemble with joy but also with questions.[140] Many were suspicious that the news would not bring what they wished. They were afraid to trust the crown and hesitant to believe what they heard – that Parliament would actually meet. Woodforde who first got wind of the reports on 8 December noted on the 13th, 'The newes of the Parliament still is confirmed'.[141] Until the issuance of the writs of summons in February, the earl of Leicester's correspondents regularly reported that although plans for Parliament apparently still held, there were as yet no writs.[142]

Observers noticed that at the same time that the king was summoning a Parliament, he was persisting in his preparations for war, his collection of shipmoney, and his reliance upon councillors thought to have little sympathy with the grievances of the public. Although some people who had been contemplating emigration to New England decided to postpone their journey, few contemporaries were openly confident that Parliament could effect reconciliation between king and subjects.[143] When Lord Keeper Coventry died in January, Charles appointed Chief Justice Finch to replace him. About the same time Sir John Coke lost his secretaryship to Sir Henry Vane.[144]

The king's support for Archbishop Laud was another sign that anyone expecting real reform might be disappointed.[145] An inveterate enemy of parliaments, Laud was thought to be responsible when the council decided in early November to break tradition and not attend the ceremonies in connection with the entry into office of a new Lord Mayor of London. Although Charles had not had a close relationship with the city and had declined the invitation for a formal entry when he had returned from the north in August, the board's action stirred talk.[146] Reports claimed that the archbishop believed London had 'affronted' the king and had dishonoured him in connection with the Scots' war and was consequently not worthy of the honour of the council's presence.[147]

Laud displayed his defensiveness rather than his vindictiveness a few months later when he attracted attention by halting the Lent readings at the Middle Temple. The reader, Edward Bagshaw, a Puritan whose conduct drew Sibthorpe's notice the preceding year, took as his topic the statute of 25 Edward III, c.4 and discussed the status of bishops in parliament.[148] When questioned, he claimed to have chosen the statute more than two years earlier and more than a year before he had heard opposition to prelacy. Why, he asked, should English bishops take offence about something that was an issue in Scotland?[149] Laud, unmoved by Bagshaw's defence, found little support at the Middle Temple. When the lawyer left town, he did so not in disgrace or defeat but as a hero, accompanied by forty to fifty horsemen.[150] The archbishop had publicly defended episcopacy but without subduing his opponent.

Joining Laud in the public limelight during the autumn and winter of 1639 was Sir Thomas Wentworth who in January was created earl of Strafford, Baron of Raby, and promoted from Lord Deputy to Lord Lieutenant of Ireland. Although he reportedly argued that Charles by summoning Parliament could wage 'effectuall warre' and consequently convinced the king in December to end eleven years of personal rule, Wentworth's views and image were like Laud's – imperious.[151] Observers marvelled that when made a peer, he chose the title Raby which was the name of the estate of Sir Henry Vane, Treasurer of the Household.[152] Soon after that a gentlewoman who brought him a petition 'cast in the old stile' was told she was 'ignorant of her duty'.[153]

Those who disagreed with him about public affairs not only lost his friendship but also gained his vigorous opposition. His fellow Yorkshireman and associate, Sir Hugh Cholmley, who had refused to pay shipmoney was affronted when he was 'barred the freedom of' entering the earl's bedchamber in London at the time of the Short Parliament. When Strafford came out, Cholmley noted, 'saluting divers gentlemen he passed me as if he knew me not, and with some scorn, which my nature could ill-digest'.[154]

Strafford's reputation led the English to watch what happened at the meeting of the Irish Parliament in March. His well-publicized success in obtaining a grant of six subsidies and a declaration of willingness to give further aid made him the focus of even greater attention when he returned to England to attend Parliament there.[155] However submissive people thought the Irish assembly was, they could not fail to wonder about the significance of its action.[156]

Contemporaries were likewise uncertain about the outcome of Parliament in England. Preparations for war continued during February and March. Negotiations between the king and the Scottish commissioners who had arrived in London in mid-February seemed to yield little progress.[157] The Venetian ambassador reported that those with the best basis for predicting thought that if Charles wanted subsidies from Parliament, he would have to sacrifice someone to it.[158] There were other signs that reform would be called for. Sheriffs discovered that as the day of opening for the session approached, people stiffened in their resistance to shipmoney.[159] At the Northamptonshire quarter sessions on 8 January 1639/40, the grand jury had presented a petition against the levy. Sheriff Sir Christopher Yelverton who himself was not enthusiastic about shipmoney defended his refusal to denounce their action by explaining that in view of the country's 'condition and state' which was, he believed, known to the board, there were clearly limits to what he as sheriff could do.[160]

Deputy lieutenants also saw signs of increasing opposition during the spring of 1640. Protesters were questioning the legality of military charges even more vigorously than they had in the wake of Parliament in 1629 and 1630.[161] Invoking their rights as freemen and arguing that the idea that a soldier might hire another to go in his place was contrary to the Petition of Right, some of the Hertfordshire trained bands petitioned their deputies that they might remain in the county. If money was wanted, they said, they would contribute that in Parliament.[162] The same notion can explain the resistance Charles encountered when he appealed for loans that same spring. Both his dismissal of Master of Requests Sir Sidney Montagu for offering too little and Montagu's firmness about his stance seemed significant to observers. They also noticed when four London aldermen went to prison because they refused to return the names of citizens in their wards who were able to contribute.[163] Although Charles raised some £232,530 in loans between 20 December and 15 May, he had had to exert pressure to do so.[164]

The conflicts between Charles and people who were unwilling to comply with his demands for money added to the political tension that was building up in anticipation of the opening of Parliament in April. Electioneering was intense in many communities. Hawkins told the earl of Leicester that at Westminster there was 'the greatest noyse about the businesse that ever was'.[165] Popular verses described the ideal candidates and condemned those who would be undesirable.[166] Reports circulated of insolence and of vigorous opposition to men who had court connections or as sheriffs had collected shipmoney.[167] While local issues or personalities dominated in some places and the intervention of patrons was decisive in others, the controversies about religion, defence and Charles's government that the Bishops' War had magnified and intensified played an important part in many of the contests. Aware of this and realizing that the outcome of the elections would give some indication about what they might expect from the session itself, people watched closely.

Also occupying much attention in the weeks before Parliament were preparation of petitions and plans for action there. Sir Robert Harley's list of almost thirty questions concerning topics that needed attention concentrated upon religious issues such as lectures put down, scandalous books licensed, the power of bishops in the courts, and altars rather than tables, but it also included the problems of vagrancy, inns and alehouses and other matters of local government.[168] Religious grievances were likewise prominent in the petitions formulated by freeholders in Essex, Northamptonshire, and Hertfordshire and by the mayor, sheriffs, aldermen, and citizens of Norwich.[169] Introducing their litany of complaints by declaring that they had been 'of late yeares ... unusually overcharged and insupportably burdened in their Consciences, Persons, Estates, and Freedomes', the petitioners from Hertfordshire attacked shipmoney, monopolies, and the absence of parliaments in addition to innovations in religion.[170] The statements from other counties were similar. Individuals like Peter Smart who remained imprisoned for his denunciation of the ceremonies at Durham, and the Oxfordshire constables who believed they had been ill-treated by the sheriff in connection with shipmoney, assembled statements to present to Parliament as did some with private business.[171]

Like the English, the Scots wished to make the most of the opportunity that Parliament offered. Fearing Charles would exhort the Lords and Commons against them, they issued an *Information from the Estates of the Kingdome of Scotland to the Kingdome of England* to strike at the 'malicious' spirits and 'popish emissaries' who were trying to alienate the king and England from them.[172] They hoped instead that Parliament would join them in pleading for redress of grievances and would refrain, as they had, from meddling with affairs in a kingdom which was not their own.[173] All the Scots wanted was peace, religion and law.[174]

Charles attempted to counter this with his *Declaration Concerning His Proceedings with his Subjects of Scotland, since the Pacification in the Camp neere Berwick* where he catalogued incidents of Scottish insolence and rebellion which, he thought, struck at the root of sovereignty and contradicted their claims about their goals. To their behaviour he contrasted his own commitment to religion and law and once again emphasized the question of obedience.[175]

As people looked to the parliamentary session, they were understandibly apprehensive. Sir Nathaniel Barnardiston who was chosen knight of the shire for Suffolk told Winthrop that he felt very unfit to bear such a heavy responsibility. If Parliament did not succeed, it 'is like to prove exceding perrelous and dangerous to this church and kingdome'.[176] Francis Kirby was one of many to pray that God might 'direct the heart of his Majesty and the house of parliament with one unanimous consent to aime at the Glory of God and saftie of this kingdome'.[177] Woodforde tells us that on 10 April, three days before the Parliament was to open, 'a general fast was held ... privately in England, Scotland, Germany ut dic. p. success of the Parliament'.[178]

When the much-heralded Parliament opened on 13 April 1640, just over eleven years after the stormy dissolution of its predecessor, its membership included both courtiers and others who had vigorously supported the king and some who had been outspoken in their opposition to his policies. In the Upper House most of the bishops including Laud, Neile, and Wren, were present as were Privy Councillors such as Lord Keeper Finch, Strafford, and Cottington and the Puritan lords Saye, Brooke, and Bedford.[179] Among those in the Commons were not only Mr Treasurer Vane, Mr Secretary Windebanke, and Mr Solicitor Herbert but also a clique of Puritans – John Pym, Sir Robert Harley, and Sir Thomas Barrington, the famed opponent of shipmoney John Hampden and his attorneys Oliver St John and Robert Holborne, and four of the MPs imprisoned in 1629, Coryton, Holles, Heyman, and Strode. Valentine whom the king had released along with Strode shortly before the session did not sit.[180]

After worshipping in Westminster Abbey, members of both Houses gathered in the Lords' chamber where Charles addressed them briefly before asking the Lord Keeper to explain the purpose of the Parliament. He wanted to 'reduce' the rebellious Scots into 'the just condicions of obedience and subjeccion', and to prove their traitorous conduct, he produced a letter allegedly revealing how they were seeking aid from the French.[181] Time and again throughout the session as in his earlier proclamations and declarations, he reiterated his diatribes against them.

For MPs the Parliament presented an opportunity to state the grievances of their 'countries' and to voice their concerns about the state of the commonwealth. As soon as their Speaker had been chosen and the formalities concluded, the Commons turned to their business. On 17 April, the second day during which they had poured out their complaints, John Pym in a speech of 'nere two hours' summarized these and arranged them in three categories: infringements of parliamentary liberties; innovations in religion; and violations of property. He pointed out the devastating impact these had on the kingdom and the urgency of obtaining redress.[182]

Being able to express objections to policies and procedures of the preceding eleven years only partially satisfied MPs, and in order to achieve the reform they also wanted, they agreed with Pym that despite demands that they begin with shipmoney or religion, they should give priority to securing the liberties and privileges of Parliament. Accordingly they inquired about Speaker Finch's conduct on 2 March 1628/9 when Charles had sent an order for the House to adjourn. Although concerned about legality in connection with this and other grievances, they were also eager to avoid getting trapped in a debate with the king about what was lawful.[183]

The Commons were busy preparing for a conference with the Lords about grievances when on 21 April Charles summoned both houses to the Banqueting House where the Lord Keeper sought to convince them to meet the king's needs for immediate supply. Going into more detail than he had on 13 April, he cited the Irish example of loyal giving and attempted to reassure those for whom shipmoney might be an impediment.[184] Three days later the king, becoming impatient that the Commons were still dealing with grievances rather than supply, personally went to the Lords to ask them for their honours and his to refrain from co-operating with the Lower House in the 'preposterous course' that ignored his pleas.[185] Although he warned them to proceed cautiously in order to avoid a 'breach', he wanted them to act upon his appeal that day.[186]

The king's request set off a long and sometimes heated debate in the House. Strafford who acted as Charles's advocate and maintained that they must trust his promise that he would allow them time to redress their grievances later, in the winter, clashed repeatedly with Saye who emphasized the Commons' privileges and their role as representatives of the country.[187] Many others spoke. Some tried to find a way out of the dilemma that the king had presented to them, but a majority eventually voted that supply should come first, that they should confer with the Lower House to that purpose, and that if that House would not be deterred from their course, the Lords should not join them.[188] Although some twenty lords dissented and some who gave their approval to the resolutions may have had reservations, the Upper House was not prepared to defy the king.[189]

Their loyalty served him poorly. His fears that the Lords might provoke a breach by announcing their view that supply should come first, proved true. The Commons believed that their privileges had been violated, and the series of conferences on that issue that ensued further postponed consideration of supply. On Saturday 2 May, Charles in another step to hasten action sent his Treasurer of the Household, Sir Henry Vane, to the Lower House with a message requesting a 'present' answer.[190] To that the Commons after a long debate returned word that they needed more time to respond.[191]

When they next met on Monday 4 May, Vane asked again that they give a 'present answer' about an immediate supply, but this time he offered the enticement that if they would vote twelve subsidies, Charles would relinquish shipmoney. The plea and the bargain proffered with it tempted many members. They weighed their grievances. Innovations in religion required attention. To some military charges seemed far more burdensome than shipmoney. The idea of buying relief troubled others. Before they agreed, they should have the legality of the levy determined. Several MPs worried about the war that would surely follow if they granted the king subsidies. Desirous of continuing the dialogue which the messages had opened, unwilling to refuse him their support, and unable to decide how to respond, they eventually rose for the day without making a definite reply.[192]

Although the Commons had not accepted Charles's offer, they were on 4 May carefully considering his appeals and, despite their concern about redress of grievances, were moving toward some action that would reassure him of their loyalty. He lost the trust that he had repeatedly asked them to give him when he denied them the opportunity to continue their deliberations. On the morning of 5 May, his patience having expired, he went in person and dissolved the Parliament.[193]

By ending this Parliament after only three weeks, Charles confirmed the doubts of any who had previously wondered whether he was willing to consider seriously the needs of his subjects. The manifold grievances that John Pym had enumerated in his lengthy speech of 17 April remained without redress. Copies of that and other speeches from the session circulated to inform people all over the kingdom about the ills that they had suffered. The Parliament's proceedings and especially its dissolution placed the history of the previous eleven years in perspective.[194] By May 1640 individuals who had complaints about policies, practices or officials could see that others also felt dissatisfied and wronged. Disappointed in their hopes for relief and aware that Charles wanted to undertake another war with Scotland, they were fearful about the future.

Despite their apprehensiveness about the session and their prayers for its success, many of the English were shocked by the dissolution. Hawkins told the earl of Leicester, 'All good men are sorry for the breach, and every one standeth at agaze what will next be done'.[195] John Eyre wrote to the earl of Rutland that he had just procured a copy of *Britain's Remembrancer* which, although it had come out twelve years before, had 'some things in it of especial note as foretelling the issue of these times'.[196] Many observers expected trouble, and by reporting the libels that appeared around London and the incidents that they heard of, they contributed to the tension and anxiety that the end of Parliament had brought. The Londoners who demonstrated against the queen mother, Laud and Strafford, 'Black Tom' as they called him, attracted much attention.[197] Even the presence of trained bands seemed not to daunt the mobs who gathered outside Lambeth Palace, calling for the archbishop to appear.[198]

The crowds who had blamed Laud for the dissolution eleven years earlier viewed him with special distaste on this occasion because the Convocations of the clergy which the king had summoned with Parliament were, contrary to custom, continuing to sit. Charles had authorized the assemblies of the two ecclesiastical provinces which traditionally met concurrently with Parliament to make canons. Not since 1604, the last time when their commission so directed, had the meeting of the clergy been the centre of such controversy as it was in 1640. In both Lords and Commons Convocation sparked disputes. The Upper House, led by Saye and Brooke, resisted complying with the bishops' request that it adjourn on the days that the clergy met. Whereas the Lords had debated the role of the prelates in their chamber, the Commons concentrated their attention on the powers of Convocation. On 21 April Dorset Puritan Sir Walter Erle who was fearful that the clergy's commission would infringe upon Parliament's protection of religion had asked for an investigation. The House was sympathetic to his concern and added an item concerning the making of canons to the grievances being prepared for a conference.[199]

Charles's decision to allow the Convocations to continue after the end of Parliament justified in retrospect the concerns that Erle and others had expressed during the session. To the legal questions about authority to make canons affecting the laity as well as the clergy critics added political questions stemming from the domination of the assembly by Laud and the bishops. The subsidies that the clergy voted to the king and the content of the canons they formulated made them appear to be oblivious to the grievances that had troubled MPs. Not only did the canons emphasize royal power and denounce resistance to it, they also confirmed many of the Laudian practices and required all clergy to take an oath, soon to be dubbed 'the etcetera oath', to uphold the 'doctrine, and discipline or government' of the Church and not to 'consent to alter' its 'government by archbishops, bishops, deans and archdeacons etc.'[200]

Contributing to the drama of the dissolution of Parliament, the Laudian triumph in Convocation, and the demonstrations of discontent in London were reports of unrest in the country and word that the council was cracking down on any suspected of resistance to royal authority.[201] Not only did the board order sheriffs who had not distrained to collect outstanding shipmoney to appear in Star Chamber, but it also had the residences of several peers searched and papers belonging to some members of both houses seized.[202] Among the MPs questioned and imprisoned in the aftermath of the Parliament were Henry Bellasis, Sir Hugh Cholmley, and Sir John Hotham all of whom, like Strafford, were Yorkshiremen.[203] Also imprisoned were London aldermen who had allegedly refused to submit the names of men who might be asked to make loans to the crown.[204] The list of people who experienced the displeasure of king and council seemed to grow steadily as the weeks passed.

Charles published *His Majesties Declaration to All His Loving Subjects of the Causes which Moved Him to Dissolve the Last Parliament* on 22 June. As he had in similar declarations in 1626 and 1629, he used the opportunity to attack the 'few sediciouslly-affected' men in the Commons whose 'audacious and insolent' conduct had forced him to abandon that course of government. Although he reiterated his promises to hear grievances, he gave people no indication that they could expect any changes in his rule.[205]

By the time the Declaration appeared, one commentator noted that 'almost generally through the kingdom the common people are sick of those parts; they labour of a suffocation of their hearts in the duty and obedience they owe to the kings service and commands ... they are stricken in the head that they rave and utter they knowe not what against his Majesties government and proceedings'.[206] Discontent was more pervasive in some localities than in others. As Windebanke believed, popular resistance frequently occurred in areas such as Northamptonshire or Essex where some lords and gentlemen were disaffected.[207]

Officials who during the summer of 1640 found their neighbours increasingly reluctant to pay shipmoney or perform military obligations did not appreciate the council's insistence that with hard work they could overcome local 'backwardness'. Sir Simonds D'Ewes who was sheriff of Suffolk at the time refrained from mentioning Parliament or raising legal questions in responding to the council's reprimands, but he suggested that instead of his negligence, they should blame the poor trade and the heavy military charges of the preceding year.[208] Some sheriffs reported receiving threats from people they sought to distrain while those who abstained from doing so and incurred the board's displeasure won sympathy from those in their community. The sheriff of Chester expected that at the quarter sessions bills of indictment would be preferred against him and all the under-officers who had assisted him in collecting shipmoney.[209] In London although the Lord Mayor undertook a house-to-house collection, people continued to hold out.[210] The city's hearing in the Star Chamber on proceedings concerning shipmoney added to the publicity that Parliament had given to the questions about it.[211]

The expectation that Charles would soon renew war against the Scots sparked mounting resistance to military preparations and charges. Accompanying and exacerbating the opposition to war and its costs were fears bred by the restiveness of the troops and by doubts about the purpose for which these might be used. From the perspective of the more widespread and serious trouble associated with soldiers in 1640 the insolencies and disorders of soldiers in the spring of 1639 seemed mild.[212] Judge Jones claimed that opposition to impressment was so great in Berkshire that in the absence of the deputy lieutenants from the assizes he had failed to get an indictment of some individuals for refusing press money and had consequently discharged them. Even the statement in his charge about the king's prerogative to ask people to serve in the wars had not moved the grand jury.[213]

Soldiers in Essex and Hertfordshire who entered churches and tore down rails showed that like many not in the army they had an intense dislike for Laudian practices.[214] With the prospect of renewed war the Convocations' proceedings gave people new cause for alarm about the way the archbishop was leading the Church. When they saw the printed books of canons, clergymen began to voice their concerns about the measures being imposed upon them. Several groups prepared petitions expressing their reservations about the meaning and about the legality of the etcetera oath. How could they, some from Yorkshire asked, bind themselves so that if changes were made in the Church they might have to disobey the monarch to whom they had sworn the oath of supremacy and whose laws instituted those reforms.[215] Dr Robert Sanderson, rector of Boothby Pagnell in Lincolnshire wrote to Laud on 13 September, reporting that he saw opposition to the oath in his own area and had had reports of protests elsewhere. Although he himself was not convinced by either of the two papers of reasons against taking the oath which he had seen, he believed, after taking a quick look, that the arguments were making a serious impact on clergy and laity who were otherwise conformable. He suggested that the king consider waiting to enforce the oath until it could be explained.[216]

Englands Complaint to Jesus Christ against the Bishops Canons, printed without authorization and thus without need for Sanderson's politic caution, declared, 'we suspect our King of being *perverted* in a *superstitious way of Gods worship* as if *he intended* to bring in some *alteration of Religion*'. Through 'bad officers' who defended innovations as not being innovations Charles was abused. Prelacy and many of the ecclesiastical practices of the preceding years were contrary to the laws and liberties which, rather than canons, were England's birthright. Critics of the canons were not disloyal. If the king would call Parliament, people would yield to him. Arranging the religious grievances from the eleven years of Charles's personal rule as a critique of the canons, the *Complaint* summarized them and argued that to return to proper order in the Church, Parliament was needed.[217]

The canons were merely one sign of the increasing popish threat. When Calybute Downing preached to the London Artillery Company on 1 September, not long after the Scots' invasion of the north of England had brought renewal of that conflict, he suggested that war might be necessary to stop the Papists. Growing evidence of Roman aggression not only gave credence to fears about Arminianism but also represented a direct source of danger.[218] Rumours circulated of popish plots to provoke trouble in Scotland and to use the disturbance there as a means of overturning law and religion in England.[219] Innovations in religion thus seemed to be portents of turmoil in the commonwealth too.

The discontent that erupted at the summer assizes attracted much attention.[220] Correspondents included lengthy accounts of these proceedings along with their reports of incidents and protests in their letters.[221] In Berkshire, the same grand jury who would not indict some men who had refused press money formulated a bold petition lamenting the dissolution of Parliament, referring to shipmoney as an illegal and insupportable charge, listing a number of other grievances, and asking for assurance that they would have the protection offered by the Petition of Right. In justification of their complaint they cited the king's words in his declaration about the causes of the dissolution where he had urged the English to present their grievances to him. If they did so, he had promised he would make reforms.[222]

In Yorkshire where the Scottish troubles were close and the burden of billeted troops heavy, gentlemen who had gathered for the assizes prepared a petition which drew considerable notice. Like the Berkshire grand jury they wanted the Petition of Right enforced.[223] Their grievances were much more serious than they had been during the Bishops' War when some of them, as deputies, had complained about the county's poverty and its suffering from the charges of that conflict. Men who had not protested then came forward to sign the petition of 1640. They had seen several of their countrymen who had been MPs questioned after the dissolution of the Parliament.[224] Cholmley who was himself one of those called by the council described the petition in his *Memoirs* as being 'in a pretty high style; for in substance (though not in plain terms) it imported, that the county would not lie longer under these pressures: and being the first action that did with a bare face complaine of the king's prerogative which went high in those times did something startle the Council'.[225]

Although Hawkins thought 'some countries speake higher', both the content and manner of the Yorkshire gentlemen's complaint irritated the crown.[226] Neither the earl of Strafford for whom the county was home and who as Lord President of the North had particular responsibility for its government nor the king could persuade the petitioners to desist. Their determination contrasted with the dutiful payment of shipmoney and adherence to royal commands that until 1639 had characterized Yorkshire. Strafford, Slingsby observed, 'now grown a stranger to his country, tho' heretofore a Patriott, seem[ed] to quarrel at ym yt they had not address'd this petition to him'.[227] Late in August the gentlemen, undaunted by the controversy their petition had provoked, appealed again, this time asking for affirmation of their right to petition and expressing concern about their militia.[228]

The Scots invasion of England on 20 August brought the simmering conflicts over religion, defence and the king's methods of government to the boiling point. Charles hoped that his subjects would rally to his support when they saw their own kingdom attacked and especially when they realized that in crossing the border the Covenanters were violating earlier statements of purpose.[229] To answer these charges the Scots explained that they were driven to desperation by some Papists and prelates who wanted to destroy their Church and nation. The chief architects of their destruction, they believed, were Laud and Strafford whose evil deeds contrasted with the favours they had gratefully received from 'good people and Body of the kingdom of England'.[230] The English Parliament had refused to contribute to war against them, and the City of London had shown its affection.[231] Since these could not protect them any longer, and since they could not silently await the cutting of their throats, they were acting. They would remain in England only until their grievances were heard in Parliament. Unlike individuals they could not look to the king for the relief he had promised in his *Declaration* about the dissolution. Their complaints were national and consequently required the attention of the English Parliament.

The Scots dispatched numerous copies, 10,000 according to some reports, of *The Intention* to England and in addition directed a separate appeal to London.[232] Their attempt to convince the English that the two kingdoms had common grievances reached people who had little enthusiasm for assuming the costs of war and hampered Charles's efforts to obtain support. Unemployment, decay of trade and shortage of money reinforced people's desire for redress of the grievances they had voiced in Parliament in the spring.[233] The king's dissolution of that Parliament, his tendency to regard petitioners as rebels rather than to listen to their cause, and his insistence upon his own honour and authority made it difficult for the English public to believe that he would protect and defend their interests. His intransigence left his subjects susceptible to the Scots' propaganda. Schooled in the practice of politics without parliament those who in the summer of 1640 took their grievances seriously knew that if they were to obtain reforms, they would have to go farther than they had previously. The Covenanters' invasion gave them an opportunity to make demands. Some were prepared to take advantage of the situation, but many remained hesitant.[234]

Among those moved to act were a group of lords who late in August petitioned the king to call a Parliament. In so appealing they were adhering to tradition and, although they did not say so, also abiding by the request he made in his *Declaration* that people should direct their complaints to him. Those peers who signed the petition included both lords who had been prominent in opposition to royal policy and practices during the 1630s and also men whose names had not been publicly associated with Puritanism or resistance. Most of them had in the Short Parliament of the spring voted against urging the Lower House to give priority to the king's supply.[235] Seven of them – Bedford, Brooke, Essex, Mandeville, Savile, Saye and Warwick – had, in corresponding with the Scots in July, refused to extend an invitation to invade England but had indicated that they would offer support if such were to occur.[236] Although a minority of the nobility, they were too important and too numerous to be ignored.

When Charles had called upon the lords to join him in suppressing the Scottish rebels in 1638/9 these men had, for the most part, cloaked any reservations that they might have had about the enterprise. A year and a half later in August 1640, they were not prepared to remain silent. Speaking for themselves and for other 'faithfull subjects', they were giving him unsolicited advice. Although when questioned by the council some of them claimed that they would not have subscribed to the petition if they had known of the Scots' invasion, others added their names after the fact of the invasion was well known.[237]

Describing their fears about the dangers currently threatening Church and state, the petitioners appealed to Charles to recognize the peril of going to war with inadequate revenue and disorderly soldiers. His plan to bring foreign, i.e. Irish troops to fight would have ill consequences. Shipmoney was unpopular and his prosecution in the Star Chamber of sheriffs who did not collect the sums due from their counties a serious grievance. Trade was weak, and his people were overburdened with charges and anxious about the increase of Popery, innovations in religion, including the recent oath and canons, the 'long intermission of parliaments' and the 'late and former' dissolutions of Parliament. Although some of the grievances cited in the petition were long-standing, most either stemmed directly from the events of 1639 and 1640 or were aggravated by those events. To avoid the troubles they foresaw if the king persisted in his current course the lords recommended that he quickly summon a Parliament to redress grievances, punish the authors of the kingdom's ills and settle the differences with the Scots without bloodshed.[238]

In petitioning Charles for a Parliament the peers took a step that he had specifically prohibited by his proclamation eleven years earlier.[239] They were telling him how to use his prerogative of summoning and dissolving that body, but they were at the same time appealing to him to employ his authority to solve the impending crisis. Petitions were a time-honoured way of addressing the monarch and parliaments, though lately unhappy, a recognized means of reconciling king and subject. If rumours were true, he was at the very time they prepared their appeal considering calling a Parliament.[240] As the abortive session of the spring had demonstrated, Lords and Commons could do nothing unless he agreed.

The petition attracted considerable attention and heralded a wave of demands that Parliament meet.[241] Charles had not satisfied the pressure for reform by his announcement in response to the lords that he would summon a Council of Peers to meet in York late in September.[242] One appeal for a Parliament came from the Yorkshire gentlemen who had only a few weeks earlier expressed concern about the charges for their trained bands. When the king requested that they provide two months' pay, they prepared a petition, citing grievances and asking that Parliament meet. The earl of Strafford convinced the majority to allow him to present that to the king, but a small group, including Cholmley and Hotham, caused a stir by refusing to accept his offer and trying to submit a petition of their own.[243] Londoners also formally entreated Charles to call Parliament. Having resisted lending him money earlier in the summer, they agreed to do so in September on carefully defined conditions which they expressed in their petition. Their fiscal interests coincided in this instance with their political concerns.[244]

The cries for Parliament almost made the Council of Peers redundant before it met. Although a group of Northamptonshire gentlemen who had on previous occasions tried to obtain relief for their countrymen met together on 15 September to prepare a petition of grievances to be taken to the council, many people believed that the council would have to be merely a prelude to more far-reaching measures for resolution of England's problems.[245] The king himself ultimately bowed to that view and announced at its opening that he would summon a Parliament, with writs dated that very day, to meet in London on 3 November.[246] With his statement Charles changed the focus of political activity and gave it new impetus. The earl of Northampton welcomed the news, 'One word of four syllables, *Parliament*, like the dew of Heaven'.[247]

Charles's decision in September 1640 to call another Parliament was very different from that he had made ten months earlier. In December 1639 he had acted in relative freedom. Times were hard then – people were complaining about grievances, the Scots were defying his efforts to subdue them, but the English were not in such large numbers failing to pay shipmoney, defaulting on their military obligations, protesting against prelates and ceremonies, and insisting that a Parliament be held. Strafford, then still Baron Wentworth, and the other councillors who had urged him to summon a Parliament for the spring of 1640 convinced him that he might thereby gain subsidies and good will without making significant concessions. By September not even the most optimistic adviser could have argued that the king had little to fear from a Parliament. The Commons would insist that grievances take precedence over supply. They would demand an end to innovations in religion, violations of property and the absence of Parliament, and seek to punish the authors of the distasteful policies and practices of the previous years. Only if he allowed reforms, could Charles achieve his goals.[248]

Because he needed money, he yielded to the calls of the English for a Parliament. By their resistance to his requests for aid, they had, thanks to the Scots' intransigence, forced him to listen to their pleas. Although he had apparently quieted the north somewhat by going there in August, he still needed much more support than he had in order to combat the Covenanters whose invasion had precipitated the crisis of August and September 1640.

Charles's failure to realize that the lords and gentlemen who were making more insistent appeals for reform during the summer of 1640 were men whose opposition was loyal and who looked to him to take the lead in redress of their grievances, forced him to summon a Parliament he did not want and one that would make reforms that he did not like. The individuals who served as JPs, sheriffs, deputy lieutenants, mayors and aldermen had no wish to overthrow order and law. Their fears of turmoil and their attachment to tradition prompted them to seek redress of the grievances of their communities. When they looked to Parliament for reform, they were reaffirming tradition and invoking a process in which king, Lords and Commons co-operated to meet the needs of all.

Their conduct and policies were radical because the king made them so. His apparent departure from the customs and procedures that the English regarded as their birthright left them facing a dilemma. They must either accept the changes that he authorized or challenge his authority. Their hesitancy to engage in outright resistance and their realization that many of the policies and practices they disliked were technically legal kept their protests subdued for a decade. Only when the Scots refused to accept the new liturgy and Charles resolved to suppress their rebellion did the politics of the English change.

NOTES

1   See M. Lee, *The Road to Revolution: Scotland under Charles I, 1625–37* (Urbana, Ill.: University of Illinois Press, 1985).
2   The Cheshire gentleman William Brereton who travelled in Scotland in 1636 was the exception. See Lee, *Road*, pp. 166–7, 196; also Schreiber, *Carlisle*.
3   See D. Stevenson, *The Scottish Revolution, 1637–1644* (Newton Abbot: David & Charles, 1973), pp. 32–3.
4   See Chapter 2.
5   See Stevenson, *Revolution*, pp. 62–3.
6   Yonge, f. 67v. In 1638 he entered *in extenso* 'The Scotts Reasons against the Service Book' (ff. 70–70v); cf. Montagu MS 4.101; Rous, p. 85; HMC, *Fourteenth Report*, app., ii, p. 49; *DeL'Isle*, pp. 127, 130, 136.
7   See Stevenson, *Revolution*, p. 57; also below. I am using 'Scots' here synonymously with 'Covenanters'.
8   e.g. HMC, *Fourteenth Report*, app., ii, p. 53; also *DeL'Isle*, pp. 156, 159; SP 16/429/38; WP, Vol. 3, pp. 512–3; Rous, p. 86; Cl C 721; *The Beast Is Wounded* (Amsterdam, 1638), STC 22032; Stevenson, *Revolution*, pp. 123–4.
9   Woodforde, p. 497; also see p. 498; Slingsby, pp. 10–11; SP 16/409/104–5.
10   SP 16/410/24; see also the king's proclamation of 27 February 1638/9 (STC 9135).
11   *God Save the King: A Sermon preached in St. Pauls Church the 27th of March 1639* (STC 24575), pp. 6, 31 ff; see also T. Morton, *Sermon Preached Before the Kings Majestie, Durham Cathedral, 5 May 1639* (STC 18196); H. Peacham, *The Duty of All True Subjects to their King: As also to their Native Countrey in time extremity and danger* (London, 1639), STC 19505; *Loyalty's Speech to England's Subjects* (London, 1639), STC 10018.
12   See Slingsby, *Diary*, pp. 10–11.
13   See Hibbard, *Popish Plot*, pp. 110–11; also see *Pigges Corantoe* (1642), STC W P2223.
14   SP 16/410/24.
15   (1639), STC 21905.
16   See Hibbard, *Popish Plot*, p. 93.
17   *Information to all good Christians*, p. 11.
18   The king's proclamation of 27 February 1638/9 (STC 9135) and his *Large Declaration* (1639), STC 21906, which printed many of the previous

statements from both sides and interpreted proceedings from the beginning of Charles's reign.

19   W. Sclater, *Death's Summons and the Saints Duty* (sermon preached in Exeter cathedral, 24 January 1638/9; printed in 1640), STC 21849, p. 49.

20   The Scots replied to the *Large Declaration* with a *Remonstrance* (22 March 1638/9), STC 21907.

21   Woodforde, p. 498; HMC, *Hastings*, Vol. 1, pp. 389–90; *A Short Relation ... to our brethern in the Kirk of England* (1638), STC 22039 (an unofficial publication); also SP 16/429/38–9; El 111 and 112. The earl of Huntingdon had a copy of the Covenanters' letter to the earl of Essex (HA 1193); see also HMC *Seventh Report*, app., p. 251 (copy of the Scots' letter to the earl of Newcastle); also BL, Add. MS 11045, ff. 3–4v; Samuel Vassall's papers (*CSPDom. 1639*, pp. 525–6, a reference I owe to Caroline Hibbard).

22   e.g. *Verney Papers*, ed. J. Bruce, Camden Society, vol. 56 (1853), pp. 228–9.

23   Cl C 236; see also Cl C 235.

24   cf. for example, HA 5524, the earl of Huntingdon's request to the earl of Manchester to present his excuses to the king for not attending Parliament because of the 'couldness and the sharpness of the weather' which aggravated his gout. Huntingdon did not make any excuse in 1639 (see below).

25   SP 16/412/48.

26   SP 16/412/124.

27   SP 16/413/55.

28   SP 16/412/134; see also A. Collins, *Letters and Memorials of State ... Collected by Sir Henry Sidney* (London, 1746), Vol. 2, p. 593.

29   HA 5549.

30   Montagu MS 4.17 (HMC, *Buccleuch*, Vol. 1, pp. 278–9).

31   See Zagorin, *Court and Country*, pp. 93, 100.

32   Newton, *Colonising*, pp. 80 ff.

33   For Saye's earlier activity, see M. Schwarz, 'Lord Saye and Sele's objections to the palatinate benevolence of 1622: some new evidence and its significance', *Albion*, vol. 4, no. 1 (1972), pp. 12–22. Concerning his opposition to shipmoney see Chapter 3. Also see M. Schwarz, 'Viscount Saye and Sele, Lord Brooke and aristocratic protest to the first bishops' war', *Canadian Journal of History*, vol. 7 (1972), pp. 17–36.

34   SP 16/413/92; 16/413/117.

35   SP 16/409/116; 16/415/65; 16/415/24.

36   Montagu MS 3.231; Montagu MS 10.4; Cope, *Montagu*, pp. 158–9.

37   Although he quibbled about how much he would give and whether that would be men and horses or money, he was prepared to give something. See below.

38   Cl C 290; he had been ill previously (Cl C 657, 658, 668). Cheynell's suggestions may reflect approaches other lords used.

39   See below.

40   Cl C 290.

41   Cope, *Montagu*, p. 159. See also Chapter 3.

42   SP 16/412/88; 16/412/95.

43 Cl C 290.
44 El 6598; also El 6596.
45 Montagu MS 4.17 (HMC, *Buccleuch*, Vol. 1, pp. 278–9).
46 El 6598.
47 El 6600, 6601.
48 El 6604.
49 El 6604, 6605, 6608. See also the list of monetary contributions (*CSPDom. Addenda, 1625–49*, pp. 604–5).
50 Cope, *Montagu*, pp. 158–60.
51 HMC *Twelfth Report*, app., iv, Vol. 1, pp. 507–8; HMC, *Fourth Report*, p. 23; Hibbard, *Popish Plot*, pp. 118–20.
52 HMC, *Twelfth Report*, app., iv, Vol. 1, pp. 508–9.
53 Montagu MS 10.5 (HMC, *Buccleuch*, Vol. 3, p. 386); cf. Kent Archives Office, U350/C2/65.
54 HMC, *Twelfth Report*, app., iv, Vol. 1, p. 508.
55 SP 16/418/99; cf. Edward Alford's objections to a proposal in 1624 that Parliament promise to assist the king 'to the uttermost' (R. Zaller, 'Edward Alford and the making of country radicalism', *JBS*, vol. 22, no. 1 (1983), p. 65.)
56 Yonge, f. 72v.
57 See Schwarz, 'Aristocratic protest', p. 27; also Cope, *Montagu*, p. 161.
58 SP 16/423/67; cf. BL, Add. MS 11045, ff. 12–13v.
59 HMC, *Twelfth Report*, app., iv, Vol. 1, p. 505.
60 See Cl C 236; HMC, *Twelfth Report*, app., iv, Vol. 1, p. 517; SP 16/423/29.
61 SP 16/418/30.
62 *Verney Papers*, p. 229.
63 *Verney Papers*, p. 205; Cl C 78, 290, 342, 348; Cornish Record Office, Buller Papers, no. 28; SP 16/418/56, 99.
64 Cl C 78. Clifton had got his own excuse previously.
65 BL, Stowe MS 743, f. 132; see also ff. 128–30.
66 He did not go to York (Kent Archives Office, U350/C2/63, 65).
67 Woodforde, p. 498.
68 Exeter, Royal Letters and Other Letters and Papers, f. 381 (Harvard film); the proclamation is probably that of 27 February, STC 9135 (see above).
69 SP 16/420/157.
70 ibid.
71 Exeter, Act Books, Vol. 8, ff. 5v, 43; Vol. 7, f. 383 (Harvard film).
72 York, House Books, Vol. 36, ff. 21–22v, 27v–31; HMC, *Twelfth Report*, app., iv, Vol. 1, p. 504; SP 16/415/78.
73 *Harley Letters*, pp. 38–9; Holmes, *Lincolnshire*, p. 137; cf. Stephen J. Stearns, 'Conscription and English society in the 1620s', *JBS*, vol. 11, no. 1 (1972) pp. 1–23.
74 See STT 1876; SP 16/417/47; 16/418/82; 16/420/67; STT 1582, 1583; SP 16/421/43; 16/422/35; 16/317/46; 16/318/6; STT 1890.
75 SP 16/413/111; 16/417/41; 16/418/1; 16/417/110; 16/414/91.
76 SP 16/409/105.

77   SP 16/418/101; STT 1893.
78   See Chapter 3.
79   e.g. SP 16/410/44, 102, 142; 16/412/9; 16/415/64.
80   I owe this point to Caroline Hibbard who shared with me her unpublished paper about the queen mother.
81   Cl C 682.
82   Montagu was probably thinking more about the difficulties of the existing arrangements than advocating any arrangement whereby the trained bands would have been sent out of the county (HMC, *Buccleuch*, Vol. 3, p. 385); see also J. Morrill, *Cheshire, 1630-1660* (Oxford: Oxford University Press, 1974), p. 30; deputies in Suffolk complained because the country had a large coast area and especially because Norfolk's trained bands were not to go (Suffolk Letter Book, ff. 92v–3); *Harley Letters*, p. 35; Pearl, *London*, p. 95; SP 16/417/41; York, House Books, Vol. 36, ff. 18, 24v. There seem to have been no protests from Hertfordshire in 1639 but there was a petition a year later (see below).
83   *Fairfax Letters*, Vol. 1, pp. 353–4; Montagu had a copy (HMC, *MSS of Lord Montagu of Beaulieu*, p. 121).
84   *Fairfax Letters*, Vol. 1, pp. 364–5; also SP 16/409/67.
85   SP 16/415/59; 16/415/64. Deputies from several countries reported that they could not increase the trained bands (SP 16/412/9; 16/410/102; 16/410/142).
86   SP 16/413/65.
87   SP 16/417/64.
88   Slingsby, *Diary*, p. 13. He later went with two light horses to serve the king.
89   SP 16/417/41.
90   STT 1884; see also STT 1890.
91   *Harley Letters*, p. 44; see also SP 16/418/95; 16/418/8.
92   Slingsby, *Diary*, p. 31; also *Fairfax Letters*, Vol. 1, pp. 367–8.
93   Woodforde, p. 498.
94   See Gordon, 'Ship-money'.
95   SP 16/417/5, 16/417/62; 16/417/64; 16/417/109; 16/418/16; 16/418/51.
96   *CSPDom. 1639–40*, p. 246, a reference I owe to Caroline Hibbard; see also Prynne, *Hidden Works*, p. 196, and below.
97   Ashton, *City and Court*, p. 198; R. Ashton, *The Crown and the Money Market, 1603-1640* (Oxford: Clarendon Press, 1960), p. 180; also Pearl, *London*, pp. 94–6; SP 16/415/65; HMC, *Buccleuch*, Vol. 3, p. 382.
98   e.g. SP 16/414/25.
99   STT 1890; see also Knowler, Vol. 2, pp. 307–11; Laud, *Works*, Vol. 7, pp. 567–8.
100   STT 1880; Sibthorpe reports this in a series of letters to Sir John Lambe, April–June 1639 (STT 1876–1893); see also above.
101   Woodforde, p. 498; also SP 16/414/163; and Chapter 2.
102   R. Clifton, 'The popular fear of Catholics during the English revolution', *Past and Present*, vol. 3 (1971), pp. 23–55.
103   STT 1876, 1877, 1880.

104   See Howell, *Newcastle*, pp. 97 ff; SP 16/409/84; 16/410/5; 16/410/99; 16/413/32; and also Cl C 236.
105   See below.
106   SP 16/415/100; 16/417/58. See also *Pigges Corantoe*, printed in 1642 but written in the spring of 1639. The disillusioned author said he could not be sure how many would go to York who were undecided about religion or about the side on which they would fight. He also wondered how many would fight without money.
107   e.g. SP 16/420/48; 16/417/97; 16/421/21; 16/421/64; Yonge, f. 73. See also the verses in *CSPDom. Addenda, 1625–49*, p. 613.
108   Rous, pp. 87–8; Essex Record Office, Essex Assize File A71, 35/81T, no. 10 (Harvard film).
109   D. Gardiner (ed.), *The Oxinden Letters, 1607–1642* (London: Constable, 1933), p. 142 (no. 121); HMC, *Gawdy*, p. 171.
110   Montagu MS 4.15; Cope, *Montagu*, pp. 161–2.
111   *CSPVen. 1636–9*, no. 582.
112   Knowler, Vol. 2, p. 246 (24 November 1638).
113   Knowler, Vol. 2, pp. 279–80.
114   SP 16/395/29; *The Covenanters' Information* (1639), STC 21905; see also above.
115   See Chapter 2.
116   e.g. N. Carpenter, *Chorazin and Bethesaida's Woe or Warning Peece* (1640), STC 4675; A. Hill, *The Peace of Enmity* (1640), STC 13467; Slingsby, pp. 10–11. Concern about the management of military affairs provided the occasion if not the inspiration for a number of publications. William Bariffe's, *Mars his Triumph* (1639), STC 1505, described military exercises, but Robert Ward's *Animadversions of Warfare* (1639), STC 25025, dedicated to the king and written because of the troubled times and 'mutations of peace', combined historical observations with practical advice about the 'well-management of the sword', i.e. providing in peace for war, the manner of fortifications, the duties of soldiers, drills, and rules for battle. Thomas Fuller's *The History of Holy Warre* (1639), STC 11464, treated the crusades rather than England's current conditions but discussed moral and political factors as well as military manoeuvres.
117   Napier, Bk. 2, chapter 14, nos 9–10 (1593), STC 18354, a reference I owe to Caroline Hibbard. (See also the prophecy noted in *CSPDom. Addenda, 1625–49*, p. 613.)
118   e.g. E. Turges, *The Christian Souldier* (1639), STC 24331.2; A. Harsnet, *Gods Summons Unto a General Repentance* (1640), STC 12875.
119   I am grateful to Barbara Donagan for sharing with me her article, 'Godly choice: puritan decision-making in seventeenth-century England', prior to its publication in the *Harvard Theological Review*; see also *Harley Letters*, p. 57.
120   SP 16/420/70.
121   Pearl, *London*, pp. 94–5.
122   Stevenson, *Revolution*, pp. 155–6. Charles assured the Covenanters who

had conceded some key points that in the future assemblies of the kirk would determine ecclesiastical matters and Parliament civil matters.

123 Woodforde, p. 498; *Harley Letters*, p. 58; *DeL'Isle*, p. 169; *CSPVen. 1636–9*, no. 674.

124 (1639), STC 12807.

125 See, for example, Holland's letter to Mandeville, HMC, *Eighth Report*, app., ii, p. 55, a reference I owe to Conrad Russell.

126 SP 16/427/31.

127 Yonge, f. 73v; SP 16/427/19; 16/427/47.

128 SP 16/427/30; see also Essex Record Office, Essex Assize File A71, 35/81 T, nos 11, 14; 35/81 H, no. 9 (Harvard film). Yonge mentions indictments in both Essex and Nottinghamshire (f. 73).

129 SP 16/435/35; see Laud, *Works*, Vol. 5, pt. 2, p. 364.

130 Bedfordshire Record Office, St John of Bletsoe MSS, no. 1361; concerning the sheriff's table, see B. Quintrell (ed.), *Proceedings of the Lancashire Justices of the Peace at the Sheriffs' Table during Assizes Week, 1578–1694*, Record Society of Lancashire and Cheshire, vol. 121 (1981), a reference I owe to Rosemary O'Day.

131 Bedfordshire Record Office, St John of Bletsoe MSS, no. 1361.

132 Dr Samuel Clarke (1582–1641), see Longden, *Northamptonshire and Rutland Clergy*; not Samuel Clarke (1599–1683), who wrote the *Lives of Divines* (DNB).

133 Although I have found no evidence that the gentlemen were later questioned for their conduct, the paper is couched as a defence of the meeting. It concludes, 'This was all that past amongst the gentlemen' except some particular arguments between Dr Clarke and Sir Miles Fleetwood about some specific points (St John of Bletsoe MSS, no. 1361).

134 Laud, *Works*, Vol. 5, pt. 2, p. 362.

135 Laud, *Works*, Vol. 5, pt. 2, pp. 369–70; Fletcher, *Sussex*, p. 242.

136 *Episcopacie by Divine Right* (1640), STC 12661; Laud, *Works*, Vol. 5, pt. 2, p. 369; see SP 16/431/2; 16/431/65.

137 *An Extraordinaire Curranto* (1639), STC 5750; 'A Famous Sea-Fight', in *The Common Muse*, eds V. DeSola Pinto and A. E. Rodway (London: Chatto & Windus, 1957), pp. 51–4; Cornish Record Office, Buller Papers, BC 24/4/52; *DeL'Isle*, pp. 195–6.

138 El 7809; see also 7810; *DeL'Isle*, pp. 172, 180, 183, 199; SP 16/429/38; 16/429/39; HMC, *Eighth Report*, app., ii, p. 55.

139 *Harley Letters*, p. 72; *DeL'Isle*, p. 201; but cf. *DeL'Isle*, p. 202; Woodforde, p. 498.

140 El 7814.

141 Woodforde, p. 498; cf. Verney MSS, Claydon letters, 18 December 1639 (Yale film).

142 *DeL'Isle*, pp. 214 ff. *passim*.

143 *WP*, Vol. 4, pp. 216–17, 219.

144 El 7817–19; *DeL'Isle*, pp. 224–5, 226.

145 *DeL'Isle*, p. 212; *WP*, Vol. 4, pp. 213–14; Verney MSS, Claydon letters, 28 January 1639/40 (Yale film).

146   See El 7810; Bergeron, 'Entries', pp. 91–7; *DeL'Isle*, p. 172.

147   El 7810; Pearl, *London*, pp. 94–5; Ashton, *City and Court*, pp. 198–9; also above.

148   E. S. Cope, 'The Short Parliament and convocation', *Journal of Ecclesiastical History*, vol. 25, no. 2 (1974), pp. 171–2; also see STT 1880.

149   SP 16/447/33.

150   ibid.

151   El 7814; see also El 7811.

152   See *DeL'Isle*, p. 224; also p. 221.

153   El 7815.

154   In addition Cholmley was removed from all commissions. Cholmley, *Memoirs*, p. 60; see also below.

155   See Gardiner, *History of England*, Vol. 9, pp. 95–6; *DeL'Isle*, p. 241; El 7830; 7831.

156   Yonge, f. 75v; El 7830.

157   El 7823, 7824, 7825; *DeL'Isle*, pp. 231, 233; WP, Vol. 4, pp. 205–6.

158   *CSPVen. 1636–9*, no. 744; cf. Verney MSS, Claydon letters, 28 January 1639/40 (Yale film).

159   SP 16/452/10; 16/452/86. See also the case of George Walker, the London minister, who was prosecuted for preaching a sermon in which he attacked shipmoney and made offensive remarks about the king and queen (*CSPDom. 1638–9*, pp. 98, 231).

160   SP 16/445/54; concerning Yelverton, Keeler, pp. 403–4; SP 16/301/43; also Cholmley, *Memoirs*, pp. 58–9; PCR, Vol. 9, pp. 355–6; also SP 16/447/46, 47. The council declared his letter 'tedious' and accused him of trying 'to prepare a way for an excuse for doing nothing'.

161   SP 16/450/75; 16/451/25; also Yonge, f. 75v; and Chapter 3.

162   *CSPDom. 1640*, pp. 95–6; also HMC, *MSS of the Marquess of Salisbury*, Vol. 22, pp. 311–13 (131.107).

163   HMC, *Twelfth Report*, app., iv, Vol. 1, p. 521; El 7825, 7832, 7833, 7835, 7837, 7838; *DeL'Isle*, p. 267; Ashton, *Money Market*, p. 181; Pearl, *London*, pp. 99–100.

164   Ashton, *Money Market*, p. 177.

165   *DeL'Isle*, p. 235. See also J. Gruenfelder, 'The election to the Short Parliament, 1640', *Early Stuart Studies*, ed. H. S. Reinmuth (Minneapolis, Minn.: University of Minnesota Press, 1970); J. Gruenfelder, *Influence in Early Stuart Elections, 1604–1610* (Columbus, Ohio, 1981) ch. 5; P. Slack, 'An election to the Short Parliament', *BIHR*, vol. 46, no. 113 (1973), pp. 108–114; WP, Vol. 4, pp. 207–8; York, House Books, Vol. 36, f. 41; see also the charges levelled in *Persecutio Undecima*, (London, 1681) p. 29.

166   e.g. BL, Add. MS 11045, f. 99v.

167   e.g. HA 5557; BL, Egerton MS 2646, f. 142; BL, Stowe MS 184, f. 10.

168   BL Loan MS 29/172, f. 251.

169   Cope and Coates, pp. 275–9, also pp. 47–8.

170   ibid., pp. 277–8.

171   ibid., pp. 280–2, 284; also pp. 283, 287.

172   (1640), STC 21916, pp. 4–5, 9.

173 *Information to all good Christians*, pp. 12–13.

174 ibid., p. 6; cf. their statement of the *Intention of the Army* (below, note 230).

175 (1640), STC 9260; see also Rushworth, *Collections*, Vol. 2, pp. 1094–5, proclamation of 30 March 1640, against pamphlets, etc. from Scotland (STC 9154).

176 *WP*, Vol. 4, pp. 217–18; see also *The Wyllys Papers*, Collections of the Connecticut Historical Society, vol. 21 (1924), letter from George Wyllys to his father, 8 April 1640 (a reference I owe to Conrad Russell).

177 *WP*, Vol. 4, pp. 200–1; see also *WP*, Vol. 4, pp. 205–6.

178 Woodforde, p. 498.

179 For the lords' attendance, see *Journals of the House of Lords*, Vol. 4, *passim*.

180 Concerning members of the Lower House see *A Return of the Names of Every Member returned to serve in each Parliament* (London, 1878), parts i and iii; and *DNB*.

181 Cope and Coates, p. 119; also pp. 53–4, 95–6, 115–23.

182 ibid., p. 234; also pp. 299–302.

183 See especially the debates of 18 and 20 April for which Sir Thomas Aston's diary gives the best account. I am grateful to Judith Maltby for sharing with me prior to its forthcoming publication by the Royal Historical Society in the Camden Series her edition of this diary which is a very important addition to the accounts of proceedings of the Short Parliament in Cope and Coates.

184 Cope and Coates, pp. 164–7, 263, 303–5.

185 ibid., pp. 69–71, 264–5, 308.

186 ibid., p. 71. After Charles had finished, the Lord Keeper told them the king wanted a decision that day.

187 Cope and Coates, pp. 71–9.

188 ibid., pp. 79–80.

189 The dissenters were: the earls of Rutland, Southampton, Bedford, Hertford, Essex, Lincoln, Warwick, Clare, Bolingbroke, Nottingham, and Bath; viscount Saye; barons Willoughby of Parham, Paget, North, Mandeville, Brooke, Robartes, Lovelace, Savile, Dunsmore, Deinecourt, Montagu, Howard of Escrick, and Wharton (SP 16/451/39).

190 Cope and Coates, pp. 187–8.

191 ibid., pp. 188–93; cf. Aston whose account is fuller.

192 Aston's account of the day's proceedings is the best available. His diary confirms the evidence of those in Cope and Coates (pp. 193–7) that the Commons were far from denying Charles's request.

193 Cope and Coates, pp. 95, 316–7; also Aston.

194 See Clarendon's story of his encounter with St John soon after the dissolution when the latter remarked with a smile that 'it must be worse before it could be better' (*History*, II.78).

195 *DeL'Isle*, p. 261; also pp. 245, 251–2, 254; *WP*, Vol. 4, pp. 243–4; HMC, *Fourteenth Report*, app., ii, p. 63; *The Wyllys Papers*, pp. 11–12.

196 HMC, *Twelfth Report*, app., iv, Vol. 1, p. 520. George Wither's *Britain's Remembrancer*.

197   HMC, *Eighth Report*, app., ii, p. 56; *WP*, Vol. 4, pp. 248–9; Rous, p. 90.
198   El 7833, 7834; Woodforde, p. 498.
199   See Cope, 'Convocation'.
200   *Constitutions and Canons Ecclesiastical* (1640), STC 10080; see also Cope, 'Convocation'.
201   El 7835.
202   *DeL'Isle*, p. 267; El 7843–4.
203   Cholmley, *Memoirs*, p. 61; Slingsby, *Diary*, p. 50; El 7832–3; Cliffe, *Yorkshire*, p. 318.
204   *DeL'Isle*, p. 267.
205   (1640), STC 9262. The Huntington's copy of the Declaration (HN 41222) has the king's comments about the House of Commons underlined with 'no' in the margin (pp. 41 ff.). See also Sanderson's sermons, July 1640 (Laud, *Works*, Vol. 1, nos x, xi).
206   El 7838.
207   SP 16/459/41; 16/454/44 and 45; also 16/455/85; 16/456/21; 16/456/34; 16/457/23; 16/458/42; 16/459/21; 16/459/32; 16/463/43.
208   SP 16/456/41; see also 16/455/35; cf. Yelverton (SP 16/445/54 and above).
209   SP 16/459/21.
210   HMC, *Twelfth Report*, app., iv, Vol. 1, p. 521; also Pearl, *London*, pp. 90–1, 102–3; Ashton, *Money Market*, pp. 181, 188; El 7842, 7843, 7844, 7845; Ashton, *City and Court*, pp. 199–200.
211   SP 16/463/32; 16/457/36.
212   Yonge, f. 75v; El 7837; 7868; HMC, *Twelfth Report*, app., iv, Vol. 1, pp. 520–2. Richard Heyrick in his Fast sermon on 8 July preached about the miseries of war, among which he named shipmoney and conduct money (*Three Sermons* (1641), STC W H1752).
213   SP 16/461/13. The grand jury at the Berkshire assizes formulated a petition against many grievances. See below.
214   SP 16/457/104; 16/459/36; 16/461/24; 16/461/25; 16/461/32; 16/467/79; HMC, *Twelfth Report*, app., iv, Vol. 1, p. 522; also see SP 16/466/44. See also *Fortunes Tennis Ball* (1640), STC 11198; El 7856; 7872; SP 16/452/99; 16/453/96; 16/454/79.
215   *CSPDom. 1640*, p. 656; also p. 567; *DeL'Isle*, p. 296; SP 16/463/70; 16/465/8; 16/461/27; 16/461/86, 88, 89, 94.
216   SP 16/467/56.
217   (1640), STC 1008; HMC, *Twelfth Report*, app., iv, Vol. 1, p. 522.
218   The sermon was printed in 1641 (STC W D2105) a reference I owe to Caroline Hibbard. See below concerning the war with the Scots.
219   See, for example, William Prynne, *Rome's Master-Piece* (1643) in Laud, *Works*, Vol. 4, pp. 465–503, a reference I owe to Caroline Hibbard; see also Hibbard, *Popish Plot*, p. 151; *The Devil's Letter Sent to Rome* (*CSPDom. Addenda, 1625–49*, pp. 624–5).
220   e.g. SP 16/460/63 (Essex); 16/463/32 and *CSPDom. 1640*, pp. 466–7 (Berkshire); SP 16/461/32, 38 (Sussex); SP 16/461/38 (Yorkshire).
221   SP 16/463/33.

222   *CSPDom. 1640*, pp. 466–7; *Declaration*, p. 44.
223   SP 16/461/38; see also Cholmley, *Memoirs*, pp. 61–2; Slingsby, *Diary*, p. 56; Rous included the petition in his diary (pp. 91–2); see also HMC, *Twelfth Report*, app., iv, Vol. 1, pp. 522–3; Cliffe, *Yorkshire*, p. 319.
224   See above.
225   Cholmley, *Memoirs*, p. 62. Vanity and time may have led him to exaggerate.
226   *DeL'Isle*, p. 311; also SP 16/464/17; El 7847.
227   Slingsby, *Diary*, p. 57.
228   Cholmley, *Memoirs*, pp. 62–4; Slingsby, *Diary*, pp. 57–8; Cliffe, *Yorkshire*, pp. 319–20. See below.
229   See above; also *DeL'Isle*, p. 315; Gardiner, *History of England*, Vol. 9, p. 189.
230   El 7847; *The Intention of the Army of the Kingdome of Scotland Declared to their Brethern of England* (Edinburgh, 1640), STC 21919.
231   *Intention*, p. 5.
232   El 7849; also El 7847; SP 16/464/57 (Cambridge); 16/464/79 (Essex); 16/465/60 (Sussex); 16/466/48 (Ipswich); 16/463/91 (London); also see HMC, *Seventh Report*, app., p. 251; SP 16/463/100; 16/465/80. SP 16/467/75 (the appeal to London).
233   HMC, *Seventh Report*, app., p. 251; also see, HMC, *Beaulieu*, p. 127; also Supple, *Commercial Crisis*, pp. 124 ff.
234   Clark, 'Gloucester', p. 186; also S. R. Gardiner (ed.), *The Hamilton Papers*, Camden Society, New Series, vol. 27 (1880), p. 264.
235   SP 16/451/39; also see above.
236   The evidence concerning the peers' dealings with the Scots is not above question. See Gardiner, *History of England*, Vol. 9, pp. 179–81 n; also see Zagorin, *Court*, p. 104; Stevenson, *Revolution*, pp. 205–6. Among the early signers of the petition were Exeter, Bedford, Hertford, Essex, Rutland, Warwick, Bolingbroke, Mulgrave, Saye and Sele, Mandeville, Howard of Escrick, Brooke, Paget, Bristol, Savile, Lincoln, North, Willoughby, Wharton, and Lovelace (SP 16/465/16; 16/465/17–19), the names vary on copies of the petition. Pym's copy includes Bath but omits Paget (Beinecke Library, Osborn files, a reference I owe to Conrad Russell); Exeter and Bristol, whose names were not on some copies, and Mulgrave are the only ones of these peers not listed among the dissenting lords in the Short Parliament.
237   SP 16/467/88; Cope, *Montagu*, p. 175.
238   Petition (SP 16/465/19); Rous includes it in his diary (pp. 93–4); see also HMC, *Fourteenth Report*, app., ii, p. 65; Cholmley, *Memoirs*, p. 62.
239   See Chapter 1.
240   El 7849.
241   e.g. SP 16/467/9, 60, and 75.
242   SP 16/466/28; 16/466/54; *DeL'Isle*, p. 325; also above and SP 16/464/82.
243   SP 16/464/82 (wrongly dated): see Cliffe, *Yorkshire*, pp. 321–3; also Cholmley, *Memoirs*, pp. 62–4; Slingsby, *Diary*, pp. 57–8.
244   Ashton, *City and Court*, pp. 199–200; Ashton, *Money Market*, pp. 181–2;

      Pearl, *London*, pp. 102–3; El 7845; SP 16/467/60; 16/467/75; 16/467/135.
245   Woodforde, p. 499.
246   Cl C 617.
247   *Hardwicke State Papers* (London, 1778), Vol. 2, p. 210. I owe this reference to Paul Hardacre.
248   I cannot accept Sheila Lambert's argument about the opening of the Long Parliament ('The opening of the Long Parliament', *Historical Journal*, vol. 27, no. 2 (1984), pp. 265–87.

Conclusion

Charles I ended a period in English political history when he announced late in September 1640 that he would summon a Parliament to meet at Westminster on 3 November. The protests that had culminated in the petitions of the preceding weeks showed that, to the public, his eleven-year personal rule had become the 'intermission of Parliaments'. He himself had made the absence of Parliament an issue when in January 1638/9 he decided to go to war against the Scots without calling one. He had magnified Parliament's political importance in 1640 by allowing the Lords and Commons to meet and then dissolving them after only three weeks – before they or their fellow countrymen believed they had had adequate opportunity to perform their time-honoured function of seeking redress for the grievances of the kingdom. His determination to renew his campaign against the Covenanters and their invasion of England in August transformed the demonstrations of discontent that had followed the dissolution of the Short Parliament into the cries of September. By yielding to these demands for Parliament, Charles, whatever his strategy may have been, gave legitimacy to the petitioners' view of the history of the preceding era.

The absence of parliaments between 1629 and 1640 shaped the politics of the period because it deprived the English of their traditional forum for discussion of public affairs. Representatives of the entire kingdom had no place to meet with each other and the king. Their consideration of the policies and practices of his rule occurred instead in smaller and informal settings without the protection of parliamentary privileges. The institutions of local government, though primarily administrative and judicial, were important in this regard because they brought together individuals who were responsible for executing royal orders. Personal contacts between family members, friends or business associates provided another means by which politics continued during the 1630s. The steady stream of seekers of favour, the others whose affairs took them to Westminster and London and the agents who made the collection and distribution of news their profession insured that people all over knew of the incidents and issues that occupied those at the hub of politics. Such ties allowed people from different communities to share concerns and examine their problems in a perspective that was not purely parochial, but the risks involved in political activities outside Parliament hampered continuing discussion among individuals who did not see each other regularly. Even close friends hesitated to commit their comments to writing.

Extra-parliamentary politics demanded either subtlety or boldness not required of those who took part in the proceedings of the Lords and Commons. People who worried about Popery, Arminianism and other innovations in religion, about charges and impositions that seemed to violate their rights or about the imprisonment of MPs and other infringements of liberties of Parliament itself discovered in the months and years following 1629 that they could do little through ordinary channels to affect the policies and practices they disliked. Letters, petitions and appeals to king and council evoked reprimands more often than changes. Neither quiet obstruction nor symbolic demonstrations of disapproval had any significant impact.

Until 1639 most people elected to grumble rather than to take more daring action. If they were uneasy about the direction of policies, they had no wish to cause disorder or incur punishment. The absence of Parliament was an implicit issue. The prelates who were introducing alterations in religion were disregarding the laws established by Parliament; statutes, and the Petition of Right, likewise protected property; in Parliament people could join together in seeking redress for a host of grievances including complaints about councillors; MPs could communicate with the king about the state of Church and commonwealth; individuals and communities could ask for solutions to particular problems. Between 1629 and 1639 the English devoted far more attention to efforts to obtain satisfaction on specific points than to their inability to look to Parliament for this purpose. Most believed that Charles would ultimately call another session.

When in 1639 he departed from custom and went to war without issuing writs of summons, he gave them cause for questioning their trust in him. With their hopes for relief diminished they were less willing to wait patiently for redress of the grievances that were by virtue of the war becoming more burdensome and taking on new meaning. Although the king described his campaign as one to subdue the rebellious Scots, the English saw that he was imposing Laudianism on that kingdom. His insistence that they support him at all costs increased their frustration and paved the way for a new era in politics.

Between the outbreak of the first Bishops' War and the summoning of Parliament a year and a half later in September 1640 the focus of politics shifted from particular complaints to the condition of England. More individuals began to voice their concerns more openly, and the absence of Parliament became an explicit issue. The session of the spring of 1640 that came to be known as the Short Parliament played a critical role in the transition because it provided an opportunity for the English to reflect on their experience over the preceding eleven years. The framework of grievances that John Pym delivered on 17 April placed the 'intermission of Parliaments' at the root of the ills that had plagued Church and commonwealth. The turmoil of the months that followed the dissolution of that Parliament seemed to prove his point. By September people had placed his argument at the centre of their petitions.

Religion dominated politics and gave it continuity during the eleven years when consideration of public affairs of necessity occurred outside Parliament. The fears that MPs expressed on 2 March 1628/9 just prior to the adjournment of that session inspired churchwardens to resist placing tables altarwise, parishioners to refuse to go to the rails to take communion, ministers to defy orders to read the Book of Sports, pamphleteers to accuse the prelates of challenging royal authority and people to flee to New England. Although some who were disciplined or called before the High Commission for religious dissent submitted, some who conformed harboured doubts about the practices being imposed. Whatever Charles and Laud may have believed, they appeared to be leading England away from Protestantism toward Rome. Their suspicions

of Puritans reverberated in questions about their intentions. By
sending plagues and judgements and by dividing the English one
from another, God seemed to be warning against policies that
permitted error and superstition. Conscientious clergy and laity
prayed about what they should do. Deciding upon action was
difficult and individuals reached different conclusions.

The polemicists' descriptions of two armies – one Puritan, the
other Arminian – facing each other in a series of battles for control
of the Church simplify the range of opinions and overestimate the
organization of the groups. Persecution created a certain sense of
fellowship among its victims and caused friends to rally around
them. Although these networks of support appeared to be undermining ecclesiastical discipline, they were more effective in reacting to it
than in altering its direction. Puritans in particular communities
occasionally co-operated to obstruct innovations, but except for the
Providence Island Company their troops were volunteers who
followed their own drummers as often as any officer. The strength
that observers attributed to them came from their commitment to
their cause.

Only a few were prepared to express their concerns about religion
openly throughout the period. Dismissed as fanatics and trouble-
makers by some, their message and their treatment by the crown won
them sympathy among people who were not necessarily in
agreement with either their words or their deeds. Prynne, Burton,
and Bastwick had by the conclusion of their trial in June 1637
become popular heroes. They, like the thousands of religious
refugees who departed for America or Europe, were symbols of the
far greater numbers of clergy and laity who had in one way or
another suffered at the hands of Laud and his minions.

The propaganda that the Covenanters sent south in 1639 sought
to capitalize upon English fears that their own religion might be
overturned and their laws and liberties endangered. The doubts
nourished by the Scots' statements helped curb enthusiasm for the
war and bring more people to resist Laudianism. When Charles
allowed Convocation to sit after he had dissolved Parliament in
May 1640 and to make the canons that imposed the etcetera oath,
he opened the floodgates of religious opposition and demonstrated,
as his opponents had argued, that Parliament was necessary to
prevent innovations.

Although people sometimes expressed uncertainty about what the king's religious policies were, they had no hesitation in concluding that these were wrong if they inclined toward the introduction of Popery in England. The strength of anti-Romanism gave a clarity and force to the politics of religion that is absent from other issues during the 1630s. The resistance that Charles encountered in his efforts to provide for the defence of the kingdom floundered upon reluctance to contest the opinions of the judges about his claims. Rather than wrestling with knotty questions about the royal prerogative and the subjects' rights and taking up a dispute that could be both costly and difficult to win, most who opposed his military or revenue-raising measures did so on grounds that were not constitutional. The public nevertheless displayed immense interest in cases where individuals like Lord Saye or John Hampden argued directly with the crown over rights.

Localism too had only limited significance in the politics of the 1630s. Cities and towns resented incursions upon their jurisdiction by counties or cathedral clergy who seemed better able to win royal support. Directives from the crown that sought to alter traditional ways of rating or to interfere in community proceedings sparked protests, and notables conducted ongoing disputes with rivals under cover of opposition or support for orders from the king and council. Yet however preoccupied the leaders of communities were with personal and parochial concerns, few ignored what was happening elsewhere. Their hunger for news and responses to events beyond their own bounds linked their words and deeds to the national political setting.

Neither localism nor constitutionalism describe the real objections of the English to the assortment of projects and charges that burdened them financially and relied upon disused customs, legal technicalities, or controversial interpretations of law. The men to whom the king turned for advice and those who executed some of his money-making schemes appeared too often to have little respect for the personal honour of nobles and gentlemen, for local pride and interests or for traditional procedures. Neither he nor they seemed to appreciate that their assumptions about the disloyalty of those who asked questions or failed to perform difficult or unreasonable tasks, alienated people who had no thought of challenging royal authority.

Those who were unhappy about aspects of Charles's personal rule formed no association to seek changes. Apart from religion most had no specific alternatives to the policies they opposed. Inspiring them were visions of an England that they believed had once existed where peace, concord and prosperity reigned, monarch and subject met frequently in Parliament and people could practise their religion, enjoy their property, earn their livelihood and obtain redress of grievances without fear of molestation.

In opposing policies and practices that were depriving them and their king of happiness the English had no desire to attack royal power. They raised points of procedure, local jurisdiction, custom and equity. Individuals and communities alike compiled evidence of their limited resources, the hardships they endured, and their previous loyal service to the crown. Experienced in techniques of delaying litigation and harassing adversaries, they applied these shamelessly to escape from military charges or reduce shipmoney assessments. If Charles's supporters were sometimes too quick to suspect disloyalty and too ready to call foot-dragging sedition, they usually had some grounds for allegations about political activity.

The most obvious opponents of the policies, practices, and personnel of the king's personal rule were the individuals who fearlessly expressed their views through unauthorized tracts. Because the crown attempted to arrest them and destroy all copies of their works, they made an impact indirectly through sensation and reports of what they did and said rather than directly. Attracting attention disproportionate to their minute numbers, they were particularly successful in exposing the prelates' pretensions with well-aimed barbs. When *Newes from Ipswich* appeared, people had heard tales about what Bishop Wren was setting out to do in his new diocese of Norwich. They were disposed to believe the worst.

A handful of lords and gentlemen likewise drew notice for their concerted resistance to Charles's policies. Lord Saye and Lord Brooke were the most unrepentant of these, but even they tried to avoid conduct that might land them in prison. Some of their puritan associates and fellow members of the Providence Island Company also hovered over the line between defiance and compliance. When called before the council for refusing to pay shipmoney or to appear at musters, they were inclined to bow to royal authority. In contrast to those who had declined to pay the Forced Loan in 1626 many of those who resisted royal exactions during the 1630s did so with little fanfare. Theirs was the politics of survival, designed to avoid costly confrontations that could not be won. Without setting an example of disobedience that if followed by the populace might be their own undoing, they were nevertheless informing their contemporaries of their own reservations about the king's demands. Some of these men and others likewise revealed their opinions by providing assistance for clergy who fell foul of the ecclesiastical hierarchy.

Ministers such as Samuel Ward of Ipswich, John Workman of Gloucester or Thomas Ball of Northampton also established reputations for struggling to remain true to their beliefs and yet avoid losing the positions that allowed them to serve those desiring religious instruction. The very sermons through which they had an opportunity to exercise influence could, if not carefully worded, be the means of their undoing. Most preachers treated politics metaphorically if at all so that the authorities would have scant evidence upon which to prosecute. Congregations drew their own conclusions. The faithful who in some instances journeyed long distances to hear ministers listened closely and reflected upon the meaning of what they had heard. People also followed the clergy's sometimes long and intricate dealings with the High Commission and noted when godly and conscientious preachers were no longer able to accept the terms imposed upon them.

Lawyers, like the clergy, had professional interests and obligations that led others to seek their advice about responses to royal policies. The complexity of the questions they dealt with and the procedural options ordinarily available to clients allowed those who wished to avoid political quagmires to do so. For each of the well-known figures such as St John, Holborn or Bagshaw who stated his opinion openly and confronted the crown, there were more lawyers who took advantage of their expertise to bury their views in the minutiae of the law, and many who affirmed the legality of the king's actions.

Though their decisions and those of members of the clergy, nobility, gentry or urban aristocracy about conformity to royal policy were personal, they were also, as the individuals involved realized, public. What the persons who served as the principal officials in the towns and counties of England during the 1630s did in that capacity had an even greater potential impact upon others. To perform their responsibilities they had to find a way of mediating between the crown's demands and those of their neighbours. When they encountered fierce local opposition to military charges, outrage at shipmoney assessments, or refusal to see Laudian practices adopted in their parishes, they had to determine whether to ignore the offensive orders, persist in enforcement, or follow another course. Through various means – negotiations, appeals to patrons, petitions, letters, delegations to the Privy Council – they tried and sometimes failed to resolve the differences that they encountered. The extent of their efforts to accomplish business and the frustrations that they experienced reveal both the strengths and weaknesses of Charles's regime. If few of these men were prepared to defy him, many had by the winter of 1638/9 come to wonder about his intentions. Duty, not affection, bound them to him.

The restraints keeping local leaders from explicitly opposing royal policy and practices had less power over others of his subjects. Sheriffs and JPs for whom the neglects of constables were a chronic headache found during the 1630s that some of these functionaries were declaring that shipmoney or military charges were illegal. Grand juries took their responsibilities seriously. They refused to be intimidated and presented unpopular policies and projects as public grievances. People who vented their spleen at constables or complained about exactions to their neighbours at the alehouse did not stop to ponder over the words with which they expressed their opinions. Those whose disrespectful comments reached the council table and led to their own subsequent appearance before the board or in the Star Chamber defined the issues which by 1640 had become the substance of petitions of grievance and parliamentary speeches.

Such rumblings of discontent posed no serious threat to Charles's rule during the 1630s. The few real outbreaks of disorder that occurred then were short-lived responses to specific conditions – food supplies or prices; unemployment; fen draining; disafforestation; distraint for shipmoney; Laudian innovations; pressing of troops. These incidents aroused fear among the king's servants, impeded the enforcement of his policies on the local level and helped to remind the community's notables that their leadership depended upon recognition from below as well as above. Although literacy could make political news more quickly accessible, political culture was still highly oral and visual.

When in 1640 opposition to Charles's regime became bolder, the dissatisfaction of the bulk of the population pressed those in positions of responsibility to insist upon redress of grievances. Although, if given more time, MPs in the Short Parliament probably would have granted subsidies to the king, their refusal to do so as quickly as he wanted owed much to the feelings that they knew they would have to face when the session ended. During the weeks that followed more sheriffs, JPs and deputy lieutenants told the council that they could not comply with orders because the people of their communities would not. Leaders who despite their own misgivings about his policies might in the summer and autumn of 1640 have given Charles another chance concluded that this was no longer feasible. They joined with those who had long before thought that Parliament must meet and make reforms.

The Scots provided them with an example that they could follow. In telling the king that he would have to observe the laws and liberties of the kingdom they were doing what the Covenanters had done earlier. Charles's stubbornness in dealing with the Scottish situation dramatized the difficulties they seemed to be facing in England. Although both politics and pride prevented any acknowledgement, the English resistance owed something to Scottish inspiration.

The war between the two kingdoms created a situation which made the Covenanters' model relevant for those in England who were unhappy with the king's policies. It also transformed English politics. Yet the issues around which people rallied in 1639 and 1640 were not new. Popery, Arminianism, and other innovations in religion, violations of property, and infringements of parliamentary liberties were grievances in 1629, and during the eleven years when Charles called no Parliament these remained concerns. Although only a few individuals were prepared to risk punishment by openly criticizing his policy and practices on these grounds, more watched anxiously to see what would happen and hoped for relief in the future. From time to time they found reason for optimism, but by 1637 the situation looked bleak. Laud and his supporters seemed to be extending their control of the Church. The presence of a papal agent suggested that Charles and his archbishop were thinking of a return to Rome. Collection of shipmoney proceeded, and the crown was preparing to prosecute John Hampden who refused to pay. Intolerant of criticism or dissent the king and his ministers seemed more concerned with raising revenue and defending royal authority than listening to the complaints of the people.

Conditions varied from one part of the kingdom to another and so did the configurations and intensity of politics. In London and Westminster the presence of the royal court and of the institutions of administration and justice made politics an important business. Where individuals or factions competed for power, disputes about

religion, defence or other issues frequently became heated and
intangled with existing rivalries. Somerset was a classic case of such
quarrelling; Newcastle upon Tyne was another. Towns like
Dorchester or Banbury where Puritanism was deeply rooted and
citizens actively involved in government were centres of resistance to
Charles's policies. The puritan lords and gentry in Essex and
Northamptonshire also gave their counties a reputation for
opposition.

The attention attracted by areas where clashes occurred or
individuals were defiant magnified the significance of those
incidents. People elsewhere had a pattern to follow if they too had
complaints. When the king and his servants responded by defending
royal authority rather than resolving the problem, they aggravated
the situation. Their perception that the English were challenging
Charles's rule became the justification for harsh reactions that
deepened grievances.

England was not on a high road to revolution or civil war during
the 1630s, but its populace was weighed down with burdens that
became intolerable when Charles set off to fight the Scots. Because
he dismissed the explicit complaints and ignored other signs of
political opposition during the preceding years, he misunderstood
the politics of 1639 and 1640 which eventually forced him to return
to parliamentary government.

Select Bibliography

MANUSCRIPT SOURCES

Bedfordshire Record Office
  St John of Bletsoe MSS, nos 1325, 1328, 1331, 1337–8, 1342, 1361–2, 1367,
    1399, 1405
Bodleian Library
  MS Ashmole 1149
  MS Firth, c.4
  MS Rawlinson 358
  MS Tanner 84
British Library
  Add. MSS 4275–6; 11044–5; 25079; 34163; 36989; 47787
  Althorp MSS A2; A18
  Egerton MSS 2645–6; 2716
  Hargrave MS 44
  Lansdowne MSS 213, 1098
  Loan MSS 29/172–3
  Stowe MSS 184; 743
Cornish Record Office
  Buller Papers, BC 24/1; 24/2; 24/4; 24/5
  Rashleigh of Stoketon, DDR(S) 1
  Trelawney Letters, NRO 5/1–4
  Tremayne Papers, DDR 5297; DDT 1981–4
Devon Record Office
  Quarter Sessions Order Books 1625–40
Duke of Buccleuch and Queensberry
  Montagu MSS 1, 3–4, 6, 10, 15, 27, 29, 30, 191
East Sussex Record Office
  Rye Corporation
    Correspondence 47/111–32

Hundred, Sessions, and Assize Books, A27/3 (1627–40)
Folger Shakespeare Library
   MS V.b.189, 'A true presentation of fore-past parliaments'
Harvard University
   Houghton Library
      Harvard MSS Eng. 1074; 1266
   Widener Library
      Film: Essex Assize File (35/70–81)
         Calendar of Essex Quarter Sessions Rolls (Q/SR 266–309)
      Film: City of Exeter, Act Books, Vols 7–8
      Mayor's Court Book
      Royal Letters and Other Letters
      Misc. Roll 103
      Minute Book, Sessions of Peace, 1629–40
Henry E. Huntington Library and Art Gallery
   Ellesmere Manuscripts 6477–859; 6873; 6879; 6895; 6963–7311; 7406–22;
      7509–16; 7564–607; 7618–82a; 7807–920; 9542
   Hastings Manuscripts, Letters, 1625–41
   Stow–Temple Manuscripts
      Letters, 1628–41
      Manorial Box 3
      Family Addenda, Boxes 1, 2
      Legal, Misc. Papers, Box 2
      Shipmoney Papers
   MSS HM 204, 728, The Case of Shipmoney
   MS HM 27514, The Mustermaster
   MS HM 1338, Commonplace Book
Kent Archives Office
   Dering MSS, U350/C2; U350/02
   Twysden's commonplace book, MS U47/47 Z1
National Library of Scotland
   Advocates MS 16.2.23
New College, Oxford
   MS Archive 9502, Woodforde's Diary
Northamptonshire Record Office
   Finch-Hatton MSS 1150–1; 3464
   Isham Correspondence, 177–233
   Northampton Borough Assembly Books, 1628–40
Nottinghamshire Record Office
   Portland MSS, DD4P 68; 70; 72; 75; 84
   Quarter Sessions Minute Books, Vols 8–10
   Borough of Nottingham Hall Book, 1629–40
Public Record Office
   Chancery Masters' Deposits, Duchess of Norfolk's Deeds (Scudamore Letters),
      C.115/M. 12, 14, 23–5, 28–37; N.1–8
   Privy Council Registers, 1631–7 (microcard edn)
   State Papers, Domestic, SP 16/138–428

Shropshire Record Office
  Bridgnorth Common Hall Order Book, 1634–85
    Third Great Leet Book
  Ludlow Corporation, 352/15
    Boxes 274–5, 293, 295
    Minute Book
  Bridgewater MSS 364–5
Somerset Record Office
  Phelips MSS, DDPH 204; 212; 219; 221–8
  Quarter Sessions Minute Books, 1627–38
  Trevelyan Papers, DD/WO Box 53, Bundle 1
University of Nottingham Library
  Clifton Manuscripts, Letters, 1629–40
Yale Center for Parliamentary History
  Film: Barrington Letters
    British Library, Egerton MS 2716
    Essex Record Office, Barrington MSS, D/DBa F/4
  Film: Coventry Council Minute Book
    Coventry, MS A. 35, Book of Matters touching shipmoney
  Film: Letters of John Holles, earl of Clare, University of Nottingham, MSS
    (NeC 15404–5)
  Film: Letter Book of Thomas Howard, first earl of Suffolk (Phillips MS 3863)
  Film: Northumberland MSS, Alnwick Castle, Vol. 14
  Film: Verney MSS, Claydon Letters, 1635–40
  Film: Diary of William Whiteway, British Library, Egerton MS 784
  Film: Diary of Walter Yonge, British Library, Additional MS 35331
York City Archives, House Books, Vols 35–6
  Chamberlains Accounts, 1629–40

PRINTED WORKS

Primary Sources
Acts of the Privy Council of England 1628—1629 (London: HMSO, 1958).
Andrewes, J., *The converted Mans New Birth* (1629), STC 565.
The arrivall and intertainements of the embassador from the Emperor of Morocco
  (1637), STC 18165.
The Articles of Peace Agreed Upon betwixt the two Crownes of Great Brittaine and
  France (1629), STC 9250.
The Articles of Peace in a Treaty at Madrit (1630), STC 9251.
Articles to Be inquired of in the Archdeaconrie of Salop, within the Diocese of
  Hereford, in the yeare 1639 (1639), STC 10217.
Articles to be Inquired of Within the Diocese of Norwich (1636), STC 10298.
Bachiler, S., *The Campe Royall* (1629), STC 1107.
Bamford, F. (ed.), *A Royalist's Notebook: The Commonplace Book of Sir John*
  Oglander (London: Constable, 1936).
Bariffe, W., *Mars his Triumph* (1639), STC 1505.

Bariffe, W., *Military Discipline* (1635), STC 1506.

Barnes, T. G. (ed.), *Somerset Assize Orders, 1629–1640*, Somerset Record Society, vol. 65 (1959).

Bastwick, J., *Apology* (1636), STC 1576.

Bastwick, J., *Letany* (1636), STC 1572.

The Beast Is Wounded (Amsterdam, 1638), STC 22032.

Bentham, J., *The Societie of the Saints* (n.d.), STC 1889.

Berington, J. (ed.), *The Memoirs of Gregorio Panzani* (Birmingham: Swinney & Walker, 1793; 1970 reprint).

Bernard, R., *The Bible-Battells or the Sacret Art Military For the rightly wageing of warre according to Holy Writ* (1629), STC 1926.

Bernard, R., *Christian See to Thy Conscience* (1631), STC 1928.

Bettey, J. H. (ed.), *Calendar of the Correspondence of the Smyth Family of Ashton Court 1548–1642*, Bristol Record Society, vol. 35 (1982).

Birch, T. (ed.), *The Court and Times of Charles I*, 2 vols (London: Henry Colburn, 1848).

Bolton, R., *Two Sermons Preached at Northampton* (1635), STC 3256.

Bond, S. (ed.), *The Chamber Order Book of Worcester, 1602–50*, Worcester Historical Society, New Series, vol. 8 (1974).

Bonsey, C. G., and Jenkins, J. G. (eds), *Ship Money Papers and Richard Grenville's Notebook,* Bucks Record Society, vol. 13 (1965).

Brabourne, T., *Defence ... of the Sabbath* (1632), STC 3473.

A Briefe Relation of Certaine speciall and most materiall passages and speeches in the Starre-Chamber, Occasioned and delivered the 14th day of June 1637 (1637), STC 1570.

Bruce, J. (ed.), *Letters and Papers of the Verney Family*, Camden Society, vol. 56 (1853).

Burges, J., *The Lawfulness of Kneeling in the Act of Receiving the Lord's Supper* (London, 1631), STC 4114.

Burton, H., *Apology of an Appeal* (1636), STC 4134.

Burton, H., *Divine Tragedie* (1636), STC 20459.

Burton, H., *For God and the King* (1636), STC 4141.

Byfield, N., *Mr. Byfield's Answer with Mr. Brerewoods Reply* (1630), STC 3622.

Byfield, R., *Doctrine of the Sabbath Vindicated* (1631), STC 4238.

Cade, A., *A Sermon Necessary for These Times* (1636), preached at Leicester, 11 October 1631, visitation, STC 4329a.

Calder, I. M. (ed.), *Letters of John Davenport* (New Haven, Conn.: Yale University Press, 1937).

Calder, I. M. (ed.), *Activities of the Puritan Faction of the Church of England 1625–33* (London: Church History Society, 1957).

Calendar of State Papers, Domestic Series, 1625–42 and *Addenda, 1625–49* (London, 1856–97).

Calendar of State Papers and Manuscripts Relating to English Affairs Existing in the Archives and Collections of Venice and Other Libraries of Northern Italy, 1625–42 (London, 1864–1947).

Cardwell, E., *Documentary Annals of the Reformed Church of England* (Oxford: Oxford University Press, 1844).

Carew, T., *Coelum Britanicum* (1634), STC 4618.

Carpenter, N., *Chorazin and Bethesaida's Woe or Warning Peece* (1640), STC 4675.

Certayne Queres propownded to the Bowers to the names of Jesus and to the Patrons thereof, wherein the auct[orities] and reasons alledged by Bishop Andrewes and his followers in defense of this ceremony are breefely examined and refuted, 4th edn (1636), BL, 873.e.9.

Certaine Statutes especially selected and commanded by his Majestie to be carefully put in execution by all Justices and other officers of the Peace (1630), STC 9342.

Charles I, *Declaration Concerning His Proceedings with his Subjects of Scotland* (1640), STC 9260.

Charles I, *His Majesties Declaration to All His Loving Subjects of the Causes Which Moved Him to Dissolve the Last Parliament* (1628), STC 9249.

Charles I, *His Majesties Declaration to All His Loving Subjects of the Causes Which Moved Him to Dissolve the Last Parliament* (1640), STC 9262.

Charles I, *Proclamation* (27 March 1629), STC 8916.

Charles I, *Proclamation* (27 February 1638/9), STC 9135.

Charles I, *Proclamation* (30 March 1640), STC 9154.

Chillingworth, W., *The Religion of Protestants* (1638), STC 5138.

Clarke, S., *The Lives of Two and Twenty English Divines* (London, 1660), STC W C4514.

Commons' Journals, Vols 1, 2.

Constitutions and Canons Ecclesiasticall Agreed upon at London and York (1640), STC 10080.

Cope, E. S., and Coates, W. H. (eds), *Proceedings of the Short Parliament of 1640*, Royal Historical Society, Camden Fourth Series, vol. 19 (1977).

The Correspondence of John Cosin, ed. G. Ornsby, part I, Surtees Society, vol. 52 (1869).

The Covenanters' Information (1639), STC 21905.

Davenport, J., *A Royall Edict for Military Exercises. Published in a Sermon preached to Captaines and Gentlemen that Exercise armes in the Artillery Garden* (London, 1629), STC 6313.

Diatelesma Nu. E., *The Moderne History of the World, expressing the principall Passages of the Christian Countries* (1637), STC 4292.

Discourse Concerning the Drayning of the Fennes (1629), STC 4270. *Divine and Politike Observations Newly Translated out of the Dutch Language wherein they were lately divulged. Upon Some Lines in the speech of the ArchB of Canterbury, pronounced in the Starre-Chamber upon June 1637* (1638), STC 15309.

Dow, C., *A Discourse of the Sabbath and the Lord's Day*, (1636), STC 7088.

Dyke, J., *A Worthy Communicant* (1636), STC 7429.

Edwards, P., and Gibson, C. (eds), *The Plays and Poems of Philip Massinger* (Oxford: Oxford University Press, 1976).

Emmison, F. G., and M. (eds), *The Ship-Money Papers of Henry Chester and Sir William Boteler, 1637–1639*, Bedfordshire Historical Record Society Publications, vol. 18 (1936).

Englands Complaint to Jesus Christ against the Bishops Canons (1641), STC W D2105.

An Examination and Confutation of a Lawless Pamphlet, Intituled a Brief Answer to a late Treatise of the Sabbath Day (1637), STC 25379.

An Extraordinaire Curranto (1639), STC 5750.

Fitz-Geoffrie, C., *The Curse of Corne-hoarders with the Blessing of Seasonable Selling* (1631), STC 10938.

The Forme of Common Prayer together with an Order of Fasting: for the averting of Gods Heavie visitation (1636), STC 16553a.

Fortunes Tennis Ball (1640), STC 11198.

Fuller, T., *Church History of Britain* (1655), STC W F2416.

Fuller, T., *The History of Holy Warre* (1639), STC 11464.

Gardiner, D. (ed.), *The Oxinden Letters, 1607–1642* (London: Constable, 1933).

Gardiner, S. R. (ed.), *The Hamilton Papers*, Camden Society, New Series, vol. 27 (1880).

Gardiner, S. R. (ed.), *Reports of Cases in the Court of Star Chamber and High Commission*, Camden Society, New Series, vol. 39 (1886).

Gardiner, S. R. (ed.), 'Speech of Sir Robert Heath, attorney general in the case of Alexander Leighton in the Star Chamber, 4 June 1630', *Camden Miscellany*, Vol. vii, Camden New Series, vol. 14 (1875).

Gibson, J. S. W., and Brinkworth, E. R. C. (eds), *Banbury Corporation Records: Tudor and Stuart*, Banbury Historical Society, vol. 15 (1977).

Gill, A., *The New Starr of the North* (1632), STC 11875.

Godwin, F., *Annales of England* (1630), STC 11947.

Goodman, F. R. (ed.), *The Diary of John Young S.T.P. Dean of Winchester* (London: SPCK, 1928).

Goombridge, M. J. (ed.), *Calendar of Chester City Council Minutes, 1603–1642*, Record Society of Lancashire and Cheshire, vol. 106 (1956).

Gouge, W., *Gods Three Arrows: Plague; Famine; Sword, in Three Treatises* (1631), STC 12116.

The Great and Famous Battel of Lutzen (1633, trans. out of the French), STC 12534.

Green, M. A. E. (ed.), *Diary of John Rous,* Camden Society, vol. 66 (1856).

Habington, W., *The Historie of Edward the Fourth, King of England* (1640), STC 12586.

Hacket, J., *Scrinia Reserata* (London, 1693).

Hall, J., *Episcopacie by Divine Right* (1640), STC 12661.

Halliwell, J. O. (ed.), *D'Ewes, Autobiography and Correspondence* (London: Richard Bentley, 1845).

Hamilton, C. L., 'The Muster-master', *Camden Miscellany*, Vol. xxvi, Camden Fourth Series, vol, 14 (1975), pp. 49–76.

Hamper, W. (ed.), *The Life, Diary, and Correspondence of Sir William Dugdale,* (London, 1827).

Hardwicke State Papers (London, 1778), Vol. 2.

Harris, M., *Brittaines Hallelujah or a Sermon of Thanksgiving for the Happy Pacification in Brittaine* (1639), STC 12807.

Harsnet, A., *Gods Summons Unto a General Repentance* (1640), STC 12875.

Hayward, J., *The Life and Raigne of King Edward the Sixt* (1630), STC 12998.

Heylyn, P., *Augustus, or an essay of those meanes and counsels, whereby the Commonwealth of Rome was altered and reduced into a Monarchy* (1632), STC 13268.

Heylyn, P., *A Briefe and Moderate Answer to the Seditious Challenges of Henry Burton*, bound with *A Coale from the Altar* (1636), STC 13270 (Folger copy).

Heylyn, P., *A Coale from the Altar* (1636), STC 13270.

Heylyn, P., *The History of the Sabbath* (2nd ed, rev., 1636), STC 13275.

Heyrick, R., *Three Sermons* (1641), STC W H1752.

Heywood, T., *The Royall King and the Loyall Subject* (London, 1637), STC 13364.

Heywood, T., *A True Description of his majesties Royall Ship* (London, 1637), STC 13367.

Hildersham, A., *Doctrine of Fasting* (London, 1633), STC 13459.

Hill, A., *The Peace of Enmity* (1640), STC 13467.

Historical Manuscripts Commission, *Calendar of the White and Black Books of the Cinque Ports, 1432–1955* (London, 1966).

Historical Manuscripts Commission, *Eighth Report*, app., ii, Manchester MSS.

Historical Manuscripts Commission, *Fourteenth Report*, app., ii, Portland MSS: Harley Papers (1894).

Historical Manuscripts Commission, *Fourth Report*, app., House of Lords MSS (1874).

Historical Manuscripts Commission, *Ninth Report*, app., ii, Diary of Robert Woodforde (1883).

Historical Manuscripts Commission, *Report on the MSS of the Duke of Buccleuch and Queensberry preserved at Montagu House*, Vols 1 and 3 (1899, 1926).

Historical Manuscripts Commission, *Report on the MSS of the Right Honourable Viscount DeL'Isle, V.C. at Penshurst Palace, Kent*, Vol. 6; Sidney Papers, 1626–1698 (1966).

Historical Manuscripts Commission, *Report on the MSS of the Gawdy Family* (1885).

Historical Manuscripts Commission, *Report on the MSS of Lord Montagu of Beaulieu* (1900).

Historical Manuscripts Commission, *Report on the MSS of the Marquess of Salisbury*, Vol. 22 (1976).

Historical Manuscripts Commission, *Report on the MSS of Reginald Rawdon Hastings*, Vols 1 and 4 (1928, 1947).

Historical Manuscripts Commission, *Second Report*, Bedford MSS (1871).

Historical Manuscripts Commission, *Seventh Report*, app., Barrington Manuscripts (1879).

Historical Manuscripts Commission, *Sixth Report*, app., Denbigh MSS (1877).

Historical Manuscripts Commission, *Thirteenth Report*, app., Nalson MSS (1891).

Historical Manuscripts Commission, *Twelfth Report*, app., i, Cowper, Vol. 2 (1888).

Historical Manuscripts Commission, *Twelfth Report*, app., iv, Rutland, Vol. 1 (1911).

Hobson, M. G., and H. E. Salter (eds), *Oxford Council Acts, 1626–1665*, Oxford Historical Society, vol. 95 (1933).

Howell, T. B. (ed.), *Complete Collection of State Trials* (London, 1816).

Hyde, Edward, earl of Clarendon, *History of the Rebellion*, ed. W. D. Macray (Oxford: Clarendon Press, 1888).

Information from the Estates of the Kingdome of Scotland to the Kingdome of England (1640), STC 21916.

Information to all good Christians within the Kingdome of England (1639), STC 21905.

Instructions for Musters and Armes, and the Use thereof. By Order from his Majesties most honourable Privie Council (27 July 1631), STC 7684.

The Intention of the Army of the Kingdome of Scotland Declared to their Brethern of England (Edinburgh, 1640), STC 21919.

Jacobson, W. (ed.), *The Works of Robert Sanderson* (Oxford: Oxford University Press, 1854).

Jennison, R., *The Cities Safetie* (1630), STC 14489.

Jennison, R., *Newcastles Call to her Neighbour and Sister Townes and Cities throughout the land to take Warning by her Sins and Sorrowes* (1637), STC 14492.

Johnson, G. W. (ed.), *The Fairfax Correspondence* (London: Richard Bentley, 1848), 2 vols.

Johnson, R., Cole, M. *et al.* (eds), *Commons Debates, 1628* (New Haven, Conn.: Yale University Press, 1977).

Journals of the House of Lords, Vol. 4.

Knowler, W. (ed.), *The Earl of Strafford's Letters and Despatches*, 2 vols, (London, 1739).

Large Declaration (1639), STC 21906.

Le Hardy, W. (ed.), *Hertfordshire County Records: Calendar to the Sessions Books* (Hertford, 1928), Vol. 5.

Lewis, T. T. (ed.), *The Letters of the Lady Brilliana Harley*, Camden Society, vol. 58 (1854).

The Life and Death of Mr. Ignatius Jurdain (London, 1654), BL, E.730(9).

'The Life of Master John Shaw', *Yorkshire Diaries and Autobiographies in the Seventeenth and Eighteenth Centuries*, Surtees Society, vol. 65 (1875).

The Lords Day, the Sabbath day or A Briefe Answer (1636), BL, 4355.b.7 (HEH photocopy).

Loyalty's Speech to England's Subjects (London, 1639), STC 10018.

Lupton, D., *London and the Countrey. Carbonadoed and Quartered into Several Characters* (1632), STC 16944.

Mayo, C. H., *The Municipal Records of the Borough of Dorchester, Dorset* (Exeter, 1908).

Mede, J., *The Name Altar* (1637), STC 17768.

The Memoirs of Sir Hugh Cholmley (London: privately printed, 1787).

Morton, T., *Sermon Preached Before the Kings Majestie, 5 May 1639* (1639), STC 18196.

Napier, J., *Plaine Discovery of the whole Revelation of Saint John* (1593), STC 18354.

Newes from Ipswich (1636), STC 20469.

Notestein, W., and Relf, F. H. (eds), *Commons Debates, 1629* (Minneapolis, Minn.: University of Minnesota Press, 1921).

Numb. Primo. The Principall Passages of Germany, Italy, France and other places (1636), STC 4293.

Orders and Directions ... for the better Administration of Justice (1630), STC 9252.

Orders ... for the preventing and remedying of the dearth of graine and victuall (1630), STC 9253.

Palmer, T., *Bristolls Military Garden* (1635), STC 19155.

Parsons, D. (ed.), *The Diary of Sir Henry Slingsby of Scriven, bart.* (London, 1836).

Paybody, T., *A Just Apologie for the Gesture of Kneeling in the Act of Receiving the Lord's Supper* (London, 1629), STC 19488.

Peacham, H., *The Complete Gentleman*, ed. V. Hetzel (Folger Shakespeare Library, 1962).

Peacham, H., *The Duty of All True Subjects to their King: As also to their Native Countrey in time extremity and danger* (London, 1639), STC 19505.

Phillips, C. B. (ed.), *Lowther Family Estate Books, 1617–1675*, Surtees Society, vol. 191 (1976–7).

Pigges Corantoe (1642), STC W P2223.

Pocklington, J., *Altare Christianum*, 2nd edn (1637), STC 20076.

Pocklington, J., *Sunday, No Sabbath* (1636), STC 2077).

Powell, R., *Depopulation Arraigned: Convicted and Condemned by the Laws of God and Man* (1636), STC 20160.

The Present Estate of Spayne (1630), STC 24929.

Primerose, D., *A Treatise of the Sabbath* (1636), STC 20387.

The Private Correspondence of Jane Lady Cornwallis, 1613–1644 (London, 1842).

Privy Council Registers, 1631–7, reproduced in facsimile (London, 1967–8).

The Priviledges and Practice of Parliaments (1628), STC 7749.

Prynne, W., *Anti-Arminianism* (1630), STC 20458.

Prynne, W., *Canterburies Doom* (1646), STC W P3917.

Prynne, W., *Hidden Workes of Darknes* (1645), STC W P3973.

Prynne, W., *Histrio Mastix* (1633), STC 20464.

Prynne, W., *An Humble Remonstrance to His Majesty against the Tax of Ship-money* (1641), HN 58925.

Prynne, W., *The Jesuits Looking-glasse* (1636) in *The Popish Royall Favourite* (1643), STC W P4039.

Prynne, W., *A Looking-Glasse for all Lordly Prelates* (1636), STC 20466.

Puget de la Serre, J., *Histoire de l'Entree de la Reyne Mere dans La Grande Bretaigne* (1639), STC 20488.

Quintrell, B. (ed.), *Proceedings of the Lancashire Justices of the Peace at the Sheriffs' Table during Assizes Week, 1578–1694*, Record Society of Lancashire and Cheshire, vol. 121 (1981).

Randol, J., *Noble Blastus. The Honor of a Lord Chamberlaine and a Good Bedchamberman or the Courtier justified in Conditions of Peace*. Sermon preached 27 March 1631 before Sir Lucius Cary at Burford Church, Oxon. (1633), STC 20684.

Ratcliff, S. C., and Johnson, H. C. (eds), *Quarter Sessions Indictment Book, Easter 1631 to Epiphany 1674*, Warwick County Records, vol. 6 (1941).

Reeve, T., *The Churches Hazzard* (London, 1632), STC 20832.

Remonstrance (22 March 1638/9), STC 21907.

Renshaw, W. C. (ed.), 'Notes from the Act Books of the archdeacon's court of Lewes', *Sussex Archaeological Society Collections*, vol. 49 (1906).

Richardson, W. H. (ed.), *The Annals of Ipswich*, by N. Bacon (Ipswich: S. H. Cowell, 1844).

Rushworth, J., *Historical Collections*, 8 vols (London, 1659-1701; 1721).

Russell, J., *The Two Famous Pitcht Battels of Lypsich and Lutzen* (Cambridge, 1634), STC 21460.

Rye, W. (ed.), *State Papers Relating to Musters, Beacons, Shipmoney, etc. in Norfolk*, Norfolk and Norwich Archaeological Society (1907).

Sachse, W. L. (ed.), *Minutes of the Norwich Court of Mayoralty, 1632-35*, Norfolk Record Society, vol. 36 (1967).

Schloer, F., *The Death of the two Renowned Kings of Sweden and Bohemia* (London, 1633), STC 21819.

Schofield, B. (ed.), *The Knyvett Letters, 1620-1644*, Norfolk Record Society, vol. 20 (1949).

Sclater, W., *Death's Summons and the Saints Duty* (1640), STC 21849.

Scott, W., and Bliss, J. (eds), *The Works of William Laud*, 7 vols in 9 (Oxford: Parker Society, 1847-60).

Searle, A. (ed.), *Barrington Family Letters, 1628-1632*, Camden Fourth Series, vol. 28 (1983).

Seddon, P. (ed.), *Letters of John Holles, 1587-1637*, Vol. 1, Thoroton Society, Record Series, vol. 31 (1975).

Shirley, J., *The Triumph of Peace* (1633), STC 2249.

A Short Relation ... to our brethern in the Kirk of England (1638), STC 22039.

Smart, P., *A Sermon Preached in the Cathedrall Church of Durham July 7, 1628* (Edinburgh, 1628), STC 22640.

Smith, S., *A Fold for Christ's Sheep* (1638), STC 22849.3.

Stephens, J., *Satyricall Essayes* (1631; orig. 1615), STC 23251.

Survey of the Kingdom of Sweden (1632), STC 23518.

The Swedish Intelligencer (1632), STC 23522.

Sydenham, H., *Sermons Upon Solemne Occasions* (1637), STC 23573.

Sym, J., *Lifes Preservative Against Self-Killing* (1637), STC 23584.

T. B., *A Preservative* (1629), STC 1071.

Taylor, J., *A Sermon preached in Saint Maries Church in Oxford* (1638), STC 23724.

Trevelyan, W. C. (ed.), *Trevelyan Papers*, part 3, Camden Society, vol. 105 (1872).

Turges, E., *The Christian Souldier* (1639), STC 24331. 2.

Two Famous Sea-Fights (London, 1639), STC 22132.

Valentine, H., *God Save the King: A Sermon preached in St. Pauls Church the 27th of March 1639* (1639), STC 24575.

Ward, R., *Animadversions of Warfare* (1639), STC 25025.

Weinstock, M. (ed.), *Weymouth and Melcombe Regis Minute Book, 1625–1660*, Dorset Record Society Publications, vol. 1 (1964).

White, F., *A Treatise of the Sabbath-Day* (2nd ed 1635), STC 25384.

Whitelocke, B., *The History of England or Memorials of English Affairs* (London, 1682).

Wildridge, T. T. (ed.), *The Hull Letters* (Hull, 1886).

Williams, J., *The Holy Table* (1636), STC 25726.

Willis Bund, J. W. (ed.), *Calendar of the Quarter Sessions*, Vol. 2, *1591–1643*, Worcester County Records (Worcester, 1900).

Winthrop Papers, Massachusetts Historical Society (1929).

The Wrens Nest Defiled (1640), STC 26016.

The Wyllys Papers, Collections of the Connecticut Historical Society, vol. 21 (1924).

Young, A. (ed.), *Chronicles of the First Planters of the Colony of Massachusetts Bay from 1623 to 1636* (Williamstown, Mass.: Corner House, reprint of 1846 edn).

Secondary Sources

Albion, G., *Charles I and the Court of Rome* (London: Burns, Oates & Washbourne, 1935).

Alexander, M., *Charles I's Lord Treasurer* (Chapel Hill, NC: University of North Carolina Press, 1975).

Anselment, R., 'Clarendon and the Caroline myth of peace', *JBS*, vol, 23, no.1 (1984), pp. 37–54.

Ashton, R., *The City and the Court, 1603–1643* (Cambridge: Cambridge University Press, 1979).

Ashton, R., *The Crown and the Money Market, 1603–1640* (Oxford: Clarendon Press, 1960).

Ashton, R., *The English Civil War: Conservatism and Revolution, 1603–1649* (London: Weidenfeld & Nicolson, 1978).

Aylmer, G., 'Attempts at administrative reform, 1625–1640', *EHR*, vol. 72, no. 283 (1957), pp. 229–59.

Aylmer, G., *The King's Servants* (New York: Columbia University Press, 1961).

Bard, N., 'The ship money case and William Fiennes, Viscount Saye and Sele', *BIHR*, vol. 50, no. 122 (1977), pp. 177–84.

Barnes, T. G., *The Clerk of the Peace in Caroline Somerset*, Leicester, Department of English Local History, Occasional Paper, no. 14 (1961).

Barnes, T. G., County politics and a Puritan *cause célèbre*: Somerset church ales, 1633', *TRHS*, Fifth Series, vol. 9 (1959), pp. 103–22.

Barnes, T. G., 'Due process and slow process in the late Elizabethan and early Stuart Star Chamber', *American Journal of Legal History* (1962), pp. 221–49, 315–46.

Barnes, T. G., *Somerset, 1625–1640* (Cambridge, Mass.: Harvard University Press, 1961).

Barnes, T. G., 'Star Chamber litigants and their counsel, 1596–1641', in *Legal Records and the Historian*, ed. J. H. Baker (London: Royal Historical Society, 1978), pp. 7–28.

Barnes, T. G., 'Star Chamber mythology,' *American Journal of Legal History* (1961), pp. 1–11.

Bergeron, D., 'Charles I's royal entries into London', *Guildhall Miscellany*, vol. 3, no. 2 (1970), pp. 91–7.

Bergeron, D., *English Civic Pageantry, 1558–1642* (London: Edward Arnold, 1971).

Bossy, J., *The English Catholic Community 1570–1850* (London: Darton, Longman & Todd, 1975).

Boynton, L., *The Elizabethan Militia* (London: Routledge & Kegan Paul, 1967).

Boynton, L., 'Martial law and the Petition of Right', *EHR*, vol. 79, no. 311 (1964), pp. 255–84.

Breen, T. H., 'Moving to the New World: the character of early Massachusetts immigration', *William and Mary Quarterly*, Third Series, vol. 30, no. 2 (1973), pp. 189–222.

Breslow, M., *A Mirror of England* (Cambridge, Mass.: Harvard University Press, 1970).

Carlton, C., *Charles I* (London: Routledge & Kegan Paul, 1983).

Carter, D. P., 'The "Exact Militia" in Lancashire, 1625–1640', *Northern History*, vol. 11 (1975), pp. 87–106.

Clark, P., 'Thomas Scott and the growth of urban opposition to the early Stuart regime', *Historical Journal*, vol. 21, no. 1 (1978), pp. 1–26.

Clark, P., and Slack, P., *English Towns in Transition, 1500–1700* (Oxford: Oxford University Press, 1976).

Clark, P., Smith, A. G. R., and Tyacke, N. (eds), *The English Commonwealth*, (Leicester: Leicester University Press, 1979).

Cliffe, J. T., *The Puritan Gentry* (London: Routledge & Kegan Paul, 1984).

Cliffe, J. T., *The Yorkshire Gentry: From the Reformation to the Civil War* (London: Athlone Press, 1969).

Clifton, R., 'The popular fear of Catholics during the English revolution', *Past and Present*, no. 52 (1971), pp. 23–55.

Cockburn, J., *A History of English Assizes* (Cambridge: Cambridge University Press, 1972).

Collinson, P., 'The beginnings of English sabbatarianism', *Studies in Church History*, Vol. 1 (1964), pp. 207–21.

Collinson, P., 'A comment: concerning the name Puritan', *Journal of Ecclesiastical History*, vol. 31, no. 4 (1980), pp. 483–8.

Collinson, P., 'Lectures by combination', *BIHR*, vol. 48, no. 18 (1975), pp. 182–213.

Collinson, P., *The Religion of Protestants* (Oxford: Clarendon Press, 1982).

Cope, E. S., *The Life of a Public Man: Edward, First Baron Montagu of Boughton, 1562–1644* (Philadelphia, American Philosophical Society, 1981).

Cope, E. S., 'Politics without Parliament: the dispute about muster masters' fees in Shropshire in the 1630s,' *Huntington Library Quarterly*, vol. 45, no. 4 (1982), pp. 271–84.

Cope, E. S., 'Public images of Parliament during its absence', *Legislative Studies Quarterly*, vol. 7, no. 2 (1982), pp. 221–34.

Cope, E. S., 'The Short Parliament and convocation', *Journal of Ecclesiastical History*, vol. 25, no. 2 (1974), pp. 167–84.

Crawford, P., *Denzil Holles, 1598–1680: A Study of his Political Career* (London: Royal Historical Society, 1979).

Darby, H. C., *The Draining of the Fens* (Cambridge: Cambridge University Press, 1940).

Donagan, B., 'The clerical patronage of Robert Rich, 2nd earl of Warwick, 1619–1642', *Proceedings of the American Philosophical Society*, vol. 120 (1976), pp. 388–419.

Donagan, B., 'A courtier's progress: greed and consistency in the life of the earl of Holland', *Historical Journal*, vol. 19, no. 2, (1976), pp. 317–53.

Donagan, B., 'Godly choice: puritan decision-making in seventeenth-century England', *Harvard Theological Review*, vol. 76, no. 3 (1983), pp. 307–34.

Donagan, B., 'Puritan ministers and laymen: professional claims and social constraints in seventeenth-century England', *Huntington Library Quarterly*, vol. 47, no. 2 (1984), pp. 81–111.

Elton, G., 'Tudor government: the points of contact: 1. Parliament', *TRHS*, Fifth Series, vol. 24 (1974), pp. 183–200.

Evans, E., 'Of the antiquity of parliaments in England', *History*, vol. 23, no. 91 (1938), pp. 206–21.

Evans, J., *Seventeenth-Century Norwich* (Oxford: Oxford University Press, 1979).

Everitt, A., *The Community of Kent and the Great Rebellion* (Leicester: Leicester University Press, 1966).

Fincham, K., 'The judges' decision on ship money in February 1637: the reaction of Kent, *BIHR*, vol. 67, no. 137 (1984), pp. 230–7.

Finlayson, M., *Historians, Puritanism, and the English Revolution* (Toronto: University of Toronto Press, 1983).

Fletcher, A., *A County Community in Peace and War: Sussex 1600–1660* (London: Longman, 1975).

Fletcher, A., 'Factionalism in town and countryside: the significance of Puritanism and Arminianism', *Studies in Church History*, vol. 16 (1979), pp. 291–300.

Fletcher, A., *The Outbreak of the English Civil War* (New York: New York University Press, 1981).

Forster, J., *Sir John Eliot*, 2nd edn (London: Chapman, 1872).

Foster, A., 'The function of a bishop: the career of Richard Neile, 1562–1640', in *Continuity and Change: Personnel and Administration of the Church of England 1500–1642*, eds R. O'Day and F. Heal (Leicester: Leicester University Press, 1976), pp. 38–53.

Foster, E. R., *The Painful Labour of Mr. Elsyng*, American Philosophical Society, Transactions, New Series, vol. 62, no. 8 (1972).

Foster, E. R., 'Printing the Petition of Right', *Huntington Library Quarterly*, vol. 38, no. 1 (1974), pp. 81–3.

Foster, S., *Notes from the Caroline Underground*, (Hamden, Conn.: Archon, 1978).

Fraser, I. H. C., 'Agitation in the Commons, 2 March 1629, and the interrogation of the leaders of the anti-court group', *BIHR*, vol. 30, no. 81 (1957), pp. 86–95.

Gardiner, S. R., *History of England* (London: Longmans, Green, 1884), Vols 6–9.

George, C. H., 'Puritanism as history and historiography', *Past and Present*, no. 41 (1968), pp. 77–104.

Gordon, M. D., 'The collection of ship-money in the reign of Charles I', *TRHS*, Third Series, vol. 4 (1910), pp. 141–62.

Green, I., 'Career prospects and clerical conformity in the early Stuart church', *Past and Present*, no. 90 (1981), pp. 71–115.

Gruenfelder, J., 'The election to the Short Parliament, 1640', *Early Stuart Studies*, ed. H. S. Reinmuth (Minneapolis, Minn.: Univerity of Minnesota Press, 1970).

Gruenfelder, J., *Influence in Early Stuart Elections, 1604–1610* (Columbus, Ohio, 1981).

Hall, B., 'Puritanism: the problem of definition', *Studies in Church History*, vol. 2, (1965), pp. 283–96.

Hamilton, C. L., 'The Shropshire muster-master's fee', *Albion*, vol. 2, no. 1 (1970), pp. 26–34.

Hammersley, G., 'The crown woods and their exploitation in the sixteenth and seventeenth centuries', *BIHR*, vol. 30, no. 82 (1957), pp. 136–61.

Hammersley, G., 'The revival of the forest laws under Charles I'. *History*, vol. 45, no. 154 (1960), pp. 85–102.

Havran, M., *Caroline Courtier: The Life of Lord Cottington* (London: Macmillan, 1973).

Havran, M., *The Catholics in Caroline England* (Stanford, Calif.: Stanford University Press, 1962).

Heineman, M., *Puritanism and Theatre: Thomas Middleton and Opposition Drama under the Early Stuarts* (Cambridge: Cambridge University Press, 1980).

Hibbard, C., 'Early Stuart catholicism: revisions and re-revisions', *Journal of Modern History*, vol. 52, no. 1 (1980), pp. 1–34.

Hibbard, C., *Charles I and the Popish Plot* (Chapel Hill, NC: University of North Carolina Press, 1983).

Hirst, D., *Representative of the People?* (Cambridge: Cambridge University Press, 1975).

Hoffman, J. G., 'Another side of "Thorough": John Cosin and administration, discipline, and finance in the Church of England, 1622–44,' *Albion*, vol. 12, no. 4 (1981), pp. 347–63.

Holmes, C., 'The county community in Stuart historiography', *JBS*, vol. 19, no. 1 (1980), pp. 54–73.

Holmes, C., *Seventeenth-century Lincolnshire* (Lincoln: History of Lincolnshire Committee, 1980).

Howell, R., *Newcastle upon Tyne and the Puritan Revolution* (Oxford: Oxford University Press, 1967).

Hulme, H., *The Life of Sir John Eliot* (London: Allen & Unwin, 1957).

Hunt, W., *The Puritan Moment: The Coming of Revolution in an English County* (Cambridge, Mass.: Harvard University Press, 1983).

Jessup, F., *Sir Roger Twysden, 1597–1672* (New York: Barnes & Noble, 1967; orig. 1965).

Jones, W. J., *Politics and the Bench* (London: Allen & Unwin, 1971).

Kalu, O., 'Continuity in change: bishops of London and religious dissent in early Stuart England', *JBS*, vol. 18, no. 1 (1978), pp. 28–45.

Kearney, H., *The Eleven Years' Tyranny of Charles I*, Historical Association, Aids for Teachers Series, no. 9 (1962).

Kearney, H., *Strafford in Ireland, 1633–41* (Manchester: Manchester University Press, 1960).

Keeler, M. F., *The Long Parliament* (Philadelphia: American Philosophical Society, 1954).

Kennedy, M., 'Charles I and local government: the drainage of the east and west fens', *Albion*, vol. 15, no. 1 (1983), pp. 19–31.

Kennedy, M., 'Fenland drainage, the central government, and local interest: Carleton and the gentlemen of South Holland', *Historical Journal*, vol. 26, no. 1 (1983), pp. 15–37.

Kent, J., 'The English village constable, 1580–1642: the nature and dilemmas of the office', *JBS*, vol. 20, no. 2 (1981), pp. 26–49.

King, P., 'Bishop Wren and the suppression of the Norwich lecturers', *Historical Journal*, vol. 11, no. 2 (1968), pp. 237–54.

Kirby, E.W., 'The Lay Feoffees: a study in militant Puritanism', *Journal of Modern History*, vol. 14, no. 1 (1942), pp. 1–25.

Lake, P., 'The collection of ship money in Cheshire during the sixteen-thirties: a case study of relations between central and local government', *Northern History*, vol. 17 (1981), pp. 44–71.

Lambert, S., 'The opening of the Long Parliament', *Historical Journal*, vol. 27, no. 2 (1984), pp. 265–87.

Lamont, W., *Godly Rule, Politics, and Religion, 1603–1660* (London: Macmillan, 1969).

Lamont, W., *Marginal Prynne* (London: Routledge & Kegan Paul, 1963).

Lamont, W., 'Puritanism as history and historiography: some further thoughts', *Past and Present*, no. 44 (1969), pp. 133–46.

Lee, M., *The Road to Revolution: Scotland under Charles I, 1625–37* (Urbana, Ill.: University of Illinois Press, 1985).

Leonard, H. M., 'Distraint of knighthood: the last phase, 1625–1641', *History*, vol. 63, no. 207 (1978), pp. 23–37.

Levack, B., *The Civil Lawyers in England, 1603–1641: a Political Study* (Oxford: Clarendon Press, 1973).

Levy, F. J., 'How information spread among the gentry', *JBS*, vol. 21, no. 1 (1982), pp. 11–34.

Lindley, K., *Fenland Riots and the English Revolution* (London: Heinemann, 1982).

MacCaffrey, W., *Exeter, 1540–1640* (Cambridge, Mass.: Harvard University Press, 2nd edn, 1975).

McGee, S., *The Godly Man in Stuart England* (New Haven, Conn.: Yale University Press, 1976).

McGee, S., 'William Laud and the outward face of religion' in R. L. DeMolen (ed.), *Leaders of the Reformation* (Selinsgrove, Pa: Susquehanna University Press, 1984), pp. 318–44.

Maguire, M., 'The attack of the common lawyers on the oath *ex officio* as administered in the ecclesiastical courts in England', in *Essays in History and*

Political Theory in Honor of Charles Howard McIlwain (Cambridge, Mass: Harvard University Press, 1936).

Marchant, R., *The Puritans and the Church Courts in the Diocese of York* (London: Longman, 1960).

Marcotte, E., 'Shrieval administration of ship money in Cheshire, 1637: limitations of early Stuart governance', *Bulletin of the John Rylands Library*, vol. 58 (1975–6), pp. 137–72.

Morrill, J., *Cheshire, 1630–1660* (Oxford: Oxford University Press, 1974).

Morrill, J., *The Cheshire Grand Jury, 1625–1649, a Social and Administrative Study*, Leicester, Department of English Local History, Occasional Papers, Third Series, no. 1 (1976).

Morrill, J. S. (ed.), *Reactions to the English Civil War 1642–1649*, (New York: St Martin's, 1982).

Morrill, J., 'The religious context of the English Civil War', *TRHS*, Fifth Series, vol. 34 (1984).

Morrill, J., *The Revolt of the Provinces* (London: Allen & Unwin, 1976).

Morrill, J., 'Sir William Brereton and England's wars of religion', *JBS*, vol. 24, no. 3 (1985), pp. 311–32.

Morrill, J., 'William Davenport and the "silent majority" of early Stuart England', *Journal of the Chester Archaeological Society* (1974), pp. 115–29.

O'Day, R., *The English Clergy: The Emergence and Consolidation of a Profession 1558–1642* (Leicester: Leicester University Press, 1979).

O'Day, R., 'The law of patronage in early modern England', *Journal of Ecclesiastical History*, vol. 26, no. 2 (1975), pp. 247–60.

Pearl, V., *London and the Outbreak of the Puritan Revolution* (Oxford: Oxford University Press, 1961).

Pettit, P. A. J., 'Charles I and the revival of forest law in Northamptonshire', *Northamptonshire Past and Present*, vol. 3, no. 2 (1961), pp. 54–62.

Pettit, P. A. J., *The Royal Forests of Northamptonshire*, Northamptonshire Record Society, vol. 23 (1968).

Prest, W., *The Inns of Court* (London: Longman, 1972).

Price, W. H., *The English Patents of Monopoly* (Boston, Mass: Houghton, Mifflin, 1906).

Quintrell, B. W., 'The making of Charles I's Book of Orders', *EHR*, vol. 95, no. 376 (1980), pp. 553–72.

Rabb, T. K., and Hirst, D. M., 'Revisionism revised: two perspectives on early Stuart parliamentary history', *Past and Present*, vol. 92 (1981), pp. 55–99.

Reid, R., *The King's Council in the North* (London: Longmans, Green, 1921).

Richardson, R. C., *Puritanism in North-West England* (Manchester: Manchester University Press, 1972).

Roberts, B. D., *Mitre and Musket* (Oxford: Oxford University Press, 1938).

Rowe, V., 'Robert, second earl of Warwick and the payment of shipmoney in Essex', in *Transactions of the Essex Archaeological Society*, vol. 1, pt. 2, Third Series (1964–5) pp. 160–3.

Russell, C. (ed.), *The Origins of the English Civil War* (London: Macmillan, 1973).

Russell, C., 'Parliamentary history in perspective', *History,* vol. 61, no. 201 (1976), pp. 1–27.

Russell, C., *Parliaments and English Politics 1621–1629* (Oxford: Oxford University Press, 1979).

Russell, C., 'The shipmoney judgements of Bramston and Davenport', *EHR,* vol. 77, no. 303 (1962), pp. 312–18.

Schwarz, M., 'Lay Anglicanism and the crisis of the English Church in the early seventeenth century', *Albion,* vol. 14, no. 1 (1982), pp. 1–19.

Schwarz, M., 'Viscount Saye and Sele, Lord Brooke and aristocratic protest to the first Bishops' War', *Canadian Journal of History,* vol. 7 (1972), pp. 17–36.

Seaver, P., *The Puritan Lectureships* (Stanford Calif.: Stanford University Press, 1970).

Seaver, P., *Wallington's World* (Stanford, Calif.: Stanford Universtiy Press, 1985).

Sharp, B., *In Contempt of All Authority* (Berkeley, Calif.: University of California Press, 1980).

Sharpe, K., 'Archbishop Laud', *History Today,* vol. 33 (August 1983), pp. 26–30.

Sharpe, K., 'Faction at the early Stuart court', *History Today,* (October 1983), pp. 39–46.

Sharpe, K. (ed.), *Faction and Parliament* (Oxford: Oxford University Press, 1978).

Sharpe, K., *Sir Robert Cotton, 1586–1631* (Oxford: Oxford University Press, 1979).

Skeel, C., *The Council in the Marches of Wales* (London: H. Rees 1904).

Slack, P., 'Books of Orders: the making of English social policy, 1577–1631', *TRHS,* Fifth Series, vol. 30 (1980), pp. 1–22.

Slack, P., 'An election to the Short Parliament', *BIHR,* vol. 46, no. 113 (1973), pp. 108–114.

Slack, P., *The Impact of Plague in Tudor and Stuart England* (London: Routledge & Kegan Paul, 1985).

Slack, P., 'Religious protest and urban authority: the case of Henry Sherfield, iconoclast, 1633', *Studies in Church History,* vol. 9 (1972), pp. 295–302.

Smuts, M., 'The puritan followers of Henrietta Maria in the 1630s', *EHR,* vol. 93, no. 366 (1978), pp. 26–45.

Spufford, M., 'The quest for heretical laity in the visitation records of Ely in the late sixteenth and early seventeenth centuries', *Studies in Church History,* vol. 9 (1972), pp. 223–30.

Stevenson, D., *The Scottish Revolution, 1637–1644* (Newton Abbot: David & Charles, 1973).

Stieg, M., *Laud's laboratory: The Diocese of Bath and Wells in the Early Seventeenth Century* (Lewisburg,: Bucknell University Press, 1982).

Supple, B., *Commercial Crisis and Change in England, 1600–1642* (Cambridge: Cambridge University Press, 1959).

Thirsk, J., *Economic Policy and Projects* (Oxford: Clarendon Press, 1978).

Tomlinson, H. (ed.), *Before the English Civil War,* (London: Macmillan, 1983).

Trevor-Roper, H. R., *Archbishop Laud, 1573–1645,* 2nd edn (New York: St Martin's, 1965).

Usher, R. G., *The Rise and Fall of the High Commission* (Oxford: Oxford University Press, 1913).

Walter, J. D., 'Grain riots and popular attitudes to the law: Maldon and the crisis of 1629', in *An Ungovernable People: The English and their Law in the Seventeenth and Eighteenth Centuries*, eds J. Brewer and J. Styles (New Brunswick, NJ: Rutgers University Press, 1980), pp. 47–84.

Wedgwood, C. V., *Thomas Wentworth, First Earl of Strafford* (New York: Macmillan, 1962).

Willcox, W., *Gloucestershire: A Study in Local Government, 1590–1640* (New Haven, Conn.: Yale University Press, 1940).

Zagorin, P., *The Court and the Country* (New York: Atheneum, 1970).

THESES

Adams, S., 'The Protestant cause: religious alliance with the West European Calvinist communities as a political issue in England 1585–1630', PhD thesis, Oxford University, 1972.

Cust, R., 'The Forced Loan and English politics, 1626–8', PhD thesis, University of London, 1984.

Hunt, W., 'The godly and the vulgar: Puritanism and social change in seventeenth-century Essex, England', PhD thesis, Harvard University, 1974.

Levy, J., 'Perceptions and beliefs: the Harleys of Brampton Bryan and the origins and outbreak of the First Civil War', PhD thesis, University of London, 1983.

Index